The People Came First

A History of Wisconsin Cooperative Extension

JERRY APPS

For additional information, plese contact
Epsilon Sigma Phi Foundation
601 Extension Building
432 N. Lake Street
Madison, WI 53706-1498
(608) 263-1096

ISBN: 1-930596-15-4

Printed in the U.S.A.

Contents

ACKNOWLEDGMENTS

Funding for this project was provided by the Alpha Sigma Chapter of Epsilon Sigma Phi, the Wisconsin Association of Extension Professionals, a generous gift from the Lenore Landry estate, and Wisconsin Cooperative Extension. Special thanks to Carl O'Connor, dean of Cooperative Extension for his support and contributions to this project, and to Mary Brintnall-Peterson, who was president of Epsilon Sigma Phi when the project was first developed. Mary helped develop the agreements for the project and work out the funding.

Rosemary Stare and Laverne Forest served as co-chairs of a special committee organized to plan and assist with the book's development. Both did yeoman's duty in helping encourage both past and present Cooperative Extension staff members to contribute items to the book.

Members of the special committee by district included the following people:

Northeast—Kathy Smith (chair), Russ Luckow, Mitch Mackey, and Dave Running.

Southeast—Carl Smith (chair), Erna Carmichael, Phyllis Northway, and Jack Trzebiatowski.

South—Jim Schroeder (chair), Al Francour, Virgil Butteris, Virginia Hall, and Don Schink.

Central—Edie Felts-Podol (chair), Thomas Gieger, Joe Tuss, Mary Ann Genson, and Pat Rychter.

North—Joan Lefebvre (chair), John Markus, Darrell Aderman, and Palmer McCoy.

Northwest—Nyla Musser (chair), Dianne Weber, Eugene Savage, Willis Erickson, Sid Bjorkman, and Tom Larson.

Statewide faculty—Marvin Beatty (chair), Mary Mennes, and Jim Everts.

Mitch Mackey and Don Schink made many contributions to the project. Unfortunately, both passed away before the project was completed.

Rita Sears and Vicki Pierce, Extension chancellor's office, helped obtain annual reports and photographs. Mary Ellen Bell, Cooperative Extension public information specialist, provided photographs, as did Robert Mitchell from the Department of Life Sciences Communication. Bill Brown, Cooperative Extension publishing unit, and Aron Larson offered advice concerning printer bids and contracts.

Many Extension agents, specialists, and administrators, both retired and currently working, sent more than 400 stories, photos, and historical bits for inclusion in the book. Without them, the book would have been impossible.

Several people assisted with the editing process, especially Lavern Forest, Rosemary Stare, and Al Beaver. This threesome read every word of the draft manuscript and offered many suggestions for improvement. Others who critiqued various segments of the draft manuscript included Carl O' Connor, Laurie Boyce, Harv Thompson, Patrick Boyle, Ellen Fitzsimmons, Gerald Campbell, Clarence Olson, and Marv Beatty. Finally, Ruth (Olson) Apps, a former county home economist and the author's wife, read every word of the manuscript at least twice, looking for errors large and small. To all these people, I offer my most sincere thank you.

THE PEOPLE CAME FIRST

INTRODUCTION

THE COOPERATIVE EXTENSION STORY

The Cooperative Extension story is about people—those who teach and those who learn, country people and urban folks. It is a story that goes back more than a hundred years.

The story is about County Extension offices located throughout the state, the staff who work in these offices, and the Extension specialists on University of Wisconsin campuses. The story is about public and private partners that assist Extension in improving the lives of people and making Wisconsin a better place to live.

The story includes county board members who receive reports, offer comments, and above all make sure that a budget is available for their County Extension office. It is about state legislators who assure that Extension is supported adequately through the University of Wisconsin. The Extension story is about Congressional representatives in the House and Senate who keep tabs on Extension operations and make sure federal funds are available.

The Extension story is made up of many stories from professionals, volunteers, office secretaries, and administrators. These stories weave together to form the rich, diverse, sometimes perplexing, and occasionally complicated story of an idea that began in the minds of Wisconsin's pioneer farmers soon after they reached the state.

People, the Extension staff who serve them, and the organization that provides a structure and budget are the major threads of the Extension story. As the story unfolded over the years, all three threads changed. In the early days, the people served were primarily farmers, and those who taught them were trained in agriculture. As the years passed, Extension also worked with non-farmers and urban people. The organization and its employees changed as the organization's focus changed.

A picture showing a 4-H member with a dairy calf was a longtime symbol for Cooperative Extension work in Wisconsin.

Extension has always focused on people. Warren Clark is shown at Portage County farmers' institute circa 1921.

The initial chapters trace the history of Extension from the middle 1800s to the year 2000. Subsequent chapters discuss the County Extension office, Extension agents and specialists, and district directors. Major historical developments include the University of Wisconsin's early involvement; the "official" establishment of Wisconsin Agricultural Extension in 1908; the passage of supportive federal legislation (Smith-Lever Act, 1914); efforts in World War I, the Depression and World War II; post-World War II challenges; reorganization into University of Wisconsin-Extension (1965); the budget challenges of the 1980s; and the ups and downs of the 1990s.

Chapter 13 recounts notable Extension programs such as dairy cow milk testing, nutrition programs, conservation education, and 4-H Club work. The development of Extension teaching approaches, from lecturing to computer use, is the topic of Chapter 14. A chapter follows on professional development, and a final chapter examines several historical themes, such as administrative leadership, the Wisconsin Idea, partnerships, and changes in program focus.

The story told in this book ends in the year 2000, but the story of Wisconsin Cooperative Extension goes on. New stories emerge each day.

Extension Professional's Creed

I believe in people and their hopes, their aspirations, and their faith; in their right to make their own plans and arrive at their own decisions; in their ability and power to enlarge their lives and plan for the happiness of those they love.

I believe that education, of which Extension is an essential part, is basic in stimulating individual initiative, self-determination, and leadership; that these are the keys to democracy and that people when given facts they understand, will act not only in their self interest, but also in the interest of society.

I believe that education is a lifelong process and the greatest university is the home; that my success as a teacher is proportional to those qualities of mind and spirit that give me welcome entrance to the homes of the families I serve.

I believe in intellectual freedom to search for and present the truth without bias and with courteous tolerance towards the views of others.

I believe that Extension is the link between the people and the ever-changing discoveries in the laboratories.

I believe in my own work and in the opportunity I have to make my life useful to humanity.

Because I believe these things, I am an Extension Professional.

Extension Professional's Creed

CHAPTER 1

EARLY HISTORY

Native Americans laid claim to most of what would become Wisconsin until the 1820s. The early exceptions were the French and British fur trading outposts and the small settlements of Green Bay, Milwaukee, and Prairie du Chien.

Great changes began when lead miners poured into the southwestern part of the region in the mid-1820s, supplanting Indians who had been mining lead since the 1700s. In the 1830s, when Wisconsin was deemed part of the Michigan territory, the number of white settlers increased rapidly. By 1836, 11,683 non-native people lived in the recently formed Wisconsin Territory—5,234 of them in Iowa County. Early miners had traveled north up the Mississippi River from southern Illinois, Kentucky, and Missouri, followed by immigrant miners from Cornwall. In 1840, the Wisconsin Territory produced 31 million pounds of lead—about half of all the lead mined in the United States.

During this time agriculture was a minor activity, carried on by native people and by some lead miners and their families. Settlers could make more money digging lead than planting corn or wheat, at least at the beginning of the lead boom. By 1839, farming was becoming increasingly important in the mining region, which consisted primarily of what was then called Iowa County. This area was later divided into the counties of Iowa, Lafayette, and Grant.

After a series of treaties were signed with various Indian tribes from 1833 to 1848, the land became available for settlement. Much of the southern part of Wisconsin was surveyed between 1831 and 1838, starting at the Fourth Principal Meridian, a line extending north from the Illinois border and now forming the boundary between Grant County on the west and Iowa and Lafayette Counties on the east. Land offices opened in Mineral Point and Green Bay in 1834. The land sold for a minimum of $1.25 per acre, and much of it was purchased by land speculators.

Word of this new land reached the East and settlers, including many farmers, began pouring into the region. The early settlers came from upper New York state, but they also came from Ohio, Pennsylvania, Vermont, New Hampshire, and other Eastern states. They were known as "Yankees." They left behind worn-out farms and were intent on making their fortunes farming Wisconsin's fertile, undisturbed soils, which were black and rich as far down as a person could dig.

These pioneer farmers were followed by wave upon wave of immigrants who arrived from Europe to seek a better life in the United States. They came from Germany, Norway, and Sweden, from Ireland, England, Switzerland, and Denmark, from Holland, Wales, Scotland, Croatia, Russia, and Poland. By 1847, the year before Wisconsin achieved statehood, the population had climbed to 210,546. By 1850, the population had reached 305,390 people. Many of them were farmers.[1]

Farm Life on the Frontier

Early Wisconsin farms were self-sufficient. A pioneer farmer had a couple of skinny cows that provided a little milk, butter, and cheese. A small flock of chickens furnished a few eggs and an occasional Sunday chicken dinner. The farmer ground his grain—generally wheat and rye—at a nearby water-powered mill to obtain his flour supply. A few pigs supplied bacon, ham, and lard. Woodlots provided fuel for the woodstoves that kept drafty cabins reasonably warm. A farmer sheared a small flock of sheep for wool, which he and his wife then cleaned, washed, scoured, combed, and spun.

Pioneer farmers broadcast their grain by hand from early settlement times until the Civil War. They cut the ripe grain with a cradle and threshed it with a flail, or had their oxen walk on it to remove the wheat kernels from the stems.

Farmers cut hay with scythes, raked it by hand and pitched it onto wagons with three-tine forks. They grew some corn and other vegetables including potatoes for home consumption. Their skinny cows ate wild grass and marsh hay. Even in winter, cows were allowed to forage for themselves. The small amount of corn that was grown was cultivated with a heavy hoe. Most farm work was done with strong arms and a sturdy back. Oxen and, later, horses pulled the plows and the high-wheeled wagons.

During the early years following statehood, wheat became the predominant crop and the major source of income for Wisconsin's farmers. Wheat soon became king. It required little attention from planting to harvest, but harvesting was extremely hard work. If he worked a long day, a skilled farmer with a cradle could cut two or three acres of wheat. The grain was then bound together by hand and hauled to the barn, where it was threshed.

Cyrus McCormick began manufacturing a fancy new horse-drawn reaper in 1846. It would cut much more grain than a man with a cradle, but the crop still had to be gathered by hand. Jerome Increase Case, from Racine, developed a threshing machine that would serve the function of the oxen that walked over the grain on the barn's threshing floor, separating the wheat kernels from the straw. Many farmers knew about these laborsaving devices, but regarded the machines as too expensive or too risky.

Logging was a major activity in northern Wisconsin from the last half of the 1800s into the early 1900s. The northern forestlands stretched from what is now Oconto County across the state through Shawano, Marathon, Clark, Chippewa, Barron, and

Polk Counties—and north to Lake Superior and the Michigan border.

When logging came to an end, these many thousands of acres of land owned by lumber companies, railroads, and land speculators came up for sale. Many people thought the land could best be used for farming. Soon everyone was promoting northern lands for farm use. The Wisconsin Central Railroad, for example, hired sales agents to work in the eastern U.S. and even in Europe. By 1895, this railroad alone had sold 300,000 acres in Taylor, Price, and Ashland Counties. The agents received one dollar for each acre they sold. Some of the land sold for five dollars an acre.[2]

At the turn of the twentieth century, a visitor to the area saw mile upon mile of giant stumps, sometimes stretching as far as the eye could see. This was hardly what a farmer wanted when he was preparing to plow and plant. Settlers soon discovered that some lands were much more suited to farming than others. For instance, because of the influence of Lake Superior, the extreme northern parts of Douglas, Bayfield, and Ashland Counties had a frost-free growing season of 120 days or more, making these good lands for oats, hay, and even corn. Vilas and Oneida, plus parts of Price, Iron, Lincoln, Langlade, and Forest Counties, had mostly sandy soils. These soils were good for garden crops, hay, and oats. They were especially good for potatoes, and cranberries thrived in certain low-lying areas.

Farther south, soils contained more clay. Some lands were so rocky that a farmer would spend days hauling stones from his fields each spring. The best pioneer farmers in the cutover were the immigrants—especially the Finns, Germans, Swedes, Norwegians, and Poles. For their part, the Yankees didn't take well to land clearing, stump pulling, or rock toting.

Agricultural Education in the Mid-1800s
Farmers learned agriculture by doing, by following the examples of their fathers and grandfathers. Women learned the ways of homemaking, with all of the attendant challenges, from their mothers and grandmothers. What one needed to know about agriculture had changed little in more than a hundred years. Farming in 1848 was essentially the same as farming in 1748. Many basic farming techniques originated in Europe, including techniques for growing crops, raising livestock, and caring for gardens. This knowledge was passed on from generation to generation.

For most farmers, education stopped at the one-room schoolhouse door. Once a farm boy or girl was old enough and strong enough to take on regular farming tasks, formal schooling ceased. High schools were essentially unknown in 1848. When it could be found, the college education of the time was formal, stiff, and had little to do with farming. The primary purpose of most colleges lay in the preparation of preachers. Beloit College opened in 1847, and a few other private colleges began in the years that followed, including St. Thomas at Sinsinawa Mound, St. Francis in Milwaukee, Lawrence in Appleton, and Carroll in Waukesha.

The University of Wisconsin was established in 1848 and began operations a year later. John H. Lathrop was named chancellor of the university; 20 boys enrolled and began study in 1849. The curriculum at this fledgling institution included ancient and modern geography, Latin, Greek, and English grammar. As early as 1851, Chancellor Lathrop urged the university to provide agricultural education. The regents support-ed the idea and the farm press thought it reasonable, but all that came of it was a few staid lectures on agricultural chemistry—scarcely what the farmers of the state need-ed or wanted. At any rate, farm boys and girls were not considered candidates for col-lege education, especially if they wished to continue farming. Most farmers agreed that too much formal education was not for them. Education was book learning, involving nothing that was practical or related to a farmer's concerns.

When great changes began occurring in agriculture, a growing belief emerged that farmers could benefit from outside help. But who would provide it? New technology began replacing human and animal power. Reapers, hay mowers, and threshing machines promised greater efficiency and productivity. By 1850, steam engines began powering threshing machines, replacing the horse sweeps.

Few farmers could afford this technology. Even if they could, many were hard pressed to understand why they should replace methods that had worked well for them, their fathers, and their grandfathers. They already knew how to plant and har-vest wheat—or so they thought. However, no one knew much about soil fertility and how it would decline with repeated wheat crops. In the early years of wheat growing, a farmer could harvest 25 bushels or more of the golden grain per acre. A few years later, he would see yields drop to only five or six bushels per acre-even when the rains came and harvest weather was cooperative. And no one knew how to control the insects and diseases that afflicted the wheat crops.

Even with reductions in crop yields, which were especially pronounced on less fer-tile soils such as those found in central Wisconsin, everyone grew wheat. Farmers in the state grew thousands of acres of it. When the railroad began laying rails into Wisconsin, starting in 1851, the problem of getting the crop to market was solved. In 1860, Wisconsin produced nearly 29 million bushels of wheat. It had become the sec-ond most important wheat-growing state in the nation.[3] The year 1860 became known as "the golden year." Wheat growers faced problems that became more serious each year after that. The farmers knew they faced problems, and most wanted to make improvements. However, they didn't know where to turn.

Wisconsin State Agricultural Society

Agricultural societies had their roots in the East, where colonial farmers saw the need to meet and exchange ideas. The first Agricultural Society began in Philadelphia in 1785, followed by a second in Charleston, South Carolina, during the same year. Many Yankee settlers in Wisconsin knew about agricultural societies in their home states and brought the idea with them.

On a Saturday evening, March 8, 1851, members of the Wisconsin legislature and many citizens of the state met at the Capitol in Madison to consider forming a Wisconsin Agricultural Society. A second meeting was held four days later to consider officers for the society. Erastus W. Drury of Fond du Lac was unanimously elected president.

First State Fair

Not long after the March meeting, the executive committee of the society met in the "village of Madison" and decided to hold the first annual cattle show and fair in Janesville. It was scheduled for Wednesday and Thursday, the first and second days of October, 1851. This was Wisconsin's first state fair, held three years after statehood.

Rufus King, then owner and editor of the Milwaukee *Sentinel,* wrote a detailed account of what occurred on each day of the fair. "An area of something over six acres, on the edge of the plateau which looks down upon the rapid and silvery Rock, and enclosed by a high board fence, constitutes the fairgrounds. Along two sides of the enclosure are pens for sheep and swine, and stands for cattle. Near the centre is a large and lofty tent for the display of fruits, flowers, fancy articles, paintings, jewelry, etc. In the open space between these centre pieces and the cattle stands on the sides, there is ample room for the exhibition and trail of all sorts of agricultural implements, as well as the display of single and matched horses."[4]

People flocked to this first state fair, anxious to exhibit their agricultural produce, but more interested in seeing their neighbors and learning something about the farming practices of others. Exhibits included samples of Wisconsin wheat, a squash from Dane County that weighed two hundred pounds, sweet potatoes, broomcorn, a barrel of "Superfine Family Flour," plus exhibits of cattle, horses, and sheep. The second day of the fair featured a plowing contest, held in a field about a quarter-mile from the fairgrounds. Ten farmers competed, eight with horses and two with oxen. Each plowed a quarter-acre.

After the plowing match, everyone hurried back to the fairgrounds to hear an address by University of Wisconsin Chancellor Lathrop. The speech was delivered in the floral tent, which "crowded to suffocation," according to Rufus King. King wrote this about Lathrop's performance: " . . . If the State Fair produced nothing else than the Chancellor's address, it would have amply repaid the Society and the Farmers of Wisconsin for the time, money, and labor expended for [sponsoring the fair]."

In summary, King wrote: "There must have been in the afternoon [of the second day] fully eight thousand persons within the enclosure; all orderly, well-behaved, and decently dressed people. There was not a single intoxicated man in the crowd; no riotous or disorderly conduct; no gambling appliances; no liquor booths; no profanity; nothing in short to offend the eye or mar the general enjoyment."[5]

Lincoln at the Fair

The state fair continued each year from 1851 to 1861, when it was halted because of the Civil War. For two years, the fair was held in Janesville. Five subsequent fairs were held in Milwaukee, two in Madison (at what is now Camp Randall), and one in Watertown. The 1859 fair was held in Milwaukee, and Abraham Lincoln was invited to speak, which he did on September 30. This took place one year before he was elected President and three years before he signed the Morrill Act of 1862, creating the Land Grant University system and the United States Department of Agriculture.

Lincoln aptly summarized the importance of agricultural fairs. ". . . They are useful in more ways than one," he observed. "They bring us together, and thereby make us better acquainted, and better friends than we otherwise would be . . . They make more pleasant and more strong and more durable the bond of social and political union among us . . . But the chief use of agricultural fairs is to aid in improving the great calling of agriculture, in all its departments and minute divisions—to make mutual exchange of agricultural discovery, information, and knowledge; so that, at the end, all may know everything, which may have been known to but one, to but a few, at the beginning—to bring together especially all which is supposed to not be generally known, because of recent discovery or invention."[6]

County and Township Agricultural Societies

When the State Agricultural Society was organized in 1851, nine county societies were already meeting. These included groups in Columbia, Dane, Iowa, Kenosha, Racine, Rock, Sheboygan, Walworth, and Waukesha Counties. By 1865, there were 37 county agricultural societies in Wisconsin. By the 1860s, many Wisconsin townships also had agricultural societies. During the same decade, 30 county agricultural societies held county fairs, the first occurring in Kenosha County on October 10, 1850, a year before the first state fair.[7]

Horticultural Societies

Many pioneer farmers in Wisconsin planted orchards and grew small fruits such as strawberries and raspberries. This was especially the case for those farmers who came from the East, where apples and various small fruits were common. On October 27, 1851, area horticulturists were invited to a meeting at the Merchants' Insurance Company in the city of Milwaukee, in order to discuss organizing the Wisconsin Horticultural Society. The object of this organization was to " . . . encourage the growth and culture of fruit and ornamental trees, flowers, and vegetables, and to disseminate useful information in reference thereto."

As had been the case with the State Agricultural Society, the horticulture people immediately began discussing times and places for holding exhibitions. They also began drawing up "the rules and regulations therefor." In addition to the exhibitions, clearly viewed as educational events, the horticultural society also collected periodicals about fruits, trees, and vegetables and catalogs from nurseries. Extracts from these publications "as they may deem useful" were provided to members.

These two organizations, one for agriculture generally and the other for horticulture, provided the foundation for agricultural education in Wisconsin. The philosophy of those who knew sharing with those who didn't was a solid one, a useful farmer-to-farmer educational approach. Until 1862, the state of Wisconsin awarded the State Agricultural Society three thousand dollars annually for premiums and "for the purchase of seeds to be gratuitously distributed." When exhibitions were halted because of the Civil War, the state support was withdrawn.[8]

Farmers, Science, and Book Learning
Farmers had long been leery of science. They were especially doubtful that science could result in improvements to farming. Information offered between the covers of a book was suspect and often scorned. However, because of the agricultural press and the appearance of books on a wide variety of agricultural topics, the door gradually began to open regarding the value of science and the printed reports of its application. In the late 1860s, one reporter wrote: "Our farmers have been steadily learning that science—that great bugbear of earlier times—is simply organized knowledge . . . In proportion as this foolish prejudice against all knowledge that has once found its way between the lids of a book, or into the column of an agricultural journal, dies away, our farmers will become more successful as individuals and respected as a class."[9]

When it appeared on the scene in 1914, Cooperative Extension relied heavily on science and the printed word to distribute its results. It still does.

Progress in Agriculture
By 1860, Wisconsin agriculture had made great strides. J.W. Hoyt, secretary of the State Agricultural Society wrote: "By a steady influx of population from the Eastern and Middle States, and from the best portions of the Old World, Wisconsin had risen, as if by magic, from the sparsely inhabited territory of twelve years before to the dignity of a great and prosperous state." [10]

The Civil War, which began in 1861, saw many of the state's young farmers march off to battle. At the same time, the demand for agricultural products increased. The Civil War therefore provided a great incentive for farmers facing severely limited manpower to begin using some of the new agricultural implements they had earlier avoided. The number of reapers and mowers sold increased dramatically during the war years. Along with reapers and mowers, farmers began using grain drills, horse-powered hay rakes, and mechanical hayforks in their barns. A mechanical revolution had begun to take place.

Wheat was king until the mid-1860s, when the chinch bug appeared and began wreaking havoc on what had been the "sure thing" crop. Potato beetles also devoured central Wisconsin potato fields, so potatoes soon became an undependable crop. Farmers began searching for alternatives. Some thought sorghum (for syrup) might be the answer. Others turned to hop culture (for the brewing industry), beginning in Sauk County. In 1867, the value of the hop crop in Sauk County alone was two and a half million dollars. Sheep growing also flourished, especially in the hilly regions of the state.

To this point in the state's agricultural history, dairy cows and cheese making had rarely been discussed. In the 1868 annual report of the State Agricultural Society, *Transactions*, Hoyt wrote: "The dairy business, as practiced on the farm, is an exceedingly laborious and trying one upon the female portion of the household."[11]

Wisconsin and the Dairy Cow

For many years, New York was the premier dairy state in the nation. Many of Wisconsin's early settlers came from New York and were familiar with dairy cows, cheese making, and dairy farming. When they arrived in this new state, they were swept along with the easy money that wheat growing provided—until the chinch bug, rust, and depleted soils took their toll on the crop.

Wisconsin farmers began searching for an alternative. Why not dairying, some of the New Yorkers asked. Their words were lost in a cloud of wheat chaff. Every farm had a few skinny milk cows, but caring for a dairy cow was clearly women's work, as was churning butter and making kitchen cheese.

Just as the Civil War forced many farmers to buy "newfangled" machines, the demise of wheat called for a similar dramatic response. There had been some early efforts at dairying in the state—a cheese factory had begun operations in 1841 in Jefferson County. However, it was actually a farm kitchen where neighbors' milk was accepted for cheese making. John J. Smith, a New Yorker, started a cheese factory in Sheboygan Falls in 1858. Chester Hazen, often credited with starting the first true cheese factory, opened a plant in Fond du Lac County in 1864.

By 1870, Wisconsin had 90 cheese factories. Ten years later, the number had expanded to 700; by 1890, it stood at 1,149.[12] This sounds like an easy and rapid transition, but it was not. Many wheat farmers didn't believe the New Yorkers who said dairy farming had a future. Each year they looked forward to another great wheat year, but none came.

The transition from wheat to dairying created one of the greatest educational challenges Wisconsin had ever faced. Not only did most of these wheat farmers know little to nothing about caring for cattle, they also had to learn to accept the idea that caring for cattle could be man's work.

Wisconsin Dairymen's Association

Dairy farmers from throughout Wisconsin gathered at the Linden House in Watertown on Thursday, February 15, 1872. Many of these farmers had recently switched from wheat growing to dairy farming, and things weren't going well.

Chester Hazen, Hiram Smith, and other dairy farmers, most of them New Yorkers, were convinced that dairy farming had a future in the state. Publisher William Dempster Hoard advocated dairy farming and called for the formation of a dairyman's association in his newspaper, the Jefferson County *Union*. He founded *Hoard's Dairyman* in 1885. G.E. Morrow, editor of *Western Farmer*, spoke at the organizational meeting and proclaimed that with a dairyman's association "a much-improved state of affairs will result."

Skeptical dairy farmers agreed, especially when they heard speakers advocate organizing for the purpose of increasing returns for their milk. Here was another example in which farmers—in this case newly minted dairy farmers—faced their problems by organizing and meeting together to share ideas. They often sought to obtain an outside perspective as well.

Land-Grant Legislation
The Northwest Ordinance of 1787 had established a huge chunk of land, out of which emerged Ohio, Indiana, Illinois, Michigan, and Wisconsin. Among other provisions, this ordinance made a strong statement about the necessity of education if a democratic form of government was to function well.

By the time Wisconsin became a state, the demand for educational opportunity was on the increase throughout the nation. Existing colleges and universities included virtually nothing related to farm life and agriculture, even though the majority of the country's citizens made their living from the land.

One of the first times the U. S. Congress assisted the country's agriculture occurred in 1839, when Congress appropriated $1,000 to distribute information and seeds to farmers. This meager appropriation would eventually lead to the establishment of the United States Department of Agriculture in 1862.[13]

Justin S. Morrill, a Vermont native, was elected to Congress in 1856. During his first year in office, he introduced a resolution to the agricultural committee, urging the members to explore the idea of establishing agricultural schools similar to West Point and the Naval Academy. The resolution died.

In 1857, Morrill introduced his first Land-Grant Bill. Under provisions of the bill, each state would receive 30,000 acres of public lands for each senator and congressman representing that state. Proceeds from the sale of these lands were to be used to establish an agricultural and mechanics college in each state. Several southern states were opposed to the bill, saying it was unconstitutional. These were the years just prior to the Civil War, when states' rights versus federal domination was a major issue. After considerable political maneuvering, Morrill's bill passed the house on a vote of 105 to 100. It later passed the Senate by a similar margin, 25 to 22. However, the bill was vetoed by President Buchanan, who said it was extravagant and would break the treasury.

In December of 1861, Morrill reintroduced the bill in the House. The Committee on Public Lands gave it an unfavorable review. Senator Wade of Ohio then introduced the bill in the Senate, where it passed 32 to 7. When it came back to the House, it succeeded in avoiding committees. It passed on a 90 to 25 vote. President Lincoln signed the bill in 1862.

The Morrill act provided for an educational institution in every state "where the leading object shall be, without excluding other scientific and classical studies and including military tactics, to teach such branches of learning as are related to agriculture and mechanic arts in such manner as the legislatures of the states may respectively prescribe in order to promote the liberal and practical education of the industrial classes in several pursuits and professions in life."[14] Iowa was the first state to accept the provisions of the act. Other northern states followed rapidly, but it was not until after the Civil War that southern states became eligible.

Because of its eight members in Congress, Wisconsin received 240,000 acres of public land within the state. The state legislature formally accepted the land grant on April 2, 1862, but legislators couldn't agree upon which institution should receive the funds and host the program. Many agricultural leaders were unhappy with the University of Wisconsin's feeble attempts to provide information for farmers. Contenders for the land-grant institution included Ripon College, Lawrence University, and the University of Wisconsin. Finally, in 1866, Wisconsin's legislature made the University of Wisconsin the formal recipient of the federal land-grant.[15]

In 1866, the legislature also sought to reorganize and enlarge the University of Wisconsin, obtaining without expense about 200 acres of land for an experimental farm. Dane County chipped in by offering a county bond issue of $40,000 for purchasing and improving lands on the experimental farm.

In addition to the land-grant legislation (Morrill Act), 1862 marked the year when Congress established the United States Department of Agriculture and passed the Homestead Act laws, which made vast areas of public lands available to settlers who did not have the financial means to purchase land.

How the land-grant legislation ever passed is a mystery. One factor was that the congressional debates, conducted in the midst of the Civil War, did not include representatives from southern states, as these men had all gone home. The essentially northern Congress simply made provisions for the southern states to receive land-grants once the Civil War was over. A second Morrill Act was passed in 1890, which provided a set of institutions throughout the south for black people.

The Importance of Newspapers and Magazines

Long before the University of Wisconsin and the College of Agriculture came on the scene, several magazines and most local newspapers carried stories and information of interest to farm families. Some Wisconsin farmers subscribed to farm publications that were published in the East, such as *The Rural New Yorker, Country Gentlemen,* and *The Monthly Horticulturist.*

In 1849, one year after Wisconsin became a state, *The Wisconsin Farmer* began publication in Racine. The *Racine Agriculturist* began publication in 1870, changing its name to *Wisconsin Agriculturist* in 1880.

William Dempster Hoard published many articles in *Hoard's Dairyman* on various aspects of dairy farming, from feeding and caring for cattle to building silos. The February 18, 1898, issue included an ad for new subscriptions and encouraged present subscribers to solicit their friends and neighbors. He used popular books on farming as prizes. Those who signed up one new subscriber received a copy of *The Dairy Calf—Breeding and Raising* by L. S. Harden; readers who enlisted three new subscribers received *The Soil* by Professor F.H. King; those who attracted four new subscribers could choose either a book entitled *Feeds and Feeding* or *Barn Building* by J. A. Sanders.

Articles published in the April 5, 1907, issue of *Hoard's Dairyman* included "Ventilation in Stables," "Keeping Milk Accounts," "Wasteful Spreading of Manure," "Living in the Country," "A Word of Caution Regarding Alfalfa," "Dairy Markets," and "Floor for a Horse Stable."

This issue, like every issue, included a large question and answer section with questions coming in from all over the region. The questions included the following:

Please tell me how to seed alfalfa?

Does skim milk from Holstein cattle contain as much protein, pound for pound, as milk from Jerseys or Guernseys?

Should a galvanized iron silo be painted on the inside, and if so, what kind of paint?

It was clear that farmers were looking for answers wherever they could find them. The farm press was one easily accessible and reliable source, and it was widely used by the state's farmers.

From the time they began arriving in the newly formed state of Wisconsin, farmers had been looking for answers to their many questions. With passage of the Land-Grant (Morrill) Act of 1862, university assistance in solving agricultural problems was on the way. In the next chapter, we see the beginning of the University of Wisconsin's involvement with agricultural education.

CHAPTER 2

THE UNIVERSITY OF WISCONSIN AND AGRICULTURAL EDUCATION: 1851-1908

I n its early years, the University of Wisconsin had little interest in agriculture and home economics education. The lectures on agricultural chemistry that Chancellor Lathrop organized in 1851 were poorly attended. They were also generally dismissed as inadequate and inappropriate for helping the state's farm families with their many problems and challenges.

The First Professor of Agriculture

The University of Wisconsin waited two more years after it received the nod for land-grant designation (1868) before it hired William W. Daniells as its first professor of agriculture and developed a course of study in agriculture. This new academic major was little different from the regular bachelor of arts major, and essentially no one enrolled. Meanwhile, Professor Daniells taught chemistry to students in other majors and managed the meager experimental farm. No one at the university was impressed by or interested in Daniells' orchard, vineyard, and grain plots, including the board of regents. During the 1870s, the experimental farm served primarily as a source of firewood for needy students' woodstoves, and as a public park for Madison citizens. This was at a time when the chinch bug, rust, and declining fertility had devastated wheat crops across the state. Farmers needed help.

The Wisconsin Agricultural Society had become totally disgusted with the university's paltry contributions to farming and agricultural education. In 1878, the society successfully lobbied the governor, asking him to appoint a farmer to the board of regents. Hiram Smith, a prominent farmer from Sheboygan Falls, was appointed and quickly began making suggestions. He argued that Professor Daniells had more than enough to do with his teaching, and that another full-time professor of agriculture should be appointed. In 1880, a full-time position was approved with these duties carefully noted by University President Bascom: "1. To give instruction in botany; 2. To superintend farm experiments and improvements; 3. To attend, in the winter months, local meetings of farmers; and 4. To build up an agricultural department."[1]

William A. Henry

Now, for the first time, it was clear that someone from the University would have responsibility for doing work in agriculture on campus, and also for taking that information off-campus to farmer meetings. In 1880, the University hired William A. Henry, who had recently completed an advanced degree in botany at Cornell University.

Interest in moving the agricultural program to another location persisted. This idea had been smoldering for years. Separation of agricultural education from other academic programs had occurred in such states as Iowa (University of Iowa/Iowa State University) and Michigan (University of Michigan/Michigan State University). In each case, the latter institutions had been designated agricultural schools. Nearly all of the agricultural organizations in Wisconsin supported separation, as did Regent Hiram Smith and W. D. Hoard. A "separatist convention" was held in 1884, but the majority of the regents held tough. In response to the threat, the regents created a committee whose charge was changing the agricultural curriculum to make it more practical and accessible to farmers. In a report filed January 20, 1885, this special committee recommended establishing a Farm Short Course, which continued to operate in 2001. The program was designed as a non-degree offering and was open to farm boys who may have had only a basic education from a one-room country school. The first short course enrolled 19 boys in a program that was the first of its type in the nation. Critics said it would surely fail, but it quickly became popular and preceded the organization of the College of Agriculture by three years.

In 1885, as the legislature considered a separation bill that would have moved agricultural education to another location, the legislative body also debated a farmers' institute bill. The separation bill failed; the farmers' institute bill passed. This was clearly a turning point for the University of Wisconsin, and for agriculture.[2]

Farmers' Institutes

In the winter of 1879-80, due to pressure from Hiram Smith and assistance from Professor Daniells, the agricultural societies came together to plan and conduct six farmers' institutes. In 1880, the first farmers' institutes were held in Galesville, Elkhorn, Auroraville, Appleton, Baraboo, and Salem. They were one- and two-day meetings, and Professor Daniells was one of the main speakers at each of them.

C. E. Estabrook of Manitowoc introduced a bill at the 1884-85 legislative session that provided continuing funding for agricultural institutes. The legislature appropriated $5,000 and assigned the funds to the Board of Regents of the University of Wisconsin. Now the farmers' institutes were official, with a budget and considerable support from farmers and lawmakers. Administratively, farmers' institutes operated as a separate division within the experiment station.

During the winter of 1885-86, thirty institutes were held throughout Wisconsin. W. H. Morrison, superintendent of the farmers' institutes wrote: "[These institutes] were well received by farmers generally, making an advance in the agricultural heart and brain, stimulating animal husbandry and improved methods in various departments of farming. The tendency of these Institutes has been to awaken inquiry, to promote comparisons of methods, to pool their experience, and create a desire for a more extended intelligence that in the end will exalt farming to a profession."[3]

Farmers' institute topics ranged from "A Plea for Fodder Corn" to "Feeding Cows for Profit"; from "Fish Culture on the Farm" to "Is it Worth While to be Honest?"; from "Mutton Breeds of Sheep" to "Beautifying Farmer's Houses"; from "What Can the Farm Do For The Girl?" to "The Farmer's Garden."

Speakers often came from great distances. At an 1886 farmers' institute, agricultural expert McClean Smith from Dayton, Ohio, spoke on the topic of selecting a breed. He talked about the importance of improved stock and why "scrub cows" were poor investments, but he also talked about proper care and feeding. "Our native scrubs are what generations of neglect and periodical short rations have made them. If it is intended the cows shall pick a living in summer along the roadside, and in winter about the straw stack, there is probably no breed that will do better or yield a better return than scrubs."[4]

Women's Programs

Cooking schools became an important part of the farmers' institutes beginning in 1892, when the first one was held in Portage under the leadership of Mrs. M. L. Clarke. From 1892 to 1907, 11 cooking schools were held each year. Starting in 1908, an annual cookbook was published. Each year, ten thousand copies were printed and distributed.

George McKerrow, superintendent of the farmer's institutes, wrote the following in a letter to Board of Regents President W. D. Hoard: "I hereby take pleasure in transmitting to you *Farmers' Institute Cook Book No. 1*. The favor with which the Farmers' Institute Bulletin report of the Cooking Schools held in connection with our Farmers' Institutes for the past 15 years has been received prompted me to advise the publication of a practical cookbook for the farm women of Wisconsin. The art of good cooking is one of the best accomplishments of the housewife; the palatability and digestibility of food has very much to do with the good health of our people."[5]

Agricultural Experiment Station

When Professor Henry arrived at the University of Wisconsin in 1880 he, along with the state's prominent farmers, realized that the state's wheat crop was steadily declining. He turned his attention instead to dairy and livestock farming. Henry promoted the silo as a means of storing winter feed for cattle. Farmers and the farm press joked about silos and silage, claiming the silo was a passing fancy. Some cheese factories even refused milk from cows that were fed silage, and a rumor developed that silage-fed cows would lose their teeth.

Clearly, research was needed to quell the rumors and misinformation. Professor Henry successfully obtained $3,000 for research on silage and the manufacturing of cane sugar and sorghum. Henry's enthusiasm and sincerity, together with his list of research projects, impressed Governor Jeremiah M. Rusk. The governor helped persuade the legislature to pass legislation establishing an agricultural experiment station. The assembly passed a bill that established the Agricultural Experiment Station and a pharmacy department on March 27, 1883. Four days later, the Senate approved the measure. Governor Rusk promptly signed it into law. The University of Wisconsin now had an agricultural experiment station and state funds to help support it.[6]

Even with the experiment station in place, Wisconsin farmers were skeptical of Henry's work and the university's concern for their problems. Henry knew he had to use approaches other than the usual classroom lectures. He had to sell the idea of agricultural research—but more importantly, as it turned out, he had to sell farmers on the value of the University of Wisconsin.

Former College of Agriculture Dean Chris L. Christensen described Henry's efforts: "[He] went among the farmers, went into their barns with them to point out the necessity of scientific feeding and to explain how a poorly producing cow could lose all the profit accruing from the milk of her healthy stablemate. He went to the sty with the farmer and showed him the folly of stuffing the animals [hogs] with corn until they were all lard and little lean, and were thus susceptible to paralysis and were poor sellers on the market. Into the chicken yard he went with the farmer to tell him the chickens' wobbly legs could be strengthened by proper diet. . . . He would go into the kitchen and eat with the farmer and his family . . .he would give them a little insight into the purpose of the agricultural school and give them from his heart much affection, for no man had a greater capacity for love of his fellow man."[7]

Henry's work set an example for all the Extension workers who followed him. He lectured, wrote bulletins, penned letters, published news articles, and made farm visits. Christensen described Henry's efforts as missionary work intended to "win the farmers to the gospel of science in farming, especially in livestock feeding." Henry's research on livestock feeding culminated in his book *Feeds and Feeding*, published in 1898. Some observers have said this was Henry's greatest contribution to the scientific development of agriculture.

In 1887 Congress passed the Hatch Act, which provided $15,000 of federal funds annually to each state for the establishment and operation of agricultural experiment stations. The funds were to go to the land-grant institutions. Now the experiment station had both federal and state funds.

College of Agriculture

With the farmers' institutes developing a solid reputation among farmers, the Agricultural Experiment Station in place and funded, and the Farm Short Course becoming popular as an on-campus educational opportunity for farm boys, it seemed appropriate to create a college of agriculture—almost as an afterthought. As historian John Jenkins wrote in his centennial history of the college: "During the spring of 1889, the Wisconsin legislature officially reorganized the state university at Madison into the College of Letters and Science, the College of Mechanics and Engineering, the College of Law, the School of Pharmacy, and the College of Agriculture. The reorganization was wholly noncontroversial, produced cordially and specifically to satisfy an official request from the Board of Regents, which itself had acceded quickly and quietly to the stated wishes of the recently appointed and highly popular University president, Thomas C. Chamberlin."[8]

The organization of the College of Agriculture was a way of bringing together various activities, courses, and programs that related to agriculture, and of tidying up some administrative clutter on the University of Wisconsin campus. With a new organization, President Chamberlin sought to expand the college's efforts in teaching, research, and outreach, as other prominent agricultural colleges such as Cornell and Rutgers had done.

Early College Research

One of the most far-reaching research projects was Stephen Moulton Babcock's milk test, developed in 1890 and discussed elsewhere in the book. In 1894, less than a year after agricultural scientist Harry L. Russell came to Wisconsin, he began work to rid Wisconsin of bovine tuberculosis. He had learned of a test for tuberculosis while working in Germany. In a classic demonstration, Russell brought in a butchered animal and showed his students that it had TB. Soon Russell was traveling the state, helping farmers diagnose the disease. Through his research, he demonstrated that prize infected cows could be used for breeding purposes if they were kept in isolation.[9]

Nutrition research led to the discovery of several vitamins. Research on silos resulted in the development of cylindrical silos that helped retard feed spoilage. Other research focused on nitrogen fixation, corn hybrids, oat varieties, artificial insemination, and the discovery of dicumarol and then "Warfarin," a rat and mouse poison. Studies were conducted about farm management, rural communities and rural life, how to most effectively conduct adult education programs, and much more. In addition to Henry, Russell, and Babcock, the great names that people still associate with the College of Agriculture include E. B. Hart, F. H. King, H. C. Taylor, Harry Steenbock, Nellie Kedzie Jones, and Charles Galpin.

In 1896, as Wisconsin established itself as a national dairy leader, the College of Agriculture wanted to demonstrate that it was solidly behind those who had abandoned wheat growing for milk cows. Henry decided that a state-of-the-art dairy barn on campus would help show the college's support. Dean Henry visited several agricultural colleges and a number of large farms in the eastern United States. Professor F. H. King traveled extensively in Canada and throughout the eastern states, collecting information on dairy barns. The college also hired J. T. W. Jennings, a Chicago architect who had been influenced by rural building designs in Normandy, France.

The College of Agriculture's dairy barn, built in 1897 at a cost of $16,000, became the site of untold numbers of research projects related to dairy cattle, breeding, feeding, and management. It soon became a symbol of the University of Wisconsin's commitment to the dairy farmers of the state, and it remained so in 2001.

By the early 1900s, farmers had begun to see the experiment station as an important source of information. Director W.A. Henry wrote the following in his 1905 report: "The Experiment Station finds its efforts spreading out more and more into every field of agricultural research and instruction. The desire and eagerness of farmers for more specific knowledge in all lines of agriculture is growing in a surprising degree, multiplying in geometrical progression with the passing years. Where once two or three letters a week measured the correspondence of the Agricultural Department of the University, now letters come by the tens of thousands annually, and where once not a line of printed material was disseminated, millions of pages of printed matter are now sent out annually."[10]

By this time, the experiment station was clearly doing Extension-style work. But the staff was not happy. Henry summarized the situation: "All these important evidences of appreciation and confidence are welcomed; but it must be remembered that such movements draw heavily upon the time and energies of those who are set apart to give most of their service to research work. We must give research that loyalty, time and energy which it is due, for the acquirement of knowledge must necessarily precede its dissemination and utilization. There is no solution to the problem, save in an increased force and the somewhat greater separation or division of duties between investigator and teacher."[11]

Agriculture Trains

During the winter of 1904-1905, the experiment station, in cooperation with the Burlington Railroad Company, ran a special agricultural lecture train over every mile of the company's lines. Experiment station staff presented lectures on dairy, seeds, and soils at each stop.

These train expeditions continued for several years. In his 1913 report, H. L. Russell wrote: "This year, several departments of the College have carried on Extension work through the medium of educational trains, which have proved unusually successful."

Three special trains traveled the state—a "Seed Special," a "Potato Train," and a "Livestock Special." The Seed Special operated from January 15 to 26, 1912, stopping at 11 towns in as many counties in southern Wisconsin. The topic was purebred seed, and the program was conducted in cooperation with the Crop Improvement Committee of the North American Council of Grain Exchanges.

In March 1912, a potato train operated in Burnett County, making four stops. A more extensive potato train, run in cooperation with the Soo Line Railroad, started at

Conrath in Rusk County on October 26, 1911, headed west to Frederic, then proceeded east to Rhinelander. The train subsequently traveled up to Ashland and south to Prentice, Stevens Point, Hancock, and Plainfield. It closed at Waupaca on November 12. At each stop, attendance ranged from 150 to 250 persons. A special potato convention was held in Waupaca at the end of the train's run, with 10 members of the experiment station staff in attendance.[12]

The livestock trains proved even more popular. The experiment station worked in cooperation with the state Livestock Breeders' Association and ran five trains, starting in the spring in the southern counties. As Russell wrote: "These trains were met at almost every scheduled stop by hundreds of farmers who were greatly interested in the exhibition of improved livestock and appliances on display in the exhibition car. Special efforts were made to demonstrate the waste and actual loss which follows the growing of poor quality of livestock of a scrub character in contradistinction to the returns secured from animals of selected breeding." The attendance at each of the train stops varied from 1,100 to 2,000 people. During the year of 1911-12, the experiment station sent out seven trains. The trains made 103 stops, and the total attendance reached 32,225 persons. They appeared in 40 counties over a period of 13 weeks.[13]

Lecture trains were used in other states as well. "These trains were composed of baggage cars for preparing demonstrational material, day coaches in which to hold meetings, and dining and sleeping cars for the professional staff. The trains operated on special schedules, making a number of stops each day . . . The idea caught the fancy of farmers, and people turned out by the thousands." In 1911, according to agricultural historian I.O. Schaub, 71 lecture trains operated in 28 states, reporting farmer attendance of over 995,000 people.[14]

Farmers' Course in Agriculture

By the early 1900s, the Farm Short Course, held in Madison each winter for young men, had become highly successful. Farmers also began pressuring the College of Agriculture to organize a weeklong farmers' course for men and women from throughout the rural regions of the state. The first farmers' course was convened in 1904. Attendees included 175 farmers from 42 counties. No one younger than the age of 25 could enroll. The course was offered free to state residents; the cost for non-residents was $10.

The bulletin announcing the course described the benefits as follows: "The farmer pupils are given definite, helpful instruction, often of a nature which cannot be gained by attending Farmers' Institutes or meetings held elsewhere at the University. The equipment of the Agricultural College in the way of apparatus, machinery, tools, livestock, books, etc. has cost far more than a hundred thousand dollars. All of this, so far as possible, is used for instruction purposes and helps immensely in rendering the lectures plain, comprehensive, and interesting to farmer students."[15]

The second farmers' course in Agriculture was held from February 14 to 24, 1905,

BULLETIN OF THE UNIVERSITY OF WISCONSIN
No. 105.

General Series	DECEMBER, 1904	No. 49

CIRCULAR OF INFORMATION

ON THE

SECOND ANNUAL

Farmers' Course in Agriculture

AND

FIRST ANNUAL

Housekeepers' Conference

AT THE

UNIVERSITY OF WISCONSIN

FEBRUARY 14-24, 1905

MADISON, WIS.
Published by the University
Bi-Monthly

Entered at the Post Office at Madison, Wisconsin, as Second-Class Matter.

1905 farmers' course in agriculture and housekeepers' conference. Later called Farm and Home Week, the program was held on the Madison campus for many years.

at the College of Agriculture in Madison. Topics taught included soil fertility and farm manure; feeding farm animals; sugar beets in Wisconsin; corn judging; milk testing and separators; spraying farm orchards; and judging and handling livestock. The program was to include a veterinary demonstration involving the dissection of a horse; a lecture on the draft horse; and a lecture by S. M. Babcock, who was well known for having developed the Babcock milk tester. Participants could visit the Washburn Observatory and "view the moon or some star through the great telescope." They could also tour "numerous museums, machine shops, laboratories, and the greatest of all in many ways, the grand library." The course attracted 227 farmers.[16]

Housekeepers' Conference

A "Housekeepers' Conference" was added to the farmers' course in 1905. This weeklong course, held at the same time as the farmers' course, was conducted in South Hall on the university campus, over the hill from the College of Agriculture. It was designed for the "entertainment and instruction of the farmer's wife and daughters," and it was conducted by members of the Department of Home Economics. The department had been organized in 1903 as part of the College of Letters and Science and was under the direction of Professor Caroline L. Hunt, who was assisted by Miss Ellen Alden Huntington. Topics covered during the week included food for health, care of children, water supplies, ventilation, care of flowers, house furnishings, and marketing. Participants could also tour a kindergarten, a hospital, the dairy department of the College of Agriculture—and Chadbourne Hall, where they could see "modern machinery for laundry work and cooking." There was no charge for any of the instruction.

For both courses, the university had made arrangements with Madison families living near the campus to provide board and room for participants at about five dollars per week. The university also arranged with the state's railroads to provide special reduced fares for those who were traveling to these courses.

The College of Agriculture and the College of Letters and Science cooperated to present this new program. The College of Agriculture provided several speakers for the Housekeepers' Conference. The university had broad aspirations for this one-week program. It wanted to attract well established farmers and their wives and provide them with practical farming and homemaking information, but the university also wanted to widen participants' horizons by offering tours and acquainting them with special features of the institution, such as the observatory and the library.[17]

Additional farmers' courses

Pressure on the College of Agriculture and the experiment station for agricultural information had become unrelenting. Each year, farmers demanded more. In response to the ever-increasing requests, the experiment station and the college decided to sponsor farmers' courses elsewhere in the state, patterned after the Madison course. Farmers' courses were often established in cooperation with county agricultural schools.

During the year of 1909-1910, more than 6,500 people enrolled in outstate farmers' courses. These were held in Jefferson, Marinette, Menomonie, Onalaska, Winneconne, Platteville, and Ashland. In addition, 1,500 people attended the Farmers', Women's, Special Dairy, and Young People's courses in Madison.[18]

Boys' and Girls' Clubs

Programs for rural young people can be traced back to New York in the middle 1850s. Horace Greeley, famed newspaper editor, sponsored a corn-growing contest with the prizes to be awarded the first week in October, 1856, at Watertown, New York. There were even earlier attempts at organizing agricultural clubs for young people. In 1828, a teacher at a boarding school in Butler County, Ohio, allotted parcels of land to his students. They grew corn, cucumbers, radishes, tomatoes, shrubbery, and flowers in competition with each other. In 1882, Delaware College sponsored a statewide corn contest for boys, with cash awards and subscriptions to *American Agriculturist* offered as prizes.[19]

By the turn of the century, educators and others began focusing on rural young people. Increasingly, out-of-school programs emerged as ways to enhance the curriculum of the one-room country school.

Liberty Hyde Bailey

Some critics were concerned that the curriculum of the one-room country school did not serve the needs of rural people. At Cornell University, educator Liberty Hyde Bailey spoke out on the problem. Bailey said that young people enrolled in country schools with a positive attitude toward rural life, but by the time they left the schools, they wanted to leave the farm. "There results a constant migration to the city, bringing about serious social and economic problems [for the country]," Bailey observed.[20]

Bailey wanted farm boys and girls to be proud of their rural heritage, not ashamed of it. Social and cultural differences between urban and farm people were probably greater at the time than they had ever been. Farm boys and girls too often heard the word "hick" or "hayseed" from their city cousins.

Other reasons emerged for establishing clubs that would serve farm boys and girls. Educators had long known that one way to approach a farmer and his wife was through his son or daughter. Let the son grow a new variety of corn, put lime on a patch of ground for alfalfa, spread fertilizer on a small plot of oats, and—if the results were positive—the parent might try the same technique. It was a clever approach, and it worked. The entire family learned when sons and daughters enrolled in early clubs devoted to corn growing, canning, clothing, or other endeavors.

Ransom Asa Moore

A Kewaunee County farm boy, rural schoolteacher, and county superintendent of schools, Ransom Asa Moore started teaching in the College of Agriculture in 1895.

In 1897, Moore became interested in seed selection as a way of improving crop varieties, and he was instrumental in helping Wisconsin become established as a leader in growing improved seeds. He was undoubtedly aware of the corn clubs for young people in other states, and he set out to start them in Wisconsin.

In the fall of 1903, Moore sold the idea of boys growing corn plots to the Richland County superintendent of schools. Moore's idea was to sponsor a corn-growing contest. He arranged for cash awards, plus a first prize of a Rock Island Planter and an Eagle Claw walking cultivator—a $40 value at the time. The contest was open to farm boys under 20 years of age. In the spring of 1904, interested boys received seed packets and printed growing instructions. They were encouraged to enter the "Great Youth Corn Growing Contest," scheduled to culminate at the Richland County Fairgrounds, September 27 to 30, 1904. Fifty boys enrolled in the contest. The local newspaper claimed that the contest drew more attention than "Big Otto's trained monkeys and a Negro ragtime band."[21]

A Need for Agricultural Extension

By 1900, the shift from wheat growing to a dairy-based farm economy was nearly complete, although farmers in many of Wisconsin's northern counties still practiced pioneer-like agriculture as they moved onto land strewn with massive stumps and debris from the logging years. Wisconsin farmers were optimistic about agriculture, and the new college of agriculture with its experiment station had begun to respond to the demands of the state's agriculturists. But the college simply couldn't keep up with the farmers' requests.

By 1907 and 1908, the experiment station was increasingly concerned about the amount of time and effort its staff members were putting into Extension activities. In his 1907 annual report, H. L. Russell wrote: "To make the results of experimental research of most value to the farmer, they must be presented in such a way as not only to engage his attention, but force the conviction upon him that he cannot afford to ignore the application. This can be done most effectually by actual demonstration work in which the principles sought to be inculcated are ocularly [visually] presented to the farmer."[22]

The experiment station's Extension activities continued to increase. In 1908, agriculture professors gave more than 100 lectures beyond their regular teaching. Dean Russell reported that the amount of correspondence and bulletin distribution had become staggering. "Some 12 stenographers have been required for the work last year [1908]. Nearly 45,000 letters were written, 23,000 manuscripts, and 102,000 mimeograph sheets of matter were prepared and sent out in compliance with requests."[23] University officials and legislators began listening to Dean Russell's call for an agricultural Extension service. In the next chapter, we see how this fledgling organization emerged.

CHAPTER 3

AGRICULTURAL EXTENSION BEGINS:
1908 TO 1914

By the early 1900s, many farmers were leery of depending solely on one income source. Wheat growing difficulties had taught them that lesson—they had become diversified farmers. A diversified farm usually had one major income source, such as dairying, but additional enterprises as well. Many farmers raised hogs, sheep, chickens, or beef cattle. Likewise, in many areas of the state, farmers not only grew forage crops such as corn and oats, but also cash crops such as potatoes and tobacco. Some even began growing peas and tomatoes for canning. And fruit crops such as apples and cranberries were becoming important economic products in certain regions of the state. In 1910, Wisconsin boasted 1,928 cheese factories. In that year, Wisconsin's cheese production exceeded New York's, making Wisconsin the leading cheese producing state in the nation.

Agricultural Extension Service
In response to considerable lobbying, the 1908 legislature appropriated $30,000 annually to operate an agricultural Extension service in Wisconsin. Russell immediately set out to establish the organization, making it a priority to ensure that "this Extension service as far as possible [be connected] with each department of the College." This first formal Agricultural Extension service was organized into two sections: demonstrations of the results of experimental or research work; and teaching courses of general agricultural information for persons unable to attend the university.[1]

Russell faced an internal struggle with the university's administration, which was attempting to revitalize General Extension activities and keep Agricultural Extension moving forward at the same time. Charles Van Hise, who became the university's president in 1904, began pushing to make all campus resources available to the people of the state, establishing what became known as "the Wisconsin Idea." The question of how to organize off-campus work was more problematic.

Louis Reber, who was in charge of the newly formed University Extension Division, later known as General Extension, wanted to separate his staff from their home academic departments. He argued that campus-based professors and researchers had neither the skills to do off-campus teaching nor the interest. Dean Russell, on the other hand, argued strongly that Agricultural Extension staff should be integral to their home departments, where they may be involved in campus teaching and research as well as off-campus teaching. Russell argued that Extension staff should be close to the research base for their teaching.[2]

The organizational wishes of both men prevailed. Agricultural Extension staff members were integrated with College of Agriculture departments. General Extension separated its people from campus departments. General Extension's organizational approach continued until (and in several cases after) the formation of the University of Wisconsin-Extension in 1965. These profoundly different philosophies of organizing proved a major challenge to the formation and successful operation of University of Wisconsin-Extension, which merged Cooperative Extension and General Extension into one organization.

Extension Plans

The experiment station published a special circular in 1909 that included a detailed description of plans for the new Agricultural Extension and what farmers could expect from it. The introduction included the following words:

"During recent years . . . a more direct and personal method has been developed at this Station which includes personal visitation and correspondence, cooperative demonstrations and experiments, and the solution of local problems by Station experts who visit the locality and study the problems on the farm."

"A special appropriation by the State Legislature has made possible better organization and expansion of this work in the College of Agriculture and Experiment Station along various lines of Extension Service. The purpose of this organization is to bring the benefits of this Station to a larger proportion of the 200,000 farmers of Wisconsin."[3] Under the direction of College of Agriculture departments, farmers could expect assistance in four areas:

(1) Demonstrations, so the farmers could see the results of research in field situations,

(2) Cooperative experiments when local conditions required special tests. These experiments would be conducted in cooperation with local farmers to determine the best methods of solving the problem.

(3) Advice through visitation and correspondence. Farmers were encouraged to write to Madison seeking answers to their questions. If the problem warranted closer inspection, a college staff person would visit the farmer.

(4) A regular series of bulletins to be published and made widely available, free of charge.

Subject areas in which farmers could expect assistance included agricultural engineering, agricultural economics, agronomy, animal husbandry, bacteriology, chemistry, dairying, horse breeding, horticulture, soils, and general lines of Extension service.

The "general lines" included such offerings as information about stump removal, cranberry investigations, agricultural lectures, rural and high school agriculture, and Extension farmers' courses.

Young People's Corn Contests

In addition to programs on pure seed dissemination, seed inspection, and weed control, agronomy included a special mention of "Young People's Corn Contests." The description read: "This work is done in cooperation with county fair associations and county superintendents. The object of these contests is to awaken in the boys and girls an interest in agricultural pursuits and to give purebred seeds the widest possible dissemination. Assistance is also given in judging the grain grown in these contests."[4]

Seeds for the contests would be provided free by the agronomy department to county fair secretaries and county superintendents. As we shall later learn, these corn contests served as one of the forerunners of the 4-H Club program.

K. L. Hatch in Charge

These new Agricultural Extension efforts, including the corn growing contests and a host of other programs for farmers, were well accepted. In 1909, Dean Russell placed K. L. Hatch in charge of Agricultural Extension activities with the job title of Extension secretary. Hatch was also responsible for agricultural education. Both agricultural education and Extension activities were placed in a department known as Agricultural Extension and Education.

Home Economics

On July 1, 1908, the department of home economics, formerly connected with the College of Letters and Science, was transferred to the College of Agriculture. The move was not without controversy. Staff members in home economics resigned.

Abby L. Marlatt, who had been with the technical high school in Providence, Rhode Island, was hired to head up this new home economics department. One of Marlatt's duties was to speak at the extremely well attended farmers' institutes that were held throughout the state. She became a very popular speaker and had many tales to tell of her outstate adventures. She recalled an occasion when she was having difficulty getting to the Northwestern train station to catch a train to a farmers' institute. When she got to the train station, the train had already left. "I have to get there," she said to the stationmaster. Institute speakers were expected to appear, no matter how much snow had fallen or how cold the weather. The stationmaster said, "Lady, the only way you'll get where you're going is to hire your own train."

"I'll do it," she said. Later, she reported that she was probably the only speaker to arrive at a farmers' institute or any Extension meeting in a private train with a special engineer and conductor. She never shared how much she paid for the trip.[5]

Even with this new Extension organization, farmers' institutes continued to have a separate superintendent and budget within the college, perhaps because the institutes had been in operation for 25 years by 1910. In 1913, Dr. Dorothy Reed Mendenhall was hired as a special lecturer. At an Osseo farmers' institute, she lectured on the subjects of "Clothing the Baby" and "The Use of Cheese in the Diet."

Farming in the North

In 1895, the legislature authorized the publication of a booklet by Dean Henry from the College of Agriculture entitled *Northern Wisconsin, A Handbook for the Homeseeker*. Here the would-be northern Wisconsin farmer could read about everything from climate to soil types, from crops to cattle raising, and even something about dairying. The book soon sold 50,000 copies. Material from this little book was found in English, German, and Norwegian pamphlets extolling the virtues of farm life in Wisconsin's cutover region.

Many publications tended to overpromote the area, meaning the reality of the north turned out to be considerably less desirable than what had been described. One writer, trying to be honest about what he saw, described some cutover land this way: "In appearance most forbidding. It showed gaunt, ghostly looking dead pines still erect, giant trunks burned off at the base in falling arrested by other dead but standing timber, half buried logs overgrown and hidden by underbrush or by groves of saplings; in short timber living and dead inextricably intermingled and nearly all worthless."[6]

Dean Russell and Secretary Hatch both saw the great potential for agricultural and home economics Extension activities. The north was opening up to farming now that the loggers had shouldered their axes and left. Thousands of acres of cutover land became available—some of it next to worthless for farming, but much of it rich and full of potential. As farmers moved onto these lands, they needed assistance. By 1911 Russell, along with the State Commission for Vocational and Industrial Education, was lobbying the legislature for money to place agricultural instructors in counties, especially in northern counties.

Seaman Knapp

The idea of county agricultural representatives was not new to Russell or Hatch. They had heard of the pioneer work of Seaman Knapp. Knapp was born in New York in 1833, just ahead of the first wave of technological change in agriculture when reapers replaced cradles, threshing machines replaced flails, and horses replaced oxen—only to have steam engines start replacing horses. This was a time when farmers began to see the value of reading, attending meetings, going on tours, and listening to lectures, instead of depending entirely on their fathers, grandfathers, and neighbors for their education.

Knapp worked in the South and developed the demonstration approach to teaching. Joseph Bailey, a Knapp biographer, wrote: "In the new type of community demonstration farm procedure, Knapp had discovered that by sending the government to the sidelines he was able to tap not only the enthusiastic cooperation of the townspeople, but also a very wholesome amount of primary social compulsion from each rural community."[7]

Seaman Knapp is most recognized for helping southern farmers control the cotton boll weevil. In 1904, Knapp organized the Farmers' Cooperative Cotton Demonstration with headquarters in Houston, Texas. Professors from Texas Agricultural College, working in cooperation with the railroads, held meetings throughout Texas. Knapp struck on the idea of appointing special agents of the Department of Agriculture to organize local committees that would assist farmers. "The agents sought to visit all their demonstrators once a month, to persuade additional farmers to sign up, to distribute selected corn and cotton seed free, and rally local businessmen to support their work."[8]

County Agricultural Representatives

W. C. Stalling was the first County Extension agent in the United States. He was hired on November 12, 1906, in Smith County, Texas. Other states soon began hiring such agents.[9]

In 1912, the new Wisconsin Agricultural Extension Service decided to add county representatives. Rather than depending on college staff to travel to the far corners of the state giving lectures and conducting demonstrations, Extension would hire representatives who would live and work in a county. In his 1913 annual report, Dean Russell wrote: "A new and most important line of Extension endeavor has been inaugurated this past year through the establishment of county agricultural representatives, who will become resident representatives of the College of Agriculture in the respective counties of the state. In the dissemination of agricultural instruction, the lecture course system has long been followed with success, but the needs of the times indicate that a more personal relation is likely to prove more effective than where the instruction is confined exclusively to the lecture platform."[10]

Russell also made a conscious decision about what to call these new county workers. He did not want them viewed as experts "upon all things agricultural." Nor did he want them called specialists, implying a narrow focus of activity. He argued that these new county workers stood "midway between the College and the man on the farm, who may desire to secure direct information relative to the problems which may arise." No mention was made of the title "agent," which would later become widely used.

Russell decided on the title "county agricultural representative." He explained the workers' role in the following manner: "[The county agricultural representative] will be of direct aid to the farmer, enabling him to establish a more productive and permanent system of agriculture. As such, he should become an economic factor in the county, but it should also be his chosen mission to awaken and develop the community spirit and help guide the social forces along the pathway of progress."[11]

These are interesting words. The role of the county representative was to be more than merely providing technical information to farmers. These new representatives were also asked to help improve rural communities.

Russell spelled out some of the specific tasks for these new Extension workers. Primarily they were to give direct aid to farmers during the summer months, and then be in charge of teaching agriculture during the winter months. The teaching would take place "in the county training school for the training of rural teachers."

Wisconsin's First County Representatives

Oneida County hired E. L. Luther in February 1912 as a county agricultural representative with headquarters in Rhinelander. The Oneida County Board had voted on November 11, 1911, to request an agricultural representative in the county. G. R. Ingalls was hired in Eau Claire County in April 1912, and F. D. Otis was employed in Barron County in August of the same year.

All three men had earlier earned their bachelor's degrees under the direction of Professor Hatch, so they were well aware of what the College of Agriculture was attempting to do by placing representatives in counties.

That first winter on the job, E. L. Luther taught a class of 15 teachers at the county training school. He also ran a 10-week short course in agriculture for 17 boys. In March, with help from the college staff in Madison, he conducted a farmers' course attended by 20 percent of Oneida County's farmers.

In an early report, Luther wrote that Oneida County needed improved livestock, liming to correct acid soils, legumes to increase the nitrogen content of soil and furnish forage, and silos to provide winter feed storage for dairy cattle. It was in these areas of need that he concentrated his teaching efforts.

In Eau Claire County, G. R. Ingalls reported on his situation: "The problems of pioneer agriculture do not obtain so strenuously here as in the new North. The dairy industry is already well established, but the problem is the 'boarder cow' that is eating up the profits of the rest of the herd."

Ingalls went on to say that he worked closely with the country schools in Eau Claire County and had "gotten the boys and girls of the farm interested in practical problems of arithmetic, such as determining the yield and profit of the individual cows in the herd." Ingalls also did considerable milk testing. In his first eight months in Eau Claire County, he signed up 32 dairy herds containing a total of 477 cows.

To make their work a bit easier, both Ingalls and Luther were provided with motorcycles. In his annual report, Dean H. L. Russell wrote about the motorcycles. "These [motorcycles] have proven very serviceable where roads are suitable, but in sandy sections travel with these has proven difficult."

According to their reports, from the time of their hiring until July 1, 1912, Ingalls

E. L. Luther was Wisconsin's first county extension agent. He served in Oneida County and made his rounds riding a two-cylinder Indian motorcycle. UW-Madison Archives.

and Luther held a total of 27 meetings in their respective counties, with an attendance of 2,700 persons. They wrote more than 400 letters, and 340 farmers came to their offices. In addition, they made 170 farm visits.[12] Mr. Otis did not begin work in Barron County until August 1912, so his efforts were not reported until the following year.

The acceptance of the county representative system spread widely. By the end of 1912, more than a dozen additional counties had requested agricultural representatives. In fact, the idea of county agricultural representives had taken hold not just in Texas and Wisconsin, but throughout the country. However, many in Wisconsin believed that its county agricultural representative plan had some distinctive features. The plan, first and foremost, was educational. Dean Russell believed that a close connection with the existing educational agencies in the counties was as important as direct work with farmers: "It was apparent at the outset that [the county representative's] work would have to be spread by the influence of other factors than merely individual service to the tiller of the soil with reference to his own personal problems."[13]

The county agricultural representatives were asked to teach at the county training schools, which would spread agricultural knowledge to the rural schoolteachers and thus to the rural children. Russell had another reason for doing this. He knew, as did many of the agriculture college professors who had long been associated with farmers' institutes, that a mature mind was sometimes a tough one to enter. As Russell wrote: "The father becomes interested in a change of methods through the child. This is particularly easy in the matter of such simple practices as seed germination and selection."[14]

These new agricultural representatives also conducted short courses in agriculture for farm boys during the winter months—typically for six to eight weeks, but in some cases for 10 weeks. Boys who had completed or left their studies at the county school were prime candidates.

Russell believed that the second distinctive feature of the Wisconsin system for county agricultural representatives was that it was totally tax-supported. There were those who believed that private money, such as funds from the railroads or from agricultural organizations, ought to be solicited to help finance the program. But Russell wrote: "At the outset, therefore, it was felt that it was not wise to trust to the reed of private philanthropy or personal support, but that we should build this type of service on the basis of a publicly supported institution. The initiative always rests with the people. If they do not want to tax themselves for this purpose, the work is not organized."[15]

In 1912, the cost to taxpayers in a county that retained an agricultural representative was between $1,000 and $1,300 a year. In 1913, Wisconsin passed a law that was introduced by Senator A. R. Potter, enabling counties to spend tax dollars on Extension work. The law authorized 10 counties to employ county agricultural representatives in 1914, with six more to follow in 1915. It provided a system for a county/state sharing of funding for agricultural representatives. Under this legislation, county boards were authorized to raise at least $1,000 a year, minimum of two years, to cover the county's contribution to these new agricultural representatives.

The preamble to the law read: "For the purpose of aiding in the agricultural development in several counties of the state, any county, except those in which country agricultural schools are maintained, is hereby authorized, through its county board, to establish and maintain an agricultural representative in accordance with the provisions of this act."

"To advise and consult, to aid in the development and improvement of agriculture and country life conditions, to offer courses of instruction for young people and adults, to aid in formation of cooperative enterprises, to promote better business methods among farmers and to give such assistance as possible in the development of agricultural teaching in the schools of the county. It shall be his duty to keep in touch with all agencies of the state or elsewhere that will enable him to utilize the most knowledge in the furtherance of his work."[16]

Between 1912 and 1916, representatives were hired in the following counties: Oneida, Eau Claire and Barron (1912); Price and Langlade (1913); Douglas, Forest,

A university agriculture professor demonstrates orchard spraying equipment on a farm near Oshkosh, about 1910.

Lincoln, Taylor, Polk, and Vilas (1914); Ashland and Walworth (1915); and Bayfield, Burnett, Portage, Rusk, and Sawyer (1916).[17]

As other counties heard about the successes of agricultural representatives, they wanted to hire their own. The first three agents, Luther, Ingalls, and Otis, were reporting great responses to their efforts. Ingalls was emphasizing cow testing, with some 1,500 cows on test. Luther was emphasizing community efforts to improve dairy herds. Otis had organized a dairy sire exchange, in order to save "the services of tested sires that would otherwise go to the block because they could not longer be used with safety in their original herds." In Price County, Griffith Richards had personally tested a large percentage of dairy cattle in the county for tuberculosis.

Extension promoted a statewide effort to improve dairy cattle feeding. One way of doing this was to encourage silo-building. County agricultural representatives were supplied with metal forms for building concrete silos, and these were loaned to groups of farmers at a low rental rate. Of course, some farmers and cheese factory operators continued to fear silage, saying that silos should be avoided. William Dempster Hoard, editor of *Hoard's Dairyman,* was still writing about the virtues of silos and why farmers should have them in 1915—some 35 years after the first ones had been built in the state.

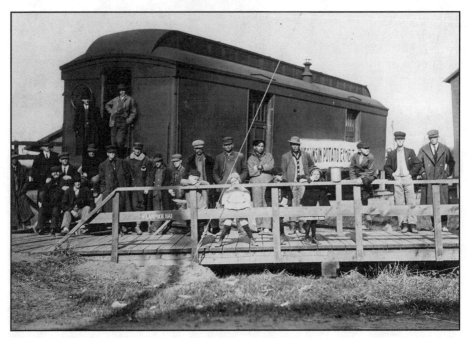

The Potato Train, an innovative way to take new information to the people

In Langlade County, F. G. Swoboda helped farmers improve their cream separators. He showed them that they were losing as much as .8 percent butterfat by using cream separators that were in poor repair.

Several agriculture representatives established demonstration plots with cooperating farmers. These tests included corn plots, use of commercial fertilizer on potatoes, the benefits of using lime when growing alfalfa, and planting hemp to eradicate quack grass.

With the exception of Walworth County, which employed a county agricultural representative in 1915, and Portage County, which employed one in 1916, all of the counties that employed early representatives were northern counties. But the southern Wisconsin counties soon began adding them as well, because it became clear that the county was emerging as the center of Extension activities, with the County Extension office the focus point. At one time the university in Madison had been the center of activity, but now the university was shifting toward a supporting role. Although the county offices could not succeed without the College of Agriculture's research and well-trained specialists, most people in the state regarded the county office as the access point for the information and assistance they had long been seeking. There were, however, holdouts that thought little of County Extension work, the University of Wisconsin, or anything else that smacked of science or new ways of doing things.

Statewide Agricultural Education Activities

In 1914 George McKerrow, longtime director of the farmers' institutes, retired. Professor C. P. Norgord of the agronomy department took his place. During the year in which McKerrow retired, 125 farmers' institutes were held—plus 41 cooking schools. The total attendance at these events amounted to 114,000 people. In 1915, 287 farmers' institutes were conducted, with 60,000 people attending. "Field meetings with automobiles" were held that summer. Seventy such meetings were held in farmers' fields, with 5,600 farmers attending.

February farmer courses in Madison continued to be useful. Dean Russell wrote: "The courses at the University in February for the farmer, the farmer's wife, and the farmer's boy have now come to be so important an agricultural and country life event that they draw over 2,000 people in attendance from practically all parts of the state."[18] The course became known as farmers' week, and later as Farm and Home Week.

Beginning in 1911, a country life conference was held each year at the same time as farmers' week. Under the direction of the rural sociology department, the conference brought together farmers, teachers, the clergy, business people, bankers, and civic leaders. President Theodore Roosevelt had earlier organized a country life conference to deal with such topics as rural unrest, doubt, isolation, and despair. Speakers from around the country spoke at a country life commission hearing in Madison in December 1908. One key point made at the hearing was that emphasis on agricultural production fell short of providing for the educational, spiritual, and social needs of rural people.[19]

Russell, too, realized that Agricultural Extension should do more than merely providing the means for farmers to earn more money. He saw the country life conference as an important way to meet broader needs. "It is evident that progress in the home, the school, and the social life of the community must keep abreast of the material and economic growth of the country, and no influence set in motion in recent years has contributed more to a healthy and vigorous growth of this idea than this most important gathering of those [who are] vitally interested in the solution of rural problems."[20]

A special livestock exposition was held during the second week of the winter farmers' course in 1913. It was developed in cooperation with the livestock and breeders' associations, and it included charts, models, and live animals. The various breed associations exhibited the best examples of their respective breeds.

In addition to the short courses held in Madison, 11 other courses were held around the state, attracting more than 9,000 people. One of the courses was held at Ripon College—a private institution. This was the first time that a state liberal arts college cooperated in providing practical information for farmers. Thirteen speakers appeared during the three-day program, and more than 900 people attended.

Special one-week schools of a more specialized nature were conducted in eight locations around the state. The 467 farmers who attended these schools each paid a $1 registration fee.

Finally, the College of Agriculture continued sponsoring an exhibit at the state fair. Russell was impressed with the importance and the power of exhibits as a way of reaching farmers. Agricultural lessons ". . . presented in a graphic and vivid manner, drive home a truth by contrast and produce a more permanent impression than when presented through the medium of the printed word."[21] Along with the college's exhibits, Russell considered the exhibition of farm products a powerful educational tool. At a glance, farmers could compare the farm products exhibited with their own— ear corn, sheaves of grain, and prize winning cattle and hogs.

Boys' and Girls' Clubs Expand

By 1910, youth corn growing exhibits appeared at 45 Wisconsin county fairs. The effort was so successful that Ransom A. Moore was able to hire an assistant to work on this new youth program. Thomas L. Bewick, a young agronomy instructor in the College of Agriculture, became the state's first college-supported farm youth leader. Interest in youth activity had spread to animal care, food preparation, and sewing, in addition to the various crop growing projects.

The name 4-H was not yet associated with farm youth organizations. Many public speakers talked about the need for public education to move beyond the three R's— reading, 'riting, and 'rithmetic. In 1905 Albert B. Storms, the president of Iowa State College, spoke at a meeting of the National Education Association. Storms talked of the need for three H's in education in order to build student character. He was referring to Head, Heart, and Hand. Booker T. Washington of Tuskegee Institute also talked about the need for the three H's. Rudyard Kipling wrote a piece called "The Children's Song." It included the following stanza:

> *Land of our Birth, our faith, our pride,*
> *For whose dear sake our fathers died;*
> *Oh Motherland, we pledge to thee,*
> *Head, heart, and hand through the years to be!*[22]

Boys' and girls' clubs were rapidly expanding across the country. They included clubs for gardening and the growing of wheat and potatoes for boys; and gardening, baking, sewing, and canning clubs for girls. In 1909 W. H. Miller, a county superintendent of schools in Mississippi, organized the first "pig club" of record. The purpose of the club was to make good use of the corn grown by corn club members. No boy was allowed to enter a pig club unless he had grown corn the previous year, "since there was no use starting a boy on pigs unless he had something to feed them."

Until this time, the cloverleaf had not been associated with boys' and girls' clubs. Wright and Page Counties in Iowa were apparently the first to use a three-leaf clover with H's on the petals. A cloverleaf emblem was given out in these counties, appearing on both a pin and a pennant for excellence in agricultural and domestic science (although some people claim it was for school attendance).

By 1910, both three- and four-leaf clovers were awarded for work in agriculture or domestic science. The four-leaf pin was given to those who completed a second year of the work.

O. H. Benson, superintendent of schools in Wright County, Iowa, was hired to work on Extension activities in the Washington office of the Farmers' Cooperative Demonstration Work in February 1911. Benson had used three- and four-leaf clovers as emblems for youth in Iowa. Girls' and boys' club leaders met in Washington in the spring of 1911 and agreed on the design for a four-leaf clover with the three H's—one each for Head, Hand, and Heart, and an additional H for Health. Thus the official emblem for boys' and girls' clubs was born. The United States Department of Agriculture, Farmers' Cooperative Demonstration Work, published a circular explaining the emblem. The four H's were to represent training that was equally aimed at the head, heart, hands, and health of every child.

Historian Franklin M. Reck wrote: "The head was to be trained to think, plan, and reason; the heart to be kind, true, and sympathetic; the hands to be useful, helpful, and skillful. . . the health H was to resist disease, enjoy life, and make for efficiency."[23] This became the official beginning of 4-H, at least as far as the universal symbol was concerned. Interest in boys' and girls' clubs continued to grow in Wisconsin and across the country.

Establishment of a Press Service
An agricultural press service was established in the College of Agriculture in January 1909. From that time forward, a weekly *University Press Bulletin* was sent to over 100 leading agricultural journals, and to 350 weekly newspapers in the state. The materials sent included reports of experimental and demonstration work, often accompanied by photographs and engravings. Dean Russell justified the new press service this way: "Recognizing that almost every farmer of the state may be reached through the medium of the agricultural and local press, the preparation and distribution of articles describing the work of this Station, results of experiments and demonstrations, with the advice of the Station staff on special topics, was considered necessary in order to extend the influence of the Station to the greater number of farmers in the state. The publication of suitable matter in such form is often of greater service than the more technical and voluminous station publication."[24]

The main reason for establishing the press service was the overwhelming number of inquiries the college had been receiving from around the state. It took considerable staff time and a large number of typists to merely answer the thousands of letters that arrived each month. Even with the press service, Russell reported that during the 1912-1913 fiscal year, college staff wrote 60,000 letters in reply to inquiries. The number would undoubtedly have been considerably larger without the press service. Russell was also well aware that researchers' often plodding reports were not read— and if they were, they were not understood by the everyday farmer looking for an answer to a practical problem.

The news releases were written in everyday, easily accessible language. We thus saw the birth of a new kind of Extension person, a journalist who was able to transform long, highly technical, sometimes obtuse and generally boring material into easily read, highly accessible short pieces targeted at the average reader.

Search for Funding

Russell and Hatch were faced with the problem of how to expand their limited resources to meet the ever-increasing demand for agricultural information. Funding, especially to expand the number of county agricultural representatives, was high on their priority list.

Wisconsin was not alone in extending its county representative program. In 1912, other midwestern states employing county agricultural representatives included Illinois, Michigan, and Iowa.

Through the 1862 Morrill Act, the federal government established agricultural colleges and the United States Department of Agriculture. The Hatch act of 1887 authorized money for experiment stations throughout the country. Logic would suggest that the federal government should provide funds for the support of Agricultural Extension. After all, agriculture had become an important part of the economy of every state in the nation.

Prior to the passage of the Smith-Lever Act (the topic for the next chapter), Agricultural Extension in Wisconsin had already established some noteworthy principles that continued over the years. In this chapter we have seen the importance of public support of County Extension through local taxes; educational programs that emphasized dealing with people's problems and questions; the connection between county-based educational programs and a research base in the College of Agriculture; the emergence of the county office as the center of Extension activity; and the cooperation of local and state governments in providing educational opportunities for rural people. We also saw the emergence of club work for rural boys and girls, and the agreement on the four-leaf clover as the symbol for the organization.

In the next chapter, we examine the passage of the Smith-Lever Act, which formally created the Cooperative Extension Service and provided a federal source of funding for it.

CHAPTER 4

YEARS OF DEVELOPMENT:
1914 TO 1930

Agricultural Extension work spread rapidly across the nation. As of June 30, 1914, 240 counties in 27 northern and western states had county agricultural representatives. Forty-two of the 48 states had approximately 1,350 men and women doing county agricultural work.[1] So far, the only funding had come from state and county coffers. The federal government had funded land grant colleges with the Morrill Act and agricultural research through the Hatch Act. Was it ready to support Agricultural Extension activities?

The Wisconsin leader Dean Harry Russell now assumed a national leadership role. In 1911 the Association of Agricultural Colleges and Experiment Stations elected him to its executive committee. Earlier he had pushed AACES to add a division on Extension. Now Russell was lobbying for federal assistance. In 1912 and 1913, he repeatedly traveled to Washington, trying to convince various congressional committees to support a bill for Agricultural Extension activities.

The Smith-Lever Act of 1914
Prior to 1914, the federal government had given some money to support County Extension activity through the Office of Farm Management within the United States Department of Agriculture. This amounted to $165,000 in 1912-1913. The Farmers' Cooperative Demonstration Work (Boll Weevil program) in the South was financed by a combination of federal and private money.

In 1909, a bill offered by the Association of American Agricultural Colleges and by experiment stations, also supported by the National Grange, was defeated in Congress. However, party control shifted in Congress as a result of the next national election. In 1911, the Smith-Lever Extension bill, with some changes, was reintroduced in the House of Representatives by Representative Asbury F. Lever of South Carolina in the Senate by Senator Hoke Smith of Georgia.

After much discussion and debate in both houses, the Smith-Lever Act finally passed on May 8, 1914. A late change in the bill stipulated that not only did land-

BULLETIN OF THE UNIVERSITY OF WISCONSIN
Serial No. 1147; General Series 930

Farmers'

AND

Home-Makers' Week

Program

Fifty Years of Dairy Progress

Let's Plan for Fifty More

AGRICULTURAL COLLEGE, MADISON
JANUARY 30 TO FEBRUARY 4
1922

REDUCED RATES ON ALL RAILROADS

Entered as second-class matter, June 10, 1898, at the post office
at Madison, Wisconsin, under the act of July 16, 1894.

Farmers' and homemakers' week program, 1922.

grant colleges and counties have responsibility for Agricultural Extension work, but the work must be done in cooperation with the United States Department of Agriculture. This was the first major attempt to legislate governmental cooperation at three levels—national, state, and county. The Smith-Lever Act said, in part, that the purpose of Extension work was "to aid in diffusing among the people of the United States useful and practical information on subjects relating to agriculture and home economics, and to encourage the application of the same."

To accomplish the work, "cooperative agricultural Extension work shall consist of the giving of instruction and practical demonstrations in agriculture and home economics to persons not attending or resident in said colleges in the several communities, and imparting to such persons information on said subjects through field demonstrations, publications, and otherwise . . ."[2]

For years, agricultural leaders and lawmakers returned to these words for guidance. Among its key points, the bill directed that those benefiting from the program could not be attending colleges; that the information offered should be practical; that it should relate to agriculture and home economics; and that those served should be involved in deciding what should be done. The latter was a bold new idea to many college and university people, who generally believed that professors knew best what people ought to learn. Now it became a two-way exchange, with all parties agreeing on plans.

Initially, each state received $10,000 annually from federal funds, with additional yearly amounts prorated on the basis of the state's rural population. Each land-grant university that received Smith-Lever funds was required to report annually to the Secretary of Agriculture regarding how the funds were spent. This was the only control the federal government had over state Extension programs—an "after the fact" reporting of how funds had been used, to ensure that the programs fell within the purposes of the act. Federal funds usually came with many strings attached, but the cooperative language of Smith-Lever placed considerable trust in the states and the counties to further the work of agriculture and home economics.

At the time and later, many writers commented on the far-reaching effects of Smith-Lever and the fundamental philosophy behind the law. In 1949, historians Edmund deS. Brunner and E. Hsin Pao Yang wrote: " . . . the Act provided federal assistance to an educational program that encompassed the whole farm family. It recognized the basic importance of agriculture, of its practitioners and their families to the nation. It set up a legal mechanism which has stood the tests of the intervening years, in large part because its philosophy and provisions were consonant with the values and attitudes of the people, particularly the farm people of the United States."[3]

The new Cooperative Extension legislation recognized the contributions women made to agriculture—caring for livestock, working in the fields, raising children, and working hand in hand with their husbands to make decisions and keep up with what was new. Production agriculture was and still is vitally important. But family and rural life were not to be overlooked. Indeed, they were to be emphasized. Thus, educational programs for men, women, and children emerged as Agricultural Extension found its financial footing and set out to prove its worth after the passage of Smith-Lever. The Wisconsin legislature quickly approved state participation in this new Cooperative Extension Service, and on June 16, 1914, the regents of the university named Dean Russell as director and K. L. Hatch as assistant director.

Over the years, many people have been confused about the title "Cooperative Extension Service," believing it must have something to do with cooperatives. Instead, the organizational title refers to the cooperation of federal, state, and county government in providing educational programming.

County Agricultural Representative Activities
Agricultural Extension in Wisconsin continued to expand. E. L. Luther, who had been working in Oneida County, was appointed state field superintendent of the entire system in 1914. His job involved coordinating the work among the several

Early county agricultural representatives:

- established cooperative creameries;
- promoted potato growing contests;
- created a cheese makers association;
- assisted with field drainage projects;
- helped control an outbreak of blackleg in cattle;
- continued testing for tuberculosis;
- checked farm cream separators;
- conducted on-farm management surveys;
- did soil analysis to determine acidity;
- advocated purebred cattle, pedigreed oats, and certified potato seed;
- organized a Tamworth Swine Association;
- encouraged silo building; assisted with county and district fairs;
- demonstrated potato spraying;
- provided plans for new dairy barns;
- organized stock judging contests;
- and helped with school fairs.

Cooperative Extension often held joint programs with the branch experiment stations. This one took place in Marshfield in about 1917.

counties with agricultural representatives, and helping new men get started. By the end of 1914, county agricultural representatives worked in 11 counties: Oneida, Eau Claire, Barron, Price, Langlade, Douglas, Forest, Lincoln, Taylor, Polk, and Vilas. All of these are northern counties. The legislature had approved 16 more for 1915, but Extension was having difficulty finding capable candidates for the county positions.

Not all farmers accepted the idea of these new "book-learned" men working in their counties. In his annual report, Dean Russell noted that "some of the farmers were inclined to be indifferent, if not actively antagonistic."

These new county agricultural representatives concentrated on teaching young people through short courses and on-farm demonstrations. They also made many farm visits. In 1914, the Vilas County representative made 403 visits, while the Douglas County representative stopped at 306 farms. Five agricultural representatives taught classes at the county training schools for country schoolteachers. Agricultural representatives taught short courses lasting from six to eight weeks in Taylor, Langlade, Eau Claire, Oneida, and Price Counties. Representatives reported that students took home and applied new ideas such as testing and grading seed corn, using purebred sires, keeping production records on cows, growing alfalfa, keeping farm cost accounting records, and applying new ideas involving farm mechanics. G. R. Ingalls, the agricultural representative in Eau Claire County, reported that a graduate of his winter class increased his corn yield on the home farm by four bushels per acre. The young man had also learned how to splice ropes, so his father was able to put off buying a new hayfork rope for a year.

F. D. Otis in Barron County reported that his county had over 1,000 cows on test and a newly organized cow testing association of 33 members. Otis also pushed planting alfalfa. He led a tour of 100 cars and 500 farmers around the county, inspecting alfalfa fields where ground limestone had been added. Otis helped bring four train carloads of limestone to the county.

In Forest County, John Swenehart helped organize a potato growers association with 90 members. Swenehart had a major challenge. Many longtime residents knew lumbering and were skeptical about farming—no matter what form it took. Same thing for Oscar Gunderson in Vilas County. He helped farmers grow potatoes after visiting almost every farmer in the county in 1914. On one of his potato demonstration plots, he harvested 135 bushels from a quarter-acre field.

In Oneida County, where W. D. Juday now worked, potato growing had advanced considerably. Eight community organizations had been formed to help farmers understand the finer points of growing potatoes. Juday helped organize a potato show in Rhinelander that offered 100 exhibits and he also created demonstration plots on the county fairgrounds that emphasized chemical fertilization of potatoes and approaches to controlling late blight. Silo building was also on Juday's agenda. He reported that farmers had built 40 silos, eight of them concrete.

In Price County, Griffith Richards organized a campaign to test cattle for tuberculosis. Thirteen herds, numbering 158 head, were tested in 1914. Richards also reported that eight of the twenty-two silos erected in the county in 1914 could be traced to his work.[4]

By 1916, county agricultural representatives numbered 18 in Wisconsin. Kenosha County, on the Illinois border, began discussing whether an agent was wanted there. County supervisors voted yes on April 11, 1917. Griffith Richards became Kenosha County's first agricultural agent, with an office located in the Chamber of Commerce Building. He had a tough job selling the scientific method and "book learning" to skeptical farmers

By 1915, county short courses were two weeks in length. They included follow-up sessions on the home farms. Farm boys showed considerable enthusiasm for these courses, with good attendance records. In Douglas County, Arvid Bong of Poplar rode a horse or walked 16 miles each day to attend the short course held at Lake Nebagamon.[5]

Professor C. J. Galpin had provided leadership for country life conferences in connection with the farmers' course in Madison. In 1915, he began advocating local country life conferences—the first ones at Platteville Normal School. They were also held at Oconto, Elkhorn, and Baraboo. The slogan for these country life conferences was "Get acquainted with your neighbor—you might like him."[6]

During 1916, agricultural work by county representatives and state-level specialists continued at a high pace. Programs included seed corn testing; treating oats for smut; treating seed potatoes for disease; encouraging the growing of legumes, especially alfalfa; and extensive work on livestock improvement and disease control for dairy cows. Testing cow production to weed out low producers continued as a high priority program, along with encouraging the use of registered bulls and balancing rations for their herds. Testing for tuberculosis received high emphasis, as did instruction on building silos. In 1917, it was estimated that Wisconsin farmers had 60,000 silos— one for every three farmers.

World War I

War had broken out in Europe when the Smith-Lever Act was signed in 1914. Many hoped that the United States would remain neutral, which seemed a possibility. But on April 6, 1917, the U.S. joined the Allies and the country was at war. Aiding in the effort proved a challenge to a Cooperative Extension Service that had barely gotten organized.

The College of Agriculture placed 27 war emergency demonstration agents in counties to help stimulate food and livestock production. Trained men were in short supply, so these new demonstration agents were agricultural college staff members, normal school instructors in agriculture, county agricultural school instructors, farmers' institute speakers, and county superintendents of schools. The college secured several thousand bushels of seed grains—wheat, oats, buckwheat, and rye—for distribution to farmers, with the goal of increasing the state's grain production. Acreage devoted to oats increased by nearly 5,000 acres, while wheat acreage increased by more than 9,000 acres.

Extension staff helped farmers obtain 36,000 bushels of seed potatoes, resulting in an increase in potato acreage of more than 8,500 acres. Agents encouraged farmers to save their heifer calves for breeding purposes rather than selling them for veal. They helped farmers sell these heifer calves to dairymen in twelve different states. One Missouri county bought 18 train carloads of Wisconsin heifer calves. The emergency agents pushed Wisconsin farmers to plant more and harvest more. Beyond obtaining seed and assisting with calf sales, agents helped organize 27 farm loan associations and helped 672 farmers obtain loans. In the midst of a labor shortage, agents helped place more than 2,000 farm laborers.[7]

Post-War Activities

The Armistice was signed on November 11, 1918. Before long, Wisconsin farmers began seeing hard times. The push to produce more crops during the war had resulted

Early county agricultural agents helped farmers with practical problems such as calibrating a grain drill.

in more produce than the markets could handle. By 1919, Cooperative Extension began shifting its program emphasis from how to produce more to how to produce more economically. On-the-farm demonstrations continued to be a popular teaching method. Marketing farm products and improving social conditions also became important program areas.

As a way to combat "the farm problem," the Farm Bureau, which was organized in 1919 and 1920, worked to create a closer relationship between farmers and county agents (such a relationship had been formed in Illinois). Dean Russell opposed the idea, believing that the College of Agriculture should not favor one farm organization over another.[8]

Changes in Farming

With low farm income and hard times, fruit and poultry production became more popular. Extension began emphasizing educational programs on pruning and spraying fruit trees, with the assistance of Extension fruit specialists Conrad Kuehner and F. R. Gifford. Poultry specialists J. G. Halpin and J. B. Hayes helped develop programs on poultry production.

The 1920s became known as Wisconsin's stump-blowing era. Thousands of acres of former forestland, now potential farmland, were covered with stumps some five feet across. Extension took on the onerous task of land clearing, which also meant the dangerous job of blasting stumps. In 1921, Wisconsin cleared 35,000 acres. In three years, 135,000 acres had been cleared. Wisconsin was able to obtain six million pounds of explosives left over from World War I for blasting stumps.

With the land free of stumps, university people asked a question that should have been asked earlier. Is all this cleared land suitable for farming? Some of it was so far north that frost-free days were few and only limited crops could be grown. Most of the soil was highly acidic, requiring huge amounts of lime before crops such as alfalfa could be grown. Some of the land was stony, sandy, and droughty.

Thoughtful people suggested returning once-forested lands back to trees. The need for lumber and pulp wood continued, jobs in the forestry industry would return, and tax delinquency on land would decrease. Farmers working on poor farms simply couldn't make it, and they quit paying taxes.[9]

Extension alfalfa specialist Larry Graber saw alfalfa acreage increase. Wisconsin grew 17,000 acres of alfalfa in 1910. By 1920, the number had reached 87,000 acres and was increasing. Farmers spread lime on their fields, but those who were close to marl lakes began devising huge machines for dredging marl from lake bottoms. Obtaining marl required considerably more labor than lime, but it was cheaper. It was also located closer to many farms. In some communities, farmers shared the hiring of a marl digger and equally divided the marl pile that resulted. Farmers hauled marl with horses and steel-wheeled wagons; they pitched it on and off the wagons with silage forks. Marl served its purpose. Acid soils now grew alfalfa, which was fast becoming the forage of choice for Wisconsin's farmers.

By 1924, alfalfa acreage had soared to over 267,000 acres, but even the wondrous alfalfa had its downside. Winter thawing and freezing lifted the alfalfa crowns from the ground and killed the plants. The 1924-25 season brought alfalfa losses to 100,000 acres.[10]

Not all county agents stayed with Extension. Some left for other opportunities, as is the case with any other organization. James Murphy was the first county agent in Walworth County, starting work in 1915. He resigned at the end of the year to manage Tilden Farms, which included 1,600 acres, 350 purebred Guernsey cows, 1,000 Chester White hogs, and 2,500 Leghorn chickens—a huge operation for its day. While working there, Murphy consulted often with the College of Agriculture's Animal Husbandry Department about feed formulation for livestock. Murphy conducted many feeding experiments on the farm and was pleased with the results. In 1921, he and his brother Lawrence founded the Murphy Products Company in Delevan, which became a well-known animal feed company in the Midwest.

Farmers' Course

The "farmers' course," which had started in 1904, continued into the 1920s. A one-week women's course was held at the same time. The courses were conducted in early

February on the College of Agriculture campus in Madison, and each year featured a different theme. A new stock pavilion was completed on the agricultural campus in 1910, at a cost of $80,000. It provided much-needed space for the farmers' course and other campus activities.

In 1914, planners selected "Solving the help problem" as the farmers' course theme. K. L. Hatch, state Extension leader, wrote: "No other problem offers more serious difficulty to Wisconsin farmers in the organization and management of their farms than does the farm help problem." The theme in 1916 was "Twenty-five years of dairy progress since the invention of the Babcock test."

In the midst of World War I, farmers' week in 1918 featured the theme "More food this year is patriotism: The nation's need—the husbandman's reward." The program announcement read: "During the past summer the war has brought about a set of conditions which our farmers must plan to meet. The shortage of farm labor, the fixing of prices of farm produce, the handling of soils so as to secure maximum return for labor expended, the breeding and feeding of livestock, the marketing of dairy products, the selection and treatment of seed—all these ever-important problems are doubly urgent on account of the war and are growing in importance daily."

The theme for the 1918 women's short course was "How food, fuel, clothing will help to win the war." An illustration of a loaf of bread in the program carried this caption: "Save a loaf a week—help win the war. Wheat saving here is life saving 'over there.'"

Two years later, with the war over, the women's short course theme was "How to reduce the high cost of living." For the men, the theme was "Keep down the cost of production." The 1922 theme of the newly titled "farmers and home-makers week," was "Fifty years of dairy progress—Let's plan for fifty more."

In 1926, the theme for the farmers' and homemakers' week was "The Triple Seal-Farmers' model: Orderly marketing, quality goods, economical production." Special features on the program included county fair day, a purebred swine sale, a horse pulling contest, music by the Mozart club, trial of the scrub bull, music by the Barron County Quartet, livestock breeders' day, music by Swiss yodelers, the coronation of Queen Alfalfa, and a short course reunion and banquet. The lead speaker was B. H. Hibbard on the topic: "What is the future of farming?" He was followed by John Jones, commissioner of agriculture, who answered the question, "Is the county fair serving Wisconsin agriculture?"

The title for the weeklong February program changed in 1929 to "Farm Folks Week." It continued to include a women's program with such topics as "worthwhile family relationships," "the value of hobbies," and a meat-cutting exhibition, to mention a few. Topics for the men included sheep feeding demonstrations, herd improvement testing for purebreds, the "mysteries of nutrition," and the Little International Livestock Show.

Boys' and Girls' Club Work

Under the direction of state 4-H Club Leader T. L. Bewick, cooperation continued between the public schools and the county superintendents, helping to expand Extension youth work. The first statewide contest for corn growing clubs was held at the state fair in 1915. In that year, 20,000 boys and girls were enrolled in corn, potato, and alfalfa clubs. The next step was organizing livestock clubs. Nearly 2,500 girls were enrolled in canning and sewing clubs.

As a special World War I emergency effort in 1917, 3,283 boys and girls signed on to cultivate war gardens, each plat being not less than two square rods in size. Some 14,862 club members grew alfalfa or some kind of grain on plats not less than four rods square. And nearly 1,650 girls in 110 clubs sewed garments "to help win the war." Also in 1917, Wisconsin boasted 39 corn clubs, 58 potato clubs, two navy bean clubs, 45 poultry clubs, 15 pig clubs, 29 calf clubs, 97 canning clubs, and 28 bread clubs. The canning clubs reportedly canned 10,742 quarts and 310 jars of jelly. Bread club members baked 828 loaves of bread.[11]

In 1917 Wisconsin had two state boys' and girls' club leaders and 235 unpaid volunteer leaders. More than 26,000 members were enrolled in 313 clubs. Leaders conducted 85 canning demonstrations, 98 field demonstrations, and 12 club fairs and festivals. The state Extension office in Madison sent out 47,535 pieces of literature to club members to aid them in carrying out their projects.

Following World War I, boys' and girls' clubs, along with all aspects of agriculture, felt the pinch of an agricultural depression. Local club members discovered that the price they received for a fattened beef animal was less than what they paid for it. National membership in boys' and girls' clubs began decreasing. In 1918 national membership exceeded 500,000; by 1920 the figure was 250,000.[12]

The clover symbol with an "H" on each petal was commonly accepted across the country, but the term "4-H club" was not popularly used until the 1920s. In 1917 the United States Department of Agriculture hired Gertrude Warren, a home economics teacher from Teachers' College at Columbia University, to head up boys' and girls' club work on the national level. She had been a New York farm girl and had participated in a nature study group sponsored by Cornell University. Through the 1920s, Warren used the name "4-H" on brochures and other printed materials released from the Washington, D.C., office. Some had wanted the organization to be known as "Junior Extension Work," but common usage prevailed. By 1924, 4-H was recognized as the official name of boys' and girls' club work in the United States.

The Capper-Ketcham Act of 1928

Although agriculture was experiencing a depression, federal funds remained at levels spelled out in the original Smith-Lever legislation of 1914. Youth leaders and others lobbied for increases, ultimately resulting in the passage of the Capper-Ketcham Act in 1928. This new legislation authorized additional funds for Cooperative Extension, with eighty percent of the money earmarked to pay the salaries of agents working in agriculture, home economics, and 4-H. Although this act provided considerably less funds than Extension workers had hoped for, it did for the first time explicitly mention boys' and girls' club work.[13]   After a brief lull in the early 1920s, 4-H club enrollment began to increase by the end of the decade. In 1930, 800,000 boys and girls belonged to 4-H in the United States.

A problem emerged between Cooperative Extension and high school vocational agricultural programs. The Smith-Hughes Act of 1917 had provided federal funds to assist high school agricultural programs. The issue was one of program overlap. It turned out to be more of a problem in southern states, where both 4-H club and vocational agriculture students met in the schools, and both groups often included the same children. Wisconsin did not have a tradition of 4-H clubs meeting in the schools during school hours.

The relationship between 4-H and vocational agriculture festered as both programs were increasing in numbers and prominence. In 1928, the national secretary of agriculture and the director of the Federal Board for Vocational Education wrote a joint memorandum of agreement after a joint committee had studied the problem. In essence, the memorandum stated that 4-H was a problem-oriented, project-based program, while vocational education was a systematic course of instruction in basic agriculture. The drafters of the memorandum said the two programs were complementary and need not compete with each other. In many states, the clarification helped both programs move forward with fewer problems.

In Wisconsin, the relationship between school-based vocational agriculture instructors and the County Extension agents responsible for 4-H work has been supportive and cooperative.

Women's Programs

The cooking schools mentioned earlier proved highly successful, demonstrating the interest of women in furthering their education. While the early county agents were all men who emphasized improving agriculture and dealing with men's problems on the farm, women's needs were far from forgotten. Wisconsin's rural women made sure of that.

The Smith-Lever legislation stated that women's programs must be included in the newly named Cooperative Extension Service. Elizabeth Kelley was hired as Wisconsin's first state leader for Extension home economics in September 1914. Soon to follow were Agnes Boeing, a clothing specialist, and Elizabeth Amery, a foods specialist. Both were hired in September 1915. Amery became the first home economics assistant boys' and girls' club leader in September 1917.

These early Extension home economics workers traveled the state from Madison headquarters and faced many challenges. They commonly worked in twos, packed their trunk with demonstration materials, and set off for a four- to six-week tour. They

Assisting rural people with indoor plumbing was an early emphasis of Extension, as this 1929 bulletin illustrates.

Circular 229   April, 1929

Turn on the Water

Extension Service of the College of Agriculture
The University of Wisconsin, Madison

usually stayed two days in a town, but occasionally it was only a one-night stand. Transportation was always a problem. If a train didn't pass through the town where the home economist was to speak, someone met her with a bobsled, a cutter, a wagon and a team of horses, or sometimes even with a more modern convenience. A state-of-the-art winter transporter was a Model T Ford with chains that ran in a continuous circle around the back and front tires. These precursors of today's snowmobiles had a top speed of eight to ten miles per hour. Even with cold weather, snowstorms, and roads that were nearly or completely impassable, as many as 600 rural women attended these meetings.

For the 1916-1917 fiscal year, home economics Extension work continued to emphasize Extension schools for women. These lasted four days in each locality. Three days were devoted to foods and the "practical work of sewing." The fourth day spotlighted child welfare. The program was typically led by a local doctor who gave "lecture demonstrations to mothers and advice on cases of malnutrition." As a follow-up, study clubs for local farm girls, and homemaker clubs were organized for older women.

Using World War I special federal funds, Cooperative Extension hired 15 emergency home demonstration agents, who worked in 17 counties under the supervision of the state leader of home economics. State home economics leader Elizabeth Kelly was called to Washington, D. C., in 1917 to work for the U. S. Food Administration. Emma Conley replaced her as Wisconsin's second state leader of home economics Extension. After one year, she too was called to Washington.

In 1918, Mrs. Nellie Kedzie Jones, who operated a dairy farm in Marathon County with her husband, became Wisconsin's third leader of home economics Extension. The 15 emergency county home economics agents and their new state leader taught many Wisconsin women how they could help win the war. They changed diets, replacing wheat flour and sugar with other ingredients; they made cottage cheese and served it in a hundred different ways. Extension brought in Susanne Crocroft, a nationally known expert on cosmetics and physical culture, who conducted workshops on the value of staying healthy.

All but one of these special County Extension home agents lost their jobs when World War I ended. Mary Brady in Marathon County was kept on, and she became the first county home agent in Wisconsin to be paid from federal, state, and county funds. For 10 more years, Marathon County was the only county to employ a home agent. Nellie Kedzie Jones added Gladys Stillman to her state staff in 1918, and she stayed on until she retired in the 1950s. Mable Jane McMurray, Mildred Hagerty, and Esther Ord were hired in 1919.

The ever-popular two-day institutes for women continued around the state, but women wanted more. By 1920, Betty Nelson had joined the state staff as foods specialist and Gladys Meloche was hired as clothing specialist. Sadie McNalty, another clothing specialist, came on staff in 1921.

These state specialists were actively involved with the farmers' institutes, but they also carried out Extension work with several counties each year. A specialist would stay for a week at a time in a selected county, then return to the county four times during the year. A county could select one topic, such as foods, clothing, or home management. Each specialist worked with four to six counties each year.

Starting in 1920, county women were encouraged to organize into smaller local groups. Each local group elected two leaders who attended one of the four center meetings conducted in each county by state home economics specialists. A county might have 20 to 90 local groups. La Crosse and Wood Counties were the first to use this plan. This marked the start of the project leader system that continued in most Wisconsin counties but with several modifications.[14]

In Monroe County, women organized a social club near Kendall in 1912. Members met every three weeks for visiting, exchanging recipes, sharing dress patterns, and doing embroidery. Soon other groups were springing up around the county. Gladys Meloche from the state office provided leadership for the groups until about 1926, when the Monroe County agriculture agent began assisting homemaker clubs.

Each state specialist prepared a set of seven outlines on the topics of foods, home management, and clothing. In addition to the subject matter content, the outlines suggested ways in which women who worked with local groups could present the material. After a county selected a topic, the specialist sent out a set of lessons a month prior to the meeting, so the local leaders could prepare. On the day of the local meeting, each member who attended received a copy.

A typical center meeting started at 10 in the morning and continued until four in the afternoon. The day's activities included games, singing, planning community projects, and receiving information. In the foods area, emphasis was placed on canning and food preservation, with special attention to the value of milk in the diet.

The home management area included lessons on rug making. In the clothing classes, women learned to use a paper dress form. Countywide homemaker achievement day meetings were held, attracting as many as 1,000 women. Some of the meetings were so large that they had to be held outdoors. The daylong program included reports from the county districts, lunch, pageants, and speakers. Much creativity was displayed; for example, many district reports were given in the form of plays.

In the mid-1920s, lessons included the proper use of pressure cookers for food preservation; how to use various pieces of electrical equipment around the home; and why and how one should keep farm accounts. The state fair in 1926 included a special program on better-fitting shoes, which continued for the following year. During the late 1920s, projects included using dress forms, cleaning sewing machines, making decorative stitches with sewing machines, and the selection of hosiery.

Farm women wanted new information, and they also enjoyed the social aspects of homemaker gatherings. The life of women on the farm had always been a lonely one. Men visited with neighbors when they took their milk to the cheese factory each day and when they hauled grain to the local mill for grinding. But if a farm woman was lucky, she got to town on Saturday night for grocery shopping. About the only chances she had to visit with her neighbors came through neighborhood card playing and the occasional quilting bee. Women also helped each other prepare meals when the threshing crews came around.

Through Extension sponsored homemaker meetings, rural women got answers to their questions, learned new homemaking skills, and had fun while they were doing it. Both state and County Extension home economists were revered by county farm women—and by the men, too. They were trusted, respected, and often viewed as members of the family. Gladys Meloche recalled the story of a man in Marathon County who came to her office and asked if she would accompany him to the railroad depot. His wife, who had been active in county homemaker activities, had died, and he was taking her back to the town where she was born for burial. "I want you to look at my wife once more. I know she would have liked to have it that way."[15]

In the 1920s, Extension agents made their rounds in Model T Fords and later in Model A Fords. The county home agents were often referred to as "a little bit of heaven sent down to earth in a Tin Lizzie," a reference to the popular nickname for Ford cars.

In the next chapter, we begin exploring two of the most critical times for Cooperative Extension in Wisconsin and throughout the nation — the Great Depression and World War II.

CHAPTER 5

CRISIS AND CHALLENGE:
1930 TO 1945

O n October 24, 1929, the stock market plummeted, setting off a succession of bank failures, bankruptcies, and job layoffs. The country sank into an abyss of economic failures and personal tragedies. Farm prices also fell, and thousands of farmers failed to pay interest on their mortgages, missed paying property taxes, and lost their farms to bankruptcy. Some farm families picked up the little they had and moved on. Many moved west, in search of work and a better life. Nationally, gross farm income reached $9.4 million in 1930. By 1932, it was $5.3 million.[1] Hogs sold for $2.95 a hundredweight in 1932; they had been priced at $11.70 in 1926. Milk dropped to ninety-five cents a hundredweight in the early 1930s, compared to $2.25 in 1929. Eggs sold for a few cents a dozen.

The Great Depression

Farmers suffered along with everyone else in the country, although those who could keep their farms always had something to eat and a roof over their heads. Farmers had heard about the soup lines in Chicago and the hundreds of people sleeping in the parks, covering themselves with old newspapers. In many cases they also saw a steady parade of destitute men stopping by their farms—men who were willing to chop wood or do most anything for a slice of bread, a cup of coffee, and a bowl of hot soup. In Milwaukee alone, an estimated 20,000 workers were unemployed by March 1930. [2]

As if the weather and the bad economy were in cahoots, the rains stopped coming for several summers in the 1930s, and the once-green western prairies that grew corn and wheat produced sandstorms that raged for days, moving the land east and south in huge, dirty yellow clouds.

Wisconsin was not spared from the drought, summer heat, and sandstorms. In 1930, the superintendent of the Hancock Experiment Station wrote in his journal: "August and September very dry. Light showers insufficient for growth, but kept crops alive. Corn ripened 10 to 15 days too soon. Peat and brush fires of considerable extent protected [crops] against frost first half of September because of haze and smoke."

In the summer of 1931, he wrote: "April 10, sandstorm, west wind; April 12, sandstorm, south wind; April 28, sandstorm, northwest wind—damage to seedlings."

His entry continued for 1931: "May 3, killing frost; May 23, killing frost. June 25 to September 10, 19 days with temperatures of 96 degrees or higher. Five days in June with maximum temperature of 103 and no rain. In July nine days with maximum temperature of 105 and little rain."

The Wisconsin weather was unrelenting during the mid-1930s. For 1934, the Hancock superintendent reported: "May 9-10, sandstorm two days and one night. Severe damage to all crops and soil. Bad drifting of sand."[3]

During these hot, dry Depression years, central Wisconsin's sandy lands were on the move. The counties of Adams, Waushara, Wood, Portage, Marquette, and parts of Waupaca suffered severe wind erosion. Piles of sand built up along the roadsides and against the field fences. A fine, talcum-powder-like dust seeped in around the windows of farm homes. No one could escape the relentless winds, the dirt, and the dust.

Harry L. Russell, longtime dean of the College of Agriculture, resigned in 1930. Chris L. Christensen took over the dean's position in March 1931. Christensen remained dean until 1943, when agricultural economist Rudolph Froker took over. In 1936, K. L. Hatch retired as Extension director. Warren Clark, who had been a county agent in Minnesota and in Portage County, Wisconsin, replaced him.

Cooperative Extension agents spent many hours working at county fairs, dairy shows, and other events that brought people together. Dairy show, 1930s.

Cooperative Extension Faces Hard Times

By 1930, most Wisconsin counties had employed Cooperative Extension agents, but little did these agents know the tough times they would face. In the introduction to his 1930-1931 annual Extension report, Associate Director K. L. Hatch wrote: "As the strongest cables are forged from the toughest metal and the brightest surfaces are burnished on the hardest stone—so the largest movements strike deep in the soil of adversity and the sturdiest men assume position of leadership at such crucial times... Today, with prices demoralized and many persons out of work, we bemoan our hardships, complain about the times, and supinely turn from the real and fancied obstacles that obstruct our paths. But we must not give up."

In the early years of the Depression, Extension worked on improving the quality of dairy products, with continued emphasis on cow testing. High-quality dairy products commanded higher prices. Extension agents teamed with cheese factories and creameries to detect problem patrons. Then the agents visited the farmer patrons and offered to help correct their problems. This was a delicate task, but agents could usually do it better than cheese factory or creamery representatives. In 1921, 187 breeders production-tested their cattle. By 1931, this number had increased to 584 breeders who worked with their local Dairy Herd Improvement Associations.

Extension also worked on improving potato quality. Extension agents helped organize cooperative machinery rings, so small growers could use modern machines for growing and handling potatoes. In 1931, potato field days were held in Wild Rose, Amherst, Antigo, and Rhinelander. Extension agents and specialists demonstrated new machines for cultivating, spraying, and managing potato operations.

The 1930-1931 Annual Extension Report discussed farm management activities. "Farming as a business is still a pioneer field," the report began. "Not many farmers keep books, nor do many farmers know at the end of the year whether they have really made or lost money, what rate of interest their capital investment has returned, or even the rate of wages that their farm operations [have] paid to them."

County agents in four counties introduced farmers to farm account books and record keeping. Later the records were summarized, and the agents visited the farmers to help solve management problems. Eight more counties participated in meetings on record keeping for dairy, sheep, hogs, and specific crops.

With dry weather, grasshoppers increased in numbers. Often the county agent had to drop everything and work with town boards and farmer committees to prepare poison bait, in hopes of saving part of an already drought-stressed crop that grasshoppers were devouring.

Even in dry weather, quack grass continued to grow. Extension agents in 1930 and 1931 demonstrated the use of mechanical quack diggers. The system was tried on 123 farms, and 93 reported almost completely killing this tough, thick-rooted weed.

Despite the hard times, the farmers' institutes continued to draw huge numbers of participants. Farmers' institutes were held in 855 communities in 1931, with 156,632 people attending. But in 1933, the state legislature refused to continue funding the institutes. The 48-year-old, highly successful program for farmers and their wives thus came to an end.[4]

During Depression years, farmers continued to find time for fun. One way was by attending corn picking contests. Grant County held a county corn-husking contest in 1937. The 1938 county contest was held on a farm near Glen Haven, featuring 21 contestants. The event drew more than 5,000 people who came to watch young men strip cobs of corn from corn plants and toss them into high-wheeled wagons. The wagons were fitted with "banging boards" that each cob hit before it fell into a wagon. The state corn-husking contest was held in Grant County in 1939 and in Richland County in 1940. Thousands of people from throughout the region attended the state contests.

Wisconsin contained 199,877 farms in 1935—the largest number the state would ever have. Major crops were corn, oats, and hay, with the latter ranking first. However, milk for cheese production was the predominant income source of farmers. In 1935, 84 percent of Wisconsin farmers worked with horses, although the number of tractors was slowly increasing. Most farms did not have electricity, indoor plumbing, or central heating.[5]

Beyond Production Agriculture

Two largely unanticipated interests developed in 1931. Many farmers wanted to improve the appearance of their farmsteads. An Extension landscape specialist sketched plans and made planting recommendations for 47 home grounds. He also visited another 191 farm homes and made suggestions for improving external appearances. In the same year, a dairy supply house conducted a contest to improve the appearance of the state's cheese factories. More than 185 cheese factories entered.

Secondly, about 10,000 rural people wrote, coached, or took part in plays and pageants or led and sang in choral groups. Twenty-eight counties provided drama programs; 20 of the 28 also offered programs for adults. A statewide annual rural drama tournament was held in Madison. The first state rural music festival was also conducted in 1931. Five counties and 5,000 people participated.[6]

Extension Staff Numbers Decline

In 1931, 57 Wisconsin counties employed 64 workers. After the fall of 1931 county board meetings took place, three workers were dismissed because of Depression-related budget problems.

By 1933, the Depression had gotten worse. Counties slashed Extension budgets, and the state cut the College of Agriculture's budget as well. At the 1932 fall county board meetings, six counties cut their Extension budgets; one more county did so in 1933.

Attempts at dropping County Extension programs came up throughout the

Depression. In 1938, the Grant County Board considered a resolution to abolish the Grant County Extension office as of December 31, 1939. The resolution stated: "It appears that a substantial saving can be effected by the abolishment of the office of the county agent and that it will be for the best interests of the taxpayers of Grant County that such office be abolished." Ben Rusy, assistant Extension supervisor, spoke at the board meeting. After his extended presentation about the values of Extension work, the motion was tabled and the matter ended. However, the county did vote to cut the Extension budget from $2,000 annually to $1,300.[7]

The New Deal

Franklin Delano Roosevelt was elected President in 1932. Within the first 100 days of his administration in 1933, he took bold steps to fight the Great Depression. His programs, cumulatively labeled the "New Deal," included a series of what were known as alphabet agencies: the WPA (Works Progress Administration); the NRA (National Recovery Administration); FDIC (Federal Deposit Insurance Corporation); SEC (Securities and Exchange Commission); TVA (Tennessee Valley Authority); CCC (Civilian Conservation Corps); and the AAA (Agricultural Adjustment Act).

Forestry programs were promoted and often supervised by Extension agents, especially during the Depression years, when thousands of trees were planted. Hand tree planting, about 1936.

Most of these these programs affected Wisconsin. The CCC, authorized in 1933, put thousands of unmarried young men ages 18 to 25 to work. The men came from families on relief, and each enrollee received $30 per month. Of this amount, $25 went to each young man's parents. The government provided room, board, clothing, and tools. In Wisconsin, these young men planted thousands of trees, created roads, and constructed buildings in Wisconsin's parks. Twelve CCC camps operated in Wisconsin's national forests, twelve in state forests, and eight in state parks.

During its first five years in Wisconsin, the CCC employed more than 60,000 persons. At its peak in 1938, 45 CCC camps operated in Wisconsin. Thirteen of the camps worked primarily on preventing soil erosion and were under the control of the Soil Conservation Service. They built terraces, performed drainage control, and planted trees.[8]

The AAA and Extension

The AAA (Agricultural Adjustment Administration) was formed after the Agricultural Adjustment Act passed in May 1933. Under the direction of Secretary of Agriculture, Henry Wallace, AAA sought to restore farm prices to their 1909 to 1914 levels. The program called for restricting farm production and subsidizing farmers who participated in the program. The government would pay farmers for not growing a crop and leaving their land unused. Extension agents were asked to explain the intricacies of the new law and at the same time encourage farmers to farm as efficiently as possible on land that was not under contract. To assist in carrying out the Agricultural Adjustment Act, several counties hired additional agents. Sixty-three of Wisconsin's 71 counties had a county agent, club agent, or adjustment agent by January 1934.

The Commodity Credit Corporation was formed to provide a crop loan and storage program, including making price support loans available and purchasing specific commodities. The program had limited success, although many farmers supported it. Farm prices did increase somewhat, but mostly because severe drought conditions prevailed from 1933 through 1936. It wasn't until World War II that farm surpluses decreased and farm income rose significantly.

In his 1934 annual report, Dean Chris L. Christensen wrote that, besides working on farm production problems, Extension helped with "social and economic problems wholly outside the field of production." These subjects included homemaking, 4-H Club work, marketing, forestry, landscaping, and various emergency projects.[9]

Relief Efforts

County agents and state specialists spent many hours on "relief efforts." During the drought years of the early- and mid-1930s, they helped enable farmers to buy hay from out of state, a project that included finding sources and arranging for lower railroad fares. The railroads agreed to reduce rates by half for hay and one-third for grain.

Thirty-eight counties were involved in this program. However, Extension people quickly realized that this would not solve the problem, so they worked to establish a Federal Feed Relief program, which was administered by the Industrial Commission. County agents helped farmers in the stricken areas prepare applications for aid. K. L. Hatch, Extension director, summed up the situation well when he wrote: "How to get along in the farming business with as little outlay as possible is the big problem with which the Extension worker is confronted."[10]

Rural Zoning Laws Passed

Among the many urban people who were unemployed, some moved to the cutover regions of the north and became subsistence farmers. They grew gardens, hunted deer, and fished—in short, they lived off the land. But they and others living in the region had trouble paying their taxes, and huge tax delinquency problems developed in several counties.

In the early 1930s the Oneida and Vilas County Boards worked with Extension and the Conservation Commission to enact rural land zoning ordinances. These were designed to control settlement outside of cities and villages. Walter Rowlands, county agent supervisor, and L. G. Sorden, Oneida County agent, led the effort. By the end of 1934, 18 counties had zoning ordinances.

Mechanization on Hold

Thanks to the farm price squeeze, horses once more became the main source of power on Wisconsin farms—even for those who had tractors. Draft horses cost less to maintain than tractors, and they always started, even when the temperature was below zero. In 1934 Extension and the College of Agriculture conducted 40 daylong programs in southern and western Wisconsin on horse-related topics, ranging from parasite control to big team hitches.

Agent Activities

In his May 15, 1933, newsletter State County Agent Leader J. F. Wojta reported on agent activities for April:

Marathon County. "Thirty-five girls enrolled for the fourteenth Marathon County Girls' Short Course under the direction of Miss (Edith) Bangham, the home agent. Gladys Meloche and Ruth Peck supervised the sewing work of the girls, each girl completing a dress."

Sheboygan County. "Miss Gunnison spent the great part of the month (April) on 4-H Club organization. Seven clubs have entered the state 4-H Drama Contest."

Ashland County. "A Welfare Garden Committee composed of one member from each ward was organized in Ashland . . . this committee will have charge of all welfare garden work in the wards."

Columbia County. "At three lamb castrating and docking demonstrations, the county agent [Harold Hovde] castrated 100 lambs. More than 800 horses have now been treated in the county for bots this spring, and 209 cattle in six herds were blood tested for contagious abortion. In addition to his soil testing and 4-H Club Work, he also distributed 5,000 pine trees to 18 farmers of his county. It is this kind of service that counts for much with the average farmer."

Wojta reported that in Marinette County, the county agent helped plan a 300-acre sugar beet project to provide employment for the many men in the county. In Ozaukee County the county agent, working with a local chicken hatchery, provided two hundred boys and girls with 50 chicks each. As payment for the chicks, each boy or girl returned seven heavy breed and nine light breed male birds to the hatchery. By April the hatchery had distributed 8,000 chicks, with 5,000 more slated for delivery in early May.

Electricity on the Farm

Rural Electrification Administration (REA) legislation passed in 1935. Before REA, the few farmers with electricity were those who had their own wind- or gasoline engine-powered generators. In some Wisconsin rural communities, village citizens had electricity (often provided by the local gristmill's generator) twenty-five years before people who lived in the country. Farmers who lived near a city or village sometimes convinced the local electrical company to string lines to their farm, but these cases were rare. In the 1930s, power companies thought providing electricity to farmers was a losing cause. "About all a farmer wants is a few bare bulbs to replace his lamps and lanterns," power company officials often said. Little did they realize the many ways that farmers would use electricity.

The REA provided low-interest loans to farm cooperatives for operating power plants and stringing power lines in rural communities. County agents helped organize these electric cooperatives. The first REA electric lines in Wisconsin were strung in Richland County during 1936-1937. By the end of 1939, REA electric lines crossed Barron, Buffalo, Columbia, Dunn, Eau Claire, Grant, Lafayette, Monroe, Oconto, Polk, Burnett, St. Croix, Chippewa, and Vernon Counties, with more soon to follow.

Twenty-Five Years of Service

In 1938 Wisconsin's Cooperative Extension celebrated twenty-five years of service. In that year, sixty-nine of Wisconsin's seventy-one county boards helped fund ninety-nine county agents, 4-H club agents, and home agents. Twenty-four of these agents were women.

According to Dean Christensen's 1939 annual report, with the Depression continuing in the late 1930s, Extension worked on three problems: 1) how to increase farm income; 2) conserving soil; and 3) helping rural people get "satisfaction and pleasure out of farm life."

To help farmers obtain higher incomes, Extension agents followed Agriculture Dean Chris Christensen's philosophy: "Success in farming, insofar as it hinges upon what happens within the line fences, often depends upon doing well a very few things. Size of farm, high production per cow, efficient feeding, good crop yields, diversification, and more alfalfa acreage may be the key to a better income. More than ever, in this time of low prices, getting better income depends upon knowing and analyzing the problems of the individual farm."[11]

Extension work included assisting local cooperatives that were in financial difficulty; providing more comprehensive market information to farmers; helping improve quality in the dairy industry; promoting the poultry industry; finding markets for surplus cattle; diversifying farms by adding sheep and hogs; controlling animal diseases; introducing hybrid corn; organizing weed control drives; destroying grasshoppers; promoting raising of vegetables and small fruits for market; and providing plans for farm buildings.

Brucellosis, or Bangs disease, had become a problem in many dairy herds. The disease resulted in cattle abortion, and it could be contracted by farmers and others who handled infected animals. The disease in humans was called undulant fever. In 1934, an intensive federal project began. County agents worked closely with AAA officials to provide information about the disease.

Soil erosion had become a serious problem during these dry Depression years. Tons of topsoil blew away. When it rained, the topsoil washed away. In 1938, the Extension Service helped organize soil conservation districts throughout the state. By the end of 1938, 10 districts were in various stages of organization. Farmers planted thousands of trees for farm forests, and to form windbreaks in those areas most susceptible to wind erosion. The trees were provided without charge by the Wisconsin Conservation Department.

In the cutover region of the state, land clearing continued. In the late 1930s, many northern Wisconsin farms had only 10 acres of cropland, with the rest still stumps. Working with county boards, Extension helped purchase and distribute huge quantities of dynamite for stump blowing. In 1938, Marinette County ordered 24,000 pounds of dynamite at car lot prices, which was distributed through the county agent's office. Some areas introduced bulldozers for stump pulling, a method that was three to ten dollars per acre less expensive than using dynamite. It was also much safer.

Home Economics

The highly respected Nellie Kedzie Jones, who became state leader of home economics Extension in 1918, retired in 1933 at the age of seventy-five. She had become a familiar figure throughout the state. Jones spoke at Extension meetings, at farmers' institutes, and nearly everywhere a crowd gathered. The people loved her.

She also worked relentlessly to increase the number of home agents in County Extension offices by speaking to county boards across the state. Her favorite theme

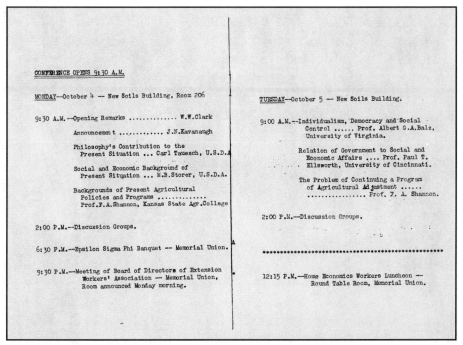

CONFERENCE OPENS 9:30 A.M.

MONDAY--October 4 -- New Soils Building, Room 206

9:30 A.M.--Opening Remarks .... W.W.Clark

Announcement .... J.N.Kavanaugh

Philosophy's Contribution to the
Present Situation ... Carl Tauesch, U.S.D.A.

Social and Economic Background of
Present Situation ... M.B.Storer, U.S.D.A.

Backgrounds of Present Agricultural
Policies and Programs ....
Prof.F.A.Shannon, Kansas State Agr.College

2:00 P.M.--Discussion Groups.

6:30 P.M.--Epsilon Sigma Phi Banquet -- Memorial Union.

9:30 P.M.--Meeting of Board of Directors of Extension
Workers' Association -- Memorial Union,
Room announced Monday morning.

TUESDAY--October 5 -- New Soils Building.

9:00 A.M.--Individualism, Democracy and Social
Control ..... Prof. Albert G.A.Balz,
University of Virginia.

Relation of Government to Social and
Economic Affairs .... Prof. Paul T.
Ellsworth, University of Cincinnati.

The Problem of Continuing a Program
of Agricultural Adjustment ......
.... Prof. F. A. Shannon.

2:00 P.M.--Discussion Groups.

12:15 P.M.--Home Economics Workers Luncheon --
Round Table Room, Memorial Union.

The 1937 Extension workers conference focused on topics related to the economic depression.

was how the home agent could ease the workload of farm women. Although only four counties added home agents during her tenure, she had planted the seeds. Marathon County retained the home agent it had hired during World War I, and Milwaukee County became the second county to employ a permanent home agent in 1928, followed by Wood in 1929, Winnebago in 1932, and Sheboygan in 1933.

Two federal acts helped provide funds for additional agents—the Capper-Ketcham Act of 1928 and the Bankhead-Jones Act of 1935. The Capper-Ketcham Act provided money for the "payment of salaries of Extension agents in the several states to further develop the Cooperative Extension system in agriculture and home economics with men, women, boys, and girls."[12]

The Bankhead-Jones Act was enacted during the depths of the Depression. The National Committee on Extension Organization and Policy argued successfully that farmers and rural people needed additional information during the difficult times they faced.[13]

During the three years (1933 to 1936) that Luella Mortenson served as state leader, 14 counties added home economics agents. In 1936, Blanche Lee from the Montana Extension Service became state home economics leader. That same year, Wisconsin

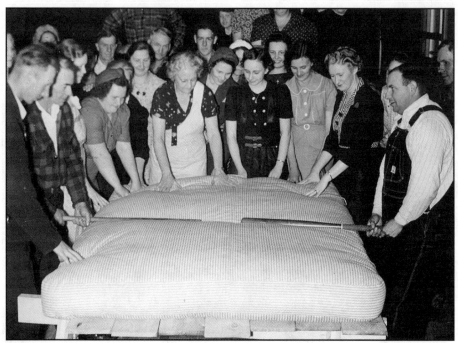

Mattress making was an important homemaker project in 1939.

had 19 home economics agents. The number jumped to 31 in 1940 and 55 in 1950.

Convincing a county board to hire a home economics agent during the Depression was not easy. Women from the Crawford County Homemakers' Association, assisted by state leader Lee, started working behind the scenes in 1938 to hire a home agent. Jessie Ward from Soldiers Grove exchanged a series of letters with Lee. In one letter Lee wrote: "I shall be very glad to tell of the advantages of having a Home Agent in Crawford County." This was written before Blanche Lee spoke at the May 18, 1939, Achievement Day meeting.

The minutes of the Crawford County Home Demonstration Council meeting of October 24, 1939, included this paragraph: "The possibility of having a Home Demonstration Agent for Crawford County was discussed. Motion was made by Mrs. Elliott that a committee of three be sent to meet with the County Agricultural Committee on Monday October 30 to discuss same. Motion seconded and carried."

The next step was for the Crawford County women to circulate a petition, which was prepared in early November 1939 and sent around the county. The petition read: "The undersigned residents of Crawford County Wisconsin do hereby respectfully petition the honorable County Board of Supervisors of said County to appropriate the sum of Seven Hundred Dollars ($700) for a portion of the cost of Home Agent's Service during the following year."

At its 1939 fall meeting, the Crawford County Board approved $700 for the employment of a county home agent. Miss Caroline M. Hubatch began her duties in the basement of the Prairie Du Chien post office on June 1, 1940.

Monroe County's homemaker clubs had been active since 1912. In 1935, Monroe County had 80 homemaker clubs with 1,500 members. Club members petitioned the county board to budget money for a home agent position, and their request was approved. Lucy Folsom began work on February 1,1936.

The first home economics agent in Grant County, Helen Davis, was not hired until January of 1944, after pressure from 4-H leaders, Farm Bureau women's groups, and homemaker club members.

In 1915, Walworth County had become the first southern Wisconsin County to hire a county agent. However, the county did not have a home agent during World War II. Walworth County women lobbied hard for the position, circulating petitions in 1944 and speaking before the county board in 1945. At the May 10, 1945, meeting of the board, a resolution to appropriate $1,200 to support a county home agent was moved and seconded but then withdrawn. At the following meeting, the board declared that the resolution had lost on a secret ballot, receiving 12 yes votes and 20 no votes. At the September 12, 1945, board meeting, a resolution to appropriate $1,500 to help support a home agent was presented. The finance committee recommended against approval, but a motion to approve the resolution passed with 22 yes votes, four no votes, and eight absent. Mrs. Alice Gillette began work as Walworth County's first county-supported home agent on December 26, 1945. The person who had served during World War I had been a temporary home agent.

Home Economics Projects

Popular Extension topics for homemakers during the Depression years included meal planning, sewing, staying well, bread making, garden planning and planting, canning, hooking rugs, repairing and refinishing furniture and, in the later years, using electricity efficiently.

Most topics dealt with shortage of goods and limited income—common themes during the 1930s. Canning meats was a popular project. The 1930-1931 state Extension report explained the need for such projects as follows: "Beef, veal, pork and mutton have all been so low in price that it seems wise to provide an ample supply by canning. Many women have learned how to cull their flocks and can the non-laying hens. With four or five kinds of meat in addition to the various vegetables from their gardens, many farm women can look with pride on storeroom shelves where is to be found a large part of the food needed during the winter."[14]

To aid farm women in becoming more self-sufficient, Extension agents and specialists did everything from conducting home butchering demonstrations to encouraging the planting of orchards.

4-H Club Work

The number of 4-H Clubs in Wisconsin continued to grow during the Depression years. Despite low cattle prices in 1931, 180 boys and girls from 15 counties showed animals at the Junior Livestock Exposition in Madison. Youthful members enrolled in corn, potato, garden, fruit, forestry, beef, dairy, baking, clothing, and canning projects, along with several others. Young people learned how to run a business meeting and participated in social activities such as singing, music, plays, and games. By 1937, six counties had hired club agents, and programs for boys and girls flourished and expanded.

In 1938, the state 4-H enrollment figure reached 30,877 members. The most popular projects were dairy and field crops. Nearly 10,000 girls enrolled in the clothing project.

World War II

Cooperative Extension continued to gain respect from the state's rural people. By 1940 the organization was doing reasonably well, employing the largest field staff ever.

December 7, 1941, changed everything once again. With the United States involved in a world war for the second time in 50 years, Cooperative Extension was asked to take on both familiar and unfamiliar activities.

Almost overnight, a cry arose for more food and fiber. By 1942 the state's dairy production reached a new high. The state produced 12 percent more pork than the year before. Poultry production was up. Farmers planted more corn, more oats, more everything. They were instructed to use more lime, use more commercial fertilizer, plant certified seed (for potatoes, corn, and oats), and join the Dairy Herd Improvement Association to keep track of dairy herd production. A few dairy farmers began using artificial breeding for their cows, something that had begun in 1939. Along with producing more and doing it more efficiently, farmers were asked to keep the quality high.

The farmers who had electricity could use electric pig brooders and automatic self-feeders, milking machines and automatic watering systems. Unfortunately, large numbers of farmers still waited for electrical lines. Many had to wait until the end of the war before they could flip on a light switch.

The government also encouraged farmers in southern Wisconsin counties to grow hemp. They planted 7,000 acres in 1942 and 32,000 acres in 1943. Hemp fiber was used for making rope, cordage, and hawsers for the navy.

During World War II about 185,000 Wisconsin farm families dealt with labor, machinery, and fertilizer shortages. They faced rationing on everything from sugar to tires. Nevertheless, they produced more milk, meat, eggs, poultry, hemp, and canned vegetables than ever before. The 1944 Dane County Extension agents' report to the county board included these words: "Dane County farmers and homemakers have met the difficulties imposed by war with 'heads up and shoulders to the wheel.' . . . Dane County farmers came through!"

Between 1941 and 1945, Extension staff nearly doubled. Eighty workers assisted with recruiting and placing farm labor. Forty more were added to help with educational programs on food production and conservation. With so many farm boys off fighting the war, labor agents scrambled to find farm help. New workers in Wisconsin included Jamaicans, Mexican nationals, and Mexican-American migrants from Texas. Ironically, German prisoners of war were placed on many Wisconsin farms to replace young men who had been drafted.

By 1945 Wisconsin had more dairy cows than any other state. It produced more milk and more cheese. The state produced more corn for silage, more peas, and more sweet corn and beets for canning. Wisconsin ranked second in alfalfa production and first in hemp acreage during the war.

Reforestation had become an Extension goal during the Depression years. Trees were planted by hand. One man with a shovel or planting spud made a slit in the ground; a person following placed a little tree in the slit and firmed the soil around it. Tree planting was slow, tedious, and backbreaking work. In 1943, encouraged by labor shortages, agricultural engineers worked with Extension forester Fred Trenk to develop a mechanical tree planter that used one operator. After design changes in 1945, the newly designed tree planter could plant 15,000 trees a day with two operators.

To improve milk quality, Extension encouraged farmers to build milk houses. Engineers drew up plans, and Extension workers conducted hundreds of meetings throughout the state. Extension agents also encouraged farmers to remodel their old dairy barns, many of which had been built in the late 1800s and early 1900s. By rearranging old barns, farmers could obtain greater efficiency in feeding, cleaning, and milking. Often the old barn needed better lighting and improved ventilation. Agricultural engineers also developed a new hay curing system that some farmers began using in 1943. By 1945, about 50 were in use around the state.

Prices for agricultural goods soared during the war. A few years earlier, farmers had been worried about losing their farms because they couldn't pay the interest on their mortgages. Now they were paying off their mortgages.[15]

Home Economics and the War

Homemaker groups continued meeting during the war. In 1945 there were 1,700 homemaker clubs in the state with more than 29,000 members. Home agents and Extension specialists held meetings at convenient locations in the counties, to which local clubs sent project leaders for training. The project leaders returned to their home clubs and taught other members. It was an efficient system that produced a large cadre of volunteer teachers.

Maintaining family health through food and nutrition programs received high priority. The programs included information about producing, preserving, and conserving the family's food supply. Pressure cooker clinics became popular. Home economics agents checked more than 4,000 pressure cooker gauges in 1945. Also popular were clinics for those who had access to local freezer-locker plants, where families could rent space to store frozen food. Home economics programs included attention to school lunch programs and helping 4-H members with food and nutrition projects. Canning continued to be an important way of preserving food. Extension reported that more than 13 million quarts of fruit, vegetables, and meats were canned or preserved every year during the war.

Sewing dresses, care of fabrics, and restyling old dresses and coats became widespread topics. Care and maintenance of sewing machines also became popular demonstration lessons. Ironically, farm families now had more money, but many items were not available because of the war. Support of the war effort demanded that many people make due with what they had. The goal was "making, not buying."[16]

Victory Gardens and Other 4-H Activities

In the midst of war, 4-H continued to flourish. In 1945 Wisconsin's 4-H enrollment exceeded 30,000 members. "Feeding a fighter" was one of 4-H's mottoes. One way to do that was through victory garden projects that encouraged and instructed members in gardening. Four-H members also helped grow canning crops such as carrots, beets, beans, sweet corn, and cucumbers for commercial canners. Clothing and food preservation projects were popular along with the dairy and poultry projects.

Along with other youth groups and rural schoolchildren, Four-H members collected milkweed pods during the war years. The floss from the pods was used to fill lifejackets for sailors and fliers. Making one life vest required the floss from two large burlap bags of milkweeds. In Grant County alone, young people collected 19,000 sacks of milkweed pods. The entire project was coordinated through the county agent's office.

Leadership development had become an important aspect of 4-H Club work. In 1945, six 4-H camps focused on developing leaderships skills.

When World War II ended, Extension had to shift gears again. A new set of challenges emerged. In the next chapter, we explore Extension operations during the post-World War II years, when one of the greatest transformations ever experienced in agriculture took place.

CHAPTER 6

GROWTH AND EXPANSION:
1945 TO 1960

As the war ended, Cooperative Extension faced the challenge of helping rural communities adjust. During the postwar years, farm numbers declined and farms got larger. In 1945 Wisconsin had 179,000 farms, down from nearly 200,000 in 1935. By 1960, farm numbers had declined to 138,000.

After the war, farmers sent their faithful draft horses out to pasture and replaced them with tractors—a new one cost less than $2,000 in 1946. REA cooperatives strung electric lines to those farmers who still lacked electricity. With electrical power, farmers soon had milking machines, milk coolers, feed grinders, fans, and much more. Combines replaced threshing machines. Forage harvesters took over for corn binders and silo fillers. Indoor plumbing arrived in farm homes. Electric or gas ranges replaced wood burning cookstoves.

One writer said: "The farm home of mid-century Wisconsin is surrounded with evidence of an advancing agriculture. The refrigerator replaced the springhouse, and modern methods of food distribution and the home freezer eliminated most home canning. Telephones, electricity, radio, television, and automobiles have all contributed to improved rural life in Wisconsin."[1]

With mechanization farmers could till more acres, milk more cows, fatten more pigs and grow more corn (now for sale off the farm as a cash crop in many parts of the state). Many people left farming in the 1940s and 1950s. Many young people who had finished high school packed their suitcases and left for college or for jobs in the cities, most of them never to return.

Extension Agricultural Programs

Helped by the College of Agriculture's research and Cooperative Extension's educational programs, artificial insemination (AI) of dairy cattle became common. In 1945, about 86,000 cows were bred with AI. By 1947 the number had increased to nearly 257,000 cows. Bulk milk tanks replaced milk cans, and bulk milk trucks roared down the country roads, replacing the old can trucks. Researchers developed a new "ring test" for Bang's disease, now commonly known as brucellosis. The presence of the disease could be spotted in a milk sample, which was followed up with a blood test of the suspected animals. Extension agents worked hard to eliminate this dreaded disease and make Wisconsin brucellosis-free. Interest in Dairy Herd Improvement Association milk testing also remained strong. Using DHIA records, it was easy to show a farmer the results of superior breeding offered by carefully selected AI bulls.

Cooperative Extension continued to emphasize milk quality. By state mandate, each Wisconsin dairy farm was required to have a milk house by November 15, 1952. Grade A milk markets demanded the ultimate in dairy cleanliness.

Paving barnyards was another way to improve milk quality. These barnyards helped keep cattle clean and out of the mud during wet weather. Al Francour, agricultural agent in La Crosse County, recalled a time when he convinced a local attorney, who owned a farm, to pave his barnyard as a demonstration project. This would allow farmers to watch the actual process.

The attorney had no farm experience and was accustomed to having other people do things for him, especially physical things. Before the day of the demonstration, the lot needed grading and required additional sand for a base. This had to take place before forms could be built and the cement poured. The attorney was on the school board, and he arranged for the local vocational agriculture class to do the preliminary work.

The demonstration was scheduled for a Wednesday. On Monday, Francour drove to the farm to check on the preliminary work. Nothing had been done. As Francour recalled: "Tuesday was a busy day. A grader was brought in to grade the yard. The agriculture students spent the afternoon hauling sand. The yard was laid out and the forms put in place. The preliminaries were completed before dark that evening."

On the day of the demonstration, the attorney/farmer stood by and watched Francour and Assistant County Agent Leonard Anderson push the cement around to fill the forms and level the lot. "Farmers attending the demonstration seemed to enjoy their Extension staff with freshly poured cement up to the tops of their boots and sweat running down their faces," Francour said.

In Wisconsin's southwestern counties, educational events featured beef cattle-breeding, feeding, disease control, and marketing. Extension helped organize the Southwest Wisconsin Beef Producer's Cooperative to improve feeder cattle marketing. A similar cooperative for feeder pigs was organized in the eastern part of the state. Preferred hog types had switched from the "lard" breeds of the Depression years to the newer, slimmer, more streamlined meat-type hogs.

Likewise, lamb pools were organized. One was headquartered in Ripon and another in Lancaster. Purpose of the lamb pools was for producers to bring their lambs together, pooling them in order to attract higher prices. Extension helped organize and promote the pools and emphasized the need for high-quality animals. "Lamb feeds" were held in various parts of the state to introduce lamb to people who had never tasted it.

The Wisconsin Extension Workers Association board, 1958.

Milk prices were low after the war, and considerable effort went into dairy promotion. The Alice in Dairyland program of the state Department of Agriculture began in 1948, with the full cooperation of Cooperative Extension.

Chemical Weed and Insect Control

Weed sprays became available after the war. Farmers, accustomed to using mechanical cultivation and hand hoeing to control weeds, now had new technology that made weed control much easier. But spraying weeds was more complicated than most farmers bargained for. They had to invest in a sprayer, purchase the proper spray, then learn how to calibrate the sprayer so it distributed the correct amount. The old saw, "If a little bit of spray is a good thing, then twice as much will be better" was bad advice when spraying weeds. Many farmers got in trouble with their wives when they sprayed 2,4-D, too close to the home garden or the flowerbeds. No one knew much about "drift" and the effects of weed killer on plants such as tomatoes, grapes, roses, and many other broad-leafed plants. Also some farmers were careless about breathing the fumes from insecticides, which may have led to health problems in later life for some of them.

In the late 1940s, Extension Specialists George Briggs (fondly known as "Soybean" Briggs) from the agronomy department and Orrin Berge from agricultural engineering traveled the state demonstrating the principles of crop spraying. The deluxe version of a sprayer was one mounted on a trailer and pulled by a tractor or even a team of horses. A gasoline engine powered the sprayer. Later versions were mounted on the back of pickup trucks.

As insecticides joined herbicides Ellsworth Fisher, an entomology specialist, joined the itinerant team. Soon Fisher, Briggs, and Berge organized sprayer schools, which continued into the late 1960s. These men produced a "sprayer service newsletter" that was distributed to thousands of Wisconsin farmers as interest in weed and insect sprays continued to grow.

Sprayer calibration, needed to ensure that the sprayer laid down the proper amount of spray, became a central feature of all sprayer schools and demonstrations. As many as 20 to 30 sprayer schools were held each year on a county-by-county basis. Because of the great demand and rather limited resources, a county could expect a sprayer school only once every two or three years. The exception was Dane County. County Agent Bill Clark insisted on having a sprayer school every year. Specialists usually acquiesced, because Clark always drew a huge crowd and the old cafeteria building at the Dane County Fairgrounds was handy. Besides, Bill Clark never cancelled a winter meeting because of bad weather. When he scheduled a meeting, there was a meeting.

Clark carried on a friendly rivalry with the campus-based specialists. He claimed he could explain to a farmer over the phone in 10 minutes how to calibrate a sprayer. One year Orrin Berge brought along a toy telephone and challenged Clark to demonstrate to the huge crowd how he would teach someone to calibrate a sprayer over the phone. Needless to say, the roomful of farmers loved the exchange.

By the 1950s computers—especially the huge mainframe models—had begun to appear on campus. They were slow, clumsy, and noisy. They overheated and made mistakes, but they also speeded up record keeping. They could do mathematical calculations many times faster than a person who was using an adding machine or a mechanical calculator.

Dairy specialists supervised the development and publishing of annual sire test results. These indicated which dairy bulls had produced offspring with the highest milk and butterfat production. By this time, artificial insemination groups were in full swing, and everyone wanted to know which bull to request when the AI technician came by to inseminate a cow. The sire report provided a "consumer's guide" to bulls.

Dealing with thousands of numbers relating to hundreds of daughters of these bulls was a monumental task. The dairy records division of the United States Department of Agriculture collected all the state records and consolidated them. They then contracted with the navy, which had the largest computer in the country at the time, to produce a sire report. Even this "state-of-the-art machine" took two weeks to produce the sire report. The late Tony Sendelbach, longtime UW dairy specialist, once mused, "What would have happened if the nation had faced a major crisis during those two weeks, and the computer was tied up analyzing bulls?"

Pacemaker Corn

What a goal! Grow corn yielding 100 bushels per acre—three times the yield of the old open-pollinated corn grown in the 1920s and 1930s. Extension specialists and county agents put together a program to push corn yields to places they had never been. The word was as follows: plant hybrids suited to your area; use appropriate amounts of fertilizer (after a soil test); follow recommended weed control practices; and hope for enough rain. Then expect your corn cribs to be fuller than they have ever been.

Everett Olsen was county agricultural agent in Richland County in the early 1950s. He recalls how district Extension leaders George Baumeister and Emil Jorgensen had spearheaded the pacemaker program statewide. In Richland County, the average corn yield in 1950 was about 35 bushels per acre, with an average of 12,000 corn plants per acre. Olsen contacted bankers and other farm lenders to help them understand this "newfangled" approach to growing corn. He and other agents taught farmers how to take soil samples, have soil tested for nitrogen, phosphorus, and potash, then fertilize according to recommendations. Olsen signed up 62 corn growers during the first year

The College of Agriculture and Cooperative Extension have been national leaders in the development and promotion of new alfalfa varieties, and of management practices that resulted in higher yields. Wood County, 1949.

of the program. These farmers grew, on average, 122 bushels per acre. Farmers throughout Richland County began copying their neighbors, and farmers throughout the state soon followed. Within a few years, the average corn production for Wisconsin was more than 100 bushels per acre.

Farm and Home Development

By the early 1950s, it was clear that increasing farm production was not a sufficiently comprehensive goal for Wisconsin farmers or for Cooperative Extension. Many other problems loomed in Wisconsin communities, ranging from soil erosion to managing farm operations more efficiently.

By the mid-1950s, 36 counties employed farm and home development agents whose job it was to work intensively with a limited number of families. Agents gave special attention to farm record keeping, record analysis, and decision-making. A farm and home development agent worked with a farm family for two or three years, or until the family had learned record keeping and the broader principles of farm management.

Associate Director Ahlgren said this about the new farm and home development programs: "Farm and Home Development is an approach which provides a means of helping farm families to learn the techniques of adjustment, record keeping, analysis and evaluation of new ideas. By evaluating their own resources and in learning how to utilize them wisely, they can project ahead and draw their own blueprints for a happier and more satisfying future."[2]

Staff Changes

Chris Christensen, dean of the College of Agriculture, resigned in 1943 and was replaced by E. B. Fred, a bacteriologist. Fred served as dean until 1945, when he became president of the University of Wisconsin. Ira Baldwin, also a bacteriologist, took over as dean in the fall of 1945. He resigned in 1948 to become vice-president of the university. Rudolph Froker, an agricultural economist, became dean and director in 1948.

Meanwhile Warren W. Clark, who had headed Cooperative Extension, retired in 1952. After several conversations, Dean Froker convinced Henry Ahlgren to take Clark's position as associate director of Cooperative Extension. Ahlgren started his new duties on October 1, 1952. Froker knew Ahlgren's reputation as an agronomist in the college agronomy department. Froker had appointed him chair of the agronomy department in 1949. Ahlgren had already made many contributions, both as a faculty member who knew how to work with people across disciplines and as someone who looked at his own discipline of agronomy in new ways. Ahlgren wrote agronomy textbooks that placed emphasis on why things happened, rather than merely reciting *how* things happened. His specialty was pasture and forage crops.

It was fortuitous that someone with Ahlgren's reputation and ability should head up Cooperative Extension at a time of great change in agriculture and rural communities, and at a time when some people had begun questioning Extension's role.

Ahlgren set out to improve the reputation of Extension staff, especially agents working in the counties. He wanted to increase agent salaries, but the university administration informed him that in order to do that, field staff would need graduate degrees. Salaries for county agents were about $3,500 a year in 1945. Home agents received about $2,500, and 4-H and assistant agents could expect about $3,000 annually. With the Cooperative Extension arrangement, about one-third of the salaries came from county budgets, one-third from state taxes, and one-third from federal Smith-Lever funds. The federal and state funds were combined at the state office, so each agent received two checks per month, one from the state and one from the county.

Ahlgren immediately set out to improve the educational level of county-based staff through an assistantship-supported graduate program within the newly reorganized Department of Agricultural and Extension Education.

Special Advisory Committee

Ahlgren wanted to keep in touch with County Extension agents and county boards. In September 1955, he appointed what he called a "special committee." The purpose of the group was to help Ahlgren and the state administrative staff wrestle with administrative problems and concerns and Extension's future direction.

In a letter to Al Francour, then county agricultural agent in La Crosse County, Ahlgren wrote: "From time to time during the past three years and especially last year I have found myself in the position of needing the judgment and wise counsel of members of our county staff on matters of importance to the future of the Agricultural Extension Service . . . I am sure you appreciate that it will probably not be wise to give much publicity to this particular matter. In fact as far as I am concerned it would be very much appreciated if you would keep the matter as reasonably confidential as possible."[3]

In addition to Francour, the members of this secret advisory committee of county agents included: W.D. Rogan (Jefferson, then Waukesha County); C.J. McAleavy (Marathon); V.W. Peroutky (Winnebago); S.S. Mathisen (Milwaukee); O.W. Meyer (Calumet); G.F. Massey (Fond du Lac); E.V. Ryall (Kenosha); Leo Shaefer (Wood); Howard Kuhn (Dunn); E.E. Anderson (St.Croix); G.I. Mullendore (Door); W.H. Dougherty (Washburn); and H.W. Kinney (Iron).

No women sat on the committee, and no positions other than agricultural agents were represented. The creation of this "secret" committee cemented Ahlgren's relationship with key county agents from around the state, which helped with internal as well as external relationships. Members also served as Ahlgren's eyes and ears.

The special advisory committee took on the task of trying to convince the legislature that Extension needed more money. In the middle 1950s, it appeared that Congress would provide the budget needed to increase county staff salaries. But to accept the federal money, the states had to provide "match money." Wisconsin didn't appear to have enough money to match the new federal dollars.

County Agent Ryall wrote the following to other committee members in 1956: "At an early district conference, the members of the Special Committee should discuss the situation with the other county agents. We could ask that each county make an effort to acquaint its state senators and assemblymen with its Extension work . . . In other words, we should try to give our legislators a picture as to the number of people we work with . . . The importance of Extension work to the economy and life of the county should be stressed . . . some idea be given as to the Extension potential, or job still to be done . . . insofar as possible, these reports should be made in person by the county agent—preferably following a meal . . . that so far as possible, each county agent become familiar with the background and personality of the legislator."

Later in his letter Ryall said: "I do not think that we should discuss state appropriations at this time. If a legislator wants to discuss finances, that is fine. But we have no way of knowing what, if any, recommendation the University will make in regard to appropriations for our work. There is no need for putting a legislator on the defensive."[4]

Rosemary Stare, who was home agent in Dodge County in 1959, recalled when Congressman Robert Kastenmeier came to the Extension office. He sat across from her desk while they discussed programs and went over her annual Extension report.

Ahlgren worked behind the scenes to direct the committee. Here was a carefully developed plan to acquaint lawmakers throughout the state with Extension's work on a county by county basis. The effort was grassroots, not Madison-based, or so it appeared. In 1958, Ahlgren renamed the special committee the "Minute Men" committee, which meant its members should be able to spring into action at a minute's notice.

In a letter written in 2000, Al Francour said this about the committee's work: "One of the real important features of this group of agents was the relationship they established with each other, plus they established a relationship with the chairmen of the Agricultural and Extension Committees of the County Boards. Most of the chairmen of the Agricultural and Extension Committees were also chairmen of county boards. This group of agents proposed that county Agricultural and Extension Committees organize into a state-wide association."

The National Scene
Cooperative Extension has a history of examining itself, trying to decide where it has been and then planning where it ought to head. In 1948, the United States Department of Agriculture and the land-grant universities published a "Joint Committee Report on Extension Programs, Policies and Goals." It began with this reminder: "The primary function of the Cooperative Extension Service in agriculture and home economics is education."[5]

After several pages chronicling Extension accomplishments, the report offers the following: "In short, whereas Extension has done much for people, it is what Extension has helped people to do for themselves that achieves the greatest results."

The report explained how Extension had been doing more than helping rural people solve their problems—and must continue to do so. It must teach people how to solve their own problems. Additionally, the report concluded, Extension has an obligation "to help rural people understand the complex social and economic problems—local, national, and international—which confront them. . . .The Smith-Lever Act clearly states that Extension's field of educational responsibility is to all the people of the United States. Hence, growing demands on Extension from nonfarm rural residents and urban residents should be met as far as resources will permit."[6] This report put into print what many Extension people and others had been thinking about, especially since the end of World War II. It addressed the need to expand Extension's audience and offerings.

Rural Development

In 1955 the U.S. Secretary of Agriculture pinpointed geographic areas in the U.S. where cash income was low. The report included several Wisconsin counties. As a result, a pilot rural development program began in Price and Sawyer Counties in 1956. The program featured development of both farm and non-farm enterprises. In Price County, a canning factory was convinced to offer bean contracts to 50 farmers who grew green beans as a cash crop. Extension helped three farmers start a broiler enterprise. Sawyer County saw a new sawmill go into operation in 1957 and another in 1958. Extension helped the maple syrup industry expand and promoted lakefront development in the county. The rural development program also helped improve health facilities, churches, and community centers and assisted with community beautification.

Home Economics

In 1947 county home agents conducted meetings, trained local leaders, wrote news releases and answered untold numbers of telephone calls about an assortment of problems related to family and home. Development and welfare of children became a major educational focus. Parent groups were organized to discuss family issues. Extension specialists wrote bulletins such as "Understanding the Grade School Child" that were widely distributed.

With electricity something new for many farm families, home agents conducted meetings and demonstrations on "the needs of the well-lighted home," "ways in which families can have good lighting," "checking light through the use of the light meter," and "converting kerosene lamps to electricity."

Demonstrations on how to use new detergents, proper care of new fabrics, and remodeling hats and other accessories continued as popular topics.

In 1952 home economics Extension emphasized the construction, selection, care and buying of clothing. In that year Extension agents worked with 56,000 home-makers in more than 2,500 organized homemaker groups.

The 1952 annual Extension report included this statement: "Social progress and human relationships have not kept pace with technological development in agricul-ture. The world is changing too fast for many of us to keep up with it. Interpreting these rapid changes is one of the goals of the Child Development and Family Relationships phase of Home Economics Extension."[7]

Foods and nutrition and home furnishings remained popular topics, along with home management. Family economics caught the attention of many farm women, especially topics about property transfer. County bar associations assisted with these offerings. Keeping farm records, a topic that Extension had emphasized for years, was catching on. Extension distributed more than 1,500 family account books in 1952.

By 1954, state home economics specialists worked less directly with farm women. They worked primarily with the county home agents to keep them up to date on subject matter and how it could be applied.

Specialists from the Federal Extension Service in Washington often came to Wisconsin on various missions. Rosemary Stare (Thornton), county home agent in Jackson County from 1951 to 1956, remembered the workshop federal worker Eunice Heywood conducted for agents on in-depth program planning. "I remember that she would take off her glasses, put the bow in her mouth, and then put them back on—16 times in five minutes."

Stare had apparently learned more than speaker quirks as she and then-County Agriculture Agent Walter Bean began gathering facts and figures. Armed with a big granite coffeepot, they met with people all around the county to learn about their problems. "We gathered problems to share with many other county agencies as well as being the basis for our programs," Stare said.

Gladys Meloche, longtime clothing specialist, said this about the changes then occurring in rural homes: "No longer is the farm woman just looking for someone to relieve her of the heavy burdens she carried in homemaking and willing to accept any program that state specialists could bring. Today, the homemakers take the lead. They have found a challenge in their job of homemaking. They look upon homemaking as a profession. They meet, discuss their problem, and decide on the program topics which they believe will be of greatest help to their community and county. They have branched out in fields of health, town government, family financial planning. Yes, they are leaders as well as good listeners."

In summing up her paper on home economics Extension from 1885 to 1954, Meloche wrote, "Two outstanding results of the home economics Extension program which are worth noting are:

1. The gradual integration of the farm, the home, and the youth programs.
2. The development of the finest system of volunteer leadership to be found

anywhere in the world."[8]

In 1957, home economics Extension conducted a survey of homemaker members. More than 6,000 women in 64 counties replied. Fifty-seven percent of the members lived on farms, 14 percent in the country but not on farms, 16 percent in cities and villages with populations under 2,500, and 13 percent in cities. Home economics programs were clearly no longer only for rural women.

By 1957 more than 46,000 women were enrolled in 3,000 homemaker groups. The programs began expanding beyond the "regular" ones such as home management, nutrition, and clothing to health programs that emphasized annual physical examinations and aid for handicapped children. They included programs in safety and consumer marketing, many of them conducted through radio and television programs. In 1957 Joan Hood worked as consumer marketing agent in Milwaukee County, while Doris Staidl held that position in Brown County. Both were heavily involved in radio, television, and newspaper writing in attempting to reach people.

4-H Programs

In 1947 Wisconsin 4-H club enrollment reached 36,486 members, including 18,200 boys and 18,286 girls. Extension agents spent about 40 percent of their time working with 4-H. Some devoted nearly all their time to 4-H; all agents spent at least some of their time working with these groups.

In 1947 Dane County alone had 1,015 4-H members in 52 clubs. One hundred fifteen volunteer 4-H leaders worked with these young people. Popular Dane County 4-H projects at the time were dairy (297), clothing (293), garden (249), foods and nutrition (129), food preservation (59), swine (55), and poultry (54).

By 1952, state 4-H enrollment had reached nearly 42,000 members. About 4,500 came from village and city homes as 4-H programs began including members who were not from farms. The clothing project attracted the most members, followed closely by dairy.

In addition to project work, 4-H members participated in a wide variety of activities, ranging from demonstration and speaking contests to taking projects to the county fair.

Shirley Felts, a farm girl from Shawano, did not know she was required to belong to a 4-H Club in order to show at the Shawano County Fair. She showed her calf, winning a prize and premium money of $24. When the fair officials found out she didn't belong to a 4-H Club, they refused to give her the money. Her father, W.H. Felts, took the matter to court and she received her check. "I think they felt sorry for me because I was planning to buy a new bike with that money I had earned," she recalled. "I lived two miles from Seneca School, and I wanted to bike instead of walk." The next year Shirley's mother helped organize a 4-H Club in Tilleda.

Later, when Felts was 16, she made the news by capturing a calf in the Shawano 4-H Rodeo, held in 1947. Some 50 people had donated dairy calves. More than 2,500 spectators watched as about 100 boys and girls tried to grab one of the calves, put a halter on it, and lead (drag) it across the finish line. If the youngster succeeded, she/he got to keep the calf and promised to show it at the next year's fair. Unfortunately, the calf Felts caught was a Holstein that would be the only black and white animal in a herd of Jerseys.

Since 1945 Extension had emphasized programs for older youth. Broadly defined, older youth included young men and women living in rural areas who were not in school and were between the ages of 18 and 30. Bruce Carter, assistant state 4-H leader, coordinated the state's older youth program. In 1952, more than 13,000 young men and women in 57 counties were involved. Older youth meetings covered public policy, good government, group relations, and recreation. Other popular topics included getting started in farming and getting married.

By the late 1950s, state 4-H enrollment approached 50,000 members. Increasingly, 4-H members came from non-farm residences.

Extension Well Respected
Largely because of the work County Extension agents and state-based specialists did through the Depression years and World War II, Cooperative Extension had become highly respected by Wisconsin's people—especially its rural people. The organization provided up-to-date information and helped farmers and their wives solve difficult problems in barn, home, and field. Extension also provided a social outlet through its many sponsored meetings, county fairs, and field days, and offered recreational and out-of-school educational opportunities for children. All through the Depression and World War II, Cooperative Extension had little competition from other educational providers or, for that matter, other recreational outlets. For many rural people, it was "the only show in town." Most country people would say it did its work well.

The County Extension agents were influential people in their counties, along with the county judge, local pastor, and the county superintendent of schools. Everyone knew their county agents and how to contact them. Farm people stopped by their offices and valued the advice they received. These were the good times for Cooperative Extension. No one questioned its value, and although there was some grumbling about raising local taxes to cover increasing Extension expenses and salaries, most people thought their tax dollars were well spent. But by the middle 1950s and into the 1960s, Extension's reputation's could no longer be taken for granted.

Fundamental Changes
Extension's audience was slowly moving to include those who did not live on farms or were not associated with farming. Four-H membership included ever-larger numbers of urban youth. Home economics programs became widely appreciated in cities as well as in the country. The rural development program, although helping to increase farm income, also helped non-farm enterprises in rural communities. The new

first year

WISCONSIN
1947 CLUB 4H WORK

CLOTHING
RECORD BOOK

PROJECT No.

NAME *Ruth E. Olson*

POST OFFICE *Westby* R. F. D. *2*

COUNTY *Vernon*

AGE *10* YEAR OF BIRTH *1937* MONTH *Aug.* DAY *23*

YEARS IN CLUB WORK, INCLUDING THIS YEAR *one*

YEARS IN CLOTHING PROJECT, INCLUDING THIS YEAR *one*

OTHER PROJECTS CARRIED THIS YEAR *Bird Project*
Dairy calf I

NAME OF CLUB *South Natwick*

PROJECT LEADER *Mrs Otto S. Olson*

DATE RECORD WAS BEGUN *May 20* 19 *47* FINISHED *Sept 23* 19 *47*

(To be signed at end of year)

This is a complete and accurate report of my work
in this project.

....

Signature of 4-H club member

Approved

Mrs. Ella Olson Parent

Mrs. Otto S. Olson Local Leader

Ethyl E. Morgan County Extension Agent

Cooperative Extension Work
College of Agriculture, University of Wisconsin
United States Department of Agriculture
Cooperating

Teaching 4-H members the value of good record keeping has long been an important part of Extension's youth programs. Vernon County, 1947.

consumer marketing agent positions were clearly designed to reach an urban audience.

Was this new trend a good thing? Some critics began to wonder. What was happening to the Agricultural Extension Service, as many continued to call it? Was Extension afraid it would no longer be needed as farm numbers continued to fall, as farmers became better educated, as feed, seed, and chemical companies sent competent field men out to work with farmers? Was expanding its audience an insurance plan, so that Extension could maintain operations and could continue asking for increases in tax dollars?

What about the federal mandate, the Smith-Lever legislation that formally established Cooperative Extension in 1914? Didn't this law specify clearly that Cooperative Extension ought work with farm men, women, and boys and girls?

The drafters of Smith-Lever did not limit those who should benefit from the organization. The first line of the Smith-Lever Act read: "That in order to aid in diffusing among the people of the United States useful and practical information on subjects relating to agriculture and home economics, and to encourage the application of the same . . ." [9]

Smith-Lever clearly said the audience should be the people of the United States, which appeared to include everyone. But the matter of content was another question. The subjects should relate "to agriculture and home economics."

The home economics people had no problem. What they were doing related to home economics no matter where people lived. But what about programs that did not seem to relate to agriculture? Here is where the debate began, a debate that continues to this day. There were those who asked then, and there are those who ask now, what "related to agriculture" means.

As Extension moved into the 1960s, questions about what Extension should do and with whom became important ones.

CHAPTER 7

NEW DIRECTIONS: 1960 TO 1975

From 1960 to 1975, Wisconsin lost 38,000 more farms. Rural communities went through massive school consolidation, with more than six thousand one-room country schools closed by the mid-1960s. The country schools had given many rural communities their identities and names, and communities mourned their passing. Country churches closed throughout Wisconsin, as did feed stores, gristmills, country stores and local cheese factories. In some ways, Cooperative Extension's challenge during these emotionally wrenching times was as great as it had ever been.

Extension's Plans
Under Henry Ahlgren's leadership, Cooperative Extension was doing well. Ahlgren had become a national Extension figure and served on the land-grant Extension Committee on Organization and Policy (ECOP), charged with developing a national plan for Cooperative Extension. "A Statement of Scope and Responsibility: The Cooperative Extension Service Today" was published in 1958. The purpose of this national report was to provide direction for Cooperative Extension and to answer critics who said that Extension was drifting. The report outlined nine areas of responsibility and reaffirmed the original mandate of the Smith-Lever legislation:
  1) Efficiency in agricultural production
  2) Efficiency in marketing, distribution, and utilization
  3) Conservation, development, and use of natural resources
  4) Management on the farm and in the home
  5) Family living
  6) Youth development
  7) Leadership development
  8) Community improvement and resource development
  9) Public affairs
The report made it clear that urban as well as rural residents could participate in Cooperative Extension programs. Many people within and outside of Extension considered this report a watershed, as it refocused Extension activity nationally.

Following the "Scope Report," Extension leaders held meetings around the country, culminating in "A Guide to Extension Programs for the Future," a more detailed action plan approved by national leaders on May 1, 1959.

Wisconsin Extension workers completed their version of the "Scope Report" in 1960. It called upon Wisconsin Cooperative Extension to emphasize the following:

1) Management on the farm and in the home
2) Conservation, wise use and development of natural resources
3) Family living
4) Youth development
5) Community improvement and resource development
6) Efficiency in agricultural production
7) Marketing, distribution and utilization of farm products
8) Public affairs
9) Leadership development

Image of Extension Conference

In spring 1962, Extension leaders from around the country gathered in Madison for a conference entitled "The Image of Extension." The National Agricultural Extension Center for Advanced Study sponsored the meeting.

Presenters examined Extension from several perspectives—agriculture, urban centers, university administration, the farm press, and more. As one might guess, the views expressed were extremely divergent. Fred Harrington, president of the University of Wisconsin said, "Cooperative Extension does not have a very satisfactory image from the campus point of view. Most professors on our land-grant faculties do not think of Cooperative Extension [as] belonging to the university at all."[1]

J.H. Florea, representing the farm press, laid out several challenges and said: "There is practically unanimous agreement, in most cases quite strongly expressed, that the agricultural Extension service has no business extending its services to urban residents."[2]

Loren Osman, farm writer for the Milwaukee *Journal*, didn't question Extension's urban programming, but he was concerned that the organization wasn't keeping up. He asked: "Can the Extension Service adjust readily to changing times? Is it backing its workers with the proper training for the urbanizing situation?"[3]

It was clear that the workshop went well beyond asking "Isn't Extension wonderful?" to focus on questions of direction and challenges that the organization faced. Although the outcomes may have been uncomfortable to some, others saw the conference as the medicine the organization needed.

In 1962, Cooperative Extension in Wisconsin celebrated the fiftieth anniversary of the passage of the Smith-Lever Act in 1912.

Civil Rights and Vietnam

In the early 1960s, civil rights demonstrations erupted in the South. In 1963, 200,000 "freedom marchers" descended on Washington, D.C. Riots in Birmingham, Alabama, resulted in Martin Luther King's arrest and in President Kennedy's decision to call out three thousand troops. In 1964, the country became immersed in Vietnam and campus demonstrations broke out across the country—including massive protests at the University of Wisconsin in Madison.

President Lyndon Johnson began pushing legislation on several fronts, especially in the areas of civil rights and programs for the poor. The Civil Rights Act, passed in 1964, made segregated schools illegal. Federal agencies and departments that discriminated would receive no funds.

This legislation sent a ripple across the country. For Cooperative Extension, it meant that the once separate but equal land-grant universities and Extension services in several southern states, which came about as a result of federal legislation dating back to 1890, had to be integrated. Alabama, North Carolina, Florida, Louisiana, Texas, and other states with "1890" institutions were affected.

The War on Poverty

President Johnson initiated the War on Poverty in 1964. He wrote: "I have called for a national war on poverty. Our objective: total victory. There are millions of Americans—one fifth of our people—who have not shared in the abundance which has been granted to most of us, and on whom the gates of opportunity have been closed."[4]

The legislation authorized a federal Office of Economic Opportunity, Job Corps, VISTA (Volunteers in Service to America), work-study for college students, community action programs, Head Start for pre-schoolers, day care services, legal services for the poor, and adult basic education programs for those who lacked literacy skills.

Cooperative Extension hoped to receive money as a result of the legislation. But there was a prevailing belief that existing agencies and organizations had failed in their work with the poor, so new organizations should be formed. The legislation gave money directly to the grassroots public or nonprofit organizations that sprang up everywhere. Workers at these organizations often thumbed their noses at established organizations and institutions.

Groups like Job Corps and VISTA called on Extension people to help them implement their programs, and VISTA asked for assistance with leader training. But some VISTA leaders told Extension that it didn't know how to work with the poor. They obviously hadn't studied Extension's history. The new community action groups were doing exactly what Extension had been doing for years.

It was not a happy time for Cooperative Extension, but the organization paid attention to what was going on and began looking anew at programs for the poor. These years provided the foundation, both in thought and action, for broad-based nutrition and family management programs and community resource development programs.

Silent Spring

By the 1960s, farmers used chemicals for everything from eliminating weeds to killing barn flies. In May 1962, Rachel Carson published *Silent Spring*. Carson's book, which questioned and often broadly accused agricultural chemicals of destroying the environment, was soon on nearly everyone's mind. In the book's foreword, she quoted Albert Schweitzer: "Man has lost the capacity to foresee and to forestall. He will end by destroying the earth." Carson went on to write: "For the first time in the history of the world, every human being is now subjected to contact with dangerous chemicals, from the moment of conception until death. In the less than two decades of their use, the synthetic pesticides have been so thoroughly distributed throughout the animate and inanimate world that they occur virtually everywhere."[5]

Extension had been researching pesticides for years and knew a great deal about them by the time *Silent Spring* arrived in bookstores and its content became the topic of news shows and the bible for environmentalists. Nonetheless, some specialists and county agents became extremely defensive. They wrote articles challenging Carson's work. DDT, an effective insecticide, had been widely used by farmers to control barn flies. It soon became one of the first chemicals banned for use in the United States.

Extension people, agricultural researchers, and other university faculty members debated the pros and cons of Carson's book, especially her conclusions. Most of the attempts to discredit her work failed. It was not a shining moment for the College of Agriculture and the Cooperative Extension Service.

Massive Organizational Change

The structure of Extension in Wisconsin changed little from the appearance of the first county agent in 1912 until 1965. All employees—field staff, specialists, and administrators—were located within the Cooperative Extension unit of the College of Agriculture. The college had long prided itself on its three functions: residence teaching (degree programs); research (the experiment station); and outreach (the Cooperative Extension Service).

This changed after Fred Harvey Harrington became president of the University of Wisconsin on August 6, 1962, upon the death of President Conrad Elvehjem, a former agriculture professor. Harrington was a history professor and became a supporter of Lyndon Johnson's various programs—especially those designed to assist the urban poor.

The successes of Cooperative Extension in rural communities impressed Harrington, and he envisioned a similar organization for urban areas. With President Johnson in Washington, Harrington believed that large amounts of new money would soon be available for higher education. In fact, in an address given at the new Irvine campus of the University of California in 1964, President Johnson talked about federal funding of urban Extension agents.[6]

Harrington decided to merge Cooperative Extension with General Extension, forming a new super-organization that would create programs for both rural and urban audiences. He also planned to include WHA radio and television in this new organization that would, he hoped, become a leader among higher education institutions with its new, radical approach.

Ordinarily, one would expect the old saw "If it ain't broke, don't fix it" to hold sway. Since the release of the Scope Report, Cooperative Extension had been riding a wave of respect and hope for better things in the future. Why tinker with the administration of the organization?

But some interesting politics developed. Gilbert Rhode sat on the board of regents when the merger proposal was presented. He was then president of the National Farmers Union, which tended to endorse Democratic policies. The National Farmers Union believed that agricultural colleges and their Extension services leaned more toward serving large commercial farms than smaller ones. He and other regents reasoned that a reorganized Extension might address some of these criticisms. Thus the regents approved Harrington's merger proposal on September 6, 1963.[7]

Harrington involved few campus people in the merger decision. He was probably unaware of how widely the agricultural faculty disagreed with the idea of a new, merged organization. In late 1963, Harrington appointed a special committee chaired by political science professor Ralph Huitt. The committee was charged with working out a merger plan. Meanwhile in 1964, due to failing health, Dean Rudoph Froker stepped down as dean of the College of Agriculture and was replaced by Glenn Pound, a noted plant pathologist. Pound took over on September 1, 1964, but not before asking President Harrington whether the 1963 Extension merger decision might be reversed. Harrington said the merger would stand.

Pound later became one of the merger's most forceful critics. It is a mystery why he didn't speak up more forcibly when he became dean. In his defense, he probably did not think the merger would be approved, especially with Ahlgren at the helm of Cooperative Extension. Perhaps Pound did not foresee the far-reaching effects the merger would have on the College of Agriculture.

The Huitt committee's report was published in May 1965. It recommended forming a single organization combining all Extension functions, led by a chancellor who would report directly to the president of the university. Cooperative Extension people became upset when they learned that the agriculture dean would no longer hold the title of "director of Cooperative Extension," and that the Extension budget—including Smith-Lever funds—would be controlled by the new Extension chancellor.

The First Chancellor

The obvious choice for Extension chancellor was Henry Ahlgren. However, some Extension staff thought the position should be filled by Lorentz Adolfson, the former dean of general Extension—or by his successor, Theodore Shannon. There were other candidates on the list, including Donald McNeil, a historian who had helped

Harrington achieve passage of Title I of the new Higher Education Act. It was this act that Harrington believed would provide huge sums of money to fund urban Extension activities.

On October 22, 1965, after several months of consideration, Harrington selected the relatively unknown McNeil to become University of Wisconsin-Extension's first chancellor. McNeil knew something about all three Extension units (Cooperative Extension, General Extension, and radio/television), but he had not worked for any of them.

McNeil set out to solidify the nuts and bolts of the new organization by establishing a "committee on organization and structure," chaired by School of Education Associate Dean and longtime adult educator Wilson Thiede.

An organizational chart was soon developed. It included two assistant chancellors, one responsible for subject matter divisions and the other to look after field and support services. The latter included responsibility for all the county and area offices. The chart included assistant chancellors to provide "administrative and coordinating services at locations outside Madison with significant faculty resources, such as UW-M [Milwaukee] and the new campuses under development at Green Bay and Kenosha-Racine [UW-Parkside]."[8]

When some people looked at the organizational chart they saw not a new, visionary organization, but an administrative nightmare. Years after the merger, in 1992, Bryant Kearl, once department chair for agricultural journalism and later a campuswide administrator, spoke to the Madison Literary Society. The title of his talk was "Who Killed the Wisconsin Idea?" After recounting example after example of agricultural successes in the laboratories and on the farms through research and Extension efforts, Kearl expressed his astonishment that the university would pull its Extension activities off the Madison campus and put them in a new organization that cut Extension people off from their campus research base. He said: "For some faculty members and departments this [new organization] may have been a relief. For the Wisconsin Idea, which obviously depended on access to the wide range of specialized knowledge available in a true university, it was a deadly blow."[9]

Besides ruffling feathers and raising questions about programming, the initial reorganization proved a costly endeavor. Gale VandeBerg recalled someone in the federal Extension Service saying that Wisconsin Cooperative Extension had the largest administrative overhead of any Cooperative Extension Service in America. VandeBerg explained that Cooperative Extension funds helped support a chancellor of Extension, two assistant chancellors, three deans, plus partial salaries for the dean of the College of Agriculture and the dean of the School of Home Economics.[10]

After studying the proposed organizational chart for UW-Extension, Dean Pound was livid. He noted that agriculture college departmental chairmen were not on the chart. Ever since the inception of Agricultural Extension, departmental chairmen had coordinated the three functions of teaching, research, and Extension. Now the Extension function had been pulled away.

Some forecast the end of Cooperative Extension as they had known it. Others said this new organization would cause departments to work together in program areas. In retrospect, people like former Chancellor Boyle believed the new organization marked the beginning of interdisciplinary programming.

The College of Agriculture had long praised its integrated departments, meaning that Extension, research, and teaching occurred in one place. General Extension departments did not have a similar history. There were campus departments of English, journalism, business, and many others, separate departments in General Extension without close ties to those "on the hill." But that was not the case in agriculture. Most "aggies" were furious with the new organizational plan.

A final bone of contention was the federal appointment for Cooperative Extension from the United States Department of Agriculture. Neither Pound nor Ahlgren thought it would go to chancellor and historian McNeil. But they were wrong. McNeil got the federal appointment, and University of Wisconsin-Extension was on its way. George Strother from General Extension and Ahlgren each became assistant chancellors. Ahlgren became responsible for field and support operations. A number of deans were appointed next to head up the main divisions of the organization: Harold Montross (liberal and professional studies); Gale VandeBerg (economic and environmental development); Glen Pulver (human resource development); Charles W. Wedemeyer (methods and media); Robert Dick (community programs); and Patrick Boyle (staff training and development).

Area and County Extension staffs that had been a part of the College of Agriculture were now in the division of community programs. District Extension supervisors reported to Robert Dick. State 4-H staff members were removed from the College of Agriculture and placed in a newly created department of youth development.

These were not just changes that took place on paper. They also meant that many people moved their offices. Agricultural Hall was no longer the center of Cooperative Extension activities for the state. The administrative center for the new organization became the Extension Building on Lake Street. Overflow staff moved into Lowell Hall, a failed student housing building that the university purchased.

The first annual conference for the newly merged organization met October 11 to 14, 1966, in Madison. Patrick Boyle chaired the planning committee. Everyone looked forward to hearing Chancellor McNeil and getting to know their new colleagues from General Extension and radio/television. Most staff members came to the meeting with an open mind about the new organization and its potential. But the experienced ones had many questions. Was the merger really necessary? What could be gained through this elaborate, bureaucratic organization with layer upon layer of administrators?

President Harrington and Chancellor McNeil had pinned their hopes on receiving a large sum of money from federal Title I funds, which would be used to create urban agents throughout the state. The idea was that any person coming into a County Extension office should have access to the entire University of Wisconsin, not just the College of Agriculture or the School of Home Economics. It was a noble thought, but it turned out to be naive, because the Title I funds were not forthcoming. The Vietnam War was raging at this time, and wars cost lots of money. McNeil thought existing county staff could perhaps broaden their clientele base a bit, doing at least some of what he had envisioned in making the university available to all. Overworked county staff did not readily cotton to the idea; they already had plenty to do. Stress levels began to rise.

Chancellor McNeil continued to press his social action agenda, praised by some and questioned by others. Cooperative Extension had some experience with controversy—the Rachel Carson episode was an example—but now controversy swirled. Many citizens were not especially pleased with the ways in which the anti-poverty programs were carried out. The controversy came to a head during state 4-H Club Week in June 1968, when a booklet entitled "Voices of Protest" was distributed to the 4-H members in attendance. The booklet contained statements from anti-war demonstrators, which some considered inflammatory.

This was a time when student protests and anti-war demonstrations increased in intensity on campus. Upstate people couldn't understand, appreciate, or accept what was going on. The university was awash in controversy. Angry citizens confronted Extension specialists with the words "Can't you control those students?" In those days, state cars were white with special license plates and easily recognized. To some university people, the cars seemed like they had bull's-eyes painted on them.

In December 1968, Chancellor Donald McNeil left to become chancellor of a new statewide system in Maine. Questions about the wisdom of the Wisconsin Extension merger returned. Because of the protests and the increasing backlash from state citizens, Harrington had lost considerable clout. The regents decided to take an active role in replacing McNeil, and pressure mounted to appoint Ahlgren as chancellor. A search committee came up with several candidates, including Ahlgren. In the midst of the search, Dean Pound of the College of Agriculture pushed to have budget and administrative control of Agricultural Extension returned to the College of Agriculture. But this was not to happen.

Ahlgren Replaces McNeil

President Harrington wasted little time in selecting Henry Ahlgren as the second chancellor for University of Wisconsin-Extension. Ahlgren took office on March 1, 1969. In the fall of 1970, Ahlgren went to Washington for a temporary assignment within the United States Department of Agriculture. In his absence, Vice Chancellor George Strother served as acting chancellor. Ahlgren did not adjust well to Washington politics and bureaucracy, and was back in Madison by October 1971.

Evans Becomes Chancellor

Henry Ahlgren retired in 1974. In November of that year, former Oklahoma Extension Vice President Jean Evans became chancellor of University of Wisconsin-Extension.

Many people still had great hopes for the Extension merger, despite its clunky organizational arrangements, its plethora of administrators, and its critics among agricultural faculty. In a 1988 interview Gale VandeBerg, longtime Cooperative Extension administrator, said: "The merger could have been the best thing that ever happened to Wisconsin, and perhaps to the nation, if it had been funded in the sixties, following the merger, with the federal monies that were expected, or if it had been funded in 1974 with six million dollars of new money from the state. It was appropriated and approved by the legislature and then put in escrow and never was released. If either of those two things happened with the right administrator, the merger would have worked, and it would have been a marvelous organization."[11]

Glenn Pound never wavered in his disdain for the Extension merger. In 1973, he wrote: "In 1965, the University merged the Cooperative Extension and General Extension Divisions into a single unit, University Extension, which was headed by a Chancellor. Since a Chancellor in the University of Wisconsin is the administrative head of a campus faculty, this administrative structure of Extension fostered a drive for separate faculty identity. This move toward separateness resulted in duplicative administrative structures, stratification of academic citizenship, and reduced program efficiency. More than these, it weakened the bonds of relationship between teaching, research, and Extension in the College of Agriculture.[12]

In spite of all the hoopla swirling around administrative change, Cooperative Extension staff continued to carry on programs old and new, as they had in the past. As some County Extension agents said, "Spend time thinking about what's going on in Madison, and you'll never get anything done."

Cooperative Extension and General Extension faculty began working on several new programming efforts. Several counties added continuing education agents to help fulfill the new University of Wisconsin-Extension's mission to make the entire university available to the people.

Center for Action on Poverty

The War on Poverty and the 1965 reorganization of Extension resulted in many new programming efforts. Don McNeil had created a Center for Action on Poverty that cut across Cooperative and General Extension interests. Dorothy Davids, a staff member in the center, recalled some of their activities in the mid-1960s. "It seems it was our goal to teach 'grassroots' people how to create change in their own communities. It was a revolutionary idea that African-Americans, Latinos, American Indians, women, physically disabled, elder, and other folks with differences actually had some ideas on what would improve their lives. It was quite a jolt, and maybe a threat to the establishment when they discovered they did not know and have all the answers. Our role seemed to be to facilitate both the power of people with differences to speak up and the people with the power to help bring about change to listen. . . . We were different, and we were learning."

Bob Bright, also a staff member in the center, wrote: "For the first time in Cooperative Extension's history, racially diverse faculty and staff were hired [in the mid-1960s] in 'sufficient' number to be noticed. . . . The Center for Action on Poverty became the lightning rod for change within Cooperative Extension as well as within other divisions. Our mission also included working with community action boards and the citizenry in a six-state region within the Midwest."

Bright noted that one of the requirements for community action board membership was that one-third of the members be representatives of the poor. Many communities resisted this membership mandate. As Bright went on to explain: "Wherever we turned, controversy ensued. Old ways of thinking and feeling were giving way to new considerations which focused on creating better relationships among diverse people." The Center's activities were often roundly criticized, with complaints piling up on Chancellor McNeil's desk. Bright said the chancellor always supported their efforts. McNeil even said at one time that he expected them to do an "inside job" on the organization—meaning to change the attitudes of Extension faculty and staff.

The Center for Action on Poverty became the Center for Leadership Development, and later was named the Community Dynamics Institute. Its programs raised questions that were not always welcomed, and it questioned existing organizations and institutions, which was not always appreciated.

During the 1960s, affirmative action became the watchword for all organizations. Donald Duxbury, a former County Extension agent, became a staff member of the Center for Action on Poverty. The director of Cooperative Extension asked him to attend a meeting in St. Louis regarding affirmative action. Duxbury learned that Wisconsin Extension representatives had failed to attend an earlier meeting in Chicago "because they deemed it unnecessary."

When Duxbury came back from St. Louis, he reported that Extension was in trouble with the federal government, and that the organization had only three months to develop a written plan for affirmative action programming. "Every county in the state was required to develop a written plan, and a follow-up review was conducted," Duxbury recalled. "Bits and pieces of change began to emerge. An official letterhead touted Extension as an organization with affirmative action programming and equal opportunity employment. Suddenly, agents in each county office received announcements of Extension job opportunities throughout the state. Here and there, a face of another color began to show up in staffing."

Wisconsin Associated County Extension Committees
In the 1960s, the special committee of county agricultural agents that Director

Ahlgren had appointed in 1955 met several times and performed grassroots lobbying with county officials and state legislators. Committee members recommended forming an organization of county agricultural and Extension committees. This new organization, called Wisconsin Associated County Extension Committees (WACEC), was incorporated on April 4, 1966.

The organization was formed "to provide a forum for the consideration of problems and policies of concern to [county board agricultural and Extension education committees], provide leadership in the identification and initiation of new Extension programs in rural and urban areas and in carrying out existing programs . . . obtaining local financial support for Extension work . . . providing leadership on legislative matters affecting Extension and acting as a liaison between state and county representatives and other public officials with respect to proposed and existing Extension programs."[13] Membership in the group included all members of county board agricultural and Extension education committees.

The organization's first meeting took place in Stevens Point on May 22 and 23, 1967. Members heard from Dean Glenn Pound from the College of Agriculture, Assistant Chancellor Henry Ahlgren, and several County Extension agents and specialists. The speakers addressed topics ranging from brucellosis and the Dairy Herd Improvement Association to alfalfa and farm management, from welfare in Milwaukee County to commercial recreation in Vilas County. At the evening banquet, which cost $3.25 per person, the group heard an address by Governor Warren P. Knowles.

In addition to an annual meeting, the Associated County Extension Committee held district meetings. There were eight Extension districts containing eight to ten counties in each district. At the district meetings, Extension continued to educate county board agriculture and Extension education committee members about Extension and its various programs and activities.

WACEC proved to be a stroke of genius. Through this organization, Cooperative Extension established a cadre of people who knew the organization, knew what it was doing, and had a say in deciding its direction. The organization also provided recognition for county agricultural and Extension committee members and helped them become acquainted with their peers across the state. WACEC members became some of Cooperative Extension's greatest local supporters, especially when it came to budget matters, at local, state, and federal levels. In 2001, WACEC was organized into six districts, with officers in each district making up the board for the statewide organization.

Agricultural Programs

Extension and the Wisconsin Department of Agriculture enjoyed a long and mostly congenial relationship. It was clear that Extension's primary role was an educational one, while the Department of Agriculture had many roles, including a regulatory function. During the winter of 1961-62, Extension worked with the Department of Agriculture to detect and eliminate sheep scabies, a parasitic infection of a sheep's skin. On a designated day in January, Extension agents throughout the state stopped at every farm with sheep. Each agent had received instructions on how to spot a sheep with scabies, as well as a scrub brush, disinfectant, and a pail. Upon leaving a farm, the routine was to wash off rubber boots with the disinfectant. The rubber boots were not provided.

Polk County agent Arno Dittbrenner did not own rubber boots, so he bought a pair and included their price in the expense account he mailed to the Madison office. The expense account came back with the boots scratched off and a note saying "personal property cannot be covered." Arno submitted an expense account the following month with a long explanation about the scabies inspection and why it required boots. This expense form was returned with the same note. The next month, Arno included this memo with his expense account: "The rubber boots are included. See if you can find them." Arno had buried the cost for the boots in with other, allowable expense items. He received full payment.

Green Lake County agents Roland Manthe (4-H) and Willis Gjermandson (agriculture) also went out that snowy, slippery day in January on their mission to detect sheep scabies. They found one flock with five infected sheep. Once a veterinarian confirmed the disease, the sheep were to be dipped in order to kill the parasite. Unfortunately, the temperature on the scheduled day for the sheep dipping was minus 20 degrees, according to Manthe. Was the dipping effective? "It got rid of the sheep scabies problem," Manthe reported, "because all five sheep died of exposure. Green Lake County was then free of sheep scabies." The outcome of the scabies adventure was more positive in most counties, and the entire state of Wisconsin was ultimately declared free of sheep scabies.

In the late 1960s, agricultural programs in many counties concentrated on crops and soils, livestock and livestock management, and farm and business management. Home economics programs featured such subjects as money management, family stability, consumer competence, human development, family health, family housing, and community resource development. Some attempts were made to work with existing welfare services to assist disadvantaged families.

Milk Marketing Orders

Throughout the 1960s, farmers and others pressured the government to do something about the complicated federal milk market orders. In the early 1960s, 83 milk marketing orders (which determined milk prices in a region) operated in the United States. U.S. Secretary of Agriculture Clifford Hardin (1969-1971) asked Truman Graf and other Extension staff to study the milk marketing situation and report back by July 1, 1972. As a result of the study Graf, an agricultural economist, recommended reducing the number of market orders from the then-operating 62 to less than ten.

Graf also recommended that pricing provisions for various classes of milk (how it was used) reflect the continuing conversion from manufacturing grade milk to Grade A milk at the farms. The changes came slowly, culminating in a 1996 Congressional act signed by President Clinton. Effective January 1, 2000, there were 11 federal milk orders in operation.

Horticulture

In the early 1960s urban people discovered the County Extension office as a place they could obtain answers to their questions about lawns, yard trees, flowers, and vegetables—everything horticultural. County agriculture agents like Dick Schuster in Green Bay, Vern Peroutky in Oshkosh, and Maury Hovland in West Bend were among the agents who began to spend time answering horticultural questions. Some farm and home development agents saw their responsibilities shifting to more horticultural work, including Richard Presney in Dane County and Gene Anderson in Bayfield County. By 1980, seven counties had horticultural agents.

Soon Extension offices became overwhelmed with horticultural questions. Extension developed an automatic phone system that allowed people to call in and receive a two- or three-minute horticultural message. Lee Hansen in Milwaukee started ed using the system in 1972, followed by Leland Smith in Kenosha County in 1973. The "Dial-a-Tape" system began in Dane County in 1974, with horticultural agent James Schroeder writing and recording several tapes.[14]

Working with Cranberry Growers

Wisconsin has a long history of cranberry growing, beginning with the first commercial bogs that opened in northern Green Lake and southern Waushara Counties in 1853. Today, cranberries are grown in 18 of Wisconsin's 72 counties, with the majority of the crop grown in Wood, Jackson, and Monroe Counties. Wisconsin led the nation in cranberry production in the late 1990s.

In 1953, the cranberry growers and Cooperative Extension began working together to solve growers' problems. George Klingbeil, Extension horticulturist, started a three-day school for cranberry growers in 1968, working with Wood County Extension agents Louis Rosandick and Tod Planer. Practical findings by Extension specialists who worked with the cranberry industry—especially with water management and weed control—were credited with helping the industry become a national leader in the 1990s. Sprinkler systems for bogs were introduced as a result of the research. Malcolm Dana, Extension horticulture specialist, worked with cranberry growers to evaluate herbicides for weed control. He also introduced more efficient uses of fertilizers. In the mid-1960s Charles Koval, Extension entomologist, helped solve the insect problems cranberry growers faced.[15]

Nyla Musser, Jackson County home economist, wrote the first cranberry bulletin with George Klingbiel. Musser also worked with Klingbiel to establish the Warrens

Cranberry Festival. At the early festivals Musser, along with Expanded Food and Nutrition Education Program workers, gave demonstrations and distributed bulletins on cooking with cranberries. The Warrens Cranberry Festival began with 20 vendors; by 2000, there were 200 vendors.

Frost Survey

For several years Arthur Peterson, Extension soils specialist, conducted runoff studies that included measuring frost depth on university property on the west side of Madison. Bob Bjorklund, a farm writer for the Wisconsin *State Journal*, called Peterson each winter and asked about frost depth. As Peterson reported: "When he called, we (usually me) went out and made a reading. One nasty, cold, windy day in December 1960, Bob called and asked the frost depth. I hated to go out, and having recently attended a funeral at Roselawn Memorial Park in Madison, I had an idea." Peterson called Roselawn and inquired about frost depth. The man he talked to asked, "Do you want the information for the north slope or the south slope?" Peterson knew he had contacted the right man.

Soon Peterson had an idea for a statewide survey. As an assignment, he asked one of his university students to contact the Wisconsin Board of Health and develop a list of funeral directors by county. Peterson then called the County Extension agents and asked them which funeral directors he should contact, thereby establishing his first mailing list. Funeral directors and cemetery officials from throughout the state provided the necessary data for the first and succeeding yearly surveys.

Peterson asked the Department of Agricultural Journalism in the College of Agriculture for help in sending out and tabulating the information, but he was told that the study was too gruesome, and he initially received no cooperation. Peterson worked with the state cartographer, who helped draw maps showing snow and frost depth, which were then released by the UW Department of Soil Science to the Associated Press and United Press International. The information was widely used and attracted great interest. Soon Peterson was working with the U.S. Department of Commerce Weather Bureau and the Wisconsin office of the statistical reporting service of the U.S. Department of Agriculture.

As yearly data were accumulated, frost depth comparisons were made. For instance, during the winter of 1960-61, with scant snow cover and severe temperatures, frost depth in northeastern and northern Wisconsin varied from 36 to 60 inches. In 1962, with heavy snow, frost depth in the same region varied from 0 to 12 inches.[16] The annual frost depth survey continued until the winter of 1999-2000, when it was eliminated as a result of USDA budget cuts.

4-H Activities

By the 1960s, 4-H members could enroll in photography, nature-conservation and horse and dog projects (emphasis on dog obedience) among others, in addition to traditional subject matter projects such as dairy, clothing, crops, and foods .

In the summer of 1965, meetings were held to start a 4-H horse show. Quin Kolb, meat and animal science specialist, and Jim Everts, assistant state 4-H Leader, organized the meetings and polled counties to see whether there was interest. The first meeting of the Wisconsin 4-H horse committee took place on December 6, 1965, and the first horse show was held at the Dane County Fairgrounds on September 10 and 11, 1966. In 1967, the state 4-H horse show was incorporated into the Wisconsin 4-H Horse Association. All currently enrolled Wisconsin 4-H horse and pony adult leaders became members of the association. The purpose of the horse show, which continued into 2001, was the education of 4-H horse project members. The Wisconsin 4-H Horse Association sponsored educational clinics, a Wisconsin pack and trail ride, a state hunt and dressage show, and other activities. [17]

In 1966, under the leadership of Norman Everson of the state 4-H staff, Ken Kuemmerlein taught arts and crafts programs for 4-H members. Ed Hugdahl provided leadership in music, and Robert Gard and Helen O'Brien taught drama workshops. These Extension specialists traveled the state, working with agents and leader groups.

Large numbers of 4-H members participated in county drama and music festivals, and in 4-H bands and choruses. State 4-H band and chorus members performed in Madison at state 4-H Club Week, at the state fair in Milwaukee, and at the National 4-H Congress in Chicago.

In January 1967, Extension developed a series of half-hour television shows (*4-H TV Action*) The programs offered information on how to prepare for emergencies such as fire, cold, tornadoes, atomic radiation, and others. The target audience was schoolchildren in grades three through six. Televsion stations carrying the programs included those in La Crosse, Eau Claire, Wausau, Rhinelander, and Green Bay—and later WHA-TV in Madison. Some 45,000 schoolchildren enrolled in the special program associated with the television shows. Prior to the showing, Extension distributed student booklets, teacher discussion guides, membership cards, and pins.

In 1969, Extension developed 10 half-hour programs on science subjects. Called *4-H TV Science*, the programs addressed topics including astronomy, animal skeletons, plants, fire, archaeology, physics, microbiology, chemistry, behavior, and meteorology. An additional television series for youth called *4-H Photo Fun* was promoted in 10 southeastern counties. These shows covered camera and film, taking photos, making stories with photographs, and more. After examining viewer surveys, Everson and Carl Smith, Milwaukee County 4-H agent, concluded that over 200,000 youth had seen at least one of the shows.

Members of 4-H also participated in demonstration contests, summer camps, fairs, style revues (for clothing members), and favorite food revues (for foods members). Prior to 1960, little 4-H work had taken place in urban centers. Carl Smith, who had been 4-H agent in Columbia County, moved to Milwaukee in 1960 and began organizing an urban 4-H program. One of his first attempts was through the Urban League. He gave a presentation about 4-H to several block leaders, and they showed some interest. But as Carl wrote: "We tried to use the traditional 4-H model-enrollment cards, record books, leader training meetings, and county activities. We soon found out that the old 4-H model was not going to work. Most volunteers could not read or write beyond the third-grade level, so they did not do paperwork such as enrollment cards. Only a few volunteer leaders attended training meetings, because they didn't want to reveal how little they knew about the various projects. Many of the volunteers said 'Organization is not one of my skills.'"

After a year of limited success, Smith decided to eliminate enrollment cards, record books and other "paperwork." He helped organize clubs based on one 4-H project each, and by 1962 had four of them operating in Milwaukee. One of the most successful was a club led by volunteer Jim Richardsen. Richardsen taught 4-Hers to make wooden flower boxes. The 4-H members made 25 of them and took them to homes in their neighborhood. The next year, this group began a "Fix up-Clean up" campaign and convinced most of the neighborhood to participate.

Smith also helped organize 4-H work at the Hillside Housing Project in the inner city. This was a government housing project for low-income families. After a lot of door knocking and personal contacts, Extension staff organized a foods project in Hillside. Twelve to fifteen kids attended the initial meetings. By the end of the school year, 110 kids were attending. To end the 4-H food project year, Extension sponsored a Hillside 4-H fair, where members were invited to bring two cookies apiece from sample recipes they were given. As Smith recalls, one of the members took the instruction literally and made the entire batch into two huge cookies.

Smith also had success working with the Sisterhood League of the Jewish Temple, which provided volunteers for the 4-H program at Hillside. Meetings were held in a small apartment within the housing complex. As Smith explained: "We were able to have three project groups at the apartment each day, five days a week. Only five or six girls per project were allowed, because each room in the apartment was very small. If a member did not attend, others could come to the meeting. Girls would line up outside the door, hoping one of the regular members would not attend so they could get into the meeting."

One day when the volunteer leader arrived at the apartment, the draperies were missing. Someone had stolen them over the weekend. Nothing else had been taken. Later that afternoon, three girls who were enrolled in the clothing project arrived wearing matching clothes made from the drapery fabric.

Other successful projects included an urban 4-H garden project, with some 350 children gardening on land provided at county institutions such as the county home on Watertown Plank Road. Milwaukee County Extension had received a grant from Sears to bus the children to their gardens. This led to an adult gardening project that was taken over by Shoots N' Roots, a nationally funded urban garden project that established as many as 3,500 gardens in Milwaukee County.

In the 1960s, Milwaukee County held its first 4-H fair at the Mayfair Shopping Mall in Wauwatosa. Seven tents in the parking lot housed horses, livestock, and poultry. Other exhibits were spread throughout the mall. Each year, a celebrity was recruited to cut the ribbon that officially opened the fair. In 1965, it was Lucy Baines Johnson, daughter of the president of the United States. In the 1970s, Milwaukee County Extension received federal money to hire five part-time 4-H staff assistants and expand what was becoming a highly innovative urban 4-H program.

Because new funds were available for urban 4-H, additional staff members were also hired in Dane, Waukesha, Kenosha, Manitowoc, Brown, Sheboygan, Outagamie, and Marathon Counties during the 1970s. In Brown County, the addition of a second agent resulted in a one-week camping experience for "at risk" youth from Green Bay schools. In Milwaukee County, Extension youth staff members were placed at the zoo and the Wehr Nature Center. In Sheboygan County, new short-term programs involved youth who had not previously been involved in 4-H. Examples included a "horseless horse" project for youth who were interested in horses but didn't own one, a "dog lovers anonymous" course, and a course in motorcycle safety. Four-H was also involved with summer school programs for migrant youth and English as a second language (ESL) programs.

During the 1970s, many counties hired their first female 4-H youth agents. Many of these women experienced blatant sexist behavior. Linda Kustka, hired as 4-H agent in Brown County, remembered the head of a fair board telling her repeatedly that he wanted to talk with the man in charge.

Staff members submitted affirmative action plans to better reach the underserved, and to affirm programming in non-discriminatory ways. County-level volunteer committees became heavily involved in setting program direction as well as planning and running county events.[18]

Family Living

Home economics programs, now regularly referred to as "family living programs," began moving beyond skill areas like clothing construction, food preparation, and family record keeping.

In 1966, a special home economics subcommittee of the Extension committee on organization and policy produced a report entitled "Focus." This special committee, which included Marlys Richert from Wisconsin Cooperative Extension, laid out future directions for home economics programming. Broad areas of emphasis included family stability, consumer competence, family housing, family health, and community resource development. These program topics were declared "areas of national concern."[19]

In response to the national planning, the entire Wisconsin family living staff assembled in Stevens Point for a three-day meeting where the family living program for Wisconsin was reorganized in areas ranging from content/subject matter to problem areas known as sub-programs. "It was a stressful meeting for many faculty members," Rosemary Stare reported.

Another task force on Extension home economics produced "Focus II" in 1974. Marlys Richert chaired the group. The report set these goals: "1. To provide states with a guide to assist with program development and administration; 2. To show how Extension home economics educational programs can contribute in resolving some of the major concerns related to the quality of life in America today; 3. To identify segments of the population which are in greatest need."[20]

Traditional homemaker members were not all pleased with the new directions "their" programs were taking. Some saw these new areas of emphasis as diminishing traditional topics such as clothing, foods, and the like. But as Ardith McDowell, a longtime homemaker member from Marquette County said: "The early projects, of course, were practical. Now they've gone into a great deal more of the enrichment projects—things that are more intellectual. I think as we become a little older, our scopes become a little broader, [and] that's very good. But I don't think that we should forget the practical things, because we always have new people coming into homemakers and young members who have not had all of those practical skills. [Of course] it's also good to have some very thought-provoking things like world concerns, government problems, and things that really tax our thoughts and our minds."[21]

College Week

In 1964, College Week for Women was launched on the Madison campus. The first year's theme was "Broader Horizons." Extension's family living education program staff and the Wisconsin Home Demonstration Council planned it. Here was an opportunity for women from around the state, no matter where they lived, to spend several days on the Madison campus, live in dormitories, and receive in-depth information on an array of topics. These topics included helping teens plan their future, improving speaking ability, considering employment, knowing oneself as a woman, citizenship roles for women, and art appreciation. In 2000 College Week, now called College Days, marked its 37th year.

In 1964 the program lasted five days; by 2000 it had been shortened to three days. At one time, the program attracted up to 1,500 people. In 2000 about 350 attended, including several men. Bonnie Hutchins, current coordinator said: "The College Days conference is a yearly highlight for many women who attend. They come back year after year, not only for the fun and friendships, but for some of their favorite instructors as well. Lois Dick, with her singalongs and Mike Leckrone [UW marching band director] never fail to fill a huge room. Joe Elder, who discusses world hotspots, has a loyal following. Harv Thompson, with his tours of theaters, is a favorite, as are Karen Goebel and other family living program faculty."[22]

Cooperative Extension Director Henry Ahlgren at College Week for Women, 1964

Expanded Food and Nutrition Program
The Expanded Food and Nutrition Education Program (EFNEP) began in 1968. Jackson County was one of the first counties to participate. The program was designed for limited-income families, especially those with young children. Its goal was to help women better manage food selection and preparation. The program was federally funded through the United States Department of Agriculture, but it was administered through County Extension offices. For a county to be eligible, it had to have a sub-stantial number of low-income families and agree to cooperate with other agencies such as county social service organizations.

During the 1970s, EFNEP programs operated in 22 of Wisconsin's 72 counties.

Campus Turmoil Continues
With the Vietnam War raging, Madison campus demonstrations escalated to the point that there was talk of closing the campus. It didn't happen, but a near war-like atmosphere prevailed, with National Guard troops on campus in February 1969 and again in May 1970. Walking down Madison's State Street in 1969 and 1970 one saw boarded up windows and felt the presence of a bunker mentality. In late summer 1970, a bomb shattered the early morning calm and blew apart Sterling Hall. The explosion

By the 1960s 4-H work was moving into urban areas, including Milwaukee. Carl Smith (left), Milwaukee 4-H Club agent, is shown with Lucy Baines Johnson at a special 4-H recognition banquet.

killed a researcher and broke many windows in the university hospital, the heating plant, and other nearby buildings. Rioting stopped. Many student rioters, although strongly opposed to the war, were also opposed to violence—especially when it resulted in death.

All the turmoil on campus and the backlash from those who didn't understand or appreciate what was happening did not help the university with its off-campus efforts. Thousands of students and others opposed the Vietnam War, but many could not accept the tactics used by some protesters, whose motto seemed to be, "Tear it down."

President Harrington, the mastermind behind the massive Extension reorganization, resigned on May 8, 1970, one of the many casualties of the "war at home," as it came to be called.

Promoting the New Extension

In early 1970s, with the campus quiet once again, Cooperative Extension renewed its efforts to help people understand University of Wisconsin-Extension. Extension published a brochure entitled "Partners for Progress," which was especially written for county government. The famous slogan, "The Wisconsin Idea—the boundaries of the campus are the boundaries of the state" appeared on the cover of the brochure.

The publication summarized the details of the Extension merger and included information about the enabling legislation (Wisconsin Statute 59.87), which said county boards "may establish and maintain an educational program in cooperation with the University of Wisconsin." It specified the requirements of a participating office—budget, office space, expense accounts, joint approval of programs and staff hiring and firing. It also listed 14 ways in which cooperating counties would benefit, starting with 4-H Club work and ending with access to Educational Telephone Network programs.[23] The brochure left readers with the impression that there was little if anything the university did that was not available to the counties. It was a bold effort but a bit overreaching, especially with budget constraints and limited county staffs.

Tourism

Tourism has been an important part of Wisconsin's economy since Chicago people first discovered the state and Twin Cities people began seeing northwestern Wisconsin as an extension of Minnesota. By the 1930s, tourist cabins and small resorts—most of them "mom and pop" operations—surrounded many of Wisconsin's numerous lakes, especially in northern and central Wisconsin and in famous resort communities like Lake Geneva.

During the 1950s and 1960s, small resorts that had enjoyed good times as fishermen returned year after year had begun to show their age. Increasingly, families vacationed together and demanded amenities beyond a log cabin on a lake with an outhouse in the woods.

Sawyer and Vilas Counties

Sherman Weiss worked as resource development agent in Sawyer County (Hayward area), starting in 1943. And Vilas County (Eagle River area) hired Herman Smith as county agricultural agent in 1947. Both men saw the great potential for tourism in their areas, but they also realized that local industry and government leaders were mostly apathetic to their efforts. Cooperative Extension leaders openly questioned whether the organization's mandate could be stretched to include working with the tourist industry.

In a 2000 interview, Herman Smith said: "We had to sneak our time in. We found the problems here were the same as in Sawyer County and all across the north."[24] Henry Ahlgren, Cooperative Extension head, wasn't too keen at first on the idea of Extension agents working with the tourism industry, but he later changed his mind. As Smith said, "Hank was good about it. He told me, 'You do what the local people want you to do. Don't be afraid.'"

Smith's early efforts were near failures. He and the county home agent set up

The last University Extension Association board, 1969–1970

meetings, but only one or two people came. As Smith said, "Somebody in Madison will find out about it and give us a mulligan for having the biggest flop in Extension. George Wright [northern Wisconsin district director] found out about it. George told us 'You guys [in the north] have got to hang together, because you got all those southern guys against you.' And we did. We held together."[25]

Not only did they hold together, they began calling on some of the "southern guys," especially Extension specialists such as Maury White and Claron Burnett, both in agricultural journalism, to help out with the program. Smith started with some of the simple things—how to write an effective letter and how to create a promotional brochure with some zing. Claron Burnett once said to Smith, "This is quite a way from agriculture, but we got time for you." Burnett drove north in the winter, and they developed some resort promotional material. "They went over big with the little people who operated resorts," Smith said. "I called them little people because they didn't have much. They would have to go to the bank to get money to paint the boats. We got some guinea pigs going, and some of them are still going."[26]

Smith mused about his efforts at upgrading resorts. "It was a long road to get the resort operators to upgrade. We had to do it piecemeal. We had resort tours. The first place I'd check was the bed. If it was not good, I'd tell them, 'Get that damn thing out of here. Buy a new bed. After riding a long way, people want a good night's rest.'"

Besides having difficulty convincing local people that he had something to offer, Smith got into a conflict with the Wisconsin Conservation Department, which apparently believed that Smith was moving into its territory. WCD Director Les Voight wanted Smith fired. Ahlgren did some behind the scenes work to smooth ruffled WCD feathers, and Smith continued his efforts to assist the tourism industry.

Soon, with the assistance of specialists from agricultural journalism, home economics, forestry, and entomology, Herman Smith and Sherman Weiss led workshops on everything from financing and good business practice to how to make structural improvements.

Extension began offering programs that included organizing community groups such as the Vilas County Chamber of Commerce, which represented 15 local chambers. Smith helped develop a two-county chamber of commerce for Vilas and Oneida Counties. By 1963, an eight-county Northwoods Council emerged as a way to cooperatively promote business in the area and "ensure communications among organizations in the region, provide legislative input with a unified voice, and . . . support and develop educational programs for members."[27]

Black River Country
Early in 1965 Eugene Savage, Jackson County agricultural agent, contacted Clark County agricultural agent John Oncken regarding a joint tourism program shared by the two counties in western Wisconsin. They agreed to a series of meetings with chamber of commerce people from Black River Falls, Neillsville, Granton, Merrillan, Alma Center, and Greenwood, plus county representatives. After four of these meetings, an association was formed to provide a communication link between resort and tourist businesses. The association also served as a way to provide educational programs for the development of tourist and travel business. The association, called Black River Country, eventually included all of Jackson and Clark Counties plus part of Eau Claire County. County boards made financial contributions to the association. Initially, the purpose of the association was to make local citizens aware of Black River Country and its attributes. Local newspapers and radio stations adopted such slogans as "Voice of the Black River Country," "Hub of the Black River Country," and more.

When it was up and running, the association had an annual budget of nearly six thousand dollars. It operated two information booths, published a weekly calendar of events in local newspapers, employed a publicity director, developed and distributed 25,000 hunting and vacation maps, sponsored a 13-week television series, presented a float at local celebrations, put up a booth at local fairs, and resulted in the formation of three new chambers of commerce. All of the association's activities were organized and operated by volunteer citizens. In 1968 the association hired an executive secretary, so Extension could withdraw from its direct support role and concentrate on educational programs. Educational programs included food service courses for restaurant employees taught by a home economics agent and tourist business training meetings led by the agricultural agents of Clark and Jackson Counties.

An early evaluation of the Black River Country organization revealed the following results: 17 small communities were brought together with a common purpose for the first time; tourist revenues increased by 10 percent in the area; communities began taking pride in their environment; and communities realized that they must provide new services to bring tourists to the area.

Eventually, Black River Country affiliated with the larger Indianhead Country, but it retained its identity as a destination with unique vacation opportunities and by serving as a first contact point for Indianhead promotions.[28]

Recreation Resources Center

In 1969, University of Wisconsin-Extension established the Recreation Resources Center. Those who helped create the center included Donald Schink, a community resource specialist, and Gale Vandeberg, Cooperative Extension director. The center received a $40,000 demonstration grant from the Upper Great Lakes Regional Development Commission.

The center had several components. Research efforts included market studies, financial analysis of campgrounds, and studies of supply and demand for Great Lakes marina slips within Wisconsin. Staff members offered workshops for restaurant operators, chambers of commerce, tavern keepers, bed and breakfast owners, and campground operators. Topics such as "how to create a brochure" and "how to write and place an ad" continued popular. They also did considerable one-on-one counseling for resort business people and others. Staff members of the center at various times included Rollin Cooper, Don Schink, Sue Sadowske, Jack Gray, Harriett Moyer, and Ayse Somersan.[29]

More Merging

Over the years, various attempts had been made to coordinate activities of the state colleges and the universities. In 1955, the legislature created a 15-member coordinating committee of higher education, charged with controlling everything from budgets to facilities planning across the two higher educational systems that existed at the time—the University of Wisconsin and the state colleges. The committee struggled to keep Wisconsin higher education in order.

Newly elected Governor Patrick Lucey wanted the University of Wisconsin system and the former state college system to become one. He figured this was necessary in order to solve the coordination problem between the two systems. The two systems didn't seem much interested in the idea. No matter. On October 8, 1971, the legislature passed a law placing the two public college and university systems under one board of regents. However, the legislature did not pass the implementation phase for the system merger until July 9, 1974.[30]

Just when Extension people began to understand the new organization that had

Wisconsin Extension Workers honorees, 1966

resulted from the 1965 merger of Cooperative Extension, General Extension, and radio-television, they were confronted with another merger. Madison faculty members and administrators were upset. They believed the new merger would diminish the prestige of the Madison campus, and that tax money for the UW in Madison would flow to former state colleges. Some "elite-leaning" faculty members said they couldn't see these "teacher colleges" carrying the name of the renowned University of Wisconsin." Glenn Pound, dean of the College of Agriculture, sent a strongly word-ed statement to Regent John M. Lavine. He wrote: "I speak to you today out of great concern over the maintenance of the academic excellence of the Madison campus, and of the Madison campus outreach to the people of the state."[31]

A new question arose: What does creation of a University of Wisconsin system mean for Extension? Donald Smith, senior vice president for academic affairs, sub-mitted draft mission statements for all the institutions in the system to the education committee of the Board of Regents in October 1973. The draft of the core mission for Extension read, in part, "The core mission of the University of Wisconsin-Extension is to coordinate and, jointly with University of Wisconsin campuses and centers, provide a program of outreach designed to bring University of Wisconsin System resources to bear upon problems confronting the people and institutions of the state. . . . Through the Extension coordinating mechanism, including faculty in every county, the resources of all institutions within the System can be applied to problems or opportunities associated with economic development, environmental quality, health care delivery, social problems, and related concerns."[32]

With the new UW system in place, system administration assumed a major role in Extension activities for the state. In 1974, Wilson Thiede was named provost for university outreach. His job was to assist and provide direction to the Extension chancellor, the chancellor for the university's two-year centers, and all the system institutions. Thiede held the position for six years.

The merger creating a University of Wisconsin system did not have a great effect on County Extension operations, at least not initially. On the other hand, Extension specialists had been primarily Madison-based, many of them holding joint appointments with UW-Madison departments. Now UW Extension was encouraged to seek Extension specialists and establish joint appointments with other UW campuses, where academic programs were consistent with Extension activities. These institutions included UW-Platteville, UW-Stout, UW-River Falls, and UW-Stevens Point.

Many Extension veterans and administrators on the Madison campus believed that establishing joint appointments with other campuses was a ploy to diminish the Madison campus's importance to Extension. Other university leaders saw the move as a way to broaden and often deepen Extension's specialist group.

By 1975, Cooperative Extension had become quite a different organization from what it had been. It was now part of University of Wisconsin-Extension; its programming began to focus on problem areas, and with new as well as traditional client groups. Some Extension specialists were located on campuses other than Madison.

More changes would face Cooperative Extension as the organization moved into the late 1970s and the 1980s.

CHAPTER 8

PROFOUND CHANGE: 1975 TO 1990

A recession in the early 1980s sent Wisconsin land prices plummeting. Some farmers who had bought and mortgaged land for $2,000 per acre found almost overnight that their land was now worth just $750 per acre. Many owed more on their land than it was worth, lost their farms as a result, and moved to the cities. Family stress was high as people who in many cases owned third- or fourth-generation farms had to sell them and move on.

Wisconsin began moving heavily into producing corn and soybeans as cash crops. In 1975, Wisconsin produced 198 million bushels of corn; by 1990 that number had reached 354 million bushels. Soybean production in 1975 was 5.2 million bushels; by 1990 it had climbed to 17.6 million bushels.[1]

Along with changes in agriculture, dramatic changes were occurring in communities and in families, as two-income families became more and more common. The early 1980s were tough times, no matter where people lived or what they did.

By 1976, University of Wisconsin-Extension, which included Cooperative Extension, had existed for a decade. Depending on who you asked, the new organization provided 10 years of refreshing change, excitement, and promise, or it was an unmitigated disaster.

College of Agriculture Dean Glen Pound saw the new organizational structure that had removed the Extension budget from the college as a monumental mistake. Many Extension people in agriculture agreed with him, but certainly not all. Marvin Beatty, a former soils specialist who was dean of Extension's field staff from 1977 to 1983, said the move "to combine UW outreach units into a separate and independent University Extension institution had far-reaching and positive effects."[2]

Gerald Campbell, professor of agricultural economics and former vice chancellor for University of Wisconsin-Extension, believed the new organization had the potential to accomplish much. "With Cooperative Extension out of the College of Agriculture in Madison, it had the opportunity to program with many partners."[3]

To an outsider looking in, the organizational structure was sheer bafflement. How could an organization operate with layer upon layer of administrators? The challenges UW-Extension faced during its first decade of existence included bringing together a staff of outreach people who had widely different traditions. Cooperative Extension included a large field staff, and these workers generally lived in the counties where they worked. General Extension people essentially lived in Madison. Cooperative Extension programs were free to participants. General Extension participants had to pay a fee for most programs.

Cooperative Extension specialists had been a part of College of Agriculture departments where research, teaching, and Extension were part of the department's mission. Most General Extension staff members were not a part of campus departments.

Many differences were subtle. How programs were determined, for instance. Cooperative Extension prided itself on working with people to find out what *they* needed. General Extension was more likely to follow a traditional higher education model of offering courses, some a week long, some a semester long, then seeing who would enroll. Both approaches worked, and both had merit. But they were different from each other.

The Vietnam War required huge amounts of federal funding—money that some believed might have gone to create an urban Extension program that would be analogous to what Cooperative Extension was in rural areas.

Program priorities for the late 1970s and early 1980s included farm and agribusiness management; human health and nutrition; small business and community economic development; environmental and natural resources conservation and management; food, fiber, and forest production; assistance to government and community leaders; and family relationships and stability.

Organizational Changes

Organizational challenges continued. Jean Evans replaced Henry Ahlgren as chancellor in 1974. Evans quickly ran into budget trouble, got cross-wise with some political decision makers, and by 1980 had lost much of the faculty's support. In that year, Robert O' Neil took over from Edwin Young as UW system president.

President O'Neil quickly discovered that University Extension was not effectively relating to the multi-campus system. He reviewed an outreach plan the regents had prepared in 1978, which essentially said that neither system administration nor Extension had moved fast enough to transfer outreach funding and responsibilities to the several campuses in the system, as the regents had suggested in a 1973 document. O'Neil's subsequent report contained several specific recommendations, including one directly related to Cooperative Extension activities: "The UW System was [referring to earlier decisions] committed to continue the existing Cooperative Extension county agent network for program delivery. UW-Extension was instructed to use more joint faculty appointments and programming contracts to share faculty resources and improve the ability of campuses and centers to function effectively within the outreach network."[4]

Chancellor Evans began feeling the squeeze. System campuses wanted more

College Week for Women, 1978. A workshop with Extension specialist in the arts Robert Gard.

Extension money, and Extension faculty felt Evans should work harder to obtain more funds for Extension. In 1980, Evans prepared a "white paper" and distributed it to the faculty. It was supposed to address background and history for Extension and make recommendations for changing the organizational structure and Extension's relationship with other UW institutions.

What it did was create a firestorm among Extension faculty members. The Extension chancellor received many letters; so did the chair of Extension's university committee, a faculty-elected group of Extension faculty.

Select Committee Appointed

With encouragement from the Extension faculty, Dwayne Rohweder, an agronomy specialist and chair of the Extension university committee, appointed a "select committee to "1. Identify serious problems facing University Extension. 2. Propose a means of solving those problems, one of which may be reorganization. 3. Formulate a faculty response to the 'White Paper,' and 4. Propose more efficient means of delivering Extension Programs."[5] After several meetings, the select committee forwarded the following statements:

"Leadership and Management: The situation is critical and the Select Committee expresses a lack of confidence in the Chancellor to deal with it. The Chancellor has not demonstrated appropriate leadership and does not evidence a likely change in capacity.

"Financial Concerns: Extension should develop a better system to manage the funds appropriated to it and tenaciously pursue various options leading to needed additional funding.

"Institutional Agreements: Extension should recommend a change to the 1973 Regent policy on joint faculty appointments to reflect current realities.

"Organizational Structure: We recommend that some aspects . . . of the reorganization proposal be adopted . . . community program statewide staff should report to the same dean as their corresponding community county program staff . . . the Director of the Cooperative Extension Service should be changed from staff to line with Deans who are responsible for Cooperative Extension programs reporting through the Director, to the Chancellor."

The paper also included some recommendations on faculty governance.[6]

The select committee's response was honest, forthright, and devastating for the Extension chancellor. No Extension person ever remembered saying that they lacked confidence in an administrator—at least not in writing.

Word spread rapidly throughout Extension and the university system, and to the state legislature. The legislature promptly ordered an audit of Extension, which began in 1981. Everyone in state government feared audits. Auditors came in, turned over every rock, opened every closet door, examined all the dirty wash, and wrote it all down for the public to read.

PAGE Committee Appointed

On May 29, 1981, President O'Neil appointed an advisory committee he called the President's Advisory Group on Extension (PAGE). Previously, in 1980, the Board of Regents had appointed a regent committee to examine UW-Extension's programs, its budgeting approach, and its relationship with institutional campuses. The new ten-member PAGE committee included Patrick Boyle, Howard Martin, and Dwayne Rohweder from UW-Extension; John Bibby, UW-Milwaukee; Joseph Corry and Thomas Yuill, UW-Madison; Marge Engelman, UW-Green Bay; Dallas Peterson, system administration; Norene Smith, UW-La Crosse; and John Morris UW-Eau Claire, who was chair of the committee. In his letter of appointment, President O'Neil made mention of the regent study committee. O'Neil wrote: "The Regent Study Committee believes that the final recommendations to the Board of Regents should reflect the judgment and insight of faculty and administrators of the UW System."[7]

In May of 1981 the regents, after conducting hearings around the state and reviewing various earlier regent policy statements, decided to hold any final recommendations until the PAGE committee reported.

On June 12, 1981, a University of Wisconsin-Extension Joint Faculty/Administration Committee sent a paper to all Extension faculty members with recommendations for the future. The recommendation on organizational change stated: "The committee recommends that the present organizational structure of University of Wisconsin-Extension be modified to provide for three separate divisions: Cooperative Extension and Related Programs, General Extension Programs, and Educational Communication."[8]

After making a few additional changes, the joint committee submitted its report to Chancellor Evans and to the President's Advisory Group on Extension (PAGE).

Some people, within and outside of the university, saw this as the appropriate time for Cooperative Extension to return to the College of Agriculture after an absence of some 15 years. But the hoped-for reunion was not going to happen.

In his letter appointing the PAGE Committee, O'Neil wrote: "A goal of the UW System is to provide access to quality non-credit educational programs to people of the state. In order for this goal to be achieved in an effective manner, I recommend that the Advisory Group proceed with the following basic assumption: A STATEWIDE AND UW SYSTEMWIDE STRUCTURE SHOULD BE MAINTAINED FOR THE EXTENSION OUTREACH FUNCTION OF THE UW SYSTEM . . ."[9]

After numerous meetings and a careful review of the Extension structure established in 1965, as well as an examination of the problems and concerns it uncovered, the PAGE committee reported to President O'Neil on December 23, 1981. In a 147-page report, the committee included everything from a brief review of Extension's history to a careful examination of current problems and concerns.

Several of their recommendations were far-reaching, but no one was surprised when they suggested that a statewide Extension organization should continue. The PAGE committee affirmed the earlier faculty suggestion that the Extension organization should contain three major units: General Extension, Cooperative Extension, and Educational Communications. To manage the Extension organization, the committee recommended a vice president for system Extension. One of the PAGE Committee's major assignments was to improve relationships with system campuses. The committee recommended five guidelines that each institution should consider in organizing for the Extension function. These ranged from appointment of an associate vice chancellor for Extension on each campus to forming an advisory group. One important recommendation, which had little effect on Cooperative Extension, was that campus-based Extension faculty should be members of a campus department. The long tradition of General Extension involved having departments that were autonomous and separate from academic departments.[10]

When President O'Neil submitted his "integrated Extension plan" to the regents, he rejected the PAGE Committee's recommendation for a system vice president for Extension and recommended keeping a UW-Extension chancellor, whose office would have responsibility for "planning, approving and monitoring statewide Extension programming."[11]

President O'Neil had agreed with the recommendation to integrate General

Extension faculty into UW system campuses. Cooperative Extension specialists were already integrated into UW-Madison, UW-Platteville, and UW-River Falls campuses. The regents approved the new plan on April 9, 1982.

A major problem with the new organization was UW-Extension's say in the distribution of Extension funds to the 13 degree-granting institutions and the 13 two-year centers each year. UW-Extension was to review each campus's plan for outreach each year and sign an agreement that included transfer of funds for Extension operations. As might be expected, campuses weren't too keen on this procedure. They didn't like the idea of dealing chancellor to chancellor, and they argued that they couldn't do long-range planning if their Extension funds were approved on a year-by-year basis.

Chancellor Evans Resigns

Meanwhile, Extension Chancellor Evans continued to struggle. As retired Extension Chancellor Patrick Boyle said: "All of the trouble that the Chancellor was having related to communicating about the major budget problems. Chancellor Evans didn't understand the political leadership in Wisconsin nor was he able to effectively communicate about the sources of the problem. He also had difficulty making timely, precise decisions. The 'no confidence' vote by the Extension faculty March 27, 1981, was a very difficult situation for him. Chancellor Evans had not developed a strong political support base, and consequently, when the budget emerged, he did not have the necessary support to identify effective solutions. In addition, the legislature was very aggressive in ordering all kinds of studies by the Audit Bureau and by the Board of Regents about what was called the 'Extension situation.'"

When Peter Pere resigned as vice chancellor in July 1981, Patrick Boyle was named acting vice chancellor. Evans, who was suffering from cancer, announced his plans to step down on July 1, 1982, the same date the new organizational plan was to take effect. Jean Evans died on November 3, 1982.

Boyle Becomes Chancellor

Patrick Boyle became acting chancellor for Extension in 1982 and was named chancellor in 1983, a post he held until his retirement in 1993. He also simultaneously held the position of director of the Cooperative Extension Service from 1984 to 1993.

Boyle was a professor in the department of agricultural and Extension education (later known as continuing and vocational education) at UW-Madison. He had become director of the division of staff development when UW-Extension was organized in 1965. Boyle had taught graduate level courses in program development and evaluation, but he had not been a County Extension agent, nor had he been an Extension specialist in an agricultural production area. Many thought he had little chance of succeeding as Extension chancellor, especially when the sky appeared to be falling—or perhaps had already fallen by 1983.

Chancellor Boyle immediately faced the results of the legislative audit, as well as a general recession in the country. As Boyle said: "I was left, after the Evans era, with a major struggle for a number of years, with a major legislative audit report [which] resulted from the budget problems that Extension was having. We also lost substantial federal money during that time because of the Graham-Rudman-Hollings budget reduction act, passed during the Reagan administration."

As the result of state legislative action and the federal cutbacks, Cooperative Extension faced severe budget problems. The effects went well beyond cutting back operating expenses and not offering salary adjustments. Extension positions had to be eliminated, both in the counties and on the state staff. Such a serious retrenchment had previously occurred in the history of Cooperative Extension only during Depression years. Staff morale plummeted. Extension workers wondered if their positions would be eliminated. Some new people bailed out after only a year or two on the job.

Extension faculty with tenure mostly stayed and rode out the storm—and a stormy time it was. County boards didn't want to lose positions. The College of Agriculture didn't want to lose specialists. As Boyle related: "The county boards said, 'Take the money out of state positions.' The College of Agriculture said, 'Take it out of the county positions because we need the staff.' So obviously we had conflict there, between the county positions and the specialist positions. The College of Agriculture wanted us to take the money out of non-agricultural program areas. It was a time when everyone was fighting for himself or herself. There was no systematic plan for handling the budget reductions. That was when we developed the 'famous' staffing plan for county offices. That plan caused a lot of animosity with the counties, because they took the plan to be reality. What we were trying to do was to project ahead if the budget reductions continued and we couldn't get some of the money restored. If we identified a position in a county and said that the county might lose the position, then we had legislators who got angry with us. It was a time that was complex and mixed with political in-fighting all over the place."

During this time Extension consolidated several county positions, and agents began working in more than one county. According to Boyle, 10 to 20 percent of the county and area positions were cut during that time. As for the specialists, Boyle said, "What we tried to do was develop a balance among the program areas. We developed criteria to use in making decisions. We tried to keep major programs. We also tried to achieve a balance between the state specialist and the county staff reductions."

As Cooperative Extension was feeling the budget bite from state and federal budget sources, so were other university units—especially the College of Agricultural and Life Sciences on the Madison campus. Add the Extension budget problem to their other budget problems, and they too were in crisis.

Recalling those difficult years, Boyle said: "The reductions were devastating for the organization because they came from both state and federal sources. It was one of the most difficult times that I can remember in all the years that I had been in Extension.

Morale was terrible because we were threatening layoffs. We had headlines in the newspapers [saying] 'Extension to cut County Agent Positions.' There was political in-fighting. We had external groups trying to influence us. Politicians were telling us, 'Don't eliminate my county agent.' A bright spot was that county budget support remained quite constant during this time."[12]

Boyle slowly worked through the crisis until, by the late 1980s, Extension was essentially back on its feet—and even prospering. As Extension historian Jim Gooch wrote: "UW-Extension Chancellor Boyle was proving to be an active lobbyist for fiscal support of Extension programming and especially for his institution's leadership role."[13]

Boyle had worked with former Chancellor Ahlgren for many years and they had become friends. Ahlgren was a master of keeping his political support base in order, and Boyle followed his example by setting out to build back a political support base that had been essentially lost in the late 1970s. One of the first things Boyle did was to hire Mark Lederer, who had many years of experience working with the legislature, understood the legislative process, knew the people, and was a good communicator. "I made [restoring political support] a high priority," Boyle said. "When I first took the job, many people were of the opinion that I couldn't do it. So to me this was a challenge. And I worked at it day and night."[14]

Boyle met with legislators one at a time. He always brought along examples of Extension programs that were operating in their districts. He told legislators they didn't have to like Extension as an organization, but they should like programs that helped their constituents. Boyle worked hard at personalizing Extension to county board members, to state legislative committees, and to legislators. "Once they started understanding our programs and how they were helping people, they were convinced," Boyle noted.

Boyle recalled a time in the late 1980s when the governor submitted a budget that recommended a major reduction of Extension funds. Extension was able to convince the legislature to eliminate the reduction. The political attitude toward Extension was beginning to change.

The regents' attitude toward Extension was also becoming positive. Boyle met several times with each regent. He sent them information about Extension nearly every month. The information always focused on the value of Extension programs to the people who lived in each regent's geographical area.

To keep county boards abreast of what was happening, Boyle worked closely with the board of directors of the Wisconsin Associated County Extension Committees (WACEC), which had been incorporated in 1966. Boyle attended every WACEC executive committee meeting, attended district meetings during the winter months, and developed a good working relationship with the WACEC group. He told board members that they might not always agree with what Extension was doing, but they should tell him what they thought Extension's programs ought to be no matter what.

Extension even began involving WACEC members on certain committees responsible for screening future Extension workers. Boyle said the group moved from being spectators to becoming involved and began to see Extension as "their" organization.

The chancellor's political bridge building included helping people see the breadth of Extension's operations. Boyle met with labor union leaders, with leaders of small businesses, with business associations, and with environmental groups. Through these efforts, he began to build a broad base of support.

Not everyone approved of his efforts. There was always the complaint that Extension was trying to do too much, and was not spending enough time with its historical audiences—farmers, rural youth, and homemaker members. Some people who were especially critical of Extension believed it wasn't devoting enough of its resources to small farmers.

Wisconsin's Three-Year Plan
As a way to show Extension staff, university campuses, regents, legislators, and others that Wisconsin's Extension program had turned the corner and had assumed a new direction, the chancellor's office produced a "Statewide Plan for Extension Programs of the UW System: 1988-1991." This 31-page document included the following goals and priorities: revitalizing the economy; building family strengths; improving agricultural profitability; improving environmental quality; and improving human health and nutrition.[15] The document illustrated the shift away from single-discipline programming and a move to issue-oriented, inter- and cross-disciplinary approaches.

National Directions
Questions about Extension viability were also being raised nationally. An evaluation of Cooperative Extension conducted from 1977 to 1979 reported that the Extension system "as a whole was not adequately prepared to provide the kinds of accountability information necessary." A special 1980 task force made up of federal and state Extension people developed a new evaluation system for measuring the results of Extension efforts. The Food and Agriculture Act of 1977 (Public Act 95-113), as amended in 1981, outlined a broadened scope for Cooperative Extension programs in the counties. The secretary of agriculture and the president of the National Association of State Universities and Land-Grant Colleges appointed a special joint study committee to "review and restate the roles and responsibilities of each of the partners in Cooperative Extension, and to produce a document that would serve as a guide for the future mission, scope, priorities, and policies of the Cooperative Extension Service." Gale VandeBerg, who was then director of Wisconsin's Cooperative Extension Service, headed up the staff/design team for the project. Professor Laverne Forest, an evaluation specialist with Wisconsin Cooperative Extension, served as project coordinator.

The committee wrestled with two major questions: What problems in the nation fall within Extension's scope? How can Extension help solve them? Six major areas were identified—the agricultural system, natural and environmental resources, community and small business development, home economics/family living, 4-H/youth education and development, and international concerns.[16]

In 1983, the Extension Service of the United States Department of Agriculture published "A Catalyst for Change—The Extension Service." It was a highly illustrated booklet proclaiming the virtues of Cooperative Extension and had been developed in response to oversight hearings held by the House of Representatives' subcommittee on department operations, research and foreign agriculture. This "Catalyst for Change" report included recommendations for a new reporting system, along with several other recommendations dealing with program direction.[17]

In November 1986, still another national "futures task force" was appointed to peer into the future and make recommendations for Cooperative Extension programming. Gail Skinner, western district Extension director, was Wisconsin's representative on the 18-member task force. The group's report, published in 1987, began with a quotation from the president of the University of Maine. "Extension currently is failing to keep up with societal changes. The primary problem of Extension appears to be, in my opinion, its present, functioning mindset, a mindset that seems to be one of survival rather than one of potential. We could say that the mindset of Extension appears to be more concerned with management than leadership; that is, more concerned with doing things right, rather than doing the right things. As a result, Extension seems to be missing much of the big picture and is beginning to slip in its role as a societal leader. To be successful in the future, Extension must decide to lead and then do so with vision and a boldness." [18]

The major outcome of this task force's work appears to be a shift, at least in words, from conducting programs based on disciplines—agronomy, dairy science, horticulture, clothing, foods—to programs based on issues. As the task force report stated: "In today's world, where the problems and concerns people face are highly complex and value laden, Extension can no longer afford [a] fragmented approach to educational programming. Its programming must make a difference in people's lives. As a result it is no longer appropriate to structure our programs around a multitude of specific and separate discipline-oriented needs. Instead, focus must be on the larger, most compelling issues facing people today, which tend to be broad-based and cross-disciplinary in nature and within the scope of the land-grant system."[19]

By this time, Wisconsin Cooperative Extension had already moved into issues programming. A new set of questions emerged. Rather than asking which problems dairy farmers were facing, the questions became broader: How can we help make agriculture profitable? How can family life be enhanced? How can the needs of young people be better addressed? What is necessary to improve a community's well being? And so on. The resulting programs were often inter-disciplinary in approach.

Wood River (Burnett County) 4-H members with Governor Tommy Thompson, 1984

Agricultural Programs

As mentioned earlier in this chapter, it was not only Extension that was in crisis during the early 1980s. Wisconsin farmers struggled with the most difficult economic situation they had seen in years—perhaps ever. Not only did they face declining land values with mortgage foreclosure threats, they also faced one of the worst spells of dry weather the state had experienced in some time.

Some County Extension agents, working with the state Department of Agriculture, organized hay lifts to help needy farmers get their livestock through the year. Russell Kiecker, agricultural and 4-H agent in Burnett County at the time, organized an emergency hay program that resulted in the delivery of more than 100 semi-truck loads of hay to the county. He organized a hay committee to assist in distribution and asked farmers who wanted hay to fill out an application form. Many practical problems emerged:

Where could they store 100 semi-truckloads of hay? They piled the hay on the courthouse lawn. "The pile of hay was so big," Kiecker said, "I thought the courthouse was going to tilt."

How could they keep the hay from being stolen? They piled the hay right in front of the sheriff's office window, so he could keep an eye on it.

How could they keep the hay dry? They found mammoth sheets of plastic, the kind used to cover silos, and stretched them over the huge haystack—but then they were faced with the problem of keeping the plastic in place. Kiecker scouted around for some old tires at the government center, but found only one-tenth of what he needed. He called a local service station and within six hours had more tires than he knew what to do with. Service stations couldn't get rid of old tires easily, and here was an opportunity.

As an aside, for some time after the hay lift was over, Kiecker encountered farmers who accused him of bringing opossums to the county. The farmers said the possums had been rolled up in the hay bales coming from the south.[20]

Dry weather was just one element of the crisis farmers faced in the 1980s. Cooperative Extension established a Strategies on Survival (SOS) program. One hundred County Extension agents worked in teams to help farm families suffering from financial hardship and family stress. Between July 1985 and June 1986, SOS provided individual counseling to 6,700 Wisconsin people—2,200 of whom had not called on Extension before. SOS offered farmers in crisis a series of alternatives—ways to continue farming, how to get off-farm income, transitions to non-farm careers, ways to manage family resources, and how to deal with stress. The 1986 Extension annual report noted the following: "Cooperative Extension faculty worked with banks, credit unions, other lenders, human service professionals, employment agencies, other educational agencies, attorneys, business organizations, chambers of commerce, local governments, agricultural groups, and the clergy."[21]

Cloud Seeding

Dry weather elicits many interesting reactions from farm people. Not only was dry weather a problem in the early 1980s, but farmers in northeastern Wisconsin had experienced severe drought problems a few years earlier. In 1977, Art Peterson, Extension soils specialist, and Extension agents from Door, Sheboygan, Calumet, Kewaunee, Brown, Manitowoc, Outagamie, Winnebago, and Fond du Lac Counties became immersed in a cloud seeding effort. The state climatologist and eventually the legislature became involved as well.

Cloud seeding caught the attention of several northeastern Wisconsin farmers who had experienced an extremely dry summer and fall in 1976 and wanted to make sure they got more rain in 1977. They had heard about cloud seeding in other parts of the country and wondered if it would work in their neck of the woods. Art Peterson chaired the agri-weather committee, which included state agencies outside of the university. He served as the point person for the effort.

A cloud seeding company in Colorado said it could obtain 50 percent more rainfall from a seeded cloud than a non-seeded one would produce. In a letter to Jerome Sickenger, a farmer in Cato, Wisconsin, an official with Colorado International Corporation explained what was necessary for cloud seeding. These requirements included a turbo-charged twin engine seeder airplane, a licensed weather modification meteorologist, an experienced weather modification pilot, silver iodide pyrotechnic seeding flares, and much more. Farmers organized a "Shower Power" cooperative, with hopes of signing up 1,200 to 1,800 members.

About 40 to 50 farmers, an official from the Colorado seeding company, and area Extension agents attended a January 14, 1977, meeting in St. Nazianz. Art Peterson shared research on cloud seeding and reaction to the proposal from the Colorado

In 1985, hundreds of tons of hay were donated by U.S. farmers to Wisconsin, which was suffering from the northern Wisconsin drought of the mid-1980s. Extension staff members organized the hay distribution.

group. At the end of his presentation, which included information from several states as well as a summary of international cloud seeding efforts, Peterson concluded as follows: ". . . The value of cloud seeding in Wisconsin based on our continental climate and the amount of moisture that is necessary for growing the crops, the amount of moisture that can normally be expected and that can be stored in the soil, I feel that it would extremely unwise, nor would I recommend that such an endeavor be undertaken by the UW-Extension Service."[22]

The cloud seeding effort became extremely controversial. A February 13, 1977, Milwaukee *Journal* article stated: "Some say it could mean the difference between success and failure on the farm this summer. Some say it would be a decidedly bad investment. Some say it would be tampering with nature and the will of God. Nobody denies it would be a gamble."

On March 4, 1977, the Cooperative Extension News Service released a news story that began: "The state climatologist and a University of Wisconsin-Extension soil scientist are skeptical about a proposed cloud seeding operation for Manitowoc, Sheboygan, and Calumet Counties."

Despite Extension's public skepticism, the cloud seeding effort moved forward. An

Assembly substitute amendment to 1977 Assembly Bill 510 was offered that would create a Council on Weather Modification. The amendment also specified that the Wisconsin Department of Agriculture be authorized to issue licenses and permits for weather modification operations. After considerable review and discussion, the legislature took no action on the amendment. According to a June 30, 1977, Milwaukee *Sentinel* article, the Shower Power cooperative had managed recruit 250 to 300 members in Brown, Calumet, Kewaunee, Manitowoc, and Sheboygan Counties. When limited rainfall arrived during the summer of 1977, interest dropped, and the matter of cloud seeding disappeared.

Cooperative Extension agents in the nine northeastern Wisconsin counties that were involved in one way or another with the cloud seeding effort learned firsthand once again what it was like to be educators in the midst of controversy. Don Peterson, Cooperative Extension statewide program chairman for agriculture/agri-business, issued a memorandum on April 7, 1977, containing the following guidance: "[A] controversy has developed as people holding differing points of view endeavor to advance or defend their respective opinions and positions. It is under these circumstances that some Extension workers concerned have found themselves embroiled in the controversy—caught in the middle as it were, as is sometimes the case in controversial public policy issues. If the Extension worker has taken a position, he may have antagonized those who advocate a different position. Even a position of neutrality has been interpreted by some to mean that 'if you're not with us, you're agin' us.' Thus, the Extension worker finds himself facing the wrath of an unhappy portion of the clientele he works hard to serve.

"Over the years and on numerous occasions, Extension workers have had to face testy situations like this, uncomfortable though they may be. Likewise, as Extension workers today, we cannot and should not back off from this issue simply because it may be controversial. Nor should we allow ourselves to be stampeded in one direction or the other. Such a situation calls for special care, caution, and courage in what we say and do. We must muster and assess the facts based on the best available research data and experience."

Don Peterson's wise advice applied not only to Extension's involvement with cloud seeding, but also to a host of other controversial issues that had not yet been uncovered.

Forage Testing

From the time when Wisconsin moved from wheat farming to dairying, forages had become (and remain) extremely important as a feed source. A long-standing challenge was how to measure the quality of forage as livestock feed. Visual assessment was common, resulting in some colorful descriptive language, from "looks good to me" on one end of the spectrum to "not worth a damn" on the other end.

In the laboratory, it was possible to use German-developed "proximate analysis" dating back to 1850 that provided a measure of crude protein and moisture level. But the process was slow and not especially accurate. Something better was needed.

In 1972, the American Forage and Grassland Council formed a forage analysis subcommittee chaired by Extension specialist Dwayne Rohweder and including dairy scientist Neal Jorgenson and other researchers from around the country. They agreed to use a 1970 analysis system developed by a New York scientist, but this test cost at least $25 and required two weeks for results.

Meanwhile Karl Norris, a USDA researcher at Beltsville, determined that an approach called "near infrared spectroscopy" (NIRs) could be used to test forages accurately and quickly. The Wisconsin Forage Council raised $25,000 by selling shares to forage producers and others in order to set up an NIRs laboratory. Gale VandeBerg, state Extension director, provided an Extension-funded loan of $116,000 for start-up purposes, to be paid back in three years. Additional support came from the College of Agriculture and Life Sciences and five commercial companies. The system was up and running in December 1981.

At the same time Terry Howard, an Extension dairy specialist, worked with county agricultural agents to enroll dairy farmers in a "Badger ration balancer" and a "least-cost ration balancer." Richard Vatthauer, Extension livestock specialist, developed a ration balancing system for beef and sheep.

It was now possible for farmers and hay dealers to obtain quick analysis of forage samples. The system also provided a vehicle for agents and specialists to discuss with farmers forage management and the use of the test in ration balancing for high-producing animals.

Starting in 1982, the NIRs system was used in conjunction with hay auctions. Previously, all farmers received about the same price for their hay from hay dealers, even if it was of superior quality. Rohweder and Richard Vilstrup, Extension animal science specialist, worked with Wisconsin's two livestock marketing cooperatives to sell tested hay. Between 1983 and 1997, these cooperatives conducted more than 800 quality-tested hay auctions. Buyers were ready to pay more for quality hay when test results were available.

As a result of efforts to improve dairy cattle feeding, and especially forage quality, Howard and Rohweder helped establish a World Super Bowl of Forage Quality at World Dairy Expo, held each year in Madison, which attracted dairy cattle people from around the world.

Agricultural Profitability

The 1987 annual Extension report explained the results of "issue" programming for increased dairy profitability. Under the leadership of Extension Specialist Allan Bringe, dairy industry professionals and milk producers were brought together with the goal of increasing milk quality and, in turn, improving farm profits. Some 30 county quality milk councils were organized, consisting of veterinarians, dairy field representatives, milk equipment dealers, agricultural lenders, dairy herd improvement supervisors, and County Extension agents. The councils focused on ways to help farmers control mastitis, a disease that lowered milk quality. As a result of the program, farmers who participated saw the incidence of mastitis drop substantially. Participating producers also began receiving milk quality premiums from their dairy plants. This was one of several programs that focused on agricultural profitability.

Urban Horticulture

Questions about gardening, flowers, and landscaping kept pouring into Extension offices. The Dial-a-Tape system, which offered callers short messages on selected topics, proved extremely popular. In Dane County alone, more than 8,000 calls were received in 1978. The most popular topics were "How to Plant Vegetables," "Making Compost," and "Setting Out Tomato Plants."

By 1980, the state-funded program operated 24 hours a day, seven days a week for Dane, Rock, La Crosse, Fond du Lac and Sheboygan Counties. Portions of the tape series were also available to Marathon, Eau Claire, and Oneida Counties, and to the River Falls area. A special dial access program operated in Milwaukee County. In 1980, to reduce the budget, the call-in system for the five-county area was cut.[23]

To meet the tremendous need for horticultural answers, Extension turned to a new system that had begun in the state of Washington in 1972, an effort called the "master gardener program." Extension horticulturists trained volunteers to answer the hundreds of horticultural calls. Waukesha and Milwaukee Counties began training master gardeners in 1976. Brown County started in 1979. James Schroeder in Dane County began training master gardeners in 1981.

Master gardeners were trained in plant propagation, disease diagnosis/control, insect control, use of pesticides, and organic gardening techniques. These topics were applied to vegetables, flowers, fruits and berries, and lawns and shrubs. For every hour of training the volunteer master gardener received, he or she worked an hour answering questions.

In Dane County, the master gardener training consisted of 42 classroom hours each year, with topics rotated over four years. This was a new idea, as other yearlong training programs covered all aspects of horticulture. In 1981, Dane County featured vegetable gardening; in 1982, houseplants and flowers; in 1983, fruits and berries; and in 1984, lawns, shrubs, and landscaping. By 1986, there were 103 master gardeners on Dane County's mailing list.[24] In 1999, the master gardening program took place in all 50 states and several foreign countries. By the same year, more than 5,500 people had been trained in Wisconsin.

Public Policy Issues

Many Extension agents became involved with public policy issues in the 1970s and 1980s. Ed Hass, department head and resource agent for Pierce County, recalled his active involvement along with the county planner in working with townships and the county on planning and zoning issues. He devoted part of his educational programming to land use issues, including exclusive agricultural zoning.

Not everyone was pleased with the effort. Hass wrote: "A group of local landowners concerned about land rights and increased governmental regulations on land circulated three petitions throughout the county at auctions, restaurants, and many other locations. The petitions asked the county board to: 1) reject exclusive agricultural zoning; 2) eliminate the county planner position; and 3) eliminate the resource agent position. After the group gathered 600 names on the petitions, the issue was placed on the agenda of the county board.

As Hass explained, Ray Anderson, who was chair of the county agriculture and Extension education committee, organized a response to the petitions. At the board meeting, the spokesperson for the petition group spoke. The Extension district director for the western district spoke about the educational role of Extension agents on public policy issues. Hass outlined his role on land use, outdoor recreation, local government education, business development, energy conservation, and natural resources.

The results of the vote were as follows: 1) table the action on exclusive agricultural zoning; 2) on a split vote, keep the county planner position; and 3) on a unanimous vote, keep the resource agent position. Reporting on the meeting, the local newspaper headline was "Don't Blame the Messenger for the Message."

Hass's experience was a good example of the often-difficult times Extension agents had when they conducted programs in the public policy arena. With such programming, tempers often ran high and people quickly took sides. This was not the case with programs on choosing oat varieties or increasing dairy cow productivity.

Environmental Quality
In response to concerns about groundwater pollution from town dumps, the U.S. Environmental Protection Agency developed strict rules that made it too costly for towns to operate them.

Extension staff began working with both counties and towns to help come up with alternatives that included developing recycling programs. Community resource development agents and county agricultural agents worked with many groups, including school and youth organizations, to help them understand the values of recycling.[25]

Community Development
Cooperative Extension became involved with several types of community development in the1960s. By the 1970s and 1980s, the programs had become quite sophisticated. Two agricultural economists, Glen Pulver and Ron Shaffer, came up with a very successful community development tool. These Extension specialists created a "Community Economic Preparedness Index." It included a series of questions community leaders could ask themselves concerning how economic opportunities could be

improved in their communities. The questions covered such subjects as whether the community had an economic development plan, a comprehensive land use plan and zoning ordinance, an industrial development corporation, and strategies for making the best use of existing commercial and industrial buildings.

Pulver and Shaffer trained and supported agents who worked with communities all over the state, following up with meetings to help communities develop plans for economic improvement.

An unusual community development program took place in northwestern Wisconsin. An agriculture and Extension committee member mentioned his concern about declining farm numbers in Burnett County to County Extension Agent Russell Kiecker. Several people sat down to discuss what they might do about the situation. They came up with the idea of a "farm lure" project that would attempt to lure farmers to Burnett County. They advertised Burnett County to farmers in New York, Pennsylvania, Ohio, and Indiana—whomever might be interested in "an opportunity to walk away from your huge farm debt, and milk cows, grow alfalfa, and continue to do what you want, debt free."

The county organized a unique promotional effort. Soon the Associated Press, a national magazine, and network television stations learned about the promotion and began discussing it nationwide. *Good Morning America* sent a helicopter load of photographers to Burnett County. Every regional television station talked about the farm lure promotion.

Older people in the county came forward to list their farms, and the county agent's office began compiling data on available farmland. The realtors in the area had never sold so many farms.

Once the Extension office had a list of farmers interested in buying Burnett County land, they invited potential buyers to visit the county. One event included 150 potential farm families from all over the United States at a county-sponsored picnic. As Kiecker said, "I didn't give any false impressions. I told them that about one week during the winter, you'll have to live with -40 degree temperatures. People from Ohio and Indiana couldn't fathom this."

As it turned out, as many farmers moved into Pierce and St. Croix Counties and other counties a little farther south as moved into Burnett County. So the program benefited the entire region.

The County Extension office faced some interesting challenges as a result of the promotion. These included a steady stream of interviews from the press, inquiries from top-level media producers in New York, and finding a place for network helicopters to land.[26]

Family Living Programs

Family living programming made a rather dramatic shift toward helping modern families resolve the issues they now faced. Nutrition programs continued with excellent results, but many other issues were considered as well. One programming effort focused on the use of credit. A team of County Extension home economists and UW-Extension specialists developed a learn at home program called "Using Credit Wisely," which was available in every county by 1989. Participating families received audiocassette tapes, accompanied by readings and worksheets that were designed to help them find solutions to their credit problems. Topics ranged from comparing credit options to considering bankruptcy.[27]

In the early 1980s, Wisconsin and the rest of the country experienced dramatic changes in health care delivery. Enrollment in health maintenance organizations (HMOs) increased from less than 150,000 in 1982 to more than one million in 1987. Consumers were bewildered by the new terminology and unfamiliar with the various types of health care systems and how these systems might affect their lives.

In 1984, utilizing $10,000 from the School of Family Resources and Consumer Sciences (later called Human Ecology), a special advisory council was formed to tackle the problem. Council members included Extension specialist Beverly Henderson and Nancy Miller from the UW School of Family Resources and Consumer Sciences. The group also included representatives from the Center for Public Representation, Wisconsin Consumers, health maintenance organizations, the Office of the Commissioner of Insurance, the Health Planning Council, and others. Resource people from the Wisconsin State Medical Society, the Coalition of Wisconsin Aging, the Wisconsin Office on Aging, the Department of Employee Trust Funds, and the Wisconsin Bureau of Health Care Financing helped prepare four bulletins that helped citizens to better understand HMOs. These were widely distributed by Extension and other cooperating organizations. This effort was part of a national effort focusing on family and economic well-being.[28]

In the early 1980s, some federal funds became available to counties for the development of child care programs. Adams and Juneau Counties didn't have licensed child care facilities at the time, so the family living agents in these two counties worked to develop a community coalition to access these funds. It was not an easy task. Both family living agents had to work with their county board members to help them understand the need for a safe place for the children of working parents. Some of the board members believed mothers should be home with their children. As Edith Felts-Podoll said, "This was a community development project that needed to be handled from a public policy perspective." On February 1, 1982, the Adams County Child Development Center opened. In 1983, child care began in the Mauston area.

4-H/Youth Programs

In the 1980s, 4-H and Extension youth programs continued to support 4-H Clubs and a variety of 4-H projects, ranging from clothing to dog obedience. But the programs also broadened their approach. Strengthening families became a focus. Research had clearly described strong families as those that have good

The 4-H dog obedience training project became popular with 4-H members.

communications, supportive friends and relatives, democratic decision making, and a sense of family pride and loyalty.

A team of Extension 4-H youth development faculty and family living education faculty developed a 100-page idea book with more than 50 home-based activities that families could do together. Wisconsin families have purchased more than 3,000 copies of the book, entitled *Family Times,* since it was first published in fall 1986. The family times program soon expanded. County 4-H youth development and family living faculty teamed up and presented programs to the Wisconsin Extension Homemaker Council, 4-H volunteer leaders, parent/teacher organizations, National Guard troop families, and churches. The Young Extension Homemakers organization (for those under age 35) decided to make "family times" a major educational program.[29] It was innovative programming that cut across disciplinary lines yet focused clearly on an issue that many people faced—how to strengthen their families.

During the 1980s, 4-H and youth staff also began focusing more on community youth development and began working collaboratively with other agencies, institutions, and organizations. Joan Lazarus and Susan Farmer, from liberal studies and the arts, added curriculum and youth leadership experiences in theater and visual arts. In 1989, 4-H celebrated its 75th anniversary with a traveling historical exhibit, extensive media coverage, and a special 4-H day at the state fair.

From 1975 to 1990, Extension in Wisconsin and throughout the nation struggled to more carefully define its purpose and clientele. To add to the difficulty, Wisconsin faced challenging economic times in the early 1980s, especially in agriculture. Budget cuts led to the elimination of Extension positions at the state and county level, and staff morale suffered.

Extension slowly regained its footing and had largely recovered by the late 1980s. Programming continued shifting from subject matter to broad themes such as revitalizing the economy, building family strengths, and improving environmental quality.

Extension was on solid ground, ready to face the last decade of the century with confidence. But more unanticipated problems would emerge in the 1990s.

CHAPTER 9

THE CENTURY ENDS:
1990 TO 2000

U nemployment rates hit record lows by the mid-1990s, as thousands of new jobs were created. Many of these positions resulted from the computer revolution. However, rural America didn't share in the prosperity. Hog prices reached Depression-level lows. Corn and soybean prices didn't cover the cost of the fertilizer needed to grow them. Milk prices went up and down, and were down at decade's end.

Wisconsin dairy farm numbers continued to decrease, as a few more farms were sold each week. Farms became larger but there were fewer of them, as farmers bought out their neighbors. In 1990, Wisconsin had 80,000 farms, including 34,000 dairy farms. Ten years later, the number of dairy farms had fallen to less than 20,000.[1]

Both parents worked in most families, even those with small children. Working parents often had no choice but to leave their children alone at home after school. Families faced the stress of juggling and negotiating work and family demands.

Wisconsin introduced welfare reform in 1998, while ending the Aid to Families with Dependent Children program. The new Wisconsin Works (or W-2) programs for limited-income families placed more emphasis on work. In many cases, spendable income did not initially increase, and employment created new expenses and stresses.

Water pollution, policies and procedures for handling solid waste, recycling programs, and land use questions became important concerns for Wisconsin's citizens.

With advances in biotechnology, new issues bubbled to the surface and demanded attention. Many involved economic, social, and ethical concerns Cooperative Extension focused on four broad program areas: 1) agriculture and agribusiness; 2) 4-H youth development; 3) community, natural resource, and economic development; and 4) family living programs.

Cooperative Extension Moving Forward
The organization had calmed down considerably under Patrick Boyle's leadership. The university had named Boyle acting chancellor of UW-Extension in 1982 and

Extension youth programs expanded in the 1990s to include community youth and family issues.

chancellor in 1983. Charles Koval assumed the position of dean of Cooperative Extension upon Gale VandeBerg's retirement in 1983. When Ayse Somersan, who had been program leader for community resource development, followed Koval into retirement, Carl O'Connor became dean of Cooperative Extension and Ellen Fitzsimmons became associate dean.

In 1990, Boyle named Gerald Campbell vice chancellor. Campbell had been associate dean for Cooperative Extension. A major responsibility for Campbell was to work with university system campuses, which he did with considerable success.

Boyle emphasized building partnerships with governmental and non-governmental groups to demonstrate the educational role of Extension and, in turn, to develop new funding sources. Boyle was committed to "issues programming," which meant working with people on community problems and issues rather than merely transferring new research from the campuses to whomever might find it useful. Teams of county and campus-based staff and other partners worked together to solve problems and introduce research findings when they became relevant. Boyle worked to redefine the Wisconsin Idea, the notion that the boundaries of the campus were the boundaries of the state. He appointed a Wisconsin Idea Commission in 1984, comprised of

Extension advocated narrow-row corn growing as a means of increasing corn yields.

Extension and campus faculty. The commission was charged with reexamining partnerships and finding new ways to define what had long been a popular idea.

Despite all the discussion that began in the early 1980s about disbanding University of Wisconsin-Extension and returning to the pre-1965 organization, Boyle was committed to making UW-Extension work. He saw great potential in the organization. In the introduction to the 1991 annual report he wrote: "A unique collaboration of state, county, and federal government, the 26 UW System universities and centers, and countless agencies, groups and individuals, Extension is the 'Wisconsin Idea'—the people's university connection. Through its divisions of Cooperative Extension, Extension Communications, and Continuing Education Extension, and its collaborative relationships with the UW System institutions, the Wisconsin counties, and countless local, state, and federal agencies and groups, Extension provides a spectrum of lifelong learning opportunities for all Wisconsin citizens."[2]

In the early 1990s, Cooperative Extension's high-priority programs included water quality, solid and hazardous waste management and recycling, families and youth at risk, profitable and sustainable agriculture, and community economic development. Some critics said these were old ideas—agriculture, home economics, 4-H, and so forth—clothed in new words. These well known and familiar categories provided a cloak for defining and dealing with new problems, some of which were coming into focus for the first time. These areas included youth at risk, problems with solid waste management, maintaining quality water, and more. These program areas also served as a way for staff to work with each other on shared interests and community needs.

From a time when faculty morale was at its lowest ever and the legislature and others were questioning Extension's worth, the organization was once more humming along, gaining respect and restoring respect where it had been lost.

Partnership Programs

Programming with partners took many forms. In Green County Michael Jones, the community resource development agent, was paid in part by the Green County tourism committee, a subset of the Green County Board. He served as liaison person with the committee and worked half-time on hospitality, recreation, and tourism programs across the county. While working with the tourism committee, Jones helped the county obtain a competitive grant, which resulted in a Wisconsin Heritage Tourism designation that emphasized the county's cheese and dairy history.

Jones helped the tourism committee produce the *Green County Tourism Scene,* a newsletter promoting the county's tourist attractions. Jones edited and made major writing contributions to the newsletter, which featured everything from "Famous Last Words—No Matter What Happens," to "Travel Gives You a Story to Tell" to tips on understanding tourists and their interests and needs.

Encouraging people to do something different was a role the university had assumed in the 1800s, when it encouraged farmers to come to the cutover region and farm. Now, the university had come full circle. It was again inviting people to return to the land—but this time just to visit.

Barn Preservation Initiative

The barn preservation effort, led by Extension Specialist Charles Law, was a partnership effort that included the State Historical Society of Wisconsin, the Wisconsin Trust for Historical Preservation, the Barns Network of Wisconsin, several private individuals, and Cooperative Extension. The purposes of the initiative were threefold: 1) to build public awareness of the need to save historical rural buildings of all kinds, including barns; 2) to deliver workshops that provided detailed information on barn restoration and preservation, including identifying resources that were available; and 3) to maintain a list of contractors and others who work on historic building preservation and make this list available to interested people.

The barn preservation initiative led to the organization of the Barns Network of Wisconsin (Barns N.O.W.). This organization of barn preservation enthusiasts published a newsletter, coordinated exhibits at farm progress days, and kept barn and rural building preservation issues in front of the public.

Wisconsin Public Television produced a special hour-long television show on Wisconsin barns, in cooperation with several members of the Barn Preservation Initiative. The program aired for the first time in 1999 and was titled "Wisconsin Barns: Stories in Wood and Stone."

Law explained the program by saying, "The aim is not to preserve useless relics from a past era. Restoring these barns preserves Wisconsin's collective sense of self and enhances rural economic development."

Responding to Family Needs
David Riley, child development specialist, was frustrated when he tried to inform the public through press releases, radio shows, newsletters, and presentations about "latchkey" children and their needs. Latchkey children were those who had no one at home when they returned from school in the afternoon, because both their parents were working. Many young children were left without supervision.

The typical response he got was, "So what?" People didn't think the results of Riley's work applied to their communities. It was a problem for Chicago or some other large city.

Riley decided to dramatically revise his approach. He helped local groups conduct their own research and assisted communities in organizing planning groups. A needs assessment questionnaire went to parents of elementary age children. When the results were summarized, many Wisconsin communities learned they had a problem. Soon the planning groups began lobbying their communities for after school activity programs, telephone reassurance lines, and self-care training for children.[3]

The program proved enormously successful. More than 100 communities became involved, which resulted in 92 new school-age programs that served 6,750 latchkey children. As Riley wrote: "To our amazement, the work led to an average of about one [child care-related] business start per month for seven years. Other outcomes included intergenerational care projects, telephone "warm-lines," and family education programs reaching 47,000 families."[4]

Beginning Farmer Program
It was difficult for a newcomer to become established in farming during the 1990s. Trempealeau County worked out a beginning farmer program to help individuals wishing to become self-employed dairy farmers. It was a cooperative effort of Trempealeau County Health Care Center, Extension, and the Wisconsin Technical College system. Dennis Frame, Trempealeau County agriculture and resource agent, served as program manager. Apprentices paid a onetime $5,000 tuition fee, then lived

Community resource development programs often involved environmental questions and land use policy and planning.

and worked on the county farm. As Frame explained: "Once selected, the apprentice works with two other apprentices in the dairy. The first year apprentice begins with the basics (milking, calves, general dairy management) and works toward becoming a herdsman. Over the course of three years, the apprentice learns about the dairy industry, agronomy, machinery, production record keeping, financial records, and labor management. While employed, the apprentice is provided a house, electricity and heat, half a beef per year, and a $15,000 annual salary."[5]

After an apprentice completed the first year of the program, the farm purchased 50 heifer calves for the apprentice, who helped select them. The calves were brought to the farm and raised by the apprentice. The heifers were bred to calve shortly after the apprentice graduated from the program and were selected to provide the core of the apprentice's own dairy herd. The first graduate of the program completed it in April 2001.

Northern Great Lakes Visitor Center
This programming partnership included the USDA Forest Service, National Park Service, State Historical Society of Wisconsin, Friends of the Center Alliance, Ltd., Northland College, and Extension. Cathy Techtmann from Extension served as edu-

cation coordinator for the visitor center. Some of her activities included a summer on the water program, school/youth environmental education programs, community Saturday programs, and a planned Elderhostel with UW-Superior. Like many new programs, these faced budget problems. Some of their financial support had to come from grants. As Techtmann wrote, "We are starting the third [year] in our three-year voyage where no Extension office has gone before."

Citizen-Based Watershed Program

Cooperative Extension has long worked with soil and water conservation. A recent collaborative effort focused attention on major river basins in Wisconsin and resulted in partnerships among Cooperative Extension, the state's Department of Natural Resources, National Resources Conservation Service, Department of Agriculture, Trade and Consumer Protection, and the Farm Services Agency.

Cooperative Extension was responsible for providing research-based educational programs that involved local citizens in making decisions within major river basins in the state. In 2001, 14 basin educators worked out of 12 offices. The facilities included the Northern Great Lakes Visitor Center in Ashland; County Extension offices in Milwaukee, Sauk, Winnebago, and Jefferson Counties; area DNR centers in Ladysmith, Wisconsin Rapids, Peshtigo, and Rhinelander; agricultural research stations at Spooner and Lancaster and at UW-Eau Claire. The DNR identified 23 river basins, and Extension basin educators covered most of them.

River basin educators helped organize volunteers in 1999 in a Wisconsin rivers cleanup project. More than 40,000 pounds of garbage and debris were collected, including tires, furniture, "Do Not Litter" signs, and a lawn mower.[6]

Summer Food Program

Florence, Wisconsin, borders Michigan and is a town with limited-income families. In 1998, the nutrition program staff and agents there decided to offer a gardening program for kids. Before long seven different partners were involved, and gardening became a comprehensive summer program. Partners included a local gardening group, the sheriff's department to help with safety issues, a local family center, a school district that provided meals and a teacher to help with the activities, an athletic group that provided physical activities and administered the grants, and the local senior apartment complex, which provided land for gardens. The planners obtained grants totaling $6,000 from the Wisconsin Promise Grant and the Wisconsin Learn and Serve Grant.

The program ran 10 weeks, with children meeting Monday and Thursday from 10 a.m. to 1 p.m. The school district prepared lunch in the school kitchen and delivered food to the site. Weekly educational themes included nutrition and gardening, physical activity, interpersonal relations, and crafts. The planners used the grant money to hire five youth coordinators who worked with the children and were trained in five

River Basin Educator Suzanne Wade (left) examines mussels with Cindy Arbiture, president of the Rock River Basin.

core areas—nurturing, protecting, educating, mentoring, and community service. Katie Tarter, Extension family nutrition educator in Florence County, was the contact person for the project. In 1999, the program won the USDA National Sunshine Award for child development activities.

Partnership with Public Television
Cooperative Extension developed special partnerships with Wisconsin Public Television. One example is the "Listen to Kids" program that focused on youth violence. Wisconsin Public Television formed a partnership with the State Bar of Wisconsin and 4-H/Youth Development to organize and carry out what became a highly successful program. The program combined watching the television special with follow-up discussions.

Internal Partnerships
Cooperative Extension employees—especially the county staff members—long ago learned how to work together. This has been particularly true since the 1980s, when some positions were eliminated and agents had to work across county lines to assist each other. By the 1990s Extension had formalized the team approach. In agriculture

and natural resources, teams were identified in beef, dairy, fruit crops, grains, swine, forage, vegetable crops, and urban agriculture/horticulture. Each team consisted of County Extension agents plus state specialists. In 2000, the dairy team focused on developing more competitiveness in the dairy industry by offering educational programs on dairy farm modernization and cow care and management.

Teams were formed to work on emerging agricultural markets, farm management, land use, marketing and risk management, and nutrient management (covering the relationship between crop production, water quality protection, and manure handling). In addition, a number of agriculture agents formed regional specialization clusters.

New Funding

Cooperative Extension has traditionally relied on three main public, tax-based funding sources—Smith-Lever funds from the federal government, state tax dollars, and money from the counties where Extension agents worked.

Special funding was available from time to time for Cooperative Extension to expand its programs and develop new ones. In 1990 and 1991, Extension in Wisconsin was granted new state funds for programs in waste management, sustainable agriculture, and new agricultural technologies. Extension established a solid and hazardous waste education center, which was a statewide effort that involved multi-campus programs. Cooperative Extension also focused new priority programs on water quality.

Retired Chancellor Patrick Boyle considers the legislation dealing with Cooperative Extension funding in the 1991-93 biennial budget to be his greatest political achievement. In the mid-1970s, Wisconsin's Department of Administration had changed a long-standing tradition of funding the annual salary adjustments on the federal portion of the budget. Thus Extension was forced to use new federal funds on salary adjustments. During some years, the new federal funding was not enough. In these cases, Extension had to reallocate base funds. In reality, this amounted to a reduction in positions. To illustrate, if the state budget process suggested a salary increase for university faculty and staff of five percent, and if federal and county budgets did not increase by five percent, then Extension was forced to fund fewer positions in order to provide the five percent increase.

Boyle was a longtime friend of then-Governor Tommy Thompson. In fact, both men grew up in Juneau County. After many discussions, Thompson agreed to include an amendment in the 1991-93 biennial budget proposal requiring the state to fund the difference between the new federal funds and the salary adjustment requirements. The governor told Boyle that he would recommend the amendment, but that Boyle needed to generate the legislative support. However, the governor's staff aggressively opposed the initiative. It was a complex issue, and many legislators misinterpreted the amendment as a request calling for the state to help solve a federal problem. In addition, many other state agencies faced the same funding problem for staff funded on federal grants, including the Department of Natural Resources and the Department of Agriculture, Trade and Consumer Protection.

After many committee and individual meetings with legislators and much help from WACEC, the legislation was approved. Subsequently, the Department of Administration and the university agreed to a cap. This legislation corrected a 20-year problem that forced position reductions when federal budget increases were inadequate to meet state salary needs.[7]

Although relying primarily on traditional sources, Extension has sought many non-traditional funding sources. Cooperative Extension's nutrition programs have received contracts for additional funding through the food stamp program, which has allowed the organization to add nutrition staff in more than three-fourths of Wisconsin's counties. New money also came from the partnership with the Department of Natural Resources that created the water basin educator positions.

In a March 7, 2000, interview Carl O'Connor, dean for Cooperative Extension, said: "We will likely continue to lose base funding from state and federal sources. Our base funding is changing radically."[8] O'Connor recognized some of the problems that came with outside dollars. "We must be careful that the tail of money doesn't wag the dog, doesn't influence Cooperative Extension too much," O'Connor cautioned. "This is where the University is caught."

Cooperative Extension has few contractual relationships with agribusiness firms. Most of its contracts are with the Department of Natural Resources, the USDA, the Department of Workforce Development (food stamp nutrition education program), and with juvenile justice. For fiscal year 2000, Cooperative Extension's budget sources broke down as follows: state funds, 42.26 percent; county funds, 27.87 percent; federal (Cooperative Extension), 19.24 percent; federal (other), 6.54 percent; and private (fees, gifts, grants), 4.08 percent.

About 89 percent of Cooperative Extension funding continued to come from traditional taxpayer sources—state, federal, and county. The total Cooperative Extension budget for fiscal 2000 was about $60.1 million.

New Audiences

As Extension developed partnerships with an array of organizations, institutions and groups, it in turn developed new audiences. For instance, in the 1990s, Cooperative Extension began working with two tribal colleges in Wisconsin, the College of the Menominee Nation in Keshena and the Lac Courte Oreilles Ojibwa Community College in Hayward.

Tribal Colleges

Extension assisted the College of the Menominee Nation in matters of economic development for the Menominee, Stockbridge-Munsee, and Potawatomi Reservations. The one-year project set out to train about 210 participants in skills needed for encouraging new enterprises and strengthening existing public and private enterprises. Activities included training in needs assessment, expanding outreach activities, conducting short-term courses, and developing a plan for economic development.

Two initiatives were planned with the Lac Courte Oreilles Ojibwa Community College, which included the Lac Courte Oreilles, Bad River, Red Cliff, and St. Croix reservations. One project focused on family resource management, nutrition education, and family development. Activities included workshops on family financial management and parenting, one-to-one-counseling on financial concerns, building a resource library, and learning how to network with other agencies.

The second project included 4-H and youth development programs on the Lac Courte Oreilles Reservation in cooperation with area youth service providers and Extension.

Urban Initiative

In 1996, a special urban initiative began in southeastern Wisconsin (Kenosha, Milwaukee, Racine, and Waukesha Counties). The purpose of the initiative was for communities to identify problems they faced and then work toward solving them. Demographic research of the region turned up the following information: 86 percent of the state's African-American population lived in the four-county area; 72 percent of the state's Hispanic population resided in the area; 41 percent of the Asian population and 20 percent of the Native American population also lived there.

Funding for the initiative came from a variety of local, state, and federal sources, including community block grants. In 1999, outside funding for the urban initiative reached $1.9 million. Partnerships and cooperation were keys to the program's success. Partners included the UW-Milwaukee, UW-Parkside, the four County Extension offices in the area, Carroll College, and a host of local agencies such as the YWCA, local elementary schools, Scout groups, and housing authorities.

Programs focused on everything from assisting recent immigrants to addressing the needs of the homeless. Several programs featured gardening and horticulture. In Kenosha County, an African heritage project was added to the county's youth gardening program. The project was started in a multi-cultural neighborhood within the city of Kenosha. Besides planting vegetables and flowers, kids between the ages of three and 16 learned about the animals, jewelry, housing, flags, and tribal headdresses of Africa. The children sold some of their produce at the Kenosha Farmers' Market and used the money to pay for the education and health care of a girl from Kenya and a boy from the Gambia. The African children have since become pen pals with the Kenosha County children.

Jose F. Vasquez, director of Cooperative Extension Urban Relations, said: "Since implementation of this initiative, Wisconsin has clearly become a recognized leader in implementing innovative programs in urban communities. We are called upon by many states to provide consultation to specific county offices or state offices on how

Members of the Extension fraternity Epsilon Sigma Phi, including (left to right) Laverne Forest, Art Peterson, Rosemary Stare, Russ Luckow, and Gale VandeBerg, served on a committee to raise funds for the Pyle Center, 1999.

to either implement urban programs or improve their current presence in urban communities."

A key element of the urban initiative, according to former Vice Chancellor Gerald Campbell, "was that it was based on a real assessment of the needs of urban area, not a list of 'what can we do in each program area that might interest urban people.' This was possible because we knew that the world we were entering was a very different one. [Extension] gave itself permission to change and respond in many new ways. It unleashed these [urban] counties from a yoke of tradition."

Family Impact Seminars
In the middle1990s, family living agents and specialists conducted programs to help policy makers understand the implications of welfare reform. Karen Bogenschneider, Extension specialist, coordinated seminars on welfare reform for more than 90 state lawmakers, legislative staff members, and agency professionals in 1994 and 1995. Working with Robert Young, Extension family demographics specialist, Bogenschneider focused on family concerns in the seminars. Some of the topics covered included policies that put families first, welfare reform, single parenthood and the well being of children, government's role in competent parenting, teenage pregnancy prevention, and juvenile crime prevention.

The seminars attracted 75 to 90 participants including legislators and their aides, representatives of state agencies, university faculty, representatives from the governor's office and staff members of legislative support bureaus.

Extension Dean Carl O'Connor, when commenting on the program said, "Our objective is not to lobby for a particular perspective. It's to encourage debate on policy options so policy makers can identify common ground where it exists."[9]

Extension agents also designed programs for affected families. In 1995, Fond du Lac was one of two pilot counties where Extension assisted with welfare reform education. Family living educators Nan Baumgartner and Barb Roder taught financial management, nutrition, time and stress management, and problem-solving skills as part of the county's JOBS program. They worked closely with the Department of Social Services. In Pierce County, the other pilot county, Lori Zierl, family living agent, trained former welfare recipients to become teaching assistants. The recipients then helped present a weeklong course on family living skills to at-risk families.

Graziers, Organic Producers, and Small Farmers

Old ideas often return in new wrappings. At one time, all of Wisconsin's dairy cattle grazed on pastureland. Farmers didn't know about hauling feed to cattle in summer rather than having them forage for it by themselves. In the 1990s, many Wisconsin farmers rediscovered grazing, and Cooperative Extension developed programs to assist them. Grazing workshops, sponsored by teams of County Extension agents and specialists, included discussion of various problems and challenges faced by farmers who were moving to "grass-based dairying." Extension also organized a forage team that focused on grazing. The team compiled a list of pasture and grazing publications on rotational grazing and pasture management. The list was made available on a forage website. Topics included pasture management, fencing, water systems, forage identification, and more. The website also contained announcements of upcoming grazing events. Dennis Cosgrove at UW-River Falls provided leadership for this project.

At one time, many Wisconsin farms were small operations of 160 acres or less—many were only 60 or 80 acres. In the 1990s, Cooperative Extension developed special programs for current "small acreage" farmers. Paul Dietmann, Extension agent in Sauk County, wrote a monthly column titled "Small Acreage Options" for the farm press. Dietmann also worked with *The Country Today*, a weekly newspaper with statewide coverage, to develop a new magazine insert that targeted the small farmer. He helped plan the insert, which was titled "Vest Pocket Farmer." Another recent innovation was an annual conference for the small farmer, which was a collaborative effort between Extension and the Southwest Badger Resource Conservation and Development Council in Platteville.

Several Wisconsin Extension agents became interested in sustainable agriculture, organic farming, pasture grazing, and smaller-scale farmers. The so-called alternative agriculture movement grew, but a rift developed between those doing and supporting conventional agriculture and those practicing alternative agriculture. Some of these efforts caused controversy within Cooperative Extension.

In a March 2001 interview, Paul Dietmann said: "Lately we've been having a philosophical discussion in Extension about 'research-based' versus 'knowledge-based' information. One of our agriculture agent colleagues, who is a confinement dairy specialist, has been criticizing me for the type of work I've been doing, and Laura Paine (crops and soils agent in Columbia County) for some of her work with graziers. This agent believes our work is not based on sound research—that it is based on anecdotal evidence and somewhat questionable knowledge."

The "anecdotal evidence" is what farmers learn on their own and are willing to share with each other—that is, knowledge-based information. Research-based information is information garnered by a researcher—often an Extension agent—under controlled and carefully planned conditions. In the early days of Extension, and before the Smith-Lever legislation that formed Cooperative Extension, much of the educational work was a combination of university research and what farmers themselves were learning.

New Uses for Newsletters
Extension has used newsletters as a teaching device for many years. By the 1990s, Extension was finding new uses for this communication tool. For instance, *Parenting the First Year* was a learn-at-home instructional newsletter for new parents. It was a follow-up of a program that family living agents Linda Boelter and Joan LeFebvre had begun in 1982. LeFebvre also wrote *Parenting Your Toddler.* In addition, family living education made a newsletter for expectant mothers called *Preparing to Parent* available in 2001.

Following the success of the 1982 newsletter, Extension Specialist David Riley produced a new edition in 1988, with the intention of obtaining statewide distribution. Wisconsin's 72 County Extension offices created partnerships with more than 350 organizations, including 77 maternity hospitals, 22 city or county health departments, 165 Kiwanis clubs, and 49 other organizations. More than $300,000 was raised each year to print and mail the newsletters to more than 40,000 Wisconsin families. Another 25,000 families received the follow-up series, *Parenting the 2nd & 3rd Years.* There was also a parenting newsletter website in English and Spanish. The latter version attracted computer users from many Latin American countries. This program won several awards from organizations devoted to preventing child abuse.

4-H Youth Programs
Throughout the 1990s, 4-H youth programs remained popular among Wisconsin's young people as leaders and administrators made changes. Those who had been 4-H members themselves, numbering in the thousands, remembered 4-H bulletins that helped guide their work. For years, most of these publications were produced in Wisconsin. By the 1990s, most 4-H literature came from a cooperative 4-H curriculum system that included 30 states. The system began in the north-central states as a

regional effort to develop new 4-H animal science materials during the 1980s. The effort proved so successful that funds generated from selling the materials were used to develop other project literature. By providing interstate collaboration on curriculum development and pilot testing, the standard for the appearance and format of 4-H materials was raised. A national 4-H curriculum jury process was initiated to provide quality control across the country.

With new computer technology, county offices managed 4-H mailing lists and enrollment information so leaders could look to the Web for information. Four-H members downloaded needed forms, obtained information about upcoming events, received project selection information, and learned about resources for various 4-H projects.

Four-H clubs became increasingly more involved in community service activities, and county 4-H youth development staff members collaborated with other agencies and institutions serving youth in their communities. Some counties, including Waupaca, Waukesha, Douglas, Jefferson, and Shawano, redirected existing resources or added new resources to the County Extension budget for staff to work more broadly in their communities. Four-H youth development broadened its statewide mission to reflect a role as community catalysts and leaders in community youth development.

A mandatory youth protection system also evolved, which meant that volunteer leaders were screened for criminal records and given special training to make certain that all youth participants were safe. Young people were also encouraged to serve with adults on community boards, become involved with youth philanthropy, serve on teen courts dealing with juvenile violations, and participate on county 4-H leader boards.

Administrative Woes
A famous baseball player once said, "It's deja vu all over again." Extension had nearly forgotten the troubling 1980s, which had brought the organization budget problems, layoffs, and a chancellor who resigned not long after receiving a vote of no confidence from the faculty.

Patrick Boyle announced his retirement in 1992, effective in August 1993. After a national search, Donald Hanna became chancellor. His background included educational technology and distance education. Hanna had trouble acclimating to the University of Wisconsin, its history, and its internal and external political climate. He struggled to respond to state government's SAVE (Study of Administrative Value and Efficiency) Commission's often strident pronouncements and challenges.

Unrest began to develop within the faculty. Chancellor Hanna then made a fatal administrative error—at least as far as many legislators and university people were concerned. In 1996 he hired a new assistant, Roberta Gassman, for $67,000, an amount that was $22,000 more than the advertised base pay. At the last minute, he changed the job description. In doing so, he broke a long-standing university rule that all hiring must be done within the limits advertised for a position, and if a job descrip-

Extension Chancellor Patrick Boyle presents an award to Ayse Somersan, Cooperative Extension dean. Boyle served as chancellor from 1983 to 1993.

tion is changed then a search for candidates must be reopened. Hanna apparently believed that he had gotten approval from UW system Senior Vice President Keith Sanders to exceed the advertised salary, but permission to change the job description remained an issue.

The press had a field day. Legislators weighed in. A *Wisconsin State Journal* reporter wrote: "State lawmakers warned Wednesday that UW-Extension may face political consequences for approving an unusually high salary for Roberta Gassman and violating university hiring rules. 'People are livid over this,' said Rep. DuWayne Johnsrud, R-Eastman."[10]

A reporter for the Janesville *Gazette* wrote: "The Hanna-Gassman controversy throws gasoline on the budget fires as the legislature prepares to debate [Governor] Thompson's executive budget request. Some lawmakers are creating links between Gassman and the budget."[11]

The timing was awful. The legislature had not gotten over the SAVE report recommendations about Extension (although SAVE had made few official recommendations about Extension, some SAVE participants used the press as a way of airing their concerns). At this time the entire university system was in the midst of seeking approval for its $5.3 billion budget request from the legislature.

Hanna resigned as chancellor on January 26, 1997, and left the office on February 3, 1997. In a July 5, 1997, letter to the editor of the *Capital Times*, Hanna wrote: "I . . . did not resign because I inappropriately offered a higher than advertised salary.

I followed the UW policy by asking for in advance and receiving approval to offer the salary that was offered. I did resign because I believed that my resignation would have the effect of allowing the UW, and particularly UW-Extension to move forward in a difficult budget year climate in the most positive way possible, without continuing controversy on the matter."[12]

Roberta Gassman resigned January 30, 1997, days before she was to start her new job as Extension communications director (with a new title of executive assistant to the chancellor). In a settlement with the university, she was given three months' severance pay of $16,925 and up to $4,000 to cover her legal expenses.

Albert Beaver, who had been in University of Wisconsin system administration since 1973 and had considerable personal credibility, was tapped to become interim chancellor. He took over on February 8, 1997. The university wanted an Extension leader immediately who knew the Wisconsin scene, knew Wisconsin politics, and was well respected inside and outside of the university. Beaver worked hard to repair political fences. He retired in 2000, with the Extension ship once more upright and on course. A national search for chancellor resulted in the hiring of Kevin Reilly, who had been vice chancellor under Beaver.

Program and Budget Challenges

A special state commission titled the Study of Administrative Value and Efficiency (SAVE Commission) was created by legislative action in the 1993 state budget. It occurred during a time when many people were talking about "reinventing" government. The commission held its first meeting in November 1993 and met 25 more times over the next 12 months. The commission drafted a report for the governor in November 1994. Its recommendations helped support budget cuts the governor needed to cover the cost of the new school funding law, which provided local school districts with two-thirds of their costs.

Some SAVE Commission members wanted an entirely new Wisconsin Idea. They sought dramatic changes in Extension and a severe budget cut, including elimination of Extension's $49 million state subsidy and making the organization entirely self-supporting.

In a special report, writers from the *Wisconsin State Journal* wrote: "The commission warned UW officials that 'growing public opinion' believes that the university's mission and structure is 'dangerously anchored' to the 19th and 20th century rather than the 21st century."

James Burgess, chair of the SAVE Commission and an Extension critic, said: "The question now is should they stop or should they do something else . . . Has Extension found simply new reasons to justify its existence?"[13]

Extension quickly helped blunt the impact of the SAVE report. A flurry of messages began arriving in SAVE offices supporting Extension's statewide activity. Joe Corry, an associate vice-chancellor for UW–Madison and an Extension historian said:

"They really pulled out all the stops and got a lot of people to say, 'Wait a minute, guys, there's some important stuff going on here.'" In response to all the cards, letters, and phone calls, Commission Chair Burgess, said: "Is anyone critical of Extension? We, the SAVE Commission, are. But it's difficult to get anyone to argue that [Extension] isn't a good thing."[14]

Extension found itself in a challenging dilemma. Some were saying the organization was outdated and had served its purpose. Other critics were saying just the opposite—that Cooperative Extension had overextended itself. In a January 1995 article, *Wisconsin State Journal* reporters wrote: "The century-old, service oriented institution with agrarian roots has become a tool for addressing issues as disparate as corporate profitability and eating disorders . . . Extension was designed to bring research-based knowledge from the University of Wisconsin to citizens of the state. But some legislators and other critics wonder whether Extension has strayed too far from its roots. They are questioning the role and scope of Extension."[15]

Mark Lederer, special assistant to the chancellor, said: "The end result was that there were only two recommendations on Extension in the final [SAVE] report. The first dealt with efforts to 'consolidate youth service functions.' It read: 'Successful 4-H programs—which foster reliability, socialization, stewardship and entrepreneurship in youth—might have an even greater positive impact if they are more closely tied to other activities.' The other recommendation had to do with duplication. It directed the Board of Regents to 'evaluate potential areas for duplication of programming, funding, and staffing.' The report specifically mentioned eight areas of review, one of which was Extension. After all the consternation, both recommendations were rather vague and meaningless in the context of the full report and how the governor and legislators received it."[16]

The 1995-1997 Budget

For the 1995-1997 state biennial budget, Governor Tommy Thompson proposed cutting the budgets of most state agencies, including the University of Wisconsin. In the initial proposal, UW-Extension's budget was to be cut five percent the first year and 10 percent the second year. Cooperative Extension would be spared a budget slash. In actuality, the budget cuts amounted to 9.3 percent the first year and 18.2 percent the second year. Although Cooperative Extension's budget was not to be cut, its state funding base was included when the overall Extension cuts were calculated. The rest of the university was to receive a 2.1 percent cut the first year and a 4.2 percent cut the second year of the biennium. Mark Lederer and other Extension officials met with the members of the legislature's joint finance committee in an attempt to convince them that Extension's cuts were excessive and would have negative effects on programs that were high priorities for the state.

Recalling the 1995-1997 budget process, Lederer said: "Extension's budget cut was reduced unintentionally by the finance committee." What happened was this. The joint finance committee reversed the governor's decision to target Extension; it then voted 15 to 1 to include Extension's budget cut in the unallotted cuts to be taken by all UW institutions. This meant the regents would have responsibility for determining the dollar amount of Extension's budget cut. Cooperative Extension was not included in these cuts, but was of course indirectly affected. During the process, the chancellor at UW-Green Bay lobbied legislators, asking that the assigned cuts should be based on the share of state tax dollars (general purpose revenue) that each institution received. The Green Bay chancellor got his wish. As a result, Extension's budget was cut $4.5 million less than it would have been under the original plan. Extension received about the same cuts (five percent per annum) as the rest of the university.

The 1997 Audit
Meanwhile, another legislative audit began in May 1996. Former state representative and later UW regent Lolita Schneiders and Senator Gary George requested it. The audit focused on the relevance of Extension education, especially in Waukesha County, which Schneiders had represented. The audit sought to shrink Extension, give greater clarity to its mission, focus its programs, and in turn reduce the cost of Extension to the state.

As Lederer reflected in 2001, "The [1997] audit itself was far less critical than had been expected and could be seen as a useful management tool." The final report recognized changes in Extension programming and the organization's ability to respond to emerging issues. But some fundamental differences remained about sources of funding, program scope, and Extension ability to reach diverse audiences.[17]

The 1997-1999 State Budget
In the governor's 1997-1999 biennial budget, further cuts were proposed for continuing education and other Extension programs, amounting to about $2.5 million for each year of the budget. Cooperative Extension was again spared, at least in the governor's budget.

Interim Chancellor Beaver understood Wisconsin politics. He immediately set out to restore some of Extension's lost budget—not a small task given the animosity that had resulted from the SAVE Commission's publicity and the problems that had swirled around former Chancellor Hanna.

Beaver sent a letter to the members of the legislature's joint finance committee on May 27, 1997, requesting that the $2.5 million targeted reduction for UW-Extension be eliminated. If that was impossible, he asked the legislators to apply the percentage reduction of base budget to the affected units only.[18] The assembly co-chair, Representative Scott Jensen, not only recommended that committee members should ignore the chancellor's request, but that the cut should include Cooperative Extension to the tune of about $1 million.

Chancellor Beaver, Mark Lederer, and others immediately set the wheels in motion to restore the money that was to be cut. When asked how he went about this seemingly overwhelming task, Beaver said: "I spent a great amount of time along with [Cooperative Extension Dean] Carl O'Connor and [Cooperative Extension Associate Dean] Ellen Fitzsimmons on developing our relationships with WACEC." Mark Lederer, special assistant to the chancellor, recalled the following: "The WACEC group held their annual meeting in Milwaukee that year [1997]. It was a hot day in June. The group discussed and then approved a resolution to oppose budget cuts for Extension."[19]

When Lederer returned to Madison, he distributed copies of the resolution to the legislators at the capitol. Lederer said that the single action of trying to cut the Cooperative Extension budget resulted in more letters and phone calls to the legislature than any other budget item. Ultimately, the legislature voted to restore Cooperative Extension's budget and eliminate half of the rest of Extension's proposed budget cut (reducing it from $2.5 million to $1 million annually).

The WACEC group held its 1998 annual meeting in Madison. As part of this meeting, they went to the capitol and met with their respective state senators and assembly representatives, to once more bring them up to date on Extension activities in the counties.

Former Chancellor Beaver reflected on the WACEC activity. "WACEC members really felt good about themselves. They felt they had made a difference in helping state-level decision makers understand Cooperative Extension, and in turn they themselves developed a much better understanding of Extension programs so they could support them at the county level."[20]

Former Chancellor Patrick Boyle, who had retired in 1993 and was appointed to the board of regents for the University of Wisconsin, suggested a lesson Extension's leadership could learn from these budget problems: "Keep your political ducks in order and your relationships with other organizations, agencies, and institutions on solid ground. Some of these partners included the Board of Regents, the University of Wisconsin system, and the universities, county agriculture and Extension education committees, federal and state agencies including the governor's office, other educational agencies including the technical colleges, K-12, business, labor, environmental groups and associations and local government groups and individuals."[21]

Extensive Program Changes

Over the years, many Cooperative Extension programs had changed—perhaps none to a greater extent than family living during the 1990s. In the early 1980s, Extension home economists, mostly faculty members, staffed family living programs in all 72 counties, with a few staff members working more than one county. During those years, 19 state specialists provided research-based support. The emphasized programs included food and nutrition education, family resource management, textiles, interiors and housing management, energy education, human development, and leadership development. The more specialized Expanded Food and Nutrition Education Program (EFNEP) reached six to ten counties, down from a high of 27.

In 2000, family living programs employed 68 faculty and 180 academic staff located in counties, and another 31 statewide specialists. The specialists were located primarily at UW-Madison and UW-Green Bay. Nearly two-thirds of the county staff and half of the state specialists were funded on grant and contract money. The largest contract program within family living was the Wisconsin Nutrition Education Program (WNEP), which accounted for almost 160 county and state staff. WNEP programming was available in 58 counties.

The nutrition education program combined funds from EFNEP and the Food Stamp Nutrition Education Program (FSNEP) of the United States Department of Agriculture. In 2000, FSNEP funds totaled $5.3 million. An additional $5.3 million in matching funds was available from county collaborators and others.

Cooperative Extension employed nearly 100 nutrition educators in 2000, some of whom were bilingual and bicultural. As State Program Leader Laurie Boyce said, "These language and teaching skills are invaluable in reaching out to new individuals and families with limited English. Cultural foods, food patterns, healthy food choice and preferences are the focus of education. We have made excellent progress in reaching diverse families. We [also] partner with nutrition programs affiliated with the Great Lakes Intertribal Council, with the Lac Courte Oreilles, and with the Menominee."[22]

In addition to emphasizing food, nutrition, and optimal health, family living programs in 2000 focused on family economic security; strengthening individuals, families, and communities; prevention of child abuse; early childhood education and related policy education.[23]

Community, Natural Resource and Economic Development (CNRED) was another program that underwent substantial change between 1980 and 2000. In 1980, the program area employed 43 agents in 42 counties, with support from 50 campus-based specialists throughout the state. CNRED worked on economic development, land use, lakes management, water quality, natural resources, environmental education, and local government education. Wastewater management and groundwater quality were also becoming important. During the lean years of the early 1980s, many Wisconsin communities had difficult economic development challenges that CNRED and other agents addressed.

In 2000, CNRED employed 62 agents in 61 counties with about 62 specialists providing support—plus 15 river basin educators. However, tax-supported funding had declined since the 1980s due to tight budgets. Like family living programs, CNRED developed partnership arrangements with other agencies such as the Department of Natural Resources to obtain new funds. These arrangements have allowed many programs such as the Solid and Hazardous Waste Education Center, the Lakes Partnership and the basin program to grow. Earlier programming issues such as land use remained extremely important, requiring staff skills in conflict management, organizational process, and planning.

Starting a New Century

When 2000 arrived with fireworks and celebration, people looked back, brushed themselves off, and declared that they had been on quite a ride for the last 10 years. Indeed, most of them had. In 1990, most people couldn't imagine that with a few key-strokes on a computer keyboard, they would have access to thousands—or millions or multi-millions—of bits of information from anywhere and everywhere in the world.

The stock market soared, breaking record after record, creating wealthy people even as the chasm between the haves and the have-nots increased. How could homeless people, street people, and hungry people be found when the unemployment rate was at record lows? But they were there.

For the most part, the agricultural economy did not fare well during the decade of the 1990s, even though agricultural productivity was high and many new technologies became available, such as genetically modified seeds, computer-assisted land evalua-tion, and much more. Rural communities suffered due to low commodity prices. As Charles Dickens wrote in *A Tale of Two Cities*, "It was the best of times; it was the worst of times, it was the age of wisdom, it was the age of foolishness, it was the epoch of belief, it was the epoch of incredulity, it was the season of Light, it was the season of Darkness." One could say the same about Wisconsin in the 1990s—and about Cooperative Extension, which rode a roller coaster of ups and downs. Credit the staff members who, in spite of administrative and political turmoil, continued to work with people, to help them with their problems, to move them toward becoming something more than they once were.

CHAPTER 10

THE COUNTY EXTENSION OFFICE

The County Extension office is the heart of Cooperative Extension and one of its most visible features. Cooperative Extension is unique in that it has an office in every county in the state. In the early days, most of these offices were located in county courthouses. Now they are located in a variety of buildings, but usually at the county seat. The number of Extension agents, other professionals, and support staff has changed over the years, but the purpose of the office has remained the same.

My first visit to an Extension office took place in 1946, when my father and I climbed the steps to the third floor of the Waushara County Courthouse in Wautoma. My father wanted to start a 4-H Club, and he knew that the County Extension office was the place to begin. As I remember the office it had but three rooms, although there may have been a storage room that I couldn't see. A woman sat at a desk in the outer room and asked us how she could help. What caught my eye immediately was a huge rack of official-looking bulletins fastened to the office wall. The bulletins offered information on just about every topic a farm family would want to know about— everything from taking care of cows to how to grow a better garden and can the vegetables that came from it.

Dad said he wanted information about starting a 4-H Club. "You'll want to talk with our county agent, Mr. Haferbecker," she said as she looked toward the open door where a pleasant-looking man sat behind a desk piled high with papers.

We entered Mr. Haferbecker's cluttered office, where some ears of corn were piled on top of a cabinet and some drying alfalfa hay was on the floor in the corner. Papers and books and bulletins were piled everywhere—on the chairs, on the floor, on the gray metal filing cabinet. Henry Haferbecker shook Dad's hand, then shook mine. After freeing some space on a couple of folding chairs, he invited us to sit as we talked about 4-H Clubs, what they were about, and how we could organize one in our country school district west of Wild Rose.

Over the next several years, I would visit that office many times on a variety of missions-turning in 4-H record books, picking up 4-H bulletins, or checking on the county fair. The place never changed. It had a messy, lived-in appearance, but a person never felt put off or out of place.

The next County Extension office I came to know well was the one in Green Lake County, also situated in the courthouse, but in the basement. It was 1957 and I had just been hired as 4-H Club agent for Green Lake County. I stopped at the reception desk promptly at eight a.m. There I met the receptionist, Jeannette. She shook my hand, said welcome, and showed me into Willys Gjermundson's long narrow office. Willy had just been promoted to county agricultural agent a few months earlier. Here, the piles of paper were shorter and more neatly piled. The appearance of neatness may have been an illusion, because this office was twice as large as the one in Wautoma.

"I'll show you around," Willie said when he got out from behind the big gunmetal gray desk.

He showed me a little room off his office that had once been the Dairy Herd Improvement Association's milk testing room. The Babcock tester and related milk-testing equipment stood nearby. Here I saw the mimeograph machine, paper cutter, and assorted office supplies. Then he showed me the bulletin rack just inside the front door–I'd missed it when I came in. It was about the same size as the one in Waushara County, and it held the same bulletins. Somehow it didn't occur to me that the bulletins would be the same in every county office in the state.

I followed Willy into another room, where two desks were pushed together. "Here's your office," Willy said. "You share with Laverne Priebe, our county home agent."

Not only did we share the office, but we looked straight at each other whenever we were both there. This didn't happen often, as we both spent most of our time in the field. At the Green Lake office in those days, there was no problem with communication between the 4-H and home economics part of the program. We each knew everything the other person was doing. We also shared the same phone.

A few years later, when I moved to Brown County in Green Bay, I got accustomed to quite a different office arrangement. The County Extension had a suite of offices on the second floor of the new federal building, where the bottom floor was the post office. The Extension offices were adjacent to the regional FBI office.

Now I had my own office and my own secretary. The outer office was a buzz of activity, with four secretaries pounding away on their typewriters and answering several phone calls at the same time. The office included five agents: Dick Schuster, county agricultural agent; June Billings, county home economics agent; Larry Tlachac, farm and home development agent; Doris Staidl, consumer marketing agent, and myself, 4-H and livestock agent. The bulletin rack, positioned next to the outer door, was about a third larger than the one in Green Lake County.

In 2001, the County Extension office was still the center of County Extension activities. In mid-March of 2001, I visited the Sauk County University of Wisconsin-Extension office on the third floor of the West Square Building, across the street from the courthouse in downtown Baraboo. There I met program assistants (once known as secretaries) Lynn Olson and Judy Lewis, who showed me around the office. Lynn had worked in the office for about 14 months. Judy had been there nearly 40 years. Lynn showed me the bulletin files, no longer on a rack by the door but contained in carefully organized file cabinets. These days, small costs are associated with each bulletin.

Lynn and Judy worked at computers that were linked to the Extension agents' computers through a networking system. I saw but one typewriter. "We use it for forms and reports," Judy said. I saw their new copy machine, which not only copied on both sides but also collated and stapled. "I remember when we had the sheets for a newsletter spread all over the counter and we put them together by hand," Judy shared. I learned about their folding machine, which makes envelope-stuffing easier. Judy said that she had worked with 13 4-H agents during her 40-year tenure, but only three agricultural agents. She also explained that they once had three secretaries in the office but with the new technology, only two were now needed.

Less than fondly, Judy remembered typing newsletters on mimeo masters and running them off on a mimeograph machine when she first started work in 1961. She also took dictation in shorthand from agents at that time. Reports were typed on an IBM electric typewriter, using onionskin and carbon paper for multiple copies. In 2001, the office received about 500 to 600 phone calls a month. E-mail was just starting to catch on. About 50 people per month stopped by in person.

Judy also remembered how she and Helen Jackson, former home economics agent, tested pressure cooker gauges with a tire pump. It took both of them to do it, and they were a little skeptical of the accuracy of their results. One of Judy's favorite stories involved a woman who called and asked how she could take the seeds out of her raspberries. This woman called regularly. She never gave her name, but she didn't need to—everyone knew who she was.

Lynn Olson recalled the time when a fellow came in with a flattened field mouse in an envelope. He wanted it identified. "It's something I won't forget," Lynn said. "Did it ever smell!"

While I talked to Lynn and Judy, Karl Hakanson, Natural Resource Educator, showed me photos of one of his "meetings from hell." It was an early evening pasture walk. The outing ended with a presentation by Doug Jackson Smith from Agriculture Technology Studies, who spoke to the group in the farmer's garage, which was dimly lit with lamps from the house. As Smith was speaking, a swallow began swooping across the garage behind him. The farm dog took after the bird. Abruptly, a cat appeared at the speaker's feet, trying to rid itself of a hairball. Smith kept on talking. "Extension people didn't let much bother them," Hakanson said.

A bit later, Community Development Agent Liz Nevers appeared, and we talked about a barn restoration meeting that Sauk County was sponsoring in May.

Paul Dietmann, agricultural agent and department head, returned from a milk quality barn meeting that some 80 farmers had attended. In his office, which has pictures of dairy and beef cows on the wall, we talked about how agriculture in Sauk

Fred Field, Juneau County agricultural agent, at an office meeting during the 1950s.

County was changing. Dairy herds ranged from 35 cows to 700 and more, he said. He noted that one farmer's hog operation included more than 800 sows.

One of Dietmann's programs was helping small farmers find alternative approaches for making a living on a farm. He had prepared a slide presentation that he called "A Bunch of Pretty Good Ideas From Small Farms." These ideas included everything from selling meat out of a farm freezer to operating an on-farm store, organic dairying, selling at farmer's markets, farm crafts, making natural wood furniture, and selling firewood.

There were books, bulletins and papers piled everywhere, just as there had been in the first County Extension office I ever visited. Yet it was a comfortable place to sit and talk as Paul told me about Sauk County, its agriculture, its tourism potential, and its environmental programs. One of the river basin educators, John Exo, was housed in the Sauk County Extension office. We also discussed opportunities for small farmers and the new emphasis on horticulture. Horticulture Agent Nancy Huffaker had just been hired.

Other agents in the office included Sue Nagelkerk, family living educator; Gretchen McCauley, 4-H and youth development agent; and summer 4-H agent Emily Roidt, who had returned for a second summer. Joyce Smidl served as family nutrition coordinator for Sauk and Richland Counties and was also located in the Sauk County Extension office.

The Sauk County office is quite typical of many Wisconsin Extension offices. Some are larger, some smaller; the size depends on location and programs offered.

USDA Suggestions for Extension Offices

In 1951, the United States Department of Agriculture published a bulletin titled "System in the County Extension Office." Here was advice about where to locate the county agent's desk and what kind of sign should appear outside the building; how to conduct the Monday morning conference and the best approaches for handling the mail and answering the phone.

The bulletin began as follows: "Extension action is organized in the county office. Here meetings are planned; news stories, radio scripts, and visual aids are prepared; and demonstrations developed. Here rural people come for advice on the latest methods of farming and homemaking. Here they bring soils and pressure-cooker gauges to be tested. Here records are kept and hundreds of bulletins are systematically filed for ready reference. . . . Rarely is the importance of the Extension office as a show window for the Extension Service fully realized. It has been called the front door to the agricultural college and the United States Department of Agriculture, for this is where the farmer and his wife make contact with these two great educational institutions." [1]

County, State and Federal Partnership

A unique feature of Cooperative Extension is the funding partnership of federal, state, and county governments. The partnership is formally recorded in Wisconsin Statute 59.56, which was passed in 1914. Among other things, it states that county boards can establish and maintain education programs in cooperation with the University of Wisconsin. The statute designates the County Extension committee (a committee of the county board), as the county's representative in the three-way partnership

Each county provides about 40 percent of the salary for county staff, along with travel expenses, clerical support, office facilities, and general supplies. The remaining 60 percent of the agents' salaries is provided by federal and state funds. Federal funds are combined with state funds at the state level. By statute, Extension agents are jointly selected by University of Wisconsin-Extension and the county.

Gerry Campbell, former vice chancellor for University of Wisconsin-Extension, said, "As the years have passed, especially since the mid-1980s, the balance of power between the county and state partner has shifted toward the county partner. This was perhaps inevitable as county government grew larger and the prevalence of county managers and the county executive system shifted the power from the county board of supervisors toward professional managers."

"These managers were generally not as sympathetic toward the Extension office as the County Extension education committee had been," Campbell went on to say. "I

In some counties, few staff changes were made over the years. Pierce County has had but three county agricultural agents: Bernard Drewiske, 1957-1985 (left); Harlan Seyforth, 1920-1957 (middle); and Greg Andrews (right), appointed in 1985 .

believe they were even more concerned with the shared partnership, which gave them little direct control over the activities and events, and the way 'their' County Extension office operated."

According to Campbell, reasons for the shift in power toward the counties include the move of Cooperative Extension from the College of Agriculture to University of Wisconsin-Extension; flat federal budgets; and an ongoing fiscal crisis in the College of Agricultural and Life Sciences, which reduced the college's capacity to contribute its share to state specialist appointments.[2]

The County Office Secretary

Anyone who has ever worked in a County Extension office or has had contact with one knows that the office secretary is the glue that holds the entire operation together.

In doing research for this book, I called an Extension office to inquire about some history of its operations. I asked to speak to one of the agents.

"What do you want to know?" the secretary asked politely. She then quietly said, "I've been here longer than any of the agents. If it's history you want, ask me." And indeed she had the answer I was looking for.

Melba Rodger, head secretary in the Marquette County Extension office for over 37 years (not the secretary I called), related some of her memories. "I really like my job, or I guess I wouldn't be here [all these years]." Melba worked from 1954 to 1960 and from 1968 on. "I have used manual typewriters, electric typewriters, and now computers. The Extension office was in the basement of the courthouse when I started in 1954. There was one light bulb in the middle of the room and one over my desk. One day a county board member came in and turned off the light to see if the lighting should be improved. It was a rainy day, so everything was dark except for the bulb over my desk. We got new lighting, and soon after [we got] a new coat of paint and new tile floors."

"When I first started in 1954," Melba said, "I worked two weeks for nothing, to see if I liked the job. Al Tschudy was county agent then. I have seen many agents come and go."

"You have to be a good listener," she explained. "Several years ago, a farmer stood by our counter and cried because his tractor motor had blown up and he couldn't afford a new one. He had been in 4-H, and I had known him for years."

"You may start out in the morning thinking you are going to get some specific thing done, and maybe you do. But people come in with their problems, and you may not finish your task until late afternoon. I guess that is what makes it interesting."

Lil Hart was an Extension office secretary for more than 30 years. "When I started working in the Jackson County Extension in the basement of the courthouse in Black River Falls, there were three agents—agriculture, home economics, and 4-H. We had very small quarters. The agents all had individual rooms but no doors for any private conversations. There was a manual typewriter—what I was used to—but they had just ordered a new IBM electric. I was a part-time secretary [hired] to replace the regular secretary when she was sick or couldn't make it to work because she lived 30 miles away."

"One of the most boggling things was getting acquainted with all those bulletins," Lil said. "Every Extension office had bulletins on a display rack in the outer office. And those monthly reports that agents had to turn in to the state office—I had to tabulate the number of visits, number of office callers and number of telephone calls and type up three copies. Two to the state and one for the file. I used carbon paper, and it was a hard job when you made a mistake."

She went on to talk about the advantages of working in close quarters and the feeling of togetherness that developed among the entire staff. Of course the coffee breaks brought everyone together as well.

"In the early 1960s, the Extension office took the lead role in many activities," Lil said. "We were right next door to the Soil Conservation Service, and they had no secretary. I did the typing for them. We had a phone in our office for their calls. I remember the jail and the Sheriff's office was just out the back door from our office. They had no secretary, so I typed their reports. We were also asked to plan various county events. I remember the ribbon cutting of Interstate 94 in Black River Falls. Actually, there were *two* ribbon cuttings of the interstate. North from Black River Falls was first. We served venison burgers and coffee for the celebration right down on the road. It took some planning."

Judy Asman worked as secretary in the Outagamie County Extension office. She wrote: "Where else can you work where you can boast that alongside of you is a shellacked cow's stomach, a cow's udder in formaldehyde, three cow's hoofs, and a cow hairball?"

Judy remembered the time when 40 German farmers came for a visit. One of the agents talked with them. As he talked, he got louder and louder, apparently hoping that volume would overcome any language barrier. Finally, one of the visiting farmers held up his hand. "I'm sorry to tell you this," the farmer said in a heavy German accent. "But we aren't deaf, we're just German."

The questions that came in every day, over the phone and from visitors, kept everyone on their toes and often in stitches. For instance, Judy remembered a woman calling and saying, "I have a problem, and I want you to promise you won't laugh when I tell you what it is." The woman was baby-sitting with her grandchild. Her daughter had a large houseplant on the porch, which the grandmother decided to bring into the living room. She no more than got it in the house when some animal in the pot began digging and kicking dirt all over the living room. In a near panic, the grandmother put her grandchild in a high chair in a corner of the room, away from the flying dirt. She called the Extension office. "How do I trap what I think is a mole in a big flowerpot in a living room?" The only mole trap Judy could find in a bulletin was a harpoon with a wicked-looking spear. She never found out what happened to the mole, the flowerpot, or the living room floor.

The questions kept coming, every day:

"I found this turkey ham in my mother's freezer. It's been there five years. Is it OK to use?"

"Prunes aren't what they used to be. Why is this?"

"I make apple cider in my garbage disposal and it's real good. Is this OK?"

"I use my dishwasher to cook fish. How does that sound to you?"

"I cooked some meat and put it in the refrigerator. Three days later I took it out, turned it over, and noticed it was green on the bottom. Is it safe to eat?"

"I bought a house with trees in the yard painted white. The previous owner liked birch trees, so he painted all the trees to look like birch. How do I remove white paint without harming the trees?"

"I bit my tongue and it hurt so bad that I forgot and left the raisins out overnight. Are they still safe to eat?"

Joyce Berg worked as secretary in Trempealeau County. She remembered the various Extension offices. "The first office was small. The farm management agent was in the main office with two secretaries. The 4-H agent, home economist, and agriculture agent had separate rooms. There was a very small room for bulletins and a copy machine.

"The next set of offices was much bigger. There was a main office where the secretaries were. Agents had their own offices. There was a bulletin room and also an ETN (educational telephone network) meeting room.

"Then we moved to an office that was said to be bigger but did not seem bigger. Each agent had his or her own room and there was a small ETN room/lunchroom. The agriculture agent and the dairy and livestock agent shared a room. In the main office were two secretaries and a family nutrition educator."

Joyce remembered starting with a manual typewriter, then moving to an electric one. She remembers well the days when she typed multiple copies with carbon paper—and the problem when she made a mistake. Now she uses a computer. "The computer is great. I save material on a disk and just go back to it to make corrections. The typewriter doesn't get used much anymore—mostly for typing envelopes and forms."

She remembers when bulletins were free, and when a small charge was first placed on them. Now they are on a compact disc, which she pulls up on her computer and runs off for the public as the materials are requested. The first copy machine in the office used a solution and "it was a mess." Now the copy machine she uses not only copies but also collates and staples the material.

Bess Schaneberg worked as Extension secretary in Trempealeau County for over 23 years. She remembers when Peter Bieri, county agricultural agent, hired her. One of the secretaries had quit and he "hired me on the spot. He was a strict boss, and I liked it that way. Mr. Bieri believed in public relations, and was ready to offer a client a cup of coffee. It's a lot different today. We have a personnel director, and everything goes through her."

The Monday Morning Conference

At nine a.m. every Monday morning, the staff in the Brown County Extension office gathered in Dick Schuster's office. Dick, who was agricultural agent during the 1950s and early 1960s, was also in charge of office operations, including making sure each staff person was well aware of what everyone else had planned that week. He would always ask, "Do you need any help?" Often someone on the staff did, and this was the opportunity to say so. If a large 4-H event was coming up, the home economics agent and the farm and home development agent might volunteer to assist the 4-H agent. Schuster usually did as well. The same was true for events that other agents were responsible for. Someone was in charge, but the person always had assistance.

Elsa Stanek, head secretary in the office during those years, sat in on the Monday morning meetings, taking notes and asking questions to make sure she understood what was going on. It was Elsa who would get the phone calls about details: When was the truck leaving for the state fair? What time did the 4-H demonstration start? What's the deadline for signing up for windbreak trees? And so on.

Each agent took notes, too, because as we traveled around the county we often got the same questions. Sometimes we had to stand in for an agent who was ill, or who had become overcommitted. This might mean giving a talk to a garden group or a homemaker meeting when we didn't expect to. The philosophy behind most County Extension offices, from the early days to the present time, was that the office had a job to do and each person was there to help get the job done. Some people roll their eyes when they hear an Extension office compared to a family, but the metaphor generally works. Of course there were and are disagreements among staff-families have their unhappy moments as well. But at the end of the day, the office members stood together, and whatever spats had surfaced stayed within the office.

Social Side of the County Office

Mid-morning coffee breaks were common in County Extension offices, serving as a respite from the telephone and office callers and a time to compare notes with each other and coordinate activities.

End-of-the-year holidays also offered opportunities for social activities. Programming had usually eased up a bit, so agents were more likely to be in the office working on reports, correspondence, and filing. Social activities were often held with other county employees. When I worked in Green Lake County, card games played in the county judge's inner office were a highlight of the week between Christmas and New Year's. In addition to the judge, players included the sheriff, the county clerk, clerk of court, county treasurer, register of deeds and, of course, the Extension agents. In those days it was an all-male activity.

Art Brehm, longtime 4-H Agent in Dodge County, recalled one of the courthouse Christmas parties he attended. He remembered that the Extension office "was stuck in the basement of the courthouse."

In the Dodge County Courthouse, people traditionally had a Christmas party in the county board room during the noon hour, shortly before the holiday. Each office took turns hosting the party. Members of the staff and the secretaries each brought food for a potluck that everyone shared.

Brehm recalled that a previous year's party had been "a pretty stiff event," so in 1955 he and the dairy agent decided it was time to liven things up. It was Extension's turn to host the party that year. The two agents volunteered to prepare the punch, and the home agent naturally provided the recipe. Brehm doctored up the punch with plenty of carbonated soda to provide a little fizz; then, upon further consideration, he decided to give the power of suggestion a try. Brehm had learned about this in Extension summer school from a rural sociologist. Accordingly, he left a few empty bottles of various kinds of spirits judiciously in the vicinity of the punch bowl. He had gotten the empty bottles from a local tavern keeper. There was no liquor in the punch.

Did the ploy work? Several department heads, including the county superintendent of schools and the county nurse, declared it was the best punch they had ever had.

Art Mitchell, the county clerk, led the carol-singing, which was heard well beyond the confines of the Dodge County Courthouse. It was a holiday party that everyone talked about for years.

Part of the social side of Extension offices was having fun and not taking the job too seriously. Merriam Sacia was office secretary in the Jackson County Extension office when my brother Darrel worked there as 4-H and horticulture agent in the early 1960s. Practical jokes were commonplace, and she had played several of them on Darrel. Although serious on the surface, Darrel has a jokester side. While the secretary was at lunch, he once wrote a phone number on a sheet of paper along with the words, "Someone has a box for you."

When she returned to the office, she called the number. Darrel overhead her asking, "Do you have a box for me?" She turned bright red when she discovered she had called the local funeral home.

Mostly, the County Extension office is a serious place where the business of County Extension work is coordinated and conducted. The county office is the hub, the center of operations. It is where the University of Wisconsin touches people on a local level. The county office turns the University of Wisconsin's research information into usable ideas and information that local people can use.

Extension agents are those who are out in the field, working directly with people. They are the topic of the next chapter.

CHAPTER 11

THE EXTENSION AGENT

C ounty Extension agents work out of County Extension offices, sometimes with multi-county responsibilities. They are the direct link between the university and the people. Like the rest of Cooperative Extension, the Extension agents' role has changed over the years. In this chapter, we'll examine the career paths of several agents, look at how agent work differs in northern and southern Wisconsin, share some agent stories, and examine other topics.

The County Extension agent's job was never easy. The hours were long, the pay was poor, and the work was never ending. In addition, the County Extension agents often had to overcome the image of the traveling salesmen. A Kenosha County historian wrote, "Most of the county agent's job was spent 'riding the circuit' throughout the county, his flivver loaded to the running boards. Into it he somehow crammed soil augers, seed corn racks, packets of litmus paper, seed germination rolls, dairy barn record sheets, caustic potash and nippers for calf and cow dehorning, dynamite sticks for ditch and stump blasting, drain tile samples, spray guns, balanced feed guides, hip boots and formaldehyde for treating seed grain. There were bundles of college bulletins, with plans for bullpens and milk houses, tied up in binder twine. His job was to sell progress to skeptical farmers who, often as not, classified the agent in the same category as liniment drummers or lightning rod salesmen." [1]

From the day in 1912 that E.L. Luther, Wisconsin's first county agent, began work in Oneida County, no one knew quite what to call this university employee who lived in the community and spread the gospel of education whenever and wherever he had an opportunity. Luther and other early employees were called county agricultural representatives. By 1920 these men—and they were all men in the early days—became known as county agricultural agents. As new program areas came along, new agent titles emerged: erosion control, recreation, dairy, forestry, farm and home development, resource development, 4-H club, 4-H and youth, livestock, farm labor, war food, horticulture, community and natural resource development The latter were known as CNRED agents-pronounced "conrad."

Titles for home economists have probably changed the most over the years. Nyla Musser, who worked nearly 35 years for Cooperative Extension, remembered the

The 1952 New Agents' Conference

changes in her own job title: "I was a home demonstration agent, a home agent, home economist, Extension home economist, family living agent, and family living educator during my career."

Today, both men and women hold agricultural, horticultural, and other positions previously held only by men. Many County Extension directors (formerly known as county office chairmen) are now women as well. In the early days, the county office chairman was always the agricultural agent, who was always a man.

It took awhile for some counties to become comfortable with women as agricultural agents and even as 4-H or horticultural agents. There were some expectations for the women agents in the office that have now changed. Edie Felts-Podoll, who is Extension director for Adams County, remembers her first Extension committee meeting. She was asked by the person who was then office chair to make coffee for the all-male staff and committee. "As a seventies woman, I was concerned that this might be a 'bad' first impression, so I said to the chair after returning from the break room, 'I just ran the grounds through again; that's how I make coffee at home.' The

office chair ran off to correct the problem, and I was never asked to make coffee again."

Elsie (Stein) Young was hired as a "war food assistant" in 1944. In a letter, she recalled: "My salary was about $250 per month plus mileage-about five cents per mile. I also got gas ration stamps and was able to buy tires, a scarcity at that time. My duties were similar to that of a home agent, in that I worked with 4-H kids and homemaker groups. I attended many of their meetings and helped form new clubs. I did some judging in other counties at their fairs, and I attended the state fair with our 4-H winners." She worked until the end of 1945.

Education by Another Name

The strength of Cooperative Extension has been its ability to provide a different kind of education without calling attention to it. Many people had unfortunate experiences with formal education, yet came to Extension with their questions and problems and left satisfied. For them, Extension was an educational institution that didn't flaunt its

An agricultural agent consults with a farmer on a farm management question.

educational objectives and used educational approaches in a far different manner than most formal educational institutions. Thus Extension avoided such terms as out-of-school education, Extension teacher, and the like.

Unlike teachers in high schools and vocational-technical schools and university instructors, the Extension agents had no pat curriculum to follow, no textbooks per se, and no timetable as to what should be taught when.

How did the Extension agent function? What did he or she teach, to whom, and when-with what outcomes? Not all Extension agents saw themselves as educators, although this has changed considerably in recent years. I once conducted an informal study, simply asking Extension agents "What do you do?" Their answers included such statements as, "I answer questions, lots of questions. They come over the phone, in person, through the mail. Never ending questions."

One agent said, "I'm an organizer. I bring people together and organize them." Another, a 4-H agent, said, "I run activities-speaking contests, demonstration contests, fairs, livestock shows." Still another responded, "I do what the local people want me to do." One more said, "For me its radio, TV, newspaper columns, speaking at meetings-I'm a communicator."

Extension agents continue to do all of these things, but today the answer to my question would likely include a reason for doing them: "I do all these things in the name of education. I am an educator."

Much has been written about Extension agents, their jobs, and their characteristics. Back in 1930, Clarence Smith and Meredith Wilson had this to say about the county agricultural agent: "In helping the farmer increase his efficiency and therefore his net income, Extension forces are striking at the very root of the matter, and the man in the Extension system closest to the farmer is the county agricultural agent." They go on to say, "The county agent has to approach his work from a considerably different angle than does the ordinary college teacher. If he leads in the county, it is not because of his authority but because of his accurate knowledge, soundness of judgment, and persuasive qualities, in individual contact, in committees, on the platform, and through the press." [2]

In 1946, the United States Department of Agriculture published a bulletin titled "The Home Demonstration Agent." In response to the question, "What is the home demonstration agent like?" the bulletin included quotations from happy customers. "She's eager to help when you need her, whether it's advice you desire on a new henhouse or facts you want about feeding the baby. If she doesn't know, she'll find out. She'd be the one I'd want around when I'm convincing my husband we need a new house. She's so human. That mortgage we'd worried about seemed easier to pay when we'd talked it over with her. She's friendly; knows our names, waves when she passes. Stops by when you've been sick or in trouble."

For 38 pages, the publication goes on explaining what home demonstration agents do and how they do it. Another excerpt: "She represents science in aiding the homemaker. She is a teacher. She uses the family approach. She passes on successful home practices. She works through rural leadership. She works through organizations. She achieves results." [3]

Changing Roles

From the beginning of county agent work, the agent knew something about many things-from caring for livestock to recommending crop varieties, from organizing a 4-H Club to producing cash crops. Agents were generalists. For many rural people, aside from the farm press and an advice-giving relative, Extension agents were *the* source of information, as well as their link to the College of Agriculture in Madison.

After 1945, the situation began changing. Former director of Extension for Iowa Marvin Anderson wrote: "Somewhere along here after World War II, we turned a corner in history. The generalist now has trouble keeping up. The agent is not so much the subject matter specialist but now needs to know more about people's needs, their problems, not to give answers but to mobilize the staff and resources to meet them." [4]

Joe Tuss, who worked as an agricultural agent in Taylor and Columbia Counties, also wrote about the changing times. "With all of this [the changes], the county agent was slowly but surely swept into the milieu of it all. Changing patterns in agriculture and accelerated emphasis on social needs [appeared] right alongside economic development. Agents had to be a part of assisting in the needs of a transforming society. Farmers were moving off the land. Farm fields in less productive areas of the state ... began to repopulate with trees and shrubs. People from the cities began to invest in lands that once were a farm. Recreation and aesthetics were booming. So now the University and its outreach programs began to heed the needs and developed specialization." [5]

Today's Extension agent tends to be more specialized. County agricultural agents may be proficient in crops or in livestock, but usually not in both. Agents work across counties, helping each other. They are in constant contact with specialists and researchers, in order to find answers to complicated problems that often go well beyond one area of knowledge.

Changing Positions

Because Wisconsin Cooperative Extension is a relatively large organization with staff in 72 counties, several area offices, and offices on multiple campuses (the largest number are located at UW-Madison), County Extension agents have had many opportunities for advancement. Many chose to stay in the county where they were hired throughout their careers. Others worked in several counties over the course of their professional life with Extension. Some left their county position, did further graduate work, and took state-level jobs in Wisconsin or elsewhere in the country. Some left Extension for other opportunities.

E.L. Luther, the first county agent in Wisconsin, left his position in Oneida County to become a county agent supervisor and eventually director of Wisconsin's farmers' institute program.

Donald Duxbury began work as a farm and home development agent in Marinette County in 1953, then moved to Sawyer County as 4-H agent in 1958. He joined the Center for Action on Poverty in the mid-1960s. As he said, "I was the only traditional Cooperative Extension agent in the center."

Elizabeth Davies worked as a county home agent in Iowa and Sauk Counties before joining the state 4-H staff in Madison, where she worked until her retirement.

Rosemary (Thornton) Stare started as a county home agent in Jackson County in 1951. After five years, she returned to graduate school, completed a graduate degree, and took a job as home economics editor at Michigan State University. A year and a half later, when she returned to a county position in Dodge County, the fellow she had dated in graduate school couldn't move. She worked for nearly two years, got married, and quit her county job. As she said, "That's what women did in those days. I became a full-time homemaker and soon a mother."

Downtown renovation leaders with a community resource development agent in the 1990s.

About two and a half years later, Stare received a call from the state leader of home economics. Would she fill in for the consumer-marketing specialist who was ill? She was asked to do weekly radio and newspaper work in a part-time position. Not long after the consumer-marketing specialist came back to work, the specialist got married and went on a honeymoon-and Stare was back to her part-time position. When the full-time specialist decided to become a full-time homemaker, Stare got the job. In addition to the media work, she counseled county home economists and showed them how to organize and teach food buying and marketing.

In 1971, Extension administration asked Stare if she would consider the job of district program leader for home economics. The position required considerable travel, but she looked forward to providing orientation for new county home economists, assisting with program planning, and working with the district director and the 4-H program leader. In 1978 she was asked to serve as acting state leader of home economics until a permanent person was hired.

When a one-year interim district director position opened, Stare applied. Up until that time, district directors had always been men. She got the position, and soon learned about working with County Extension education committees, hiring staff, working on salary adjustments, and all the rest. After the regular district director returned, Stare resumed her district program leader position, but a year later she was back as acting state home economics leader while Extension searched for a permanent employee. After two searches and three years, a new state leader was finally hired. About two years later, the state leader resigned and returned to teaching and research. Stare was back as acting state leader of home economics for two more years. Then she took early retirement.

As times changed and program areas shifted, many County Extension agents changed directions as well. Several county agricultural agents became resource development agents.

Joe Tuss made several job changes during his career. He grew up on a farm in northern Wisconsin and is a World War II veteran. Tuss graduated from the University of Wisconsin in 1950 and started his Extension career as Taylor County 4-H agent in the same year. However, he was called back into service for the Korean Conflict. He returned to Taylor County as agricultural agent in 1951, where he worked until 1963. From 1963 to 1972, Tuss was county agricultural agent in Columbia County.

Tuss became a district director in 1972, a position he held until 1979. At that time Gary Rhode, secretary for the Department of Agriculture, Trade and Consumer Protection, asked Tuss to serve as deputy director, which he did until 1982 when he retired.

Joe Tuss, like so many other County Extension agents, was highly respected and even revered by county people. When Tuss applied for the district director position, Jack Kelly, farm editor of the Portage *Daily Register*, wrote the following in support of Tuss: "Joe [Tuss's] involvement in county affairs—economic, social, cultural, and recreational—approaches the incredible."

With a childhood background in Outagamie County's 4-H program, Alice Kempen attended Stout State University, received a degree in home economics, and accepted a county home economist position in Oneida County. During her first year in Oneida County, she received no paid vacation; after the second year she was granted one-week's vacation, but was to receive no salary adjustment. Harvey Becker, who was the county agricultural agent, told the Agricultural and Extension Education Committee to give Alice his salary adjustment. The county increased its share of Kempen's salary from $50 to $75 per month.

With Becker's retirement, a resource agent was hired. The resource agent began working with the more prestigious organizations in the county, leaving Kempen to work with the restaurant association, the lodging association, and so forth. This work got her interested in family-owned recreational businesses. Soon she finished a master's degree in hotel/restaurant management. When she returned to the county, her title was changed to area food management education agent. As Kempen said: "They tried to make your position sound more important than the salary that went with the job. Try to put 'area food management education agent' on a name badge!"

Rock County 4-H youth development summer enrichment

Once again she returned to graduate school, this time to receive a master's of business education. She enrolled in a weekend program, which meant she traveled to Madison every other weekend for five semesters, leaving on Friday afternoon and returning to Rhinelander on Sunday afternoon. "It was worth it," she said. "I enjoyed working with people who had a dream. A dream to start their own business. They challenged me, and I challenged the reality of their business ideas."

Gale VandeBerg grew up on a farm in Clark County, where he attended a one-room country school. He enrolled in the University of Wisconsin in 1939 and began teaching vocational agriculture at Dorchester upon his graduation in 1943. In 1945 he began work in Outagamie County as an emergency war foods assistant. He did this until 1946, when he became assistant, then 4-H agent, then associate county agent. He left the county to do graduate work. In 1952, he earned a master of science degree from Cornell University and returned to Outagamie County as agricultural agent and county office chairman.

Extension Director Henry Ahlgren invited VandeBerg to Madison in 1954, to help establish an undergraduate, graduate, and in-service training program for Cooperative Extension. During that time, VandeBerg worked part-time on a Ph.D. degree. He resigned the position in 1956 to finish his degree, which he did in 1957. He was immediately offered a position as associate professor in the National Extension Center for Advanced Study.

In 1960 VandeBerg, now a full professor, returned to Cooperative Extension as an assistant director. When University of Wisconsin-Extension was formed in 1965, VandeBerg became dean of the Division of Economic and Environmental Development, and in 1970 became assistant chancellor and state director of Cooperative Extension. In 1980, with yet another Extension reorganization, VandeBerg became dean and state director of the Cooperative Extension Service. He retired in 1983.

These are but a few of the hundreds of stories of how Extension careers twisted and turned over the years. By and large, the organization provided many opportunities for Extension agents to develop their interests.

The preceding examples might suggest that county staffs were constantly shifting, but this was not the case. Some counties experienced few changes. Pierce County had but three agricultural agents in 80 years: Harlan G. Seyfoth (1920 to 1957), Bernie Drewiske (1957 to 1985), and Greg Andrews (1985 to the present).

North and South

Where Wisconsin's north begins is a never-ending debate. Some say Stevens Point, some say Wausau, some believe Highway 8 is the dividing line. Aside from the debate, there are cultural, geographical, environmental, economic, and historical differences between northern and southern Wisconsin. The Extension agents who live in the north know this well.

Donald Schink, a longtime County Extension agent and Extension specialist who is now deceased, wrote: "These northern Wisconsin agents deserve special mention in the story of Wisconsin Extension. They played a role much different from those in the south. These northern agents were thrown into the cut-over country. As George Strother [former associate Extension chancellor] said at a state Extension meeting: 'The real problem was the cut-over mentality of the people. There was a void of leadership.' Our agents were forced to play the leadership role. They headed the county fairs, the forestry committee, etc., etc. It was quite a different role than [the one] played by southern and eastern Wisconsin agents."

Northern agents continue to be a breed apart. Russell Kiecker was county agricultural and 4-H agent in Burnett County from 1970 to 1995. He then served five more years at Spooner, where he was an area agricultural agent. In a 2001 phone interview, he said: "We are all by ourselves up here. Very little administration. We always said the Madison artillery couldn't reach us. They [the state office] just didn't have the long-range firepower. We were pretty much allowed to work on our own. We did work a lot with agents in neighboring counties. We needed them and all the expertise they had. Teamwork was a big part of what we did. Lots of times the state initiatives didn't really apply to us, so we would look at these initiatives and tailor them to our needs here in the north-so we didn't get in too much trouble with state Extension administration."

Successful northern agents understood the culture. Don Duxbury worked in the north for several years. In a 2001 letter, he wrote: "Extension has lost most of its characters. Herman Smith, Vilas County agent, was a classic character. Newell 'Dad' Stephenson, Florence County agent, played straight man for many of their extracurricular activities. They took up chewing tobacco to raise the ante of expectations others had of them. During pregnant pauses at annual Extension conferences (always in Madison in those days) you could hear the 'splat' of tobacco juice resounding against the bottom of a makeshift spittoon, an empty coffee tin. Their antics prompted speakers to refrain from frequent and unnecessary pauses."

Being a character didn't mean an agent avoided raising difficult issues. Duxbury recalled a breakfast meeting he attended with Smith and Stephenson. A Farm and Home Administration employee joined the group. Stephenson asked him how many loans he'd lost. The FHA man quickly replied, "In the last ten years, we haven't lost a

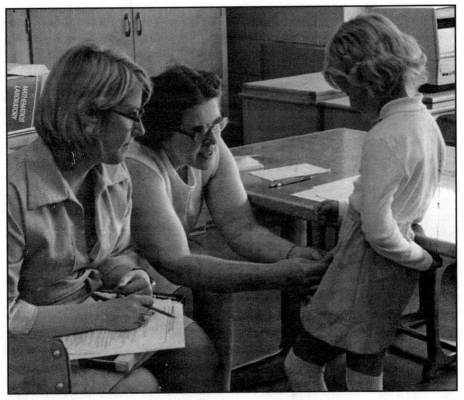

Signe Sorle judges dress review in Burnett County, 1970s.

loan." After a short pause, Smith looked the man in the eye and said, "You must be lending money to the wrong people—certainly not to those who need help."

Often, the northern agents were skeptical of southern agents and especially skeptical of new specialists and administrators who hadn't grown up or spent time in the north.

In 1957 Jim Everts, a livestock specialist, agreed to do a meat-cutting demonstration with homemaker members and speak to a young farmer group in Ashland County. "As I drove north toward Ashland County," Everts recalled, "I began to think Ashland must be just a few miles south of the North Pole. After arriving in Ashland and anxious to meet Dave Holt, I hurried to the courthouse, as I knew he was expecting me. I found Dave at the end of a huge office, which I later learned had been the courtroom before remodeling. As I entered his office and began to walk toward his desk, Dave, a small man no more than five feet-five, stood up and extended his hand to me. Dave's first words were, 'Young man, I am the county agent, the home economics agent, 4-H agent, and supervisor of the county highway crew. To whom do you wish to speak?' Later I learned Dave was making more than a point with a youngster from the ivory tower, as his influence in Ashland was very deep and real."

Norman Everson joined the state 4-H staff in fall of 1961 and became district 4-H program leader for the south-central, central, and northern district. George Wright, then district leader for the northern district, contacted Everson at the annual Extension conference in October and suggested that Everson delay visiting the northern district Extension offices until January, adding only a couple of visits per year would be adequate. He implied that the northern agents didn't want to be bothered with visits from program leaders.

During the second week of January 1962, Everson drove north for a series of meetings. He attended a district 4-H leaders meeting in Phillips, then followed Dave Holt to Ashland, where he stayed in a motel on Lake Superior. The next morning the temperature was -37 degrees. Everson woke up to hear Holt doing his live radio broadcast. Everson's car started and he drove to the courthouse, where he waited for Holt, whose car had stalled at the radio station. When Holt arrived, he asked, "Now what program did you want to talk about?" But before they talked, Holt called Harry Lowe in Bayfield County to check on the weather there.

Everson's next stop was Bayfield County. As Everson said, "They chatted about the weather and other things for some time while I sat there wanting to talk about 4-H programs. When their conversation was over, it was time for me to leave for Washburn." No discussion of 4-H took place.

Everson drove to Washburn and was greeted by agents Harry Lowe, Gene Anderson and Ardala Littlefield, who was recently employed and wanted to talk about 4-H programs. Before they could start talking, someone announced that it was time for a coffee break. After an extended break, Lowe asked Everson if he was going to Hurley to see Herb Kinney. Everson said he was. Lowe got on the phone with Kinney, inquiring about the weather, and announced that Everson would soon be on his way. Now it was lunchtime, and Everson was off to Hurley. There had been little talk about 4-H in Bayfield County. The temperature at noon was -25 degrees.

Everson met Kinney at the Iron County Extension office in time for the afternoon coffee break. As Everson said, "We walked to a cafe near the courthouse. Everybody in the cafe knew Herb and wanted to chat a little with him. We did talk some about 4-H. Herb was the only Extension agent in Iron County at the time."

That evening Everson drove to Wausau, meeting the next day met with the Marathon County staff. He spent some time with Joe Tuss and Al Lietzke on Thursday, after which he drove back to Madison.

When Everson went to his office in Agriculture Hall on Friday morning, state 4-H leader Frank Campbell asked about his trip north. "I don't think I accomplished very much," Everson admitted. "I hardly talked about 4-H."

What Everson didn't know was that Campbell had already gotten a call from one of the northern counties. "Norm is OK," the caller had said. "We can work with him. We will accept him here."

As Everson said later: "I guess I learned that acceptance has to come first."

John Preissing, a former community resource development agent in Burnett County, got to know Mark Pettis, a small business owner in the area. Pettis came to Preissing for help in establishing a lodging tax. Preissing developed a public policy educational packet, which members of the county tourism promotional council (including Pettis) used to promote the idea. The idea proved highly controversial. Many people were just plain against it. Pettis and Preissing developed a close working relationship because of this and other projects. Pettis went on to become assemblyman for the 28th Assembly District. Preissing now serves as director for the northern district. "To this day," he wrote in a 2001 letter, "Representative Pettis maintains a positive, cordial relationship with UW-Extension."

Northern agents generally got to know their people well and did things for them that went well beyond the usual Extension activities. Russell Kiecker knew an older lady who had lost her husband several years ago. She lived in a shack six miles from town, under the most primitive conditions. She fed bears behind her house, and she raised flowers. Kiecker stopped by a few times during the summer in order to see her flowers and talk with her. The woman had little income. She earned some money from a perpetual yard sale-the items remained covered with snow in the winter.

One day in December, the woman stopped by Kiecker's office. She was crying. "Russell, I don't know what to do," she told him. She had been arrested for driving under the influence, not a first offense, and faced a huge fine or jail time.

"I don't have the money for the fine," she said.

Kiecker suggested that the two of them go talk to the judge. The judge, who also knew the woman, said, "Why don't you take the jail time? It's only three months, then you won't have to pay anything."

She said she'd have to think about it. Back in Kiecker's office, she asked, "Russell, what should I do?"

"Take the jail time," Kiecker advised. "It's winter. When you get out, it'll be spring and you can go back to your house.

"She had a good time in jail," Kiecker said. "She read books. She had a shower every day. Good meals. She gained weight. And they made sure she got her medication. When they needed something done around the jail, she helped out. She got along fine."

Stories from the Field

It was June 17, 1957, when I walked into the Extension office in the courthouse basement in Green Lake. I had gotten out of the army a year earlier, and I had just completed a Master of Science degree at the University of Wisconsin. It was a few minutes before eight a.m. Willys Gjermundson was waiting for me and fidgeting, apparently because I hadn't appeared earlier. I quickly learned that, even though the office opened at eight a.m.; agents were expected to arrive by 7:30.

I was briefly introduced to Jeanette the office secretary, and to Lavern Priebe, the county home agent. Then Willie, as everyone called him, announced that he and I and a couple of carloads of 4-H leaders were driving to the Adams County 4-H camp at Patrick's Lake. Green Lake County's 4-H members camped there for a couple of weeks each summer, and we were expected to help with the annual cleanup.

After an hour or so of driving we arrived at Patrick's Lake, which had once been a Civilian Conservation Corps camp. It was a rather primitive camp with no indoor plumbing and only the most minimal electric lighting.

"Got lots of work today," Willy announced to the 4-H leaders and me as we gathered around him for instruction. "Got to dig new pits for the privies, got to sweep out and dust the dormitories, got to clean up the kitchen . . ." He went on with a long list of jobs.

I volunteered to dig toilet pits, first the boys' and then the girls'. A couple of 4-H leaders worked with me—surprised, I think, that I would do it, and even more surprised that I knew how to use a shovel and knew what digging a toilet pit was all about. I didn't tell them that I grew up on a farm with an outhouse, and that every few years we had to dig a new pit.

That day of outhouse pit digging left me with a couple of blisters and a sore back, but it cemented my relationship with a core group of 4-H leaders who supported me every step of the way.

Edie Felts-Podoll has a similar memory, except it involves the county fair. "Two weeks after I was hired, I was taken to the fairgrounds and instructed by the secretary to wash the shelving units. Surprised, I mumbled under my breath, 'I went to college for this?' Little did I know that was just one of the many necessary jobs that were assigned to me that college had not prepared me for. However, I learned that rolling up your sleeves and working side by side with the people will put you in a better position to get help on projects that your college training *did* help you develop."

Joe Walker, longtime county agricultural agent in Waupaca, had a memorable first day on the job as well. The year was 1958, and he was to take a load of 4-H dairy members to the state fair. He met the 4-H members at various places, loading them and their suitcases and heading off to Milwaukee. There was so much luggage that Walker's trunk door wouldn't close, so he tied it down. When they arrived at State Fair Park, all had their luggage except for Harvey, a big, happy, quiet kid. His suitcase was no place to be found.

Walker and Harvey went to a nearby J. C. Penney store, where Walker bought the young man a couple of sets of underwear, a pair of overalls, shirts, socks, and a new toothbrush. Harvey was all set to show his cattle at the fair.

Walker called the sheriff's office in Waupaca, and one of the deputies found Harvey's suitcase. It was battered, but still in one piece. When Harvey returned home, he got his clothing back.

In a 2001 letter, Walker wrote: "This young man and his parents became very good friends with me. A few years later Harvey, all dressed up in his own suit, graduated from the University of Wisconsin with a major in agricultural engineering. I felt my few dollars spent for Harvey's clothing at the state fair had been a great investment."

Steve Kohlstedt, agriculture/resource agent in Richland County, recalled the fellow who contacted him about a problem with microscopic mites. "This fellow insisted that he and his wife were being attacked by microscopic mites that only came out at night, when he and his wife were sleeping. He further stated that the biting and pinching kept him and his wife awake all night. I drove to their house and took dust samples and sent them to Phil Pellitteri, Extension entomologist. There were no mites.

"The couple questioned our abilities. I went back to the couple's home and asked them how were they trying to control the mites. I learned they were spraying each other with a concentrated fly spray from head to toe before they went to bed. At this point, I suggested they see a dermatologist. There were no mites, but they were both reacting to the insecticide with a bad rash. After a couple of weeks with the dermatologist, the couple was back to as close to normal as they would ever get."

Karen Dickrell, family living educator and department head in Outagamie County, recalls the time when she was asked to make a presentation at a county board meeting. When she got the agenda for the meeting, her presentation was listed as "special odor of business."

In 1981, Matthew Glewen began working as county agricultural agent in Calumet County. During his first week on the job, a person walked into the office with an avocado. He wanted to sprout it by putting it in water. "Which way is up?" the person asked. "I'll find out and call you back," Matthew said as he wrote down the telephone number. Just then, the maintenance man walked in to collect the wastepaper. He saw the avocado on the desk and asked what it was doing there. Glewen explained the situation. "Here. This end is up," the maintenance man said. Thus Glewen learned that the County Extension agent must rely on many sources of information, some of which are often overlooked.

Tom O'Connell, longtime county agricultural agent in Dane County, recalled the time he was asked to show a movie at a meeting. When he arrived at the meeting place, he discovered that he had forgotten the take-up reel. Being a typical, "make do" agent, O'Connell collected the film in a wastepaper basket. He didn't say what comments he got from the people in attendance.

Mary Lukas, Sawyer County home economist, was known to speed a bit as she drove on the county's often deserted roads on her way to a meeting. Co-worker Don Duxbury recalled the following incident: "One spring morning, Mary said goodbye to the office staff and drove off to one of her meetings. As Mary came down Zesiger's hill, she hit a patch of loose gravel being worked on by a highway crew. Mary rolled her mostly new Buick one complete turn in front of the highway crew. They checked to see if Mary was all right, and she seemed fine. They pulled the car out of the ditch. Mary turned the key in the ignition, the car started, and she was off to her meeting at the Meteor Town Hall."

"News of the rollover reached the Sawyer County Courthouse via the highway crew," Duxbury added. "Later, when the staff heard her cheery voice down the hallway, everyone rushed to the window to get a glimpse of the Buick. We saw a few dents in the roof and a cracked windshield. Someone asked her how the meeting went. 'Well, I was supposed to make an angel food cake, but I found most of the eggs were broken. So I changed the recipe to yellow cake.' Mary never had a problem adapting to circumstances."

Many agents tell stories about winter driving. JoAnn Gruber-Hagen was 4-H agent in Marathon County in the early 1970s. One Friday evening she agreed to lead a discussion on parenting issues with the Marathon County Young Farmers group at a member's home west of Wausau. It snowed all evening, and when the meeting was over she left for Hayward for the weekend. She hadn't been to this home before, so she hadn't remembered how far it was to the intersection where she could get back to Highway 29. After driving for some time in what had become a raging blizzard, she realized she had gone too far. She tried to turn around and got stuck. She dug her winter clothes out of the trunk and changed while standing in the middle of the road. "You could have been as modest as you'd want and still have had no qualms about changing in the middle of that road that night," she said.

Gruber-Hagen started walking and finally found a house with a light on. She waded through deep snowdrifts to the door and got help and directions back to the highway. She had been turned around 180 degrees; what she believed was north was really south. It should have taken her 10 minutes to get back to the highway, but it took four hours. The trip to Hayward was equally treacherous. She arrived in Hayward at six a.m., just in time to go skiing with her friends.

Roland Richards began work as farm and home development agent in Waukesha County in 1956. During his first year, he held a meeting on winter wheat production. Jack (not his real name) came up to Richards after the meeting and said he had a problem and wanted to talk about it privately. Jack said he was having difficulty with his marriage. It seems his wife had gotten pregnant by a different man, and Jack wondered what Richards would suggest. Jack didn't want a divorce. Richards mulled over the question, concluding that Professor J. James, Agricultural Education Department, had never covered this problem in his agricultural education course. Finally, Richards thought he should say something, so he suggested Jack find a good time to tell his wife how much he loved her. He should also take her to a Friday night fish fry regularly, take her dancing, and maybe give her a bouquet of flowers once in a while.

The couple stayed together, and Jack became a recognized leader in the agricultural community. At Richards' retirement in 1983, Jack came up to him and said, "I just had to come and say thank you one more time." In those days, farm and home development meant more than agricultural records and meetings about winter wheat.

In 1993, corn had progressed very slowly in Pierce County due to a cool, wet growing season. Farmers prodded Greg Andrews, county agricultural agent, to hold a corn silage field day. Farmers were worried about an early frost of immature corn and wanted to know what to do to save what little crop they had.

For the field day, Andrews planned a demonstration showing the effects of early frost on corn. In a cornfield, he erected panels around three corn plants to simulate an early frost with dry ice, but no expert in Madison or anywhere else knew how much dry ice he needed. He and his assistant, Lee Milligan, placed two pounds of dry ice inside the panels and attached a thermometer to a string that was suspended from the top of one of the panels. They waited two hours, but the temperature scarcely budged. With lunchtime near, they added another two pounds of dry ice and headed off to eat.

When they got back from lunch, Andrews lifted out the thermometer to check the temperature. Milligan asked what it said. Andrews said he didn't know, because all the mercury had collected below the -50 degree mark. The corn was frozen solid. Andrews' conclusion: When trying to replicate frost conditions, "it takes more than two pounds of dry ice but less than four."

A Word About Spouses

We can't talk about County Extension agents without at least mentioning their spouses. Extension agents' families were involved with Extension, too, in ways often not acknowledged. Extension agents worked evenings, weekends, just about anytime. They drove thousands of miles, in all kinds of weather and all seasons. When Lou Musser, spouse of Extension worker Nyla Musser, was asked to pinpoint his most memorable moment related to Cooperative Extension, he had a revealing answer: "When my wife retired." He recalled the many nights of waiting and wondering when Nyla would return home, worried because of the long distances she traveled and the ever-present possibility of hitting a deer. Nyla worked as home economics agent in Jackson County for many years.

In a 2000 letter, Beverly Everson wrote: "Our third child in three years was born while Norm was 4-H agent in Green County. It was during the state fair. He picked the baby and me up from the hospital, delivered us at home, and took off to the fair for three days. Talk about dedication."

Steven Kohlstedt, agriculture/resource agent for Richland County said, "I'm sure there were lots of times that my wife Geralyn wished I had a different occupation. But my family has never asked, 'Why are you doing this or that?' or 'I wish you had never started that program,' [because it] was controversial and resulted in nasty phone calls at home)."

That's a Good Question. What Do You Think?

County office secretaries fielded many questions, but Extension agents got their share, too. Many of the questions came as surprises. Faye Malek, family living educator from Manitowoc County, completed a master's degree in May of 1999. She had spent five years working on the degree, and upon completing it was ready for about anything. On her first day in the office, the phone rang. As she answered the telephone, she anticipated a challenging, family-oriented question. "Hello, this is Faye Malek, family living educator. Can I help you?"

"You sure can," the person replied. "How do I get fly dirt off my windows?" As Malek mused later: "A new $10,000 education, five years of stress, all pumped, and I get a fly dirt question. I still laugh about it. It really puts into perspective that we are called on to assist in many ways."

The agents confront a never-ending myriad of everyday problems:

"How do I get rid of bats?"

"I have a skunk in my basement. What do I do?"

"A snake is in my outhouse. What do you recommend?"

"How do I rid my woodshed of snakes?"

"How do I dry my nuts?"

"I have ants in my clothing. How do I get rid of them?"

"I let milk stand out all day. Do you suppose it's still good?"

Beyond eliciting chuckles here and there, these questions and stories say much about people, and about Extension agents' responses. Every question gets treated as a serious inquiry.

The next part of the Extension story involves Extension specialists and district directors.

Here are a few of the problems to which agents have responded over the years:

"I have bugs all over my house. Come see me," a caller urged. Nyla Musser went to the house but found no bugs. "I'll bring you the bugs in a jar," she was told. The jar contained dust balls. "Send the jar to Madison," the person insisted. Results came back. Dust balls.

"How do you get skunk odor out of dressed chickens? A skunk got into my henhouse and sprayed the chickens. I butchered them right away, but now all the meat smells like skunk." Mary Mennes' answer: Soak the meat in tomato juice. The caller shouldn't have killed the chickens. Fresh air would have solved the problem in a day or two.

"I dropped my aluminum shovel, and it went through the blower into my upright silo. What do I do?" Clarence Olson's answer: "Get a bunch of plastic bags and run them into the blower to mark where the shovel pieces are. Then throw away a foot or so of corn silage when you come to the pieces of plastic."

This one didn't help. "I can't do that," the caller said. "I've put in two more loads since the shovel went through."

A caller had just run over someone's goose and wanted to pay the owner what the goose was worth. "What is the market price of goose?" he asked agent Janet Cismoski. Her answer: "Check the cost of a whole turkey at a local grocery store and pad it a little."

A woman once called Cismoski about some fish her father had caught several days earlier in Wyoming. He had brought them home in the trunk of his car. "Is the fish still good?" the woman wanted to know. Cismoski: "I still can't believe the smell alone wouldn't have given the correct answer."

CHAPTER 12

SPECIALISTS AND DISTRICT DIRECTORS

E xtension agents were amply backed up by Extension specialists, a cadre of university faculty well versed in specific subject matter areas and located on a campus in the same academic departments where research was carried out. District directors, with different titles over the years, served as coordinators—links between state and county government, troubleshooters, and supervisors of county staffs.

Extension Specialists

In a 1930 book on Agricultural Extension[1] the authors said this about specialists: "They are the people the county agents depend upon to keep them up-to-date on the latest findings in science as they apply to agriculture and home economics and help them develop sound county and local Extension programs. They take the complicated results of agricultural research and simplify them so that the farmer may understand and apply them to his everyday affairs. They tone up the whole Extension service, keeping the county agents alert and their teaching accurate. They are as essential to the Extension Service as are the specialists in medicine and surgery to those professions."

Over the years, Extension specialists have helped County Extension with many types of programs. By the year 2000, specialists often worked as partners with county staff, many of whom also have specialized training.

Specialists had a broader role, too. An April, 2000, document titled "Extension: Partnership in Education" included the following description of the Extension specialists' role: "Extension specialists on campuses of the University of Wisconsin system teach, conduct applied research, and interpret research of other scholars in response to local and state needs. These specialists provide statewide educational leadership in their discipline and serve as resource people to Extension offices, state agencies, the legislature, professional associations, business and industry, and other state and national groups."

The first recorded Extension specialist in Wisconsin was Frank Kleinhienz, a sheep specialist who began work in 1902. Other early specialists included Ransom Moore (agronomy), 1903 to 1945; George Humphrey (dairy), 1903 to 1942; A. L. Stone (seed and weeds), 1903 to 1939; James G. Fuller (horses), 1904 to 1951; and D. H. Otis (farm management), 1905 to 1919.

Many Extension specialists became legends in their time, and some "old-timers" still remember their speeches, and their way of entertaining and educating an audience at the same time.

These Extension specialists included:

- George "Soybean" Briggs (agronomy);
- Gerald Annin (poultry);
- James Crowley (dairy);
- Charlotte Dunn (nutrition);
- Robert Ellarson (wildlife management);
- Robert Gard (arts);
- Agnes Hanson (4-H);
- Barry Hayes (poultry);
- Lenore Landry (clothing);
- Wakelin McNeel (4-H);
- Gladys Meloche (clothing);
- Walter Rowlands (land use);
- James Schwalbach (arts);
- Randall Swanson (agricultural engineering);
- Verne Varney (4-H);
- Art Wileden (rural sociology); and
- George Ziegler (landscape specialist).

Many more could be listed.

Some County Extension agents thought specialists had rather romantic jobs. They got to the travel the state, stay in motels, eat in fine restaurants, and meet all kinds of interesting people. I didn't know how unromantic the job really was until I became a specialist myself.

Specialists did travel. They still do—a lot. In the early days, they traveled by train. Gladys Meloche, a former Extension clothing specialist, described the trips: "Hotels were not equipped as well as they are today. The only heat was frequently the big pot-bellied stove in the lobby, and these workers were told to leave their room doors open in order to get a little heat. Often they were entertained in private homes and were given the spare bedroom, which was heated only when the rare guest came. The windows were nailed shut for the winter, and paper [was] pasted around the edge to keep out the cold draughts. There was a washbowl and pitcher for the morning wash, and the comfort station was the 'chic sales' building on the back of the lot."[2]

Later the automobile provided transportation, becoming a portable office, visual aids storage unit, and a source of emergency food and shelter as some specialists carried tents and sleeping bags with them. With automobiles, Extension specialists often left Madison on a Monday morning, spoke at some event each day all week, and drove back to Madison on Friday night—only to do it again the following week. This was especially so during the winter months, when the meeting schedule was heaviest.

As an example, here is the 1976-77 schedule for a series of two-day dairy schools conducted for farm women. The workshop dates were: Chippewa County, October 12 and 19; St. Croix County, October 13 and 20; Polk County, October 14 and 21; Buffalo County, October 15 and 22; Sheboygan County, November 1 and 8; Calumet County, November 2 and 9; Manitowoc County, November 3 and 10; and Kewaunee County, November 4 and 11. The staff for these workshops included the county agricultural agent, the county home economics agent, the area DHIA technician, plus four Extension specialists and campus faculty: John Anderson (Extension veterinarian); Robert Bradley (UW Madison food sciences and industries); Robert Cropp (UW Platteville agricultural industries); Anton Sendelbach (Extension dairyman) and Clarence Olson (Extension dairyman).

The schedule was similar for January, February, and March, when dairy schools were held in Wood, Taylor, Lincoln, Marathon, Portage, Waushara, Waupaca, Shawano, Marinette, Green Lake, Sauk, Marquette, Adams, and Juneau Counties. A total of 44 dairy schools were held in 22 counties during that winter.

Extension specialists usually worked in teams as they traveled the state. Mary Mennes was hired as a food service management specialist in 1962. She recalled her work with the "Meat for Modern Living" program, which involved meat and animal science specialists, nutrition specialists, and county agricultural and home economics agents from the counties where the programs were presented. In addition, representatives from the National Livestock and Meat Board, the Wisconsin Livestock Council, and the Wisconsin Department of Agriculture were involved.

Mennes said she learned how to plan as she worked with food and nutrition specialist Charlotte Dunn. Together, they developed the most elaborate plan she had ever seen. The program included a three-hour lecture/demonstration on a stage, alternating meat cutting demonstrations and cooking demonstrations. As Mennes said: "In three hours, we prepared 10 different beef and pork recipes and had them ready for display to the audience at the end-beautifully garnished and with handouts of meat buying and cooking information. The entire three hours was laid out in the plan, right down to the last detail on cooking equipment, serving dishes, and garnishes."

Mennes, a new specialist at the time, explained that the real experience was working with her teammates. Quin Kolb, a meat and animal science specialist, had quickly developed a reputation as an articulate and charismatic teacher. Charlotte Dunn, Mennes explained, was a larger than life role model. "Charlotte not only seemed to know all there was to know about food, but she also knew the owner of every decent motel in the state, every good place to eat, the best places to get good deals on appliances and cookware, and every good ol' boy north of St. Louis."

What were these "Meat for Modern Living" programs like from the specialist's

Introduction of weed spraying for corn, 1956. Art Peterson and Don Peterson, Extension specialists, helped establish field demonstrations.

perspective? As Mennes explained: "We loaded enough equipment and supplies for three well-equipped kitchens into [Charlotte's] Chevy and away we went-to Antigo, Green Bay, Park Falls, Wausau, Chilton, Stevens Point, Barron-a total of 16 or 18 cities. Audiences ranged from a low of 200 to as many as 700. Local sponsors donated door prizes, including one time a 'spanferkel.' I must admit that was new to me. I'd never done a demonstration on a stage overlooking a naked 50-pound pig."

Robert Hall was Extension veterinarian in Wisconsin for 24 years, retiring in 1985. He was often part of an Extension team that traveled the state doing meetings and workshops for dairy and livestock breeders. As Hall said, "On the production side of animal sciences, producers always gave this subject [animal health] high ratings when it came to their interest and importance."

Hall saw the specialist role change over the years, especially in his area of veterinary science. "State funding for research has dwindled and there is more emphasis on grantsmanship, with funding coming from [federal sources] and other basic research organizations. The research is more human than livestock oriented ... applied research for transfer to the animal owners almost dried up during my career. Commercial companies are producing much of the applied research that universities produced. It is tough to be an Extension veterinarian willing and able to transfer knowledge to the county agent when the well is dry."[3]

Historically, Extension specialists often carved out a specialty that assisted one segment of Wisconsin agriculture. For instance, Extension entomologist Walter Gojmerac researched and conducted Extension programs on beekeeping and honey production, in addition to working with general entomology concerns. Beekeeping has a long tradition in Wisconsin, as Gojmerac explains in his book on the history of honey production in the state.[4] A 1916 Extension bulletin was titled "Better Queens Produce Better Bees: Why Keep Mongrel Bees?" Interest in beekeeping continued over the years and, as Gojmerac said, "By 1948, the University of Wisconsin was recognized as a world leader in apiculture (beekeeping)."

George Briggs became famous as a promoter of soybean growing. In fact, it's claimed he never went anywhere without a few soybeans in his pocket. Walter Rowlands was an expert in land use planning. Robert Gard, a quiet man from Kansas, taught hundreds of rural people how to write and how to act in local plays. Jim Schwalbach taught them how to paint. Jim Crowley, a popular after-dinner speaker, told thousands of farmers how to better feed their cows. And home economists such as Charlotte Dunn appropriately scared the bejabbers out of women who didn't prepare meats properly—especially poultry.

Specialist Stories

Don Schink, now deceased, recalled an occasion when the Recreation Resources Center bought a new overhead projector—a beautiful machine. He and Rollin Cooper traipsed off to a meeting in Barron County shortly afterward. "The place was packed," Schink said. "The only problem was that two Extension specialists couldn't figure out how to turn the projector on. Finally some kid came up and said, 'Why don't you push this little bar?' [When] he did, the projector came on."

Jim Everts was hired as livestock specialist in the animal husbandry department of the College of Agriculture in 1956. Many calls came into the department for specialist help; most went to the established specialists. However, Oneida County Agricultural Agent Harvey Becker asked for Jim, the new guy. He had lined up a meeting of hog farmers and sheep men, and had arranged for a stop at the Red Dot Beef farm on the way to Rhinelander.

After the farm stop, Jim met Harvey for lunch and they drove to the meeting site. One farmer came in, then two more. "Everybody is here," Becker announced. "Let's get started." Jim answered questions and listened to concerns. That evening, Becker and Everts were off to a sheep meeting about 20 miles south of Rhinelander. Twenty farmers arrived, and Jim gave his presentation. After an animated discussion of deer and bear hunting following the meeting, Everts and Becker headed back toward Rhinelander. When they got back in the car, Becker asked Everts if he would mind stopping at a sheep farm on the way back. Everts agreed to do it. As he explained,

Elwood Brickbauer, Extension specialist, at a corn meeting in mid 1970s

"With an old lantern and a flashlight we inspected the flock of about one hundred ewes and talked until after midnight. As we drove back to Rhinelander, Becker said, 'Jim, you may never again have this depth of educational penetration in a county. You have met every beef, hog, and sheep farmer in Oneida County today.'"

When Al Anderson was Extension agent in Juneau County, he regularly called Phil Pellitteri, Extension entomologist. Phil was well known for his ability to deal with almost anything related to insects. He had an especially uncanny ability to identify insects from the briefest of phone descriptions.

One day, a woman brought in a strange creature about the size of a nickel, asking for Anderson's help in identifying it. It had a center and several legs and was real fuzzy. Anderson said it looked something like a starfish. "I was describing this to Phil over the phone," Anderson recalled. "For the first time, I stumped him. Then I turned it over and told Pellitteri that on the bottom side it was shiny. 'Al,' he said, 'you've had it upside down. What you've got is the larva of the Hag Moth.'"

Truman Graf and Bill Dobson, agricultural economists, were invited to Russia shortly after the Berlin Wall came down. They were working on marketing programs, and they had been warned to be watchful because the Russian KGB was still wary of foreigners. They heard that a colleague who had taken a photograph of a farmer's market lost all his possessions, including his passport.

The area where they worked had rather primitive housing. They were to sleep in a tiny room that barely held two beds. A small anteroom served as an entryway. After a long day of translations, they both went to bed early and fell sound asleep. When Graf awakened the next morning, Dobson and his bed had disappeared. Graf immediately suspected the KGB. He surmised that they had come in the middle of night and spirited off Dobson, his bed, and all his belongings.

Graf dressed quickly and opened the door to the anteroom. There was Dobson, sound asleep. Graf awakened him and asked what happened. "It's a little quieter in here," Dobson replied. When Graf's snoring had become unbearable, Dobson got up, pushed his bed through the door, gathered up his belongings, and went back to sleep. Graf hadn't stirred.

Joe Walker, longtime agricultural agent in Waupaca County, recalled the time when he had set up a series of meetings on alfalfa, corn, and other common central Wisconsin crops. He had invited Extension Agronomist Dwayne Rohweder, known as "Mr. Alfalfa," to be guest speaker for the first meeting, which was scheduled for one p.m. at Cedar Springs Resort near Manawa. It had been snowing most of the previous night, and the roads were treacherous. Rohweder, who had experienced a career's worth of bad roads, arrived at Walker's home on time. Walker considered the situation and said, "Anyone with any smarts would have cancelled this meeting." Nevertheless, he and Rohweder jumped into Walker's car and headed for Manawa. The visibility was so bad that they often couldn't see the road.

When they arrived at the meeting hall, there was but one car in the parking lot. It looked like a wasted effort. Upon entering the resort, they quickly learned differently. Some 50 or 60 farmers were there waiting. They had gotten together and rode their snowmobiles to the meeting, parking them out back. The meeting came off as planned.

Extension Specialist Dick Vilstrup recalled a similar incident with bad weather. He and Bob Cropp, another specialist, drove from Madison to a cooperative director meeting in Oconto Falls. They drove four-and-a-half hours (160 miles) in a fierce snowstorm, finally arriving at a country tavern where the meeting was to be held. They stumbled into the tavern, toting their projector and screen.

"Meeting's been called off," the bartender said. "But tell you what, let me call the Extension office, some of the cooperative guys, and the local radio station."

Soon snowmobiles, RVs and four-wheel-drive pickups with snowplows began to arrive. The meeting went off as planned, the food was consumed, and over 30 cooperative directors had taken a step toward becoming certified by the UW Center for Cooperatives.

Donald Schink recalled a time when he was an Extension agent in Jefferson County. He was asked to introduce four specialists who had driven out separately from Madison and didn't stay to hear each other's speeches. The first specialist got up, told a story, and got a good laugh. The second specialist told the same story and got some response, but not much. The third specialist, with the same story got groans. The fourth—and mercifully last—specialist got up and told the very same story, which had been the story of the week on the agriculture campus. He was booed.

Some older, well-established County Extension agents were brusque with specialists, especially if they visited counties unannounced. If you were a specialist and planned to visit a county, you'd better announce your attentions to the county agent before you arrived.

In 1961, the State Board of Health had contacted the UW Soil Science Department for assistance. Subdivisions with septic tanks had serious problems, especially in western Milwaukee and eastern Waukesha Counties. Marvin Beatty, soil specialist, was assigned the task. Harold Johnson, Board of Health sanitary engineer, worked with Beatty as they inspected a farm that had been proposed for a subdivision. Beatty quickly determined that the water table was too high, ensuring that septic systems would almost surely fail.

Beatty and Johnson talked about the need to educate developers, surveyors, and others so they could avoid these problems. Beatty knew Bill Rogan, Waukesha County agent, and his reputation for acting cool toward specialists. Despite this, Beatty took Johnson to the county agent's office, where they met a crusty Rogan. They explained the situation and as Beatty said, "Bill's crust disappeared like ice in August. He saw an opportunity to have the Waukesha County Extension office gain new relevance to the problems and issues of an urbanizing county."

Extension specialists have long known how to deal with adversity. Laverne Forest, a staff development specialist, recalled a snowy trip from Green Bay to Madison. A Minnesota native, he'd had lots of experience driving on snowy roads and he, along with most Extension specialists, subscribed to that unwritten Extension motto: "No matter what, when a meeting was set, you got there."

It was December 15, 1970. He and Doris Staidl had gone to a program planning training meeting in Green Bay for newly employed agents. At the end of the meeting, Doris stayed on in Green Bay but Laverne started back to Madison. Listening to the fleet car's radio, Laverne heard the weather forecast predicting snow. Outside, a few flurries were falling, their intensity increasing somewhat as he drove by Appleton and on south. By the time he got to Oshkosh, snow had already covered the ground.

The radio weather people were saying this was the biggest snowfall of the season so far, but Laverne continued on. With some difficulty because of the now-heavy snow, he found the Highway 26 turnoff to Rosendale. He noticed that there were fewer cars and trucks—and those that were on the highway were moving much more slowly. The snow continued, steadily increasing in intensity.

At Waupun, the snow had built up to four inches or so. By the time he got to Beaver Dam it was dark, and what traffic there was had slowed to 15 miles per hour in snow that was now eight inches deep. Laverne drove into a truck stop for a cup of coffee, then drove back onto the highway, confident of his driving skills in snowy weather. At Sun Prairie, the snow had reached 10 inches, but he crept on. Years earlier, he had learned to keep going when driving in heavy snow—don't stop, and make sure no one is stopped in front of you.

Northern Wisconsin agents gather for meeting in 1984 with specialists Al Bringe, Bob Cropp, and Roy Ax.

Laverne finally arrived safely at the fleet car office in Madison. He transferred to his own car and continued out of town, toward his home in Fitchburg. Twelve inches of snow had accumulated, and it was still coming down. There were no cars on the streets. He could see his home in the distance, so he relaxed, turned into his drive, and slid into the ditch. He had driven 140 miles without incident, but he slid off the road 100 feet from his house. The next day, he learned that 18 inches of snow had fallen.

Jack Gray, a specialist with the Recreation Resources Center, left an all day marketing workshop in Superior for a presentation the same evening at a Chetek Chamber of Commerce banquet. On the way he hit a deer, which ended up sitting beside him on the passenger seat. Jack had the state car towed back to Superior (the record does not indicate whether it was towed with or without the deer). Gray borrowed another car from the University of Wisconsin-Superior and continued on toward Chetek. He missed the banquet, but he arrived in plenty of time to deliver his presentation. He said he didn't care for banquet chicken anyway.

Gray had developed a reputation, especially with the camping and resort people. Don Schink recalled a meeting in Wisconsin Dells with campground managers. Someone asked Gray if he had ever made a mistake. He said that he had once, back in 1956. A young campground owner in the back of the room stood up and called in a loud voice: "Daddy!" Schink said it was only time he remembered that Jack Gray was at a loss for words.

Extension specialists, experiment station staff, and County Extension agents often worked together on projects. Agents Bill Dougherty, Sherm Weise, and Harry Lowe once arranged for a shipment of six carloads of western ewes, which were to arrive at the rail station in Spooner for distribution to northern Wisconsin producers.

As Carl Rydberg from the Spooner experiment station pulled his full truck away from the first rail car being unloaded, one old western ewe felt left behind and jumped to the ground in the city of Spooner. Livestock specialist Dick Vilstrup, Rydberg, and all the local kids and dogs tried to capture the elusive ewe. After a chase through the railroad roundhouse and down the main street, Dougherty suggested tying another ewe to a rail car, in order to lure and capture the errant western ewe.

As the Spooner newspaper reported, the idea was great, but the educators' knot failed. In short order, they had *two* ewes roaming the streets of Spooner. Hours later, the ewes were finally captured and hauled to the Spooner Experiment Station.

Times of Controversy

County Extension agents often got caught up in controversy. So did the specialists. Controversy for specialists goes back to the time of the first specialists and such concerns as testing milk ("Whose side are you on, the milk plant's or the farmer's?"). There were battles over tuberculosis, mastitis, and brucellosis—all serious dairy and livestock health problems. Advocating the building of siloes and milk houses sparked controversy ("We never had one before, why do we need one now?") And of course there was a considerable flurry of excitement when Rachel Carson declared that certain pesticides killed eagles and hawks and drifted into places where they didn't belong, including groundwater. In the 1990s, controversies swirled around the bovine growth hormone BST, which enhanced milk production, and genetic engineering of such crops as potatoes, corn, and soybeans. Land use planning was an early issue that Extension agents and specialists faced, and they continue to deal with it as environmentalists, land developers, and farmers often square off against each other.

Entomologist Specialist Walter Gojmerac and his colleague Ellsworth Fisher were caught in the milieu of Rachel Carson's work. Gojmerac wrote: "As with any controversy, just like a pancake, each one has two sides." The angry questions began rolling in about pesticides contaminating food, killing songbirds, and upsetting the ecology of nature. Callers complained about the killing of honeybees when insecticides were sprayed. In the late 1950s and 1960s, Dutch Elm disease swept through the state. Common practice involved spraying trees with DDT to kill the European bark beetle, the culprit that carried the disease from one tree to another. However, DDT killed more than beetles, and the calls came in to County Extension offices—and to Gojmerac.

Gojmerac was also involved with many "ticklish" situations involving food contamination. Here are some examples:

A truckload of Wisconsin milk once arrived in Georgia with insects floating on the top. The Georgia company called the Wisconsin dairy and refused payment. Gojmerac determined that because the truck left Wisconsin in cold mid-February weather, the insects could not have come from Wisconsin.

A food plant received a shipment of new glass jars with insects inside some of them. The food plant accused the supplier of providing contaminated jars. Gojmerac identified the unwanted intruders as grain-feeding insects. He reviewed the trip tickets of the trucking firm and discovered that the truck had previously hauled grain. The trucking firm assumed responsibility for the problem.

The late Claron Burnett, a specialist in agricultural journalism, was often called on to help other specialists prepare visual aids. He recalled the time when overhead projectors were just coming on the scene and educators were beginning to use them. Burnett was asked to make some overhead transparencies for Lenore Landry, clothing specialist, on clothing selection for women. The first batch of transparencies was comprised only of words, including the statement: "Overweight women should select dresses and other garments with vertical stripes or design."

Landry picked up the transparencies and was soon back with a picture to include with the set. It was a drawing of an overweight woman "with a rear that appeared to be about three feet wide," according to Burnett. "Lenore had sketched the woman in slacks with wide vertical stripes, so anyone would not ignore stripes, vertical or horizontal. I didn't know Lenore had such artistic ability. She probably convinced all audiences to pay more attention to diets as well as clothing."

District Directors

E.L. Luther, Wisconsin's first Extension agent, also became the first county agent supervisor on January 1, 1914. His job was to oversee the handful of new agents who had been hired to work mostly in the northern counties of the state. He was to show them the ropes, help them stay connected to each other, and answer their many questions.

Early county agent supervisors arranged for new agents to spend time with experienced agents and helped them learn a variety of teaching approaches. These supervisors used monthly newsletters to keep agents informed about what their peers were doing and what was happening at the College of Agriculture.

J. F. Wojta, was state county agent leader in the 1930s. In his May 15, 1933, monthly newsletter, Wojta wrote: "From the Agronomy Department: Assistance and information will be given on the use of emergency hays, better pastures, and infield inspection of grains, farm tours, [and] field demonstrations concerning weed control . . . help to arrange for demonstration of grain varieties and new crops such as lespedeza, canary grass, hybrid corn, and alfalfa for seed production. Drop a line to

State staff at mid-1970s district meeting. Left to right, Rosemary Stare, James Everts, Curtis Gear, John Woeste.

Crop Specialist G. M. Briggs for further information. From the Soils Department: C. J. Chapman, Specialist in Soils, has completed plans and made arrangements to conduct a pasture demonstration in Milwaukee County on a 10-acre field, which constitutes the entire source of summer feed for a herd of 15 dairy cows. The pasture will be divided with a fence into two halves. One half will be fertilized with pure nitrogen fertilizer and the other a check. The whole herd will be rotated back and forth from fertilized to unfertilized areas. Records will be kept as to pounds of milk produced and number of days the herd grazes on each portion."

Wojta ended his newsletters with bits of philosophical advice:

"Study and serve the people.

"The County Extension worker's word should be as good as his bond if he would have others confide in him. He assumes leadership among those to which the duty takes him.

"Doing one's work is like sowing a seed, if it is not done at the right time, its growth will have a tendency to be forever out of season. Summer will not be long enough to bring to maturity the fruit of delayed action.

"To do work well it requires an enlistment of all powers of application, such as conservation, perseverance, singleness of purpose and other qualities as enter into the composition of a competent man or woman."

In 2000, Cooperative Extension had six district directors: John Preissing (interim), north district; Yvonne Horton, northeast district; Sue Buck, central district; Paul

Brings (interim), southeast district; Mike Perkl, west district; and Dick Pederson, south district. Jose Vasquez was director of urban relations.

As of 2000, district director responsibilities included being " the official representatives between the university and Extension education committees, local government bodies, and public and private organizations. [They are to] provide leadership for selection and retention of county personnel, participate in program development and evaluation, administer district human and fiscal resources, and conduct external relations."[5] The official duties, rather stuffily and bureaucratically stated, were nonetheless extremely important for Cooperative Extension's health and vitality in the counties.

Exactly what does a district director do during a typical week? I asked Sue Buck, director of the central district. "In any given week, district directors can be involved in any of the following: County Extension committee meetings, signing leave statements, travel expense reports, professional development requests, conducting preliminary and final interviews before hiring faculty and staff. Orient new staff. Organize and participate in district meetings. Attend Cooperative Extension administrative committee meetings. Deal with personnel issues (put out fires). Help with website development for computer access. Do civil rights reviews. Participate in state audio conferences from the Dean's ETN meeting to other committee meetings. Attend district resource management team meetings. Provide leadership for Cooperative Extension's standing committees (five at the present time). Do special committee work on endowment campaigns, leadership development, and evaluation."

Much of the work is behind the scenes and confidential, especially work on personnel questions. Although all of the above sounds like serious work, and it is, district directors do things just like most other people. John Preissing, director of the north district, tells the following story about himself:

"I drove out on Interstate 90, on my way to a meeting. As with most district directors, we eat a lot of road food. Although convenient, nutritionists advise us to eat in other ways, for health and safety reasons. I was wearing my suitcoat and tie, with a bottle of pop in my lap, speeding down Interstate 90—at the legal speed limit, of course. I opened my bottle of pop in my lap and the pop shot out of the bottle like a cannon. All the pop from the twenty-ouncer landed back in my lap and on the seat of my car, [where it] seeped into my pants. And was it cold. I just had to sit there and take it, since I was moving down the highway with no place to stop."

Gale VandeBerg remembers fondly his contacts with district directors when he worked as a County Extension agent. "District supervisors, later called district leaders and now district directors, provide invaluable personal counsel to County Extension personnel in addition to their administrative roles."

Ray Pallett was VandeBerg's district supervisor when Gale began work in Outagamie County in 1945. Gale and his wife invited Pallett over to dinner one night, and as they sat visiting in the living room, Pallett explained the new federal retirement system option that had just become available to County Extension agents. The federal retirement program required a five percent salary deduction-and for a short time, agents could pay back to when they were first hired to gain additional benefits. VandeBerg, who had two young children and a third on the way, told Pallett he didn't have the money. The amount needed was $600. "Gale, trust me," Pallett told VandeBerg. "I know what it can amount to. I would advise you to go to the bank, get a $600 loan, and make the payment. Some day you will thank me for that advice."

VandeBerg took out the loan. Years later, when he retired, he saw the value of the loan. But he never had a chance to thank Pallett, who died of cancer a few years after the discussion took place in VandeBerg's living room.

Rosemary Stare was the first female district director. She was hired as an interim district director in 1979. After 65 years of males only in the position, some people with whom she worked couldn't fathom a female district director—and they made their thoughts known.

One of Stare's responsibilities involved working with the Moraine Park Technical Institute in Fond du Lac, serving in a liaison role. Questions were raised about Stare's ability and background for doing this. Donald Peterson, associate dean for Cooperative Extension, sent off a carefully worded, no-nonsense letter to the chairperson of the agri-biotechnology division at Moraine Park. In the letter, Peterson wrote: "While Rosemary does not have the agricultural background and perspective that Ernie (Northeast District Director Ernie Ehrbar) has, she brings to her new responsibilities as district director many years of Extension experience at county, district, and state levels. She has frequently worked with Agricultural Extension personnel on joint programs and has, therefore, a practical insightful grasp of agricultural programming and relationships in particular, and interagency relationships in general. Moreover, she is a person who possesses intelligence, good judgment, and common sense, qualities that transcend all others in our interagency working relationships."[6]

Peterson's letter did the trick. Less than a week later, he received a letter from the individual at Moraine Park who had raised questions about Rosemary. The letter-writer wrote: "As to working with Rosemary Stare, I have absolutely no 'hang-ups' because I think she is definitely a very well qualified and enthusiastic individual. Since meeting her . . . I think it would be a pleasure to work with her, and I will look forward to doing exactly that in the future. Everything that you have described about her I completely agree with."[7] One wonders what went on behind the scenes that week, and the nature of the phone calls that were made. Women have been a part of the district director group ever since. In 2000, two of the six district directors were women.

District directors often did special things for the agents they supervised. Ruth Olson was hired as "agent at large" in Sauk County in 1959, primarily because there was no opening in a county. She worked for a month without a paycheck. She mentioned this to Home Agent Marian Litscher, who in turn talked to Stan Rynearson, county office chairman. Rynearson called District Director Oscar Woelfel and told him about the paycheck problem.

Woelfel arrived in Baraboo the next day, with check in hand. "Someone forgot to put you on the payroll," he explained. Olson didn't know where he got the money, but she could now pay the rent. Woelfel apologized for what had happened and went on his way.

Often in the background until problems bubble to the surface, district directors have long served as a critical link between the county staff and various levels of government and client groups that Extension comes into contact with. In many ways, the directors are Extension's unsung heroes.

CHAPTER 13

NOTABLE PROGRAMS

From its beginnings, Cooperative Extension has worked with communities and individuals on a host of problems and concerns. This chapter contains a sampling of Cooperative Extension programs that have been carried on over a number of years with substantial results.

Environmental Programs

Cooperative Extension has a long history in soil and water conservation education and in the related areas of zoning, land use, watershed management, lakes, and solid waste management.

SOIL AND WATER CONSERVATION

In 1937, federal law authorized creation of soil and water conservation districts in each state. A 1939 amendment authorized county boards to establish county-wide soil and water conservation districts. The county boards' agricultural committees provided leadership and direction for this work. Trempealeau County organized the first such district in Wisconsin in 1938, followed by Crawford and La Crosse Counties in 1939. By 1956, Wisconsin had become the eighteenth state to be fully organized into soil and water conservation districts.

In the late 1940s and early 1950s, Cooperative Extension became heavily involved in soil conservation activities. Extension appointed four area erosion control agents—Ed Baker, Newal Stephenson, Don Neindorf, and Ingwald Hembre. These men assisted counties in developing conservation education programs on erosion control.

In 1954 the federal government passed Public Law 566, the Watershed Protection and Flood Prevention Act. This legislation provided federal money allowing local soil and water conservation districts to sponsor various watershed projects. Several agencies cooperated in implementing these projects, including the Department of Natural Resources, Department of Transportation, Federal Corps of Engineers, Soil Conservation Service, and Cooperative Extension, which was asked to provide educational leadership and organization for erosion control projects. Vernon County was the first to have all of its lands in watersheds.

Lowell Klessig, Extension specialist (center) with representatives of the Wisconsin Federation of Lakes and the Wisconsin Association of Lake Districts

Later laws modified this early, far-reaching 1939 legislation. In 1982, new legislation abolished the existing soil and water conservation districts and transferred responsibility and authority over the districts to county government. Counties were to create land conservation committees to direct soil and water programs.

The state Board of Soil and Water Conservation had been attached to the University of Wisconsin for many years. With the 1982 legislation, the board was moved to the state Department of Agriculture, which directed soil and water conservation programs at the state level. As a result of this action, Cooperative Extension agents had no official responsibilities for soil and water conservation work. Educational programs on soil and water conservation remained important, however, and in some ways became more important as the years passed.[1]

It took some farmers a while to believe that soil erosion was a problem on their farms. Al Francour, La Crosse County agricultural agent, flew farmers over their properties. He could then show the farmer how his neighbors used strip cropping and point out where erosion was occurring. At the time (1951), few farm people had ever ridden in an airplane.

Francour recalled taking two farmers on a ride in a four-seater Piper Cub. To reach the farms, the plane had to climb over the high bluffs along the Mississippi River. "As we approached the bluffs, I suspect we were only a couple hundred feet above them,"

Francour said. "Just as we were on top, the plane hit an air pocket and dropped straight down. I heard a groan from the seats behind us [Francour sat up front with the pilot]. One farmer held his seat belt with both hands. His eyes were wide and he yelled, 'If this things drops any further, I'm getting out.' The remainder of the flight was fine."

WATERSHED PROGRAMS: A CASE STUDY

Eugene Savage, retired county agricultural agent from Jackson County, was heavily involved in the development of the Trout River watershed project, which began in 1956 and was completed in 1962. He also worked with the Beaver Creek watershed project, which started in 1963 but was abandoned as a funded project in the 1970s because of federal budget cutbacks and changes in priorities.

In a comprehensive report on Jackson County's organized watershed associations, Savage explained that the purpose of the associations was to prevent erosion and flooding. The Watershed Protection and Flood Prevention Act (PL 566) was written to assist local associations with watershed work. The report also demonstrated the careful and detailed research necessary to apply for supporting federal funds, and the disappointment that resulted when they weren't forthcoming. The application for funds included a detailed account of the watershed's problems with floodwater and sediment damage, including bridge destruction and erosion of stream banks and farm-lands. Even without federal assistance, many people became aware of watershed problems by working on developing the proposals.[2]

CLEAN SWEEP

In 1989 Pierce County conducted its first household clean sweep program, led by County Extension staff and a group of community leaders. County Agricultural Agent Greg Andrews and Community, Natural Resource, and Economic Development (CNRED) Agent Ed Hass followed a plan they had learned about in Minnesota. They worked with the Department of Natural Resources, Department of Agriculture, Trade and Consumer Protection, state legislators, and local officials to plan and carry out the program. Local support came from the Farm Bureau, Farmers Union, the National Farmers Organization, St. Croix Valley Sierra Club, Pierce-St. Croix Counties League of Women Voters, the College of Agriculture at UW-River Falls, and local agribusi-nesses. On November 3, 1990, the agricultural clean sweep collection program was held at the County Highway Building in Ellsworth. They collected more than 5,000 pounds of unwanted and hazardous agricultural chemicals. A state grant of $26,147 covered the disposal cost. Pierce County Extension Agent Ed Hass believed this was the first coun-ty-wide agricultural clean sweep program in the state.[3]

SOLID WASTE MANAGEMENT

At one time, getting rid of solid waste meant loading it on a wagon, hauling it to a far corner of the farm, and dumping it in a gully—or toting it out to the brushiest part of a woodlot and dumping it. Out of sight, out of mind.

As the years passed, most municipalities developed landfills. In 1984, there were 986 in Wisconsin. New federal and state laws required communities to change how they managed waste materials, including establishing recycling plans and closing most landfills. Only 83 licensed landfills remained in the state in 1992.

These new laws challenged Cooperative Extension agents and specialists to establish educational programs that would assist individuals and communities in complying with the legislation. Extension formed the Wisconsin Extension Solid and Hazardous Waste Education Center (SHWEC) to help County Extension staff obtain the necessary resources. In 1991, SHWEC pollution prevention specialists provided training for County Extension agents on industrial hazardous waste and pollution prevention. In 1992 SHWEC worked with County Extension offices in reaching 300 Wisconsin companies. Center activities included assisting companies with pollution prevention audits, establishing telephone hotlines that provided regulatory information, offering waste reduction training programs, and providing video teleconferences as a means of introducing new technologies and methods.[4]

LAND USE PLANNING

Land use planning has always been a contentious issue in Wisconsin. Many landowners believed they had the right to do with their land what they pleased. Yet everyone is familiar with development that has run amok. Farms eaten up by housing development. Strip malls. Livestock farmers conflicting with new city neighbors who "always wanted a home in the country," and much more.

In 1995 Donald Last, an Extension natural resource policy specialist based at UW-Stevens Point, met with others to form a statewide organization for land use planning. This meeting and further discussions resulted in "1000 Friends of Wisconsin," a group comprised of citizens interested in responsible land use. They helped engineer Wisconsin's "smart growth" land use law, which requires every town, city, and village in Wisconsin to have a land use plan by 2010. As Last said: "The public was far ahead of state political leaders on this issue, and our group was able to tap into and organize public sentiment in order to nudge them forward with action."[5]

Many County Extension agents and Extension specialists have worked on zoning problems over the years. In early 1965 Archie Brovold, Extension agent in Buffalo County, called Marvin Beatty and Doug Yanggen for assistance. Beatty was a soils specialist, while Yanggen was a land use specialist. The problem was potential development on the floodplain of the Mississippi River.

Brovold called several meetings of area citizens to discuss zoning the floodplain and possibly zoning the bluffs and the land just below to allow no residential use. At one meeting, an old farmer agreed with the proposal. He had seen huge boulders crashing down the bluffs.

At another meeting, several developers appeared and objected. They were selling lots along the Mississippi River, on lands that had been designated by the specialists as flood prone. The developers didn't agree with the specialists' conclusions.

On the day when the county board met in April 1965 to vote on the zoning plan, the developers were nowhere to be seen. The same was true of the lots. The river had flooded and forced the closing of Highway 35. The zoning ordinance passed by a large majority.

INLAND LAKE PROGRAM

Until 1968, lake management did not exist in any comprehensive way. As early as the late 1800s, property owners around some lakes had organized into voluntary associations. But state policy makers did not accept direct citizen participation in lake management decisions. They believed that private interests would supersede a statewide concern.

When Cooperative Extension became involved in lake management in 1968, it assumed that local citizens armed with assistance and knowledge could and should make decisions. In 1968 Harold (Bud) Jordahl, Ray Penn, and others said the inland lakes could provide the economic engine for the economically depressed cutover region of the northern lake states. Jordahl helped secure funding from the Upper Great Lakes Regional Commission for a project to demonstrate lake management techniques, and to determine who might implement these techniques. Research concluded that only lake property owners "have enough passion, are close enough to the resource, and [are] numerous enough to take on that challenge."

Steve Born was director of the Inland Lake Demonstration Project. After five years of research, he proposed legislation allowing lake property owners to form lake districts and tax themselves to provide lake protection or rehabilitation. The legislation also provided state cost-sharing for feasibility studies and implementation projects.

Lowell Klessig and Bob Sterrett (later replaced by Ron Hennings and the late George Gibson) were hired as Extension's first lake management specialists. They held hundreds of meetings to explore the ramifications of the new law. A Wisconsin Association of Lake Districts emerged, which later merged with the older Federation of Lakes to form the Wisconsin Association of Lakes (WAL). The Wisconsin lakes partnership now included the Department of Natural Resources, Extension, and the Wisconsin Association of Lakes.

Facing budget problems in 1981, the state legislature cut all funds for lake management, including staff support for DNR and Extension. WAL hired a lobbyist and secured funding out of the gasoline taxes paid by boaters. Not only were grants to lake communities restored, but funds were also obtained for additional DNR and Extension staff.

A youth component was added in subsequent budgets, and in 2000 a quarterly newsletter called *Lake Tides* went to some 20,000 property owners. Local lake management organizations now exist on about 700 lakes in the state.

In the mid-1990s, WAL needed a pool of local people willing to lead county lake associations and serve on the board for WAL. Lowell Klessig, who had served a stint as executive director of the Wisconsin Rural Leadership Program, helped develop a Wisconsin Lake Leaders Institute, which consisted of three seminars. The seminars provided facts about lake management. They also helped instill a passion about caring for Wisconsin's lakes.[6]

WATER QUALITY PROGRAMS

Extension's water quality programs took a variety of forms. A five-year demonstration project near Green Bay sought to reduce runoff in the East River, the Fox River, and Green Bay itself by demonstrating that farmers could reduce their use of commercial fertilizer and pesticides without decreasing crop yields. In other words, farmers could increase profits and also contribute to water quality. Fifty-two farmers used integrated crop management (ICM) techniques on a total of 16,000 acres. The ICM program included soil testing, nitrogen crediting, and crop scouting—approaches that let farmers determine when they needed to add additional fertilizer or pesticides.[7]

Nutrition Education Programs

The first bulletin published by the Cooperative Extension Service was called "Canning for Pleasure and Profit," published on July 15, 1915. One of the first Extension specialists, food specialist Elizabeth Amery, was hired two months later. During World War I, emergency county home economists were hired to, among other things, teach farm women how to replace wheat flour and sugar in their diets, as these items were needed for the war effort.

Through the Depression years and during World War II, Extension taught thousands of women how to prepare and preserve nutritious food for their families. The foods project was always a popular one for 4-H members.

At the earliest homemaker clubs, formed in 1915, members exchanged recipes and looked forward to new ideas about food preparation and preservation and healthy diets. Foods and nutrition education has always been a high priority program for Cooperative Extension. It remains so.

EXPANDED FOOD AND NUTRITION PROGRAM

The July 1970 issue of *Extension Service Review* included an article on the Expanded Food and Nutrition Program (EFNEP). "The Expanded Food and Nutrition Education Program took Extension back to its beginning by giving knowledge to those who needed it and helping them use it to manage their resources for a better life. Extension picked up a neglected audience and brought it into the mainstream of life . . . the overall objective of the Expanded Food and Nutrition Program—to take another neglected audience and give it the knowledge, confidence and ability to step into the mainstream of life—was fulfilled."[8]

An expanded food and nutrition program began in 1968.

Through EFNEP, Extension reached out to low-income persons. The first program in Wisconsin began in Jackson County in 1968; by 1978, 13 counties were participating. EFNEP hired program assistants, many of whom represented the people they served, to help with the program. It was funded by the U.S. Department of Agriculture and administered by Cooperative Extension. County Extension home economists provided on-the-job training and supervised program assistants who taught nutrition and budgeting to low-income homemakers and youth. The program assistants lived in the communities where they worked. In 1988, 41 program assistants taught approximately 1,800 homemakers and 2,100 young people. In that year, EFNEP programs were available in 20 Wisconsin counties, with the majority of the participants in southeastern Wisconsin.

The family profile for EFNEP participants revealed the following:

    *79 percent had annual incomes below the poverty level;

    *71 percent received food stamps;

    *70 percent were enrolled in the federal supplemental food program for women, infants, and children at nutritional risk (WIC);

    *59 percent had children under six years of age;

    *43 percent of the families were minorities.[9]

Wisconsin Nutrition Education Program

Nutrition education programming expanded in 1988, when the Brown County Extension office received a matching grant of $8,300 from the federal food stamp program to target high-risk people and food stamp recipients by providing them with basic nutrition information. Marilyn Herman, Brown County Extension home economist, supervised the program. It was a cooperative endeavor between county and state level Extension and the Wisconsin Department of Health and Family Services' Bureau of Economic Assistance, which administered the food stamp program. Ten-minute topics were prepared for continuous demonstrations (six per hour) in the waiting rooms of the food stamp office, homeless shelters, Salvation Army, Domestic Violence Center, YMCA, commodity food program, Hmong Community Center and the community clinic.[10]

In 1999, 37 percent of the participants were families with young children; 40 percent were school age youth; 15 percent were older adults; and six percent were single adults between the ages of 18 and 65. Nine percent of the participants were African American, six percent Hispanic, five percent Asian, four percent Native American, and the remainder were white.[11]

The program was designed to help participants make food choices consistent with the dietary guidelines for Americans and the food guide pyramid; manage their food resources and use thrifty shopping practices for nutritious foods; and use safe handling, preparation, and storage practices.[12]

In 2000, 38 county-level projects existed, with several programs serving more than one county. In all, 58 counties have been involved. This nutrition education program was a partnership between the Food and Nutrition Service of the United States Department of Agriculture, the Wisconsin Department of Workforce Development, and Cooperative Extension. County Extension offices employed nutrition educators who worked closely with county family living professionals and state specialist advisors. As in the EFNEP program, nutrition educators were often residents of the communities where they taught.

Nutrition educators used a variety of teaching approaches, including skits, educational games, educational displays, and sessions in classrooms at local elementary schools.

Homemaker Organization

Cooking schools started in 1892 and were offered through 1907 as a part of farmers' institutes held around the state. The Department of Home Economics, then operating within the College of Letters and Science, offered a ten-day housekeepers conference for wives and daughters of farmers who attended the Madison farmers' course. But it was a long trip to Madison, and if a husband came for the farmers' course, someone generally had to stay home and do the chores. As a result, attendance by more than one family member often presented difficulties.

Rosemary Thornton

Circular 4H 3   (Revised June 1940)   December, 1936

Clothing
CLUB **4H** WORK

Geneva Amundson

Project I

Let's begin with these which we can make with ease

The girl who chooses clothing is taking an interest in a project which will always be helpful to her. The clothing requirements are planned so that a girl not only learns clothing construction, but also the principles of good design. Since it is true that a well dressed girl gains poise and confidence in herself, it is important that she becomes conscious of her appearance early in life.

We are going to have fun along with our work in our clothing project this first year. And why shouldn't we since our requirements are in line with what we 4-H girls think about—namely, how to make ourselves more attractive? Why shouldn't we be concerned with our appearance when appropriate dress, a knowledge of color, line and design are so important in a modern girl's thinking.

The requirements for this year are listed in the projects on page 2. This circular is merely an outline of the requirements. Information on, use of sewing machine, selecting patterns, cutting and fitting, choice of material and construction processes are given in the Clothing Handbook. Let's complete every leaf of the clover and be an achievement member by:

1. Making the things listed and carrying on the work according to directions;

2. Filling out the clothing record book completely including story, grooming score card, health page, summary and proper signatures;

3. Making a public exhibit; and

4. Attending and participating in the club meetings.

Extension Service of the College of Agriculture
The University of Wisconsin, Madison

4-H clothing bulletin, 1936

State Homemakers Chorus, Green Lake, 1953

After the Smith Lever Act passed in 1914, the College of Agriculture began sending home economics specialists out to the counties, where they offered educational programs for farm women. By 1915, women were encouraged to organize into smaller groups. Each group sent two representatives to a training meeting, where they received instruction from a home economics Extension specialist. These were the first homemaker groups in Wisconsin, and there were hundreds of them. Nellie Kedzie Jones, an early state home economics leader, reportedly organized 690 homemaker clubs in 43 counties in 1932 alone.[13]

In February 1939, during Farm and Home Week in Madison, homemaker representatives discussed organizing a state home demonstration council. The purpose of the council was to: "1) provide representatives of rural women at important state meetings and on important state committees concerned with problems which affect homes and families and rural communities; 2) develop an awareness of national and international interests and needs; 3) develop leadership abilities of rural women; and 4) facilitate statewide acquaintance of rural women."[14] In 1995, the Wisconsin Extension

Homemaker Organization changed its name to Wisconsin Association for Home and Community Education.

For many years, Extension agents assisted homemaker clubs by providing—often with specialist assistance—leader training programs for representatives from the clubs, essentially following the system started in 1915. As counties added home economics agents, these agents assumed major responsibility for working with homemaker clubs.

As Extension family living programs broadened and added new client groups, County Extension agents had less time to work with homemaker clubs and their leaders, but the homemaker groups continued nonetheless. Winnie Joos, 2000 state HCE president, wrote: "Family lifestyles and communication have changed since the beginning of our organization. Family values were important in the lives of our families and through leadership skills that were available gave us challenges to extend our education in many different areas. Leader meetings were of such value to people in the rural communities. [The organization] provided tremendous friendships, a lot of camaraderie, also learning and enrichment programs along the way. Looking back over the years we were doing more of the 'how-to' programs and today we are doing more 'why.' Programs have changed. We are altogether a different kind of organization than when we first [began]. We are interested in the communities in which we live—ways of making them better by providing educational opportunities for women to grow and become better leaders in their communities. When the organization was first formed, it was mostly rural, [but] now it has spread to the urban areas."[15]

Some HCE-sponsored community projects include helping Wisconsin's sister state, Nicaragua. This program, called Wisconsin Nicaragua Partners of the Americas, Inc., began in the early 1980s. Homemaker members collect sewing materials, including sewing machines, which are regularly shipped to some 66 sewing centers in Nicaragua. The sewing centers provide opportunities for women to learn skills that will provide income while they remain in their homes and communities. The homemaker organization has also collaborated with Wisconsin Public Television to promote its "First Book" program for pre-school children.

The homemaker organization has made a tremendous contribution to the lives of Wisconsin's women. For years, rural women's lives were difficult and lonely. Homemaker clubs helped them learn skills to make their work easier and also provided a social outlet. By the 1960s, many suburban and urban women were also forming homemaker clubs. They realized they could also benefit from the university's up-to-date information on everything from clothing care and food safety to understanding infants and caring for the elderly. Along the way, they learned leadership and teaching skills as they took turns attending training meetings and bringing back information to their local clubs.

Leadership Development

Very early in its history, Cooperative Extension recognized the importance of developing leadership. Before there was a formal Extension service, when agricultural professors climbed on a train and met with farmers at stops throughout the state, local agricultural leaders were an important part of the process. These local leaders often weren't even known to the professors who depended on them to try new ideas. Long after the professors returned to Madison, they heard from farmers who had planted a new grain variety, tried a new cow feeding approach, or put up a new silo. These farmers were not called leaders, but their neighbors usually followed their example. "If it works for Emil, then we'll try it" was a typical sentiment. Much later, rural sociologists began labeling individuals as farmer leaders, innovators, and early adopters.

Home Economics Leaders

Before counties hired home economists, specialists traveled to a county and met with key leaders who were members of local homemaker clubs. These key leaders returned to their clubs and shared the information they received with the other members in homemaker clubs throughout the state.

This strategy was a way of assisting professional Extension employees, but it also served to develop a cadre of volunteer teachers throughout the state. The specialists,

```
            DAIRY SCHOOL FOR FARM WOMEN

                   P R O G R A M                                DAIRY SCHOOL FOR FARM WOMEN

Friday, October 15          Friday, October 22
                                                         Friday, Oct. 15 & Friday, Oct. 22, has
10:00-10:15  Program plans & County   10:00-10:45  Your role in the partner-   been set for the Buffalo County Dairy
             dairy information                      ship                       School for Farm Women.
             Archie Brovold                         Diane M. Johnson
             Buffalo County                         Buffalo County             Women are an indispensible part of
             Agricultural Agent                     Extension Home Economist    most dairy farm operations & they par-
                                                                                ticipate in many important farm deci-
10:15-10:45  Dairy outlook & related  10:45-11:45  Wisconsin USDA sire         sions. This two-day school will help
             issues                                 selection guide             farm women with such tasks as raising
             Dr. Robert Cropp, Extension            Dr. Anton Sendelbach, Extension  calves, keeping the herd healthy,
             Ag Economist, UW-Platteville           Dairyman, UW-Madison        keeping useful records, maintaining
                                                                                production & quality, & developing
10:45-11:45  Why have milk cows?      11:45-12:45  Noon Lunch                  sound breeding programs.
             What to expect from DHIA re-
             cords                     12:45- 1:15  Cleaning milking equip-     The meeting will be held at the River
             Dr. Clarence Olson, Extension          ment                        Road Inn on Highway 35 between Alma &
             Dairyman, UW-Madison                   Dr. Robert Bradley, Extension  Cochrane from 10:00 AM to 3:00 PM. The
                                                    Food Scientist, UW-Madison  enrollment fee of $7.00 covers program
11:45-12:45  Noon Lunch                                                         materials & both noon lunches, inclu-
                                       1:15- 2:00  Milk quality tests run by    ding tip.
12:45- 1:00  How we test your milk                 your plant
             Area DHIA Technicial                   Dr. Robert Bradley          Register before October 8th at the
                                                                                University Extension Office, Court-
1:00- 1:30   Herd health & simple      2:00- 2:30  Put it all together for      house Annex, Alma, Wisconsin 54610.
             medication                             better farming              If you have any questions, contact
             Dr. John Anderson, Extension           Dr. Clarence Olson          Archie Brovold or Diane Johnson,
             Veterinarian, UW-Madison                                           University Extension, Courthouse Annex,
                                       2:30- 3:00  Graduation & wind-up         Alma, Wisconsin 54610 or phone: (608)
1:30- 2:30   Study & discussion of                 Archie Brovold              685-4560.
             problems on keeping calves             Diane Johnson
             healthy                                Buffalo County Extension Staff
             Dr. John Anderson

2:30- 3:00   Guides for feeding &
             using records
             Dr. Clarence Olson
```

The dairy school for farm women was a popular program in the 1970s. Shown is a program schedule for a 1976 workshop conducted in Buffalo County.

and later the county home economists (now called family living agents), provided new information to volunteer leaders, but they also helped the volunteers learn teaching approaches, how to do demonstrations, and how to prepare various teaching aids. Specialists and Extension home economists modeled teaching techniques that volunteer leaders could emulate in their presentations to local homemaker clubs. Many of these volunteers became excellent teachers.

4-H LEADERS

The 4-H program depended on volunteer leaders for its success. A local 4-H club was directed by a volunteer leader, who might be assisted by several project leaders—persons willing to help youngsters with specific projects such as dairy, woodworking, sewing, foods, and so on. Many 4-H clubs also had activity leaders who helped with music, drama, public speaking, and related 4-H activities.

As was the case for women's programs, 4-H volunteer leaders met occasionally for leader training, to be updated on project subject matter, and to keep abreast of upcoming 4-H events such as county speaking contests, fairs, demonstration contests, 4-H camps, and the like.

After World War II, the number of 4-H leaders in Wisconsin increased greatly.

Many new Extension agents were hired, and the 4-H program received more attention. New 4-H projects emerged, such as horses, photography, and several others, and the need for volunteer leaders in turn increased.

Extension hired several specialists who were to work with 4-H as a major emphasis in such areas as woodworking, dairy, the arts, clothing, and foods. These specialists developed teaching aids such as slide and audiotape sets and attractive 4-H bulletins, and they often helped conduct leader training meetings in the counties.

In the early 1960s Glen Barquest, an agricultural engineer and former County Extension agent, helped develop the key leader idea. He suggested that each county should recruit someone knowledgeable about a project and experienced as a volunteer leader—an individual capable of helping new project leaders get started. In some counties, the key leader title was given to volunteers who were county-wide leaders for horse, dog, tractor, or cat projects.

When Henry Ahlgren became associate director of Cooperative Extension in 1952, he worked to elevate the county 4-H agent position to a career level, upgrading it from its former assistant county agent role. With appropriate rewards and recognition, 4-H agents began staying longer and were able to develop long-term volunteer leader recruiting and training programs.

In the 1970s and early 1980s, Extension began promoting the idea that 4-H volunteer leaders could assume management roles. These leaders were asked to help plan, organize, and conduct 4-H events at county, district, and state levels. These events included fairs, shows, revues, sales, fund-raisers, exchanges, leader forums, and meetings of the state 4-H Congress. Program management also included helping Extension with literature distribution, promotions, awards and recognition, county leader associations, and serving on district and state leadership councils.

In 1985 the W. K. Kellogg Foundation provided funds to 12 states to increase and improve 4-H volunteer leadership programs. Wisconsin received $86,000 for the first year of the five-year project. Part of the project included research to determine what volunteer 4-H leaders were doing beyond working with local 4-H clubs. In 1985, some 13,500 volunteer 4-H leaders served in program management roles. Extension developed several videotapes intended to encourage volunteer leaders to accept program management roles.[16]

LOCAL COMMUNITY LEADERSHIP DEVELOPMENT

Several Wisconsin counties sponsored local leadership development efforts for emerging community leaders. The city of Merrill in Lincoln County was an example. Local leaders from education, health, agriculture, business, and industry met with volunteers for several sessions to learn about leadership strategies, and to learn more about their own community and where it was headed. The local chamber of commerce worked with the County Extension office in conducting the program.

HOW TO COOPERATE IN HOME MAKING

The American housewife can no longer remain apart from world affairs. Today, every garment she buys and every meal she cooks has some bearing on international markets and relations. The home of today must face new and difficult problems. What they are and how the housewife may meet them—from the standpoint of both economy and of well-being for the family—are suggested in this short course.

How to reduce the cost of products in the home by the greater use of cooperative stores, laundries, and kitchens figures in the short course as a possible solution of the home problems.

How the wiser use of public markets and wider use of parcels post in direct buying from the producer may be an aid will be discussed.

Efficient and scientific planning of meals are considered as factors which may aid in reducing the cost of home-keeping.

The possibility of reducing labor in the farm home will be demonstrated with labor-saving equipment and power machinery. Intelligent reference to saving time for living and playing with the children will be emphasized.

Cutting the cost of clothing by using short-cut methods in making new garments, and simple renovation and dyeing in preserving the old, will be the subject of several demonstrations.

The value to the state of maintaining health, especially that of children in the pre-school age, is emphasized in lectures and demonstrations. These deal with the underlying principles of child feeding and the practical importance of the hot school lunch—in city and in rural schools—and of feeding clinics. In connection with this subject we are very fortunate in securing the services of Miss Amy L. Daniels of the Child Welfare Research Station of Iowa.

Room and board may be secured near the University at reasonable rates.

Upon reaching Madison, take a Wingra Park street car and come directly to the College of Agriculture.

For further particulars address:

MISS ABBY L. MARLATT,
Director Course in Home Economics,
University of Wisconsin, Madison, Wis.

WOMEN'S SHORT COURSE

Tuesday, February 1

RELATION OF FARM AND HOUSE TO WORLD MARKET NEEDS

Morning
9:00 Registration   Room 18, Home Economics Building
10:00 Greeting and Plan of Work
            MRS. NELLIE KEDZIE JONES
11:00 The World's Food Supply DR. ALONZO E. TAYLOR
            University of Pennsylvania
            Auditorium, Agricultural Hall
Afternoon—Auditorium, Chemistry Building
2:00 The World's Cereal Market—
            Woman's Share in Wise Use of Cereals in
            the Diet—A demonstration on meals
            showing "Breads as 50% of the Diet"
                MISS A. L. MARLATT
                MISS ELIZABETH MILLER
3:00 Use of Wisconsin Products as an Aid in
            Decreasing Costs
            An exhibition of "Made in Wisconsin
            Products"   MRS. NELLIE KEDZIE JONES
                MRS. EDNA D. WALKER
3:45 Relation of Canning to World Market
            Supply   MISS DOROTHY ROBERTS
4:30 Play Hour in Gymnasium—Lathrop Hall
                PHYSICAL EDUCATION STAFF
Night
8:00 The World's Buying Power
                DR. ALONZO E. TAYLOR
                Auditorium, Agricultural Hall

Wednesday, February 2
HOW TO REDUCE THE COSTS OF SUPPLIES
Morning—Room 18, Home Economics Building
9:00 How to Get the Most Food Value for Your
            Money
A marketing lesson   MISS WINIFRED L. NEUBBAUM

Women's short course emphasized the world market, 1921.

WISCONSIN RURAL LEADERSHIP PROGRAM

In 1980 Leo Walsh, then dean of the College of Agricultural and Life Sciences, was invited with others to attend an informal meeting in Spokane, Washington, conducted by the W.K. Kellogg Foundation. The meeting offered information about Kellogg-sponsored leadership programs in Michigan, Washington, Montana, California, and Pennsylvania. On January 9, 1981, the Agricultural and Natural Resource Consortium of the UW system approved writing a proposal for a Wisconsin rural leadership program. Al Beaver, UW system administrator at the time, chaired the meeting. Gale VandeBerg, director of Cooperative Extension, was asked to contact faculty and further develop the idea and the proposal for Kellogg. UW-Extension was to coordinate and administer the project. Richard Barrows, professor of agricultural economics and an Extension specialist, agreed to contact state leaders and develop the proposal. Barrows, who had worked with farmland preservation and had many statewide contacts, was a key person in getting the program off the ground.

After several meetings in 1982 and 1983, a proposal was submitted to the W. K. Kellogg Foundation. In September 1983, a board of directors was officially organized, which then approved a curriculum proposal and a fund-raising strategy to meet cost sharing requirements. Richard Barrows served as executive director. Group I participants were selected in April 1984 and attended their first seminar in July of the same year.

The program went beyond agriculture. Board members and participants came from tourism, agriculture, business, government, and health. There were urban participants, Native Americans, blacks, and Hispanics. It was designed primarily for women and men who were in the early part of their careers, but past participants have ranged from 21 to 55 years old. The purpose was to develop leaders with broad perspectives who could serve their communities. Past participants have served on school boards, town boards, county boards, the state legislature, farm organization boards, and national and international committees and organizations. By 2000, 230 Wisconsin leaders had participated in the program.[17]

According to Gerald Campbell, who has been associated with the program for many years, key aspects included the following:

- UW faculty served as executive director for two-year blocks of time.
- A UW faculty member chaired the planning committees for each seminar conducted.
- The curriculum committee included lay and university people who shaped the two-year curricula.
- Participants in the leadership program were encouraged to obtain community support for their program costs.[18]

James Massey, general manager and editor of *The Country Today*, wrote: "From 1990 to 1992, I was a participant in the Wisconsin Rural Leadership Program. It was an experience like none I've had before or since. During the two years, the 30 of us in our class participated in seminars on a variety of topics, from economic development to health care to education. We traveled to Washington, D.C., California, and Brazil, besides participating in eight in-state seminars. We looked at issues from all sides and learned from some of the foremost experts in the field we were addressing. I would guess there's no other program in Wisconsin that compares in terms of breadth and information disseminated. I made some lasting friendships during my two years in the program and have valuable contacts that I have used many times since. I believe I gained the leadership skills I needed to become the editor and general manager of a statewide farm newspaper."[19]

International travel was a part of each leadership group's experience. Unplanned things often happened on such trips. Al Anderson served as executive director for rural leadership groups seven and eight. He later worked with the Center for Community Economic Development. In April 2000, the leadership group traveled to Turkey. The on-site leader there was Ayse Somersan, who had been dean of Cooperative Extension and was from Turkey.

As the group was traveling on a long bus trip from one city to another, someone on the bus asked if they would have a chance to meet with "ordinary" country folks. They had been talking with politicians, university professors, and civic leaders.

"We were high up in the mountains, going through a pass on our way to the second city," Anderson related. "Every so often, we'd pass through a mountain village. In one of these villages, population about 300, Somersan asked the bus driver to pull over." People on the bus watched as Somersan talked with a woman who was carrying a bundle of firewood. Soon Somersan motioned for everyone to get off the bus. The Turkish woman had invited all 38 of them in for tea.

Somersan had explained that many in her group were farmers and would like to see some of the agriculture in the area. The Turkish woman said they didn't look like farmers. Somersan told the group this and one of the fellows, a dairy farmer from near Monticello, walked up to the woman and held out his hands, palms up. She looked at his hands, and a big grin spread across her face. Then she held her hands out to him. The group spent about half an hour in the village. They saw the farm animals. They met the village president, who insisted the group stay for dinner, which would include a freshly slaughtered sheep.

The village president was disappointed when they didn't stay to eat. As they climbed back on the bus, another woman came rushing out of her house with five loaves of bread for the group to take with them.[20]

Funding for the Wisconsin Rural Leadership Program came from a long-term endowment that the board raised, support from UW campuses, plus private and participant contributions. Later in the program's history, support also included a line item budget allocation from the state.

4-H Camping

Some might question 4-H camping as a notable program, but those youngsters who had an opportunity to spend a few days at a 4-H camp had an experience that they never forgot.

The first 4-H camp in southwest Wisconsin was held in 1940, at Wyalusing State Park in Grant County. Sixty 4-H members from Grant and Crawford County attended. Wakelin McNeel and Grace Rowntree from the state office assisted the county agents with the camp program.

By 1947, 24 counties held camps for club members. Seven counties—Adams, Burnett, Langlade, Marinette, Oconto, Polk, and Rusk—had established their own 4-H camps. The other 17 counties used the facilities of these county camps or rented camps from churches, Boy Scouts, or the YMCA. In 1947, five district camps were held for older 4-H members, officers, and junior and adult learners from every county in the state. These were primarily leadership training camps.[21]

Camps were also conducted around specific topics. For example, conservation camps were regularly held at a site in Manitowoc County and at the Trees for Tomorrow camp in Northern Wisconsin.

The camps were the first trip away from home for many 4-H members. They slept in a bunk house (several 4-H camps had been former Civilian Conservation Camps), ate in a mess hall, and sat around a campfire singing songs and roasting marshmallows. Many 4-H members had heard about the good times Boy Scouts and Girl Scouts had at camps. Now they had an opportunity to experience something similar.

One feature of 4-H camps, making them different from many other youth camps, was that boys and girls camped together. They slept in different dorms, of course, but all ate together and participated in the same activities. In addition to planned educational programs, 4-H camps provided opportunities for isolated farm kids to develop social skills. Parents of 4-H campers served as camp counselors, along with older 4-H members.

Many of the camping stories are memorable—especially those shared by 4-H and home economics agents, who usually served as camp directors. When I was 4-H agent in Green Lake County, we camped at Patrick's Lake in Adams County. It was a former CCC camp best described as primitive, but it offered a nice view of the lake. One of my challenges as camp director was maintaining water safety. We had a firm set of rules—no child was to go out beyond a certain point in the lake. I always sat in a boat during swimming time, prepared to act in any emergency.

We had one swimming session in the morning and another in the afternoon. During one session, I was called away from my place in the boat to respond to a minor emergency on shore. When I returned to my appointed vigil, I spotted a young man way beyond the well-defined limits. His name was Clyde, if I remember correctly.

I immediately began calling for him to swim back to safer waters. But he remained where he was, with a smile on his face. I surmised that he must be treading water and looking forward to a confrontation with a 4-H Agent. I rowed out to him.

"What are you doing way out here?" I said to him in exasperation.

"Oh, nothing much," he replied.

"Well, climb in the boat," I ordered.

"Why?" he said, a bigger smile spreading across his face.

"Because you'll drown."

"Hardly. I'm standing on the bottom," he replied. He then proceeded to walk to shore. It had been a dry year, and much of Patrick Lake was no deeper than five feet.

Camp Upham Woods is the state 4-H Camp, located north of Wisconsin Dells on the Wisconsin River. The property encompasses more than 300 acres, including 200-acre Black Hawk Island. It is situated on the pre-glacial channel of the river, which has little traffic. Mrs. Caroline V. Hughes and Mrs. Carl Henry Davis, daughters of Horace and Mary Greene Upham, deeded the land to the University of Wisconsin in 1941 in memory of their parents. The Upham family had owned the land for many years.

The deed stipulated the following: "The lands are to be used as an outdoor laboratory and camp for youth, such as 4-H Clubs and other people cooperating with the University of Wisconsin in the advancement of conservation, of agriculture, or rural culture—to stimulate in Wisconsin's youth an appreciation for nature and all things natural."[22]

Donald Schink was 4-H agent in Adams County in 1951 and 1952. He remembered camping there before any buildings were constructed. Campers slept in tents pitched on permanent wood bases in an area near the softball field.

In 1952, 17 different groups camped at Upham Woods, and Wakelin McNeil served as the first Upham Woods director. By 1952 more than 1,500 4-H clubs from all parts of Wisconsin had contributed to the development of Upham Woods, including the construction of several cabins and a lodge.[23]

When Marvin Hansen became director, a campfire burned near the lodge constantly. Here, young and old alike took a break from camp activities to talk with one or two others, or just to watch the flames and see the smoke rise above the pine trees.

In 2000, Upham Woods was a popular camping place for school and 4-H groups and for many others who used its well-developed facilities.

Building Cooperatives in Rural Wisconsin

From Cooperative Extension's early days, agents and specialists spent many hours helping farmers organize cooperatives. They provided encouragement, training, and leadership, and often served as advisors and officers to fledgling cooperative organizations.

The emergence of Wisconsin's cooperatives has gone through several stages. The years from 1910 to 1930 were a time of development and organization. Many small, local cooperatives emerged during these years, including cheese factory co-ops, creamery co-ops, community dairy herd improvement associations (DHIAs), the Central Livestock Association, Equity, Wisconsin Wool Growers, and more.

Between 1930 and 1945, more cooperatives emerged, including the Production Credit Association (farm credit), land banks, Lake-to-Lake (dairy cooperative), Consolidated Badger, Badger Breeders, several small artificial breeding cooperatives (AIs), grain elevators, supply cooperatives, rural electric cooperatives, Dairyland Power, and more.

County Extension agents worked long and hard helping to organize local electric cooperatives. In a 1938 report, the Dairyland Power Company included the following quote from the Eau Claire *Leader* newspaper: "To the wonderful jacks-of-all-trades, the county agricultural agents. Nearly every rural electrification project in the state has had the whole-hearted and splendid assistance and cooperation of a county agent."

The postwar years from 1945 to 1955 were a time of reactivation after the war. They were also years of reorganization and growth. Emerging and growing cooperatives included Associated Milk Producers (AMPI), Land O' Lakes, FS-Growmark, Wisconsin Dairies, and more.

Between 1955 and 1970, a number of livestock and marketing cooperatives were organized. During these years lamb pools, feeder cattle sales, the Wisconsin Feeder Pig Cooperative, the Horse Council, American Feeder Pig, Tel-A-Auctions, and dairy beef sales cooperatives emerged.

Mergers and consolidations marked the years from 1970 to 1990. The mergers included Morning Glory and Associated Milk Producers; Wisconsin Dairies and Hiawatha; A G Cooperative and Golden Plump; Production Credit Association and Land Banks; farm supply cooperatives; Land O' Lakes and Lake to Lake (dairy cooperatives). Newly formed were Cooperative Resources International and the Wisconsin Federation of Cooperatives.

Wisconsin had become a national leader in the cooperative movement by the 1950s. There were cooperative cheese factories, milk plants, farm supply stores, feed mills, dairy herd improvement co-ops, telephone and electric co-ops, shipping and marketing associations, artificial breeding cooperatives, rural insurance and production credit associations. A cooperative hospital was organized in Wild Rose in the 1940s.

As the years passed, smaller cooperatives joined to form statewide and regional organizations like Land O' Lakes, Foremost Dairy, CENEX, Growmark, Equity, Farm Credit Banks, MSI Insurance, Wisconsin Federation of Cooperatives, Accelerated Genetics, and many more. Extension specialists including Truman Graf, Frank Groves, Jim Crowley, Bob Cropp, and Dick Vilstrup were often called on to assist with these mergers and consolidations. Many tense meetings were held to convince members of the need to close outdated facilities and consolidate services. Mergers required the support of two-thirds of the members, and often meant loss of identity and proximity to local facilities.

Extension agents were often recruited to build and organize cooperatives, and some were even hired as managers. Examples included Truman Torgerson (Lake to Lake), Ken Wallin (Badger Breeders), Lyle Lamphere (Central Livestock Association), and Norbert Brandt (Midwest Livestock and American Feeder Pig Cooperative).

In Wisconsin's livestock industry alone, Extension agents and specialists helped organize 15 Wisconsin Equity and Central Livestock lamb pools throughout the state, the Great Lakes Wool Growers, eight Wisconsin feeder cattle cooperatives, the Wisconsin Feeder Pig Cooperative, Wisconsin Horse Council, Wisconsin Pork Producers, Wisconsin Cattlemen's Association, Wisconsin Beef Council, Wisconsin Sheep Breeders, Wisconsin Agribusiness Council, and many dairy, beef, and hog breed associations.

In 1963 Extension specialists Frank Groves, Vernon Schneider, and Dick Vilstrup worked with agents in 20 counties to develop the first intensive educational programs for cooperative directors in the nation. The specialists gained the close cooperation of the Wisconsin Council of Agricultural Cooperatives and the Wisconsin Association of Cooperatives. Later these two groups merged into the Wisconsin Federation of Cooperatives (WFC). Over 5,000 directors of Wisconsin's marketing, supply, and service cooperatives were involved in the training programs. On average, the cooperative directors were involved in five to seven cooperatives and often served on school, town, church, and county boards. These were truly community leaders, and through the training program, Extension had direct contacts with them.

Gary Rohde, John Cottingham, Bob Cropp, and Tom Schomisch later joined the training team of Groves, Vilstrup, and Schneider. Working with County Extension agents and the WFC, these specialists developed a director certification program, designed youth and young leadership seminars, organized board chairmen and presidents' conferences, and helped organize the Cooperative Development Council. During this time, the UW Center for Cooperatives was formed. In 2000, Bob Cropp served as director.

The cooperative leadership training techniques developed by these Extension specialists have been recognized nationally. The program received the USDA Extension Superior Service Award in 1979, and Dick Vilstrup was inducted into the National Cooperative Hall of Fame in 1998. These training techniques have been adopted nationwide and in Canada, Europe, and Central America.[24]

Milk Production Testing

As dairy farming took hold in the 1870s and 1880s, most people believed that 100 pounds of milk from one cow would make as much butter or cheese as 100 pounds from another cow. Everyone focused on the amount of milk that a cow produced, not the butterfat content of the milk.

About the only way to measure butterfat content in the 1880s was with a complicated and expensive laboratory analysis that no farmer, cheese plant, or creamery could afford. Stephen Moulton Babcock changed all that. He came to the College of Agriculture in 1888. Dean Henry asked him to look for a method to measure the fat content of milk. Like many researchers before him, Babcock tried many approaches. Some worked, but most didn't. One method Babcock tried worked well; however, the test from one cow in the college's herd, Sylvia, did not check out. Sylvia was a Jersey. Babcock refused to promote this test until it would work for every cow in the college's herd—including Sylvia.

Babcock discovered that when he added concentrated sulfuric acid to milk, all the fat in the milk could be recovered. The acid, in solution with non-fat solids, generated heat that melted the fat and allowed it to rise to the surface. With a moderate amount of centrifugal force, the fat collected in the neck of a graduated test bottle, so the percentage of butterfat could be readily seen. The year was 1890. From that time forward, it was possible to accurately measure the butterfat content of milk, even from Jersey cows that usually produced more butterfat than Holsteins and some other breeds.

Before the Babcock test, dairy plants had no easy way of measuring the fat content of milk and no uniform way of paying farmers for their milk. Babcock, an unassuming researcher, never patented his invention. Soon his milk test was used widely.[25]

With a milk test available, it seemed likely that farmers would want to have their cows tested—if for no other reason than doing so would allow them to cull the low producers. But that was not generally the case. It took years before farmers accepted milk testing as a management tool, even though milk plants had long used the

Babcock test to determine equitable payments to farmers.

The breeders of purebred dairy cattle showed greater interest in milk testing, because production records were then a requirement for registry of their cows. The annual experiment station report for 1908 included this summary: "The Extension work in testing officially the milk production of purebred dairy stock continues to increase year by year under Professor F. W. Woll's direction. The total number of tests conducted on all kinds and breeds being 1,290 on 421 cows. At present 12 supervisors are employed under Civil Service rules, the breeders whose cows are tested pay the expenses connected with the same."

Later in the report one reads: "There is much need that the farmers interested in general dairying take up the work of testing their cows to ascertain whether or not they are profitable. This work can be better accomplished by the organization of cow testing associations. As this line of Extension effort is being pushed at the present time by the Wisconsin Dairymen's Association, there is not the necessity for the College developing the same, but the need of such work is yet very great throughout many portions of the state."[26]

Dairy Herd Improvement (DHI) organizations began with 31 herds in Michigan in 1906. A few months later, a DHI organization began in Fond du Lac County in Wisconsin. The purpose of DHI, later organized by county agricultural agents, was threefold: to help cull poor producers; to feed more correctly; and to increase potential production through better breeding and selection of herd replacements. An important aim of DHI was to increase genetic potential and rid Wisconsin farms of "scrub sires."

By 1931, annual bull sales included bulls from dams with known records of performance. "In Winnebago County the [DHI] association . . . conducted three bull sales . . . of the 46 bulls sold, 39 were from tested dams who produced 400 pounds of butterfat or more a year.[27] In 1931, Wisconsin had 102 Dairy Herd Improvement Associations with 2,437 members testing 48,879 cows.[28]

Due to the Depression, farmers faced low prices for their products. Extension agents tried to show farmers how milk testing could make or break a dairy business. A Wood County study conducted in 1931 and 1932 confirmed the value of testing. On farms where cows averaged under 250 pounds of butterfat a year, milk cost $1.92 a hundred to produce. On farms where cows averaged over 300 pounds of butterfat a year, the cost of production was $1.45 per hundred pounds.

Nevertheless, the Depression took its toll on milk testing. By 1934, the number of cow testing associations had declined to 67, even though the number of milk cows in the state had increased by about 13 percent.[29]

George O'Connor, county agricultural agent for Crawford County, said the following about Dairy Herd Improvement in a 1938 report: "The Dairy Herd Improvement Association was reorganized with full membership and has been operating in fine shape under John Huebsch, the field man. It is hoped that by another year, one or more new associations will be organized and operating. It is felt that in order to make the best of our crops that are fed to dairy cows, and to increase the efficiency of the dairy herd, we must have records on each cow. The records are a guide in feeding, they are the determining factor in culling out a herd, and they are very essential as an index to pick out cows that one wants to raise heifer calves from, and lastly over a period of years, the value of a sire is determined."[30]

By the 1960s, dairy records had become computerized. Extension dairy specialists Eugene Starkey, Anton Sendelbach, and Clarence Olson worked with County Extension agents and DHI staff to help make dairy production records readily available and understandable to farmer participants.

County Extension agents served as the local educational arm for DHI organizations. In the early days, the milk-testing laboratory was part of the county agent's office, where a technician did the actual testing. Two kinds of DHI milk tests evolved, one called "official" and the other "owner-sampler." For the official test, the DHI fieldman came to the farm and, while the farmer milked his cows (both evening and morning), the fieldman took milk samples from each one and put them in test bottles. The fieldman also weighed the amount of milk from each cow. Once the milk was tested, computerized production reports for each cow were sent to the farmer. The official test was used primarily by purebred breeders who were interested in selling breeding stock. In the early days of the official DHI test, the fieldman arrived at a farmer's place in late afternoon, ate supper with the farm family, did the milk testing, stayed overnight, tested again in the morning, ate breakfast, and went on his way.

Owner-sampler testing meant the fieldman dropped off the test bottles for the farmer, who took the samples and weighed the milk. The following day the fieldman picked up the test bottles and weight records, later providing the farmer with a complete computerized production record for each cow.

In the mid-1970s, three other options were added:

1) Dairy Herd Improvement Registry for purebred breeders who were willing to pay an added fee to have copies of their cow and herd data sent directly to their national breed association.

2) Alternate AM-PM Records, in which milk weights and samples were taken from only one milking. This worked well for a farmer with a large herd.

3) Milk Only Records for those farmers who did not want butterfat tests but were interested in maximizing milk output.[31]

Both the number of Dairy Herd Improvement programs and the number of participants increased over the years, but not dramatically. When computers became available for analyzing dairy records in the 1960s, farmers were able to receive more complete records for each of their cows.

In 1961 Clarence Olson, who had been Extension dairyman in North Dakota, was hired as a dairy specialist to work on Wisconsin's DHI educational efforts. Olson said that Wisconsin's DHI program showed a net gain every month from 1969 until

1972, when more farmers quit than joined. With field research, Olson learned that farmers quit DHI because they weren't convinced the program was worth the bother or the cost.

This finding led to a campaign to increase DHI participation. Olson assembled a state DHI campaign committee representing 20 organizations, including county agricultural agents, vocational agriculture instructors, DHI supervisors, artificial insemination organizations, and others. The slogan for the campaign was "Over Six in '76," meaning over 600,000 cows on test. The campaign resulted in 619,373 cows on test in 1976, with 709,270 on test by 1978.[32]

Olson also learned that women usually kept the farm records and often helped on test day to collect samples and do the weighing. So he set up an extensive series of "dairy schools for women" aimed at increasing their knowledge of using DHI records to improve dairy profits. Olson began these dairy schools in 1975. They ran from 10 a.m. to 3 p.m. on two days, a week apart. In 1976 he scheduled 18 schools. Working with other specialists and County Extension agents, Olson tried to limit the attendance to 50, so there would be ample opportunity for questions. "Due to the demand, we had to allow as many as 90 in some classes," he said later. "We took these schools to where the students lived and scheduled them on a county basis."

When asked to characterize the women who attended these workshops, Olson said: "Women arrived on time. They didn't sleep during the meetings. They took notes. And they asked lots of questions."[33]

Topics discussed at the dairy schools included herd health; procedures used by milk plants to test milk; keeping healthy calves; guidelines for feeding; aids in keeping farm records; sire selection guidelines; cleaning milking equipment; DHI records; and dairy outlook. The staff at the schools included a veterinarian, a breeding specialist, an economist, a home economics agent, a county agricultural agent and an Extension dairy specialist. The theme for these schools was "Partners in Better Dairying." Following completion of the program, each participant received a diploma.

By the mid-1970s, local DHI Centers had switched from the Babcock test to an electronic device called the Milko-Tester. With this device, the butterfat content of each cow could be measured in 30 seconds. The process used a photocell, which converted the amount of light penetrating a thin film of milk into a percentage of butterfat. Olson's field work accelerated the acceptance of this new test by farmers and milk plants.

A few years later, machine improvement allowed measuring both the level of milk protein and butterfat in less than 15 seconds. Dramatic changes resulted in DHI services. Local DHI laboratories merged, forming area and regional DHI laboratories. The mergers enabled the larger laboratories to more easily recoup the cost of the new machine. With a rapid and reliable protein test, milk plants began paying farmers premiums for milk with higher protein levels. About the same time, University of

Wisconsin research identified a strong relationship between somatic cell count (SCC) and the health status of the cow (presence or absence of mastitis).

Allen Bringe, Extension dairyman, led the effort to provide SCC testing through DHI services and helped identify the relationship of SCC to milk quality. Milk plants quickly added another premium bonus for producers of high-quality milk based on SCC tests.

These new milk tests also helped farmers who marketed their milk to cheese plants. Higher protein milk yielded more cheese per one hundred pounds of milk. Milk with low SCC resulted in cheese of higher quality.

Protein levels became a factor in the genetic selection of breeding animals, and dairy herd management approaches to lower SCC levels set the stage for less emphasis on traditional DHI, which focused only on high production per cow. New developments in milking parlors, with the ability to create a computer readout of milk yield for each cow on a dairy basis, began to compete with DHI—especially in larger herds. Cow enrollment in DHI peaked at 853,651 (17,029 herds) in 1985 . In April 2001, DHI enrollment had dropped to about 500,000 cows. The computing center that served DHI members in Wisconsin became a subsidiary of Cooperative Resources International, which served dairymen in several states.

Like many other Cooperative Extension efforts, milk testing has evolved from an effort organized and promoted by county agricultural agents to one in which Cooperative Extension's role involves support rather than direct involvement.

Rural Arts

In 1900, the arts were mainly available in cities, especially the theatre. Music was more widespread, because it was a part of most church services. Literature was limited, as there were few libraries and bookstores in Wisconsin at the time. Newspapers were quite widespread, providing a means for citizens to keep up with what was happening in the community, the state, and the world. But most people did not consider newspapers art.

Rural communities had few art opportunities. Many rural communities included local farmer-musicians who played at weddings and birthday parties, and at dances held in homes, town halls, and one-room schoolhouses. Most communities had storytellers, but no one considered them artists. A few people kept journals. Some even wrote poetry, but they usually didn't share their work with anyone. Naturally talented men and women painted, carved wood, did weaving, and engaged in other crafts, but they were often reluctant to show their work to others.

Certain ethnic groups—the Welsh in particular—conducted singing schools and held singing competitions. All of this went on with little organization and essentially no assistance from the University of Wisconsin.

Preparing for a rural art show, Jackson County, 1952

ART PROGRAMS

In March 1931, Chris L. Christensen became dean of the College of Agriculture. He is credited with encouraging a number of arts programs for Wisconsin's rural people. Influenced by the Danish Folk Schools, Christensen believed that rural people should have an opportunity to study art and poetry as well as learning how to improve their cattle and field crops.

In 1936, Christensen hired John Steuart Curry as artist-in-residence, which marked the beginning of the Wisconsin Rural Arts Program. Curry was followed by Aaron Bohrod, who started in September 1948 and served as artist-in-residence until he retired in 1974. The artist-in-residence program was unique in the nation, especially within a college of agriculture.

In 1936, James Schwalbach began broadcasting a program called *Let's Draw*, which was beamed via radio to listeners in country schools and provided instruction on the basics of drawing along with art appreciation. Using word pictures and music, together with print materials sent ahead of time to the schools, Schwalbach inspired kids to draw in new and creative ways. During the 1936-37 school year, Schwalbach enrolled 108 classes representing a listenership of 2,400 students. By 1952, enrollment had increased to 4,320 classes representing 95,040 students.[34]

The Wisconsin Rural Art Association was organized in the late 1930s, and Wisconsin's first rural art show was held in 1940. UW Rural Sociologist John Barton served as coordinator, and 16 paintings were exhibited from 16 counties. The organization (later known as the Wisconsin Rural Artists Association), was still operating in 2001 with Leslee Nelson as director.

THEATER AND WRITING PROGRAMS

In the midst of the Depression, Cooperative Extension made great strides in bringing educational programs in the arts to Wisconsin's rural people. In 1931, 28 counties held drama programs—20 of them for adult farm people. Twelve winners of these county contests performed in Madison as part of a state drama tournament. In 1932, Wisconsin rural people entered 10 plays in the second rural playwriting contest.[35]

Twenty-six counties conducted drama programs for adults and 25 counties sponsored drama programs for young people in 1938. Seven plays were selected to perform at the 11th annual Wisconsin Rural Drama Festival, which was held during Farm and Home Week.

Robert Gard, now deceased, arrived in Wisconsin in 1945 to work as a writing and drama Extension specialist in the College of Agriculture. He was a Kansas farm boy who had studied at Cornell University and worked in Alberta, Canada, and New York. He had a background in rural drama, but he was also a writer and a rural folklorist.

Following his interest in playwriting and drama, Gard encouraged and helped many communities organize theater groups—a Wisconsin tradition that went back to the 1890s. By 1950, more than 100 theater groups had been organized in the state. In 1966, the National Endowment for the Arts awarded a three-year grant to Extension's theater program. The purpose was to develop interest and participation in the arts in communities of 10,000 or less. Gard selected five target communities: Portage, Waupun, Rhinelander, Spring Green, and Adams-Friendship. He assisted them with special arts programming.[36]

Gard was an organizing genius. His way of moving an idea along was to organize a group of people and give the idea a name. Shortly after he arrived, he created the "Wisconsin Idea Theater," a clever way of labeling the notion of making the university available in every corner of the state to cultural arts endeavors. In 1948, Gard helped organize the Wisconsin Rural Writers, later known as the Wisconsin Regional Writers. By 2000, the group had about 800 members. Gard also encouraged the organization of local writing groups, and soon they were found all over the state. He met with these local groups as he had time, encouraging them and discussing the basics of good writing. He suggested that people write about their life experiences, either as nonfiction, fiction, or poetry. In a gentle, supportive way, he moved people to go beyond the limits they had set for themselves to produce works that surprised everyone, especially the authors.

Robert Gard helped organize the Council for Wisconsin Writers in 1964. Continuing into the 2000s, the organization provided recognition and awards for Wisconsin writers. Gard also helped organize the Wisconsin Fellowship of Poets, another organization that remained active in 2000.

In 1964, Gard helped organize the School of the Arts at Rhinelander. Gard's long-time friend, Extension administrator, writer, and former Oneida County agricultural agent L. G. Sorden, suggested Rhinelander as the site for a weeklong school, which continued into the new century. Gard directed the school himself until 1980. Darrell Aderman served as director from 1981 to1984, and current director Harv Thompson began in 1985. Instructors with longtime ties to Extension included Helen O'Brien, Kenneth Kuemmerlein, Ed Kamarck, Karen Cowan, and Jerry Apps. In 2001, more than 350 students from Wisconsin and 13 other states studied writing, drama, art, music, folk arts, woodcarving, and related topics at the school.

Dave Peterson, one of Gard's proteges, helped realize another of Gard's visions in the early 1960s. This was a touring theatre company that would serve communities statewide, presenting professional productions based on Wisconsin history, folklore, and music. Peterson created shows such as *Down River, Hodag, Badger Ballads* and *Son of the Inland Seas*. In the course of 35 years, more than 4,000 performances were presented at county fairs, community theaters, state parks, and schools.

Drama programs have always been popular with 4-H members. Helen O'Brien led much of the 4-H effort, followed by Joan Lazarus.

Music

Wisconsin's first state rural music festival was held in 1931. Additionally, five counties held county festivals in which about 5,000 rural people took part.[37]

Also in 1931, Professor Edgar B. "Pop" Gordon began a radio show on WHA called "Journeys in Music Land," which was part of the Wisconsin School of the Air series that also included "Afield with Ranger Mac." The latter was conducted by Wakelin McNeel, state 4-H leader. Thousands of country schoolchildren participated in these broadcasts by listening to music and by working on nature projects in their schools.

Nineteen music conferences were held in nine counties in 1938, and Extension specialists conducted music leadership training schools in eight counties.[38]

Emmett R. Sarig began as head of the Extension music department in 1950. Cooperative Extension paid part of his salary to develop music programs for 4-H and homemaker's clubs throughout the state. For the next 40 years, music played a prominent role in the 4-H program and, to a lesser degree, the homemaker's organization. State 4-H Bands and Choruses were organized, and these ensembles performed at annual 4-H and homemaker meetings and at the state fair in Milwaukee. Over the years, various faculty from the Extension music department were assigned to Cooperative Extension programs. They included Ed Hugdahl, Robert Swan, and David Peterson, along with several part-time instructors who were hired to work on special projects.

Throughout the 1980s and 1990s, Karen Cowan fostered a statewide dance activity through 4-H, the Wisconsin Dance Council, and numerous workshops and classes. Harv Thompson followed Gard in promoting theater programs in all 72 counties and on all college campuses, both public and private.

In 2000, Susan Farmer led art education programs. Marshall Cook, Christine DeSmit, and Laurel Yourke provided workshops and classes on writing techniques. Harv Thompson worked with drama programs.

One of Gard's last organizational efforts was creating the Robert E. Gard Wisconsin Idea Foundation, which was founded in 1981. Each year, the foundation presents an award of excellence to someone who has made an outstanding contribution to the arts.

With the Extension merger in 1965, the arts faculty was moved out of the College of Agriculture. As a result, many of the arts programs had to pay their own way, and funding became a serious problem. Some programs continue, such as the School of the Arts and various programs in drama, writing and art. Others have closed down.[39]

The people who started the arts programs in the College of Agriculture and in Cooperative Extension had a vision and a commitment to the importance of the arts. Initially, it was unheard of that such programs be part of an agricultural organization's mission. These agricultural staff members created a solid foundation of organizations and a commitment to the arts that continues into the 2000s, even though Cooperative Extension has changed dramatically over the years, some funding sources have dried up, and many new teaching approaches have evolved. From the early days to more contemporary times, Wisconsin people have valued the arts in their lives, recognizing that creative activity helps make them whole persons. Wisconsin citizens have long looked to Cooperative Extension as a valued source for the arts and art education.

Central Sands

An old-timer once said that a crow needed to carry its lunch when it flew over central Wisconsin's sand counties. Farmers had worked these sandy lands, trying to grow potatoes or alfalfa or attempting to make a living milking cows. They had problems during wet years and worse problems during dry ones. Many lost their farms during the Depression and the drought years, as the winds blew and the sky turned dirty gray. Land could be purchased for $15 an acre—or in some cases for back taxes. Those who bought these sand farms were thought foolish, for the central sands grew little more than jack pine and sandburs, and had been declared worthless by many who were familiar with the area.

The College of Agriculture's experimental farm began operations at Hancock in 1916, on land owned by a Hancock development company. Early research focused on helping general livestock farmers make a living on droughty sands. In 1922, the university purchased 95 acres from the development company; by 1934, the university had acquired two more parcels for a total of 223 acres. More land was added later. For the next 20 years, research focused on dairy feeding, pasture use, soil fertility management, and studies with shelterbelts to control wind erosion.

Many people knew about the vast water resources located just a few feet below the surface in the area, but it wasn't until aluminum pipe became available in the late 1940s that irrigation became feasible.[40]

A pivotal meeting was held at the research station on January 13, 1954, when a group of university Extension specialists, College of Agriculture faculty, and area County Extension agents met to discuss the possibility of irrigated vegetable growing in central Wisconsin—specifically, in the counties of Waupaca, Juneau, Waushara, Portage, Marquette, Wood, and Adams. John Schoenemann, Extension horticulturist, chaired the meeting.[41]

This meeting and subsequent meetings and actions resulted in one of the largest transformations of any area of the state—from land considered worthless or nearly so by realtors, business people, and others to one of the most productive vegetable-growing areas in the United States.

With sufficient water, researchers demonstrated that yields of potatoes, sweet corn, peas, cucumbers, and green beans could be tripled, and sometimes increased fourfold. Researchers concentrated on the genetics and physiology of sweet corn quality, development of early maturing, frost-tolerant corn varieties, herbicide evaluations on various crops, improvement of potato cultivars, genetic improvement of cucumbers and snap beans, fertilizer studies, and much more. In 2000, about one-third of the station's research was focused on potatoes. Researchers there also studied alfalfa, clover, soybeans, sweet corn, cucumbers, snap beans, field corn, rye, sorghum-sudan grass, asparagus, peas, melons, cabbage, tomatoes, jack pine, and poplar trees.

Extension agents in the area worked with farmer-producers to help them understand irrigation technology and how to grow crops under irrigated conditions. Soon the area became known as the "Golden Sands." Vegetable processing companies were opened in the area, employment opportunities increased manyfold. No longer did the crows need to pack a lunch when flying over the area.

This chapter has discussed but a few of the "notable" Cooperative Extension programs. Space limitations prevent the addition of others, but they are all good examples of people working together with the university—and often with other organizations and agencies—to solve a problem or meet a community need.

CHAPTER 14

TEACHING APPROACHES

I n the beginning it was the lecture. A strong-voiced agriculture professor climbed on the back of a high-wheeled wagon as people gathered around to hear his message. Imagine what it was like without a microphone or visual aids! Nothing but the man and his voice. And what voices these early Extension teachers must have had, for they drew hundreds of people to their lectures. Farmers thirsting for new information about wheat growing and cattle raising, about the newfangled idea of commercial fertilizers, about silos and how they would provide winter feed storage for cattle.

These itinerant teachers followed in the footsteps of the great Lyceum and Chautauqua speakers who preceded them. Indeed, a few of these men had been Chautauqua speakers and knew the tricks of keeping an audience entertained while they were taught.

Farmers were a skeptical lot; they still are. Many of them wanted more than merely hearing about some new research project. They wanted to see how the idea worked, preferably how it worked on a neighbor's farm. If it worked for their neighbor, then they might try it. Farmers said, or at least thought, "Show me, don't just tell me."

Enter the demonstration approach.

Demonstrations

The demonstration approach is widely associated with Cooperative Extension work. For many years, when people thought about Extension, they thought about demonstrations.

Extension used two basic kinds of demonstrations: those that showed someone how to do something (method demonstrations); and those that showed the outcomes of doing something (results demonstrations). Method demonstrations included everything from how to sew a shirt or bake a cake to how to lead a discussion, take a soil sample, or test the hardness of water used in the home. For many years, Extension home economists were called "home demonstration agents," because they so often used the demonstration method in their work. Very early in 4-H club work, members were taught how to give method demonstrations. Soon 4-H members were competing locally and statewide in demonstration contests that determined who could do the best job of showing how to do something.

The results demonstration goes back to Seaman Knapp, fondly referred to as the "schoolmaster of American agriculture." Knapp worked in Texas in 1904, trying to help Texas farmers deal with the boll weevil, which raised havoc with the cotton crop. He also assisted farmers in improving agriculture generally. By working with local farmers, Knapp established demonstrations in which farmers followed the instructions of an agricultural scientist. He also made arrangements to compensate the farmer for any losses if the demonstration didn't work.

Knapp's famous and often-quoted remark came from this effort: "What a man hears he may doubt, what he sees he may possibly doubt, but what he does himself he cannot doubt."[1] The Extension section of the experiment station knew the importance of demonstrations. In his 1909 report, Dean Russell wrote: "As our experience with the demonstrative lines of Extension work increase, it becomes more and more apparent that better results are obtained where the instruction is given by demonstration so far as the nature of the work will permit. Habits of thought have a strong tendency to become fixed. We are apt to do the things we need to do in the same old way, and it is difficult to change methods that have long been in vogue. An actual demonstration, however, affords the most convincing proof and will carry conviction where frequently all other methods fail."[2]

Russell reported demonstrations on fertilizer application, orchard spraying, potato spraying, cranberry spraying, TB post-mortems on cattle, and demonstrations to show the crops and fruits that would grow in far northern Wisconsin. The latter demonstrations were conducted at the Ashland, Iron River, and Superior branch experiment stations.

Both method and result demonstrations became an important and widely used teaching strategy in Wisconsin and every other state. They took many forms. County Extension offices maintained demonstration kitchens to show food preparation and preservation approaches. County agricultural agents set up demonstration plots on farms to compare oats, corn, and forage varieties, to illustrate the results of different amounts of fertilizers, or to show how to improve an old pasture. They conducted demonstrations on how to judge cattle, sheep, and hogs. In 1947, Dane County agent R. V. Hurley conducted "managed milking demonstrations." At each demonstration, held at farms around Dane County, Hurley brought in fieldmen from the various milking machine companies to show how to best handle the cow and the machine. These demonstrations proved so popular that a county-wide "managed milking contest" was held at the Dane County Junior Fairgrounds, with 500 farmers attending. In 1947, the Dane County agent held a total of 63 demonstrations with 3,199 people attending.

An unusual demonstration was conducted in La Crosse County on October 29, 1951. The demonstration was a joint effort between the Extension office (Al

Nyla Musser, Jackson County home economist, wrote this early cranberry bulletin in 1972. Bulletins have always been important teaching aids for Extension.

1972

THE LITTLE BERRY (CRANBERRY) THAT COUNTS

Cranberry Recipes

Prepared by:
Nyla E. Musser
Jackson County
Extension Home Economist

Francour, county agricultural agent) and the La Crosse County soil conservation office (Lyle Molstad). The purpose of this highly publicized educational event was to show how a drainage ditch could be dug by using dynamite. The news article in the La Crosse *Tribune* began, "Events at the Elmer Kastenschmidt farm six miles east of Mindora started off with a bang Thursday afternoon when an 80-foot ditch was blasted to open a field drainage demonstration."

Blasting ditches was a new venture for Francour, and he quickly learned that you needed a license to use dynamite in Wisconsin. In fact, you couldn't even buy the blasting material without a license. Francour had been studying a USDA bulletin that described in great detail the use of dynamite for blasting drainage ditches, and he figured he knew how to do it. He would just follow the instructions in the bulletin. He also learned that by driving across the river to Minnesota, he could freely buy dynamite—Minnesota had different rules than Wisconsin. Francour bought a case of dynamite at a farm supply store in Caledonia, Minnesota. A tiling company from Mason City, Iowa, had the contract for tiling the farm where the demonstration was to be held. The dynamite would be used to blast the outlet ditch for the drainage system.

On the day of the demonstration Francour and the SCS man, with the dynamite bulletin in hand, began placing sticks of dynamite about 18 inches apart and burying them about nine to twelve inches.

With more than 100 farmers looking on and the press watching, Francour made some preliminary comments about this new approach to ditch digging that didn't require heavy equipment and long hours of work with a shovel. Then it was time to set off the dynamite. No one knew if it would work, and whether what the bulletin prescribed was appropriate for a river county in western Wisconsin. The danger of it all apparently hadn't entered anyone's mind. With a tremendous explosion that shook the earth where the participants stood, a plume of dirt, mud, and water lifted 100 feet or more into the air. Then there was silence as people, most of whom had not expected such an explosion, slowly moved forward to see the results. The dynamite had blasted a ditch five to six feet deep, and the soil was laid out on each side eight to ten feet across the top. The demonstration had worked perfectly. Today, Francour questions his use of dynamite. Would he do something like that again? "Never," he says.

Extension-sponsored meetings were usually associated with demonstrations. People gathered to learn how to do something, or they came together to see the results of something—to determine whether a certain weed spray had worked as advertised, for example.

The Meeting

Meetings of two or more people were and continue to be one of the most popular teaching approaches for Extension. Meetings ranged from a handful of people sitting around a cookstove in a farmer's kitchen to several hundred gathered in a farmer's field to hear the latest about new crop varieties and how to grow them.

Meetings took many forms. For years, Extension followed the successful pattern of the farmers' institutes, where people in a community came to hear an assortment of agricultural experts speak on topics ranging from feeding dairy cows to keeping farm records. Many daylong Extension meetings were held in high school gymnasiums or in churches. An area bank provided a free lunch, and local businesses offered door prizes such as motor oil, fly spray, flashlights, or caps that prominently displayed the company's logo.

As the years passed, meeting topics became more focused. An entire day might be devoted to dairy cattle management. Discussion of hogs, sheep, or beef cattle took place on another day. The typical format presented a speaker who used visuals of various kinds to keep his audience engaged and awake, followed by a lively question and answer period. Sometimes the format was a panel discussion in which several speakers provided a variety of perspectives on a given topic, followed by open discussion. The country school was the site of many smaller meetings. At such gatherings the county agent might be invited to talk on a particular topic, or on a problem that was prevalent in the community. The agent might discuss what to do when the corn crop froze before it ripened, what to use as a windbreak to prevent wind erosion, or how to stop an infestation of grasshoppers.

In the course of the year, a County Extension agent conducted or attended an enormous number of meetings. For instance, the Dane County Extension staff in 1969 included seven members. According to their 1969 report to the county board, they collectively attended 1,376 meetings. Of this total, 516 were listed as meetings held to train local leaders.

Tours and Field Days

Tours have always been a popular teaching approach. A tour might mean the Extension agent had lined up five farmers around his county who had put in new milking equipment or built a different kind of dairy barn, or did something else that other farmers were interested in learning more about. The agent and the tour group drove from farm to farm, with the agent and the local farmer explaining what had been done, how it had been done, and what it cost. Tours were highly effective for farmers who were trying to make a decision about whether and how to do something. They could see how someone else had resolved the same decision.

Field days meant farmers gathered at one place—often one of the College of Agriculture's research facilities—to see new crop varieties or new crop management approaches, to gather weed control ideas, and more. E. L. Luther, who had moved from his agent job in Oneida County to heading up the farmers' institute program, attended a field day at the Hancock research station in 1930. Luther wrote an article for the Hancock newspaper containing the following impressions: "The sub-station farm looks the best that it ever looked when it was opened to receive visitors on Wednesday, August 6. It looked like a real farm. Where I got anklets of sandburs eight years ago was [now] a fine field of potatoes, green looking and vigorous. Close by was a field of corn as good as I have seen in Wisconsin this year. Just over there was a sweet clover pasture. Yonder alfalfa. Scarcely a weed anywhere."

He went on to talk about the people who attended—250 carfuls "from far and wide." They "came to see what science carefully worked out could do to help them with their personal problems. They came to get good information from the station and they got it."

Emil Jorgensen, county agent for Waushara County, also reported on this field day. He said attendance was nearly one thousand farm folks. Jorgensen wrote: "Threshing machines were deserted and other farm work neglected that they might drive many miles in the scorching hot sun to study and examine the year's results at the station farm. The morning was spent in studying the several necessary machines used in the successful operation of this extremely sandy farm. A field inspection trip was conducted in the afternoon, following the large after dinner group meeting."

The afternoon program opened with music by a male quartet known as the Wild Rose Band, three of whose members were professors from the College of Agriculture. The music was followed by a discussion led by O. B. Jensen of the National Fertilizer Association and a presentation by Professor Grantham of Michigan State College. Two professors from the Home Economics Department in Madison met with the women who attended the field day.

This was a rather typical field day for the times, attracting large numbers of farm people. These gatherings took place all over the state and they continued into the 2000s. Farm Progress Days was an offshoot of some of the earlier field days—a kind of hybrid show that combined displays from commercial exhibitors with field demonstrations from the College of Agriculture and Cooperative Extension.

Farm Progress Days

By the late 1990s, Farm Progress Days was billed as the largest agricultural show in Wisconsin and one of the largest in the nation. It was a three-day event that moved around the state and showcased the latest innovations in production agriculture, usually incorporating practical application of recent research findings.

The first Farm Progress Days was held in Waupaca County in 1954. The event operated as a non-profit educational organization, with a board of directors that oversaw each year's show. The board consisted of representatives from state and federal agencies involved in agriculture and natural resources, University of Wisconsin members, plus farmer and agribusiness representatives.

Since its beginning, Farm Progress Days has been held in 35 counties, with several hosting it more than once. By 2000, the show included more than 600 commercial and educational exhibitors in a "tent city" consisting of several acres of tents set up for the three-day show.

The 2000 Farm Progress Days was held in Fond du Lac County, where it had been in 1973. Show visitors saw the newest in dairy cow shelter design, the most up-to-date equipment for forage handling, plus many exhibits illustrating how computers and technology were influencing agriculture. Those attending also saw farming from an earlier day, with a display of antique tractors and farm machinery, an operating threshing machine, and an exhibit by the Barns Network of Wisconsin, a group devoted to the preservation of rural buildings.

Attendance at Farm Progress Days is so large (in the thousands) that the state patrol and local law enforcement people close roads and design special travel strategies to accommodate the visitors.

Fairs

County fairs preceded Cooperative Extension by many years. As reported earlier, the first county fair in Wisconsin was held in Kenosha County in 1850, just two years after Wisconsin became a state. By the 1860s, some 30 county fairs existed.

When County Extension agents were hired starting in 1912, it seemed reasonable that they provide leadership for the fairs. In many counties, the county agricultural agent became the fair secretary. Some County Extension offices moved to the fairground for the duration of their county fair, and all of the agents and support staff were heavily involved with fair activities. Extension agents also served as judges for many fairs in their regions. Nyla Musser, who served as county home economics agent in Outagamie and then in Jackson County, recalled some unusual occurrences while she was judging at fairs. She once judged a jar of cucumber pickles and wondered how they could possibly look so green. She opened the jar to discover that they had been

General managers of Farm Progress Days:
• Alfred J. Wojta, 1954-1959;
• F.V. Burcalow, 1960-1962;
• Randall Swanson, 1963-1968;
• George L. Wright, 1969-1976;
• Lyndon A. Brooks, 1977-1984;
• Al Francour, 1985-1992;
• Glenn S. Thompson, 1993-.

Board of Directors chairs for Farm Progress Days:
• Henry Ahlgren, 1954-1975;
• Donald R. Peterson, 1975-1993;
• Neal A. Jorgenson, 1993-2000; and
• Richard M. Klemme, 2000-.

Farm Progress Days managers, 1954 to 1993

canned in kerosene. On another occasion, a jar of peaches looked perfect. She discovered that the peaches had come from store-purchased cans. This exhibitor had removed the peaches from their cans, put them in jars, then heated and sealed them. Musser pointed out that face-to-face judging of 4-H projects with the children present eliminated the occasional shenanigan.

A judge of 4-H vegetable projects recalled finding a cabbage that was supposedly home grown but had a price on the stem; another found an exhibit of what were clearly store-bought carrots.

The stories associated with fairs are legion. Russ Kiecker, longtime agricultural and 4-H agent in Burnett County, tells the story of Charlie Brown (his real name) who farmed not far from Webster, Wisconsin. Brown had never been fond of the government, and had been cool toward Cooperative Extension. Nevertheless, Kiecker made a point of visiting him occasionally, and they had come to like each other.

The Burnett County Fair at Webster was on, and it was almost closing time one evening when Charlie Brown appeared on the fairgrounds. Kiecker walked up to him and said, "Sure nice to see you."

"Well, dammit, I couldn't stay away," Brown said. "I was out there cultivating and I had my tractor radio on and I was listening to you talk about the fair. You were talking about all this stuff going on at the Webster Fair. I've lived here for almost 60 years, and I've never been to the Webster Fair. You talked about that rooster with the red comb. It was a red comb that you'd never seen before. You talked about that like I just had to come and see it. I'm gonna tag along with you, and you show me that rooster."

As Kiecker explained: "Charlie Brown had never been to the fair, and he was standing on the fairgrounds wearing a new pair of bib overalls. And he wanted to see that rooster. I took him over there. I took that rooster out of the cage, and I showed it to him. It was a beautiful rooster. He looked at that bird and he looked and [he] continued looking. Then he said, 'I guess I saw everything.' He went home."

Ian Meeker, 4-H and youth development educator in Bayfield County, shared a story written by 4-H member Kristen Tetzner about "Big Red," the market steer. The year was 1996. Kristen looked forward to showing Big Red and then selling him at the market sale. But on Thursday of the fair at Iron River, Big Red took off for the woods. The steer missed the judging, missed the showmanship contest, and of course missed the sale.

When word got around that the big steer had run off, everyone pitched in to help find him. Many people hiked through the woods, but there was no trace of the steer. A fellow went up in his airplane. Still no steer.

George Vernon from Northern Clearing suggested that Kristen sell the big animal at the sale, sight unseen. As Kristen said, "If Big Red came back, fine—the buyer had himself a steer. If he didn't, what did we have to lose?

George Vernon and Jim Ogilvie from M & I Bank bid together on Big Red and purchased him, if he should ever turn up.

A week after the steer disappeared, he returned to the fairgrounds on his own. As Kristen said, "He must have tired of eating pine needles. John Benson from Delta herded up the steer, got him into a cattle trailer, and hauled him home [to Kristen's farm]." She kept him until mid-October, when the buyers picked him up.

"This was my most emotional fair," Kristen wrote. "Everyone was so good to me. It felt like a big family. We were all competing with each other, but deep down we were there because of our love for the fair. None of us wanted to see another fail, no matter how badly we wanted to succeed ourselves. I think we all learned a little something extra that year."

Gayle Nelson from Pierce County Extension remembers when country singer Tanya Tucker was making the rounds of county fairs. She arrived in Pierce County to do a grandstand show. Tucker was only 14 or 15 then, but she undoubtedly expected slightly better accommodations than those available at the fairgrounds. The fair committee had moved a trailer to the fairgrounds for an office, and this was to be Tucker's dressing room. There was no running water, so someone took the vegetable drawer out of the refrigerator, filled it with water, and gave Tucker some paper towels. "Now she's rich and famous," Nelson wrote. "I wonder if she remembers times like these."

Farm Visits

Norman Rockwell, arguably the most famous painter of Americana, is most remembered for his *Saturday Evening Post* covers. On July 24, 1948, he did an oil painting for the *Post* entitled "The County Agent." For those of us who fondly remember the many farm visits we made as Extension agents, the painting said it all. In the painting the county agent, wearing a tan shirt, rumpled pants, and a crumpled felt hat, is showing a young 4-Her how to determine the weight of her Guernsey calf by using a tape measure. She holds the lead rope, her 4-H record book under her arm, listening carefully to what the county agent is saying. Meanwhile her brother stands by patiently, holding a chicken, and a sister waits to show the agent her newly sewn dress. The mother watches, a proud look on her face, while the father leans against the barn door with his hands in his pockets, observing what is going on. On the far right, with a hint of skepticism on his face, stands what appears to be the grandfather, his hands folded behind his back. The farm dog and a black barn cat look on, and a half-dozen chickens scratch in the straw.

When making a farm visit, the agent met the entire family and could learn much about their problems and successes. Unfortunately, as time passed, Extension agents had less time for farm visits. In response, they tried to reach larger numbers of people through newsletters, meetings, and (later) radio and television. Something was lost when farm visits all but disappeared. The informality of a one-to-one meeting across the kitchen table, in the dairy barn, or over a fence, let people know that County Extension agents were real people who cared about a person's problems. It is more difficult to convey such a feeling in a large gathering, and it's even more difficult via radio, television, or computer.

Bulletins

The popular television show *Green Acres* aired from September 15, 1965, until 1971. The show featured Oliver Wendell Douglas, played by Eddie Albert, and his wife Lisa Douglas, played by Eva Gabor. They had moved to a rundown farm near Hooterville, and they soon met County Extension Agent Hank Kimball. Whenever someone had a question, Kimball pulled out a bulletin. What little success Kimball had depended on the printed word—in this case, the Extension bulletin. While few real county agents have relied exclusively on bulletins, these publications have always been an important Extension tool.

The history of bulletins in Wisconsin goes back to a time when the College of Agriculture and its fledgling experiment station had become overwhelmed with letters from farmers. In 1908, Dean Russell wrote: "The amount of correspondence connected with the work of the college is rapidly increasing each year. More and more people of all classes are looking to the Station and college for help on all matters in any way relating to agriculture. Very frequently these requests entail considerable search for definite data to answer satisfactorily the matter in question."[3]

In 1908, 12 stenographers typed 45,000 letters answering questions that had arrived at the College of Agriculture. Agriculture professors spent untold hours digging out the answers to questions covering everything related to farming and farm life. One way to address the ever-increasing flood of letters was the bulletin. Agriculture professors were soon writing bulletins, many on topics related to the questions they were receiving, but others based on the results of research the college was conducting. However, there were always questions for which there were no bulletins—thus the large number of letters received by the College of Agriculture.

Bulletins quickly became an important teaching tool. From 1883 to 1905, the College of Agriculture Experiment Station published 132 different bulletins on topics ranging from experimental calf-feeding to ensilage and the feed value of whey. As many as 30,000 copies of a bulletin were printed. During the 1904-1905 year, the Experiment station published 13 bulletins, including a 92-page bulletin on silo construction.

During the year 1906-1907, the experiment station published 15 bulletins. More than 20,000 copies were printed in several cases. The longest bulletin, titled "A Report on Horse-Breeding Industry of Wisconsin," contained 162 pages. The shortest was a 16-page publication discussing the relative value of shelled corn and cornmeal for fattening pigs.

With the passage of the Smith-Lever legislation in 1914, Cooperative Extension itself began publishing bulletins. These early publications were called "stencil bulletins." They featured crude, hand-drawn illustrations. They were printed on poor-quality paper with crude and reproduced on mimeograph machines.

The first one published in Wisconsin came out on July 15, 1915, and was titled "Canning for Pleasure and Profit." It was written by Elizabeth Kelley, the new home economics director for Extension. The 19-page tract was intended for use by home canning clubs. Kelley also penned the second bulletin, "Twelve Lessons in Sewing," which was published in October 1915. The third one, "How to Cure Seed Corn," was written by R.A, Moore and J.J. Garland. It included detailed instructions for making a seed corn tree. The instructions: fashion together an upright pole, pound headless nails into it, and push the cobs of corn to be dried over the nails.

Bulletin number 38, published on December 20, 1920, was titled "A Nitro Starch Mixture for Land Clearing." It included a detailed report on how to blow stumps out of the ground. As John Swenehart, the author, explained: "New methods, devices and processes constantly are being devised to push the stump line back. Some are accepted, many are rejected, while still others play a minor part in the program of development in the cut-over sections of upper Wisconsin."[4]

This bulletin described tests conducted on white pine stumps in the vicinity of

One of hundreds of bulletins produced by Cooperative Extension over the years. This one appeared in 1948.

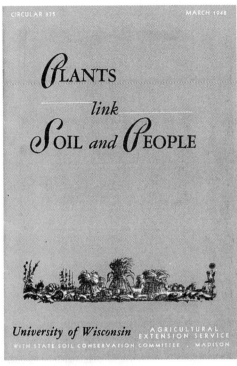

CIRCULAR 375   MARCH 1948

*P*LANTS

link

*S*OIL *and* *P*EOPLE

University of Wisconsin AGRICULTURAL EXTENSION SERVICE
WITH STATE SOIL CONSERVATION COMMITTEE · MADISON

Bayfield and Salmo. Varying portions of a nitro starch mixture were packed into cartridges, then shot at from a distance of 80 feet with a Savage 303 high-powered rifle. The cartridge-packed explosives were shot to pieces, but they didn't detonate. Ordinary dynamite would explode given similar treatment. The experiment demonstrated that this new explosive mixture was safer than dynamite as a stump blower.

Cooperative Extension produced thousands of bulletins on almost as many topics. Until the 1980s, they were offered free to the public. Subsequently, the price for a carefully edited and designed, four-color bulletin was only a fraction of the cost of producing it.

Bulletins were especially useful as adjuncts for various home economics programs. If, for example, a county home economist was demonstrating how to use meats in home cooking, she sent attendees home with "Meats in Our Meals," which covered the topic in much greater depth than she could manage at one meeting.

In 4-H Club work, the bulletin served a role similar to that of a textbook in school. For many years, the state 4-H office had its own publication department with an editor who solicited manuscripts from Extension specialists, then edited, designed, and prepared them for printing. The agricultural journalism presses did the actual printing, but the 4-H office stored and distributed them.

When a 4-H member signed up for a project, he or she received a packet of materials that contained forms for keeping records, plus a bulletin that provided background material. Bulletins were also bibles for the volunteer 4-H leaders, who depended on them for the in-depth knowledge they needed for teaching children about a particular project. The 4-H bulletins—especially those for young people—had an open design and many illustrations. They were high quality, and members often saved them and used them for reference for years afterward.

Many 4-H bulletins were developed in a series: "Meats in our Meals," "Fruits in our Meals," "Vegetables in our Meals," "Milk and Eggs in our Meals," "Breads and Cereals in our Meals." This series provided ongoing emphasis to the food groups for 4-H members who participated for several years. Often the county home agents encouraged Extension homemakers to have a foods project lesson on the same topic emphasized in 4-H. Together with project training for 4-H foods leaders, this meant that the leaders and mothers had information to help members and provided repetition and reinforcement of basic nutrition information.

In 2000, popular 4-H bulletins included the following titles: "Adventures with Your Camera," "Action! Making Videos and Movies," "Horses and Horsemanship," "Dig into Dairy," "Bite into Beef," "Sew for the Fun of It," "You're the Chef," "Living With Others," and many more.

Examples of general Cooperative Extension bulletins in 2000 included "Commercial Vegetable Production in Wisconsin," "Lawn Aeration and Topdressing," "Forage Variety Update for Wisconsin—1999 Trial Results," "The Wisconsin Storm Water Manual," and many more. Cost of the bulletins mentioned ranged from 50 cents to $15.

During the earlier years of radio, bulletins were published to supplement radio programs. Titles included "About Rural Life," "Cook With Milk," "Have You Had Your Eggs Today?" "Renewing Permanent Pasture," "60 Ways to Use Wisconsin Apples," and more. One of the more interesting ones was a radio circular entitled "How to Gain Weight." Published in 1930, the bulletin included this advice: "Make every meal a large one; a fourth meal often helps." Further advice included, "Drink at least a pint of milk a day, and if the underweight is still growing, preferably a quart . . . Eat fat and lots of butter and cream. Weight for weight, pure fat has two and one quarter times as much fuel value as pure carbohydrate or protein. It is not difficult to slip in [extra] fat at a meal. Potatoes and other vegetables are excellent carriers of butter. Mayonnaise or French dressing may be liberally used on salads. Cream may be served with desserts."[5]

Radio

Wisconsin has long been a national leader in educational broadcasting. In 1917, University of Wisconsin physics professor Earle M. Terry, along with several students, successfully transmitted music and voice using handmade vacuum tubes. Later that year, University of Wisconsin station 9XM began broadcasting. In January 1922, 9XM received a new license and call letters, thereby becoming WHA. The first commercial radio station did not begin operations until 1920, in Pittsburgh, Pennsylvania. But interest in the medium grew rapidly. By 1922, 537 commercial stations were broadcasting in the U.S.[6] Cooperative Extension was actively involved in broadcasting by the late 1920s, especially over WHA. Both a daily farm program and a daily homemaker show came on the air in 1924.

Extension Associate Director K. L. Hatch, reporting for 1930-31, wrote: "Two separate programs—a farm program and a homemakers' program—are given each weekday. Included in these programs are timely topics of farm and home; farm

County and state staff have used radio effectively as a teaching device. Here, Poultry Specialist J. B. "Barry" Hayes appears on a WHA radio show in 1944. The topic was chick feeders.

questions and answers; timely farm news; and a daily weather report. Through the cooperation of the weather bureau, the forecast is expanded in the summer months to cover weather predictions of three or four days for the benefit of haymaker and harvesters."[7]

Presenting the programs were staff members of the College of Agriculture, County Extension agents, and representatives of the federal-state crop reporting service and the Wisconsin Department of Agriculture and Markets.

By 1939, WHA farm and homemaker programs were also broadcast over WLBL, another station near Auburndale, which greatly expanded the radio audience. In 1947, the portable tape recorder was used for the first time by Wisconsin Extension radio broadcasters, enabling them to capture farm news on the spot.

From 1930 to 1935, Ken Gapen served as farm radio broadcaster on WHA. He was followed by Milton Bliss, who worked from 1935 to 1950 with the exception of a two- year leave on a foreign service assignment. Maury White, who had been a farm radio broadcaster at Ohio State University, took over in 1951 and worked until 1968. "I was given the leeway and freedom to broadcast what I wanted," White recalled. "I regularly involved Extension specialists and administrators such as Dean Glenn Pound, Extension Director Henry Ahlgren, staff from the Soil Conservation Service, the State Department of Agriculture, and even the Treasury Department [during the Korean War, when bond sales were promoted]."

Like every other professional, Maury had some less than proud experiences. He recalled a day when he drove to Sparta to tape a radio program and forgot his tape recorder back in Madison. He hustled around, found someone who had a recorder, borrowed some tape, and was back in business.

White believed his greatest contribution was helping to bring Extension specialists into homes throughout the state. "After hearing them a few times on radio, people felt like they knew these specialists."[8] Ultimately, Maury White became known as the "Voice of Wisconsin Agriculture," a title still associated with him in his retirement.

Larry Meiller began his radio career when Maury White taught at the Colorado State University summer school in 1967. White asked Meiller, who had been one of White's students, to do the half-hour noon show. During those years, the noon show consisted of farm markets, farm news from the wire services and the Extension news service, plus two guests each day who were allowed five to seven minutes each. The talk was about alfalfa, cows, fertilizer, weed control—anything related to agriculture. In 1978 the show became an hour, airing from noon to 1 p.m. After 1978, Meiller worked with a series of co-hosts including Jim Collins, Chris Sterling, and Rhonda Allen. "We tried to combine features that would attract a broader audience," Meiller said.

In 1978, Jack Mitchell from Wisconsin Public Radio asked Meiller if he was interested in doing a call-in talk show. Meiller said he was and suggested a format that included advice about agriculture, the outdoors, health and exercise, and nutrition—the things that affect the daily lives of people. At that time, Meiller's co-host was Jeanne Dosch.

Meiller believes that this was the first public radio call-in program in the nation. He remembers the first broadcast well. "My guests were Dick Bristol and John Skinner, both from the College of Agriculture and Life Sciences, to talk about pet care. I was kind of nervous, because I had no idea if anyone would call in. But the lines lit up. The first caller was a woman from Stevens Point. She asked, 'How do I tell if my cat is a male or a female?' Dick Bristol leaned into the microphone as only he could and said, 'You pick up its tail.'"

In the 1980s, the noon show switched from 11 a.m. to 1 p.m., then to to its current time slot from 11 a.m. to 12:30 p.m. in order to make room for *Chapter a Day.*

After 34 years of public radio work, Meiller is likely the dean among those hosts who feature agriculture and related topics. "I really enjoy the show," Meiller said. "It's great fun working with Extension people." Extension specialists are regular guests on his show, including Scott Craven, John Merrill, Sue Nitzke, Phil Pellitteri, and others.

Meiller also brings in experts on a variety of topics. He recalls when he invited a person on the show who was an expert in stress management. Before the program began, everything was fine, but when they went on the air and she received her first question, she froze. "She stressed out when she got the first question," Meiller said.

Meiller improvised. He tried to answer the questions himself, then asked his guest whether his answer was right. All he got out of her was a "yes." This went on for some time before she calmed down enough to answer questions on her own. Later, Meiller received several letters. "Why don't you let your guest answer the questions herself?" listeners inquired.

The worst situation he remembers was when he was doing a call-in, his guest didn't show up, and the telephone lines were down. He opened the microphone and began ad-libbing. An engineer rushed into the studio. "I had a guy on the floor between my legs, working on the phone lines as I kept blabbering away. Finally, [morning program host] Tom Clark rushed into the studio, and [we] talked together until the phone lines were finally repaired."

In 2000, Meiller's listening audience was about 150,000 people each day. The program went out on two AM and ten FM stations, reaching beyond Wisconsin into Michigan, Iowa, Minnesota, and Illinois. Since 2000, the program has been on the Web, so people can hear the program on their computers. "We are expanding our Web presence," Meiller said. "One thing we are doing is offering programs on demand. My show will go to an 'audio vault' where a person who may have missed my live show can go to hear it. Not quite ready yet, but it is coming quickly."

In addition to the noon radio program, Meiller also supervised a radio tape service that provided audiotapes to about 100 commercial radio stations in Wisconsin on agriculture and related topics. Jeanne Geurink did most of the interviewing for these approximately four-minute tapes.[9]

The agricultural journalism department hired Aline Hazard in 1933 to establish a women's radio program on WHA. In 1965, after Aline Hazard had completed 33 years in radio, Jean Fewster replaced her. Norma Simpson took over in 1968. By this time, the women's program was called *Accent on Living*. Eventually, both the farm and women's programs broadened and adopted a call-in format. The programs were no longer identified specifically with agriculture or homemaker concerns. When Margaret Andreson took over the women's program, it began dealing with people's questions related to current public issues and events.[10]

During the 1940s and 1950s, the state radio network expanded beyond AM stations WHA in Madison and WLBL in Auburndale to include seven FM stations. With the AM and FM stations, broadcasts reached about every corner of the state. By 2000, Wisconsin Public Radio, including its Ideas Network and its extensive classical music programming, blanketed Wisconsin and considerable territory in Illinois, Iowa, Michigan, and Minnesota. It was an important educational force for University of Wisconsin-Extension.

In addition to the state radio network, many County Extension agents did regular radio programs on commercial stations. When I worked as Extension agent in Brown County, I prepared two radio programs per week, lasting five minutes each. Thankfully, I was able to do them on tape and did not need to appear at the radio station twice weekly. When I worked in Green Lake County, the Ripon radio station had just come on the air (in 1958). There, the Extension staff appeared in person at the station once a week.

Radio became an essential part of weekly activities for many Extension agents. They used the medium to share new ideas and new research results distributed by the agricultural journalism department to county offices. Agents used the radio to announce upcoming events, such as meetings and workshops. And radio was also a useful tool for talking about local problems and questions that the Extension agent learned about during the week.

Newspapers

Some 163 bulletins were published before the College of Agriculture and the experiment station began utilizing professional editors. When the Department of Agricultural Journalism began in 1908, J. Clyde Marquis was appointed as agricultural editor. In his first year, Marquis took charge of the college's publications and sent out press releases through the newly formed University Press Bureau. These regular news releases, along with the bulletins, eased the workload of the university people who had been answering thousands of letters from farmers. Now, many farmers' questions could be answered by reading agricultural news items in the state's newspapers.

Professor Marquis moved on to *Country Gentleman* magazine in 1911, and John Y. Beaty took over. In addition to becoming agricultural editor, he also assumed the title of instructor of agricultural journalism, offering three basic journalism courses for campus students. Beaty had some definite opinions about writing for the farm press, including the following: "The main difference . . .between newspaper journalism and agricultural journalism is that farm papers want instructive articles. Each article must tell not only the value of the plan but the details of how to carry out the plan. It benefits a farmer little to know that a certain [agricultural] method will increase his profits. But it benefits him much if he can both know the value of the method and the details of putting the method into practice on the farm. . . . I believe the most essential thing in teaching agricultural journalism is to show the students what is worth writing about and what is worth saying about that thing. Of course some emphasis must be laid upon the use of English, but this comes in as secondary to the other."[11]

Beaty was a very active agricultural editor. He mailed college news and agricultural information weekly through the University Press Bureau to 446 papers in Wisconsin and 312 outside the state. He edited two columns of agricultural information for the Western Newspapers Union, which served 121 Wisconsin county papers. He edited 13 regular bulletins, 11 research bulletins, 12 circulars of information, two country life conference reports, five college catalogs, and a laboratory manual. He lasted one year.

The Department of Agricultural Journalism continued to offer a variety of press services. The Extension director's 1930-31 annual report devoted a section to press releases. "The subject matter for press uses includes news of Extension activities,

Extension agents have written newspaper columns as an important adjunct to their teaching. Weekly column, Kenosha County.

results of Extension work, and the interpretation of scientific investigations that apply to methods on the farm and in the farm home. In the preparation of this material, emphasis is placed upon a popular style. Information on home economic subjects is prepared in popular form and brought to Wisconsin homemakers through the medium of both weekly and daily papers. At least four such releases, explaining approved home practices in cookery, nutrition, clothing, health, housing, and home management, are sent out each week from the Extension editor's office. These press services are sent regularly each week to 342 weekly newspapers in Wisconsin. The 42 daily papers receive material suitable to daily press use as often as occasion demands."[12]

County Extension agents quickly learned the value of the press. Many agents wrote (and still write) weekly columns for their local newspapers on a wide range of topics. The College of Agriculture news service regularly sent them releases about new research and information on wide-ranging topics in agriculture, home economics, and farm life in general. This information could provide the core for a good column. Unfortunately, some agents used the college material just as they received it. The resulting columns were often boring, and were filled with, "This specialist said this, and this researcher said that."

SUNDAY, JUNE 18, 2000

Today's Family
BY ELLEN SHIFLET

4-H Camp:
Mentoring in Action

Three fun-filled days at Camp Timberlee in East Troy on the surface might look like carefree days away from home, chores, jobs and parental supervision. It was for the almost 200 campers who recently returned from the 2000 4-H camp experience. For everyone else involved in providing a positive experience for the campers, however, it is a mentoring program in action.

Mentors: Interested friends who share activities, usually outside school hours, offering individual attention, fun and guidance in life skills (as defined by the Mentor's Guide, produced by the Wisconsin Clearinghouse for Prevention Resources).

Encouraged by research demonstrating the effectiveness of mentoring in boosting self-esteem and school success, organizations throughout Wisconsin are working to match young people with adults and older teens to build on the power of relationships. These agencies are working to implement successful program strategies such as:
● recruiting adult volunteers, often with the focus of attracting males
● training mentors about the challenges they will face
● supporting mentors as they encounter some challenges in working with their young charges.

What is Racine County 4-H Camp all about? All of the above.

Campers are arranged in cabin groups by grades three through seven and are supervised by youth in grades eight through 12. Campers have a counselor, generally someone who has been a camper themselves, who supervises activities assisted by a counselor in training. These cabin groups spend the first two days at camp moving as a group, rotating from craft activity to beach time to horseback riding, and sitting as a group at all meals. The groups create their cabin chant, and create and star in the cabin skit for the Thursday night program. The counselors are the campers' first line of defense; they help ward off homesickness, escort campers to the nurse if

Agents soon discovered that their readers wanted more. Readers especially appreciated a homey touch and a practical approach, as if the agent was sitting across the kitchen table from them. Rural editors by and large were a group of curmudgeons. They knew what they wanted in their papers, and if an agent couldn't supply it, the agent's column wasn't published. Sometimes an editor would take a neophyte agent columnist aside and offer some column writing basics—mostly consisting of what had been missed in the formal writing courses the agent had taken.

When I worked in Brown County, I was asked to write two weekly columns—one for the weekly papers and one for the Friday edition of the Green Bay *Press Gazette*. Ray Pagel was farm editor. He was an excellent writer and, as it turned out, an excellent teacher. When he saw some of my early columns, he came over to my office and proceeded to give me a short course in column writing, right down to the use of commas and when to include a anecdote. He sometimes returned my columns to me for rewrites, especially in the early days. He used a red pencil, as I recall, and some columns had more red than black on them. But he stuck with me, and I learned something about column writing, which I continued to do for 20 years—well past the time I worked in Brown County.

Occasionally, local editors simply refused to carry agent columns. Maury White, a longtime agricultural journalist, taught column writing as part of a summer short course for several years. Eileen Neidermeier, home economics agent for Marathon County, attended one of his classes and said she couldn't convince the editor of a large county newspaper to even consider her columns. "When I called and asked if he might be interested in a weekly column, he said, 'Hell, no! I have too many columns to run now,'" Neidermeier said.

Maury suggested that she adopt a different strategy. "Eileen," he advised, "don't ask him if he would run your column. Send him a couple of completed columns." That's what she did when she returned to Marathon County.

Maury saw her not long afterward. She was eager to tell him what happened: "I sent a couple of my columns to this fellow's office, and a few days later he appeared in my office in person. He dropped the columns on my desk and said, in his gruff newspaper editor's voice, 'Hell yes!'" From that time forward, Neidermeier's column appeared every week in the newspaper.[13]

Weekly columns remained popular in 2001. Despite the abundance of electronic media, many people read newspapers and gained much from agent columns. In Racine County alone, Family Living Agent Beverlee Baker continued to write a column for the Racine *Journal Times* titled "Today's Family." She addressed topics including children's perceptions of parents and their work, child development, and many others. Patti Nagai, horticulture agent, wrote columns with such titles as "Winter Blahs? Brighten Interiors with Houseplants" and "Make the Effort Now for a Better Lawn Next Spring." Peter Wagner, community resource development agent, did columns on building with the environment in mind and how an energy audit can help save money on fuel and electricity. Ellen Shiflet, 4-H youth development agent, contributed columns on everything from 4-H camp to a research project that studied adult attitudes toward youth.

Newsletters
Newsletters provided ongoing contact between the County Extension office and regular participants in its programs. In many counties, newsletters went to groups with which Extension worked—dairymen, homemaker organizations, 4-H leaders, those interested in gardening, and so on.

A 2000 Manitowoc County Extension newsletter reported on how various volunteer groups had helped clean up after a widespread May 12, 2000, storm. The storm had destroyed buildings and scattered tons of debris across farmers' cornfields and pastures, and along ditches. The newsletter served as a recognition and thank you for the 550 volunteers in the county who offered their services. The newsletter also included some information on June dairy month activities, among them a "Breakfast on the Farm" event scheduled for June 25th.

Sauk County Extension published *Sauk County Clover Comments* for 4-H families, *New and Views* for homemaker members, and *Country Connections* for rural families interested in "harvesting" tourist dollars.

Some people have questioned whether the costs of producing and mailing a regular newsletter have paid off. In 1984 Linda Boelter, Extension home economist in Oneida County, and Joan E. LeFebvre, area Extension home economist for Vilas, Florence, and Forest Counties, surveyed 200 new parents who received a 12-issue *Parenting the First Year* newsletter. These home economists wondered if the old idea of a newsletter would still work. They learned that over half of these new parents had no previous contact with Cooperative Extension. More than 50 percent of those responding said the newsletter provided "a lot of help," and the average new parent had tried eight of the eleven activities designed to increase parent-child interaction and stimulate the child's development. Many of these new parents wanted additional written information.[14] This newsletter continued into the 2000s, with Dave Riley in charge of updating.

Television
By the late 1940s and early 1950s, commercial television stations had begun broadcasting throughout Wisconsin—especially in the Milwaukee, Madison, Green Bay, La Crosse and Eau Claire areas. In 1952, WHA-TV began broadcasting from improvised studios in the old chemical engineering building at UW-Madison. In the beginning, it broadcast only two half-hour programs daily to a tiny audience. By the 1980s and 1990s, Wisconsin Public Television had become a leader in the nation in broadcasting everything from history and gardening information to news analysis, public affairs programs, and educational programming focused on the performing and cultural arts.

The Department of Agricultural Journalism produced several films and was involved early in TV production. Maury White (left) and Fritz Albert.

Many Extension specialists and County Extension agents did television shows on a variety of topics related to agriculture, homemaking, and other subjects. Extension programs on gardening were popular.

Extension people also became regulars on commercial TV stations. Many of these stations employed farm directors who were always looking for program ideas. The shows were generally 30 minutes long, but some were longer. The broadcast work was done in the studio, under the hot, often stifling lights necessary to create a sharp image. Extension people learned the rules of appearing on television—don't wear white, don't wear checks, and use uncluttered visuals with special gray backgrounds.

Donald Duxbury, a northern Wisconsin agent, recalled that in 1956 three counties from Wisconsin and Michigan combined resources for an early television training session for Extension agents. It was held in Marinette. Maury White, radio and TV farm director from Madison, and Margaret McKeegan, Extension editor for home economics from East Lansing, Michigan, conducted the two-day workshop.

As Duxbury recalled, "We learned to move in slow motion on camera. Items close to the camera lens were handled with care. Informational charts were constructed in rectangular shapes. Gray paper with blue ink for on-camera use was ideal."

Duxbury returned home, anxious to try out his TV skills. He took two hens to the television studio to demonstrate the visual differences between a hen that lays eggs and one that doesn't. Duxbury recalled the show: "As I removed the chickens from the crate, one flew up onto a steel beam just under the rafters of the studio. I proceeded to show how one could observe feather changes, color around the eyes, and presence of yellow color on legs—all of which would indicate poor production. The camera operator in this one-camera studio zoomed the focus on the chicken sitting on the steel beam. I can't remember which chicken was sitting under the rafters. But I do remember I never got that chicken back."

Nyla Musser recalled her early television days when she first started work in Jackson County in 1960. "I did programs in Eau Claire and La Crosse," she said. "At first it was a short three- to four-minute presentation. [It] hardly seemed worthwhile to drive 45 to 50 miles, but the agricultural committee thought it was a good way to get out the Cooperative Extension message. How right they were. Then the programs expanded to half an hour. Sometimes I split the program into two segments, and sometimes I did the entire 30 minutes. Sometimes I did it alone, and sometimes I brought along a guest."

Extension people learned along with the station managers, as television became widespread and more people had television sets than had telephones. The stories about early TV programs and the disasters and near-disasters that occurred are legend among Extension people. Everyone discovered that what you did and how you did it, and what you said and how you said it, could not be erased and done over—which is what an agent could do when preparing a radio recording.

In the early 1960s, Green Bay commercial television stations carried live farm and home shows. These shows, which aired at noon, were half an hour long and took place in the station's studio. In the fall of 1961, during the Northeastern Wisconsin Livestock Show, the farm director at WBAY-TV called me. I was 4-H and livestock agent in Brown County at the time, and he asked if I could bring a 4-H member and a live animal to the studio to talk about the livestock show. We agreed on a 4-H member with a market lamb, because the lamb would be easy to transport and would likely present few problems in the studio when the bright lights came on and the huge cameras began dollying around. The 4-H member, a young woman, the lamb, a carefully trimmed and blocked Shropshire, and I, an overconfident television performer, arrived at the station a few minutes before the program was to air. After a look at the lamb and its handler, the farm director breathed a sigh of relief, knowing that what had happened the previous year when a beef steer tore up the studio was quite impossible with this much smaller, more easily controlled animal. The farm director informed us that Alice in Dairyland would be joining us for the show, but said she might be late because of a speaking engagement.

The lights came up, the lamb didn't move, and the program began. Everything was going even better than planned. The bright lights and the warmth in the studio seemed to make the lamb sleepy. The farm director and I began talking with the young 4-Her about her lamb, how she cared for it, what she thought of the livestock show, and what she was learning—that sort of thing. Just then, Alice in Dairyland was ushered onto the set. She wore a full-length formal gown with a beautiful corsage pinned on the right, a few inches down from the top of her left shoulder.

The farm director welcomed her to the program, then our attention turned back to the 4-Her and her Shropshire lamb. Alice in Dairyland, who was apparently not highly knowledgeable about lambs and their habits, bent over to pet the animal. She no more than got the words "Isn't this a cute lamb" out of her mouth when the lamb, now wide awake and alert, took a huge bite out of her corsage. Alice in Dairyland let out a muffled shriek, remembering she was on live TV, and her face promptly turned a bright red. There was a long moment of embarrassing silence as the lamb chewed on its mouthful of carnations and greens.

All of us have those moments when after we say something we immediately know we shouldn't have said. This was one of those times, on live television. To break the silence, I blurted out, "That lamb surely has good taste."

Alice in Dairyland's face turned an even brighter red. The farm director's face turned white. The floor crew burst into laughter, and the 4-Her began to snicker. After an agonizingly long time, the station flipped to a commercial.

According to people who had watched the show, this performance became the standard against which all other farm shows were measured.

Home Economics Answering Service

Erna Carmichael, longtime home economist in Milwaukee County, recalled the widely used home economics answering service. Callers could call during certain hours and the home economist would personally answer their questions. The canning/freezing season and the holiday cooking times were busiest. As many as 75 calls were taken in a three-hour period.

Many of the questions related to food safety. Carmichael recalled the time when a woman called and asked if it was safe to make chili from three pounds of ground meat that had been left in the car overnight. It was the middle of the August, and the night-time temperature had not gone lower than 75 degrees. The home economist explained that bacteria grow rapidly in warm conditions, especially in ground meat.

"How sick would you get if you ate spoiled meat?" the caller asked.

The home economist replied that you would become extremely ill and might even die. The conversation ended when the caller said, "I think I'll try it out on my husband. If he doesn't get sick, I'll feed to the rest of the family. I hate to throw out ground chuck."

By the 1970s, the Milwaukee County Extension staff had developed their own dial-a-tape program, using converted automobile tape decks and some grant money to record the messages. The choice of tapes was based on the most frequent telephone questions received. The Milwaukee *Journal* publicized the system, and it was an immediate success. The most popular tapes were: how to thaw a frozen turkey; how to organize a rummage sale; how to freeze string beans; the costs of disposable versus cloth diapers; and when was the proper time to harvest squash. The system included 250 additional messages.

The dial-a-message service also included horticulture topics. The most popular dial-a-garden tip was how to freeze tomatoes. This tape received 1,700 calls in one day.

Educational Telephone Network

In 1965, a telephone network consisting of 200 linked sites became available. It was initially established to make continuing education programs available to Wisconsin physicians in their home communities. By using it, they could participate without leaving their work sites.

Think of the system as a giant party-line telephone, where everyone could listen in and could, by pressing a button on a special microphone, raise questions that everyone on the line could hear.

ETN as it was commonly called, soon became available to many other groups, especially Cooperative Extension. Now it was possible for an Extension specialist to work from an ETN site in Madison and offer material to groups of people gathered at ETN sites around the state.

Soon specialists became quite adept at using the medium effectively. For instance, Ruth Diez and Lenore Landry did a series on textiles and new textile legislation that achieved national recognition. They put together packets of textile samples and other materials, which they sent to each listening site. County home economists served as moderators and on-site teachers for these programs. Because ETN was a telephone network, it was possible to patch in national experts from all around the country, which is what Landry and Diez did for this series.

In 1966, UW-Extension leased dedicated phone lines from the Wisconsin Telephone Company. These lines were available 24 hours per day, but early problems with the system presented challenges. In the middle of a presentation, an occasional mystery voice would come on the line. It was often a long-distance caller who got shunted to the wrong place. Sometimes in the middle of a presentation, with several people gathered at the listening site, the phone would go dead. And that was it. No more program.

It took a while for Extension agents and specialists to learn how to use the medium effectively. And it was difficult for many listeners to adjust to a system that seemed like radio but was less convenient because they had to drive to a listening site, usually the local courthouse. Some people never did adjust to ETN, which later became known as the Educational Teleconferencing Network. They much preferred having the person in the room with them, so they could "look them in the eye." But most put up with it because they knew it allowed them to gather and exchange information in a way that had previously been impossible. Besides, it was relatively inexpensive for all concerned. A farmer didn't have to travel farther than the county seat to obtain a wide array of information.

County Extension agents often became the keepers of the key. They were asked to make the listening site available to an array of groups, including many that were not directly related to Extension programs. Understandably, some agents grumbled until other arrangements were made for opening and closing buildings in the evenings.

By the 1990s, WisLine was available. This telephone conference call service could link three to 68 locations anywhere in the world. Another innovation was WisView, which combined audio teleconferencing with a computer-based display of charts, text, and color pictures.[15]

In addition to providing an opportunity for innovative programming, the ETN system served as an administrative tool for the state Extension office, allowing staff members to maintain regular contact with county and area-based staff around the state. The equipment has been updated several times, and the failures and problems experienced earlier have become rare.

Satellite Network

In September 1991, the WisSat satellite system began operations. Satellite dishes were erected near every Extension office in Wisconsin plus a few more, positioned from Superior to Kenosha, from La Crosse to Sturgeon Bay—75 sites in all. In addition to being used for Extension programs, the system is used by other educational institutions and government agencies plus the general public on a time and space available basis.

According to Bill Lawrence, satellite program manager, there was a steady annual growth in satellite program transmission between 1991 and 2000. During those 10 years, 814 satellite programs were initiated or produced by Digital Education/Digital Media Unit—a satellite program-producing unit within University of Wisconsin-Extension.[16]

Examples of satellite programs included "Explore New 4-H Projects," "Successful

The computer had become a widely used teaching tool by the 1980s.

Cider Making: Sanitation Is the Key," "Fish Plant Sanitation," "Family Estate Planning," and "4-H Money: Handle With Care."

Satellite videoconferencing became a valuable teaching tool. Videoconferences contained taped material, live presentations, or a combination of the two. Telephone connections allowed viewers to call in and talk with presenters during the conference. In many situations, a local moderator conducted an on-site discussion before and after the videoconference. Instructional Communications System, a unit within UW-Extension, assisted Extension staff and others who used satellite videoconferences with basic information and technical help.

Computers and the Internet
By the mid-1980s, Extension offices began replacing their dependable electric IBM typewriters (and other brands) with word processing computers. Words were no longer typed; they were now processed. Carbon paper became obsolete because the computer printer spilled out as many copies as were needed—provided the printer's pin-driven, fanfold paper didn't jump a cog and jam.

Secretaries remember letters, reports, and newsletters carefully created on a computer screen that disappeared, never to be seen again. At least when they used a typewriter, the material never disappeared.

In the 1990s, electronic mail (E-mail) became popular. Type a few lines on the screen, push a button, and an electronic message went whizzing to its recipient—no stamp, no envelope, no delay. County Extension agents could quickly communicate with each other and with other people no matter where they lived in the world, as long as the message recipients had a computer. People with computers and questions could E-mail the local Extension office or even a specialist to get the answer.

The Internet was up and running by the mid-1990s. People with a computer and Internet access had access to an overwhelming amount of information with a few keystrokes and lots of patience.

Cooperative Extension soon began creating websites so local people could obtain detailed information about their local Extension offices, including how to contact the agents and which current programs were available. Site visitors could click again to see an assortment of options at the state level, including current Cooperative Extension news releases, publication lists, available 4-H projects, even a brief explanation of Cooperative Extension's organization and purpose.

Joan Cybela, distance education specialist for Cooperative Extension, made the following observations: "The computer has become a central tool for all that we do. I can't imagine going back to a computerless way of getting the job done, and yet I revel in escaping from it for R & R. The computer is rarely a tool in and of itself anymore. Its interconnectivity is the magic link to our productivity in using it. Yes, word processing is standalone, but more often than not the product of word processing is shared in some way electronically with others, whether for publishing, committee feedback/redrafts, edits, or just to communicate with others across the state or around the world. It is an integral part of the media mix, one vital piece among other vital pieces. Text documents that were initially desktop published are now downloaded from the Web for use as print learning resources. Learners and facilitators connect via the Web to discuss ideas, follow up, clarify assignments, or share other Web-based resources. Computers have also become powerful (and sometimes mentally deadly) presentation tools for Extension, using software packages such as Power Point (Microsoft) to create and communicate information. Again, we can communicate ideas in a room or electronically send them around the world."

Distance Education

In the mid-1960s, adult education professionals began using the term "distance education" to mean educational programs that were offered using various electronic media. Distance education began long before the 1960s at the University of Wisconsin, with correspondence study offered in 1891. By 1906, a full-time staff person, W. H. Lighty, managed the "learning through the mail" program. A second historical leg for distance education was radio station 9XM, which began broadcasting in 1917 and became WHA.

In 1995, the state budget authorized construction of a $15 million addition to the

The Pyle Center on the University of Wisconsin-Madison campus is a state-of-the-art multimedia educational facility and is widely used by Extension staff.

former Wisconsin Center building, making it a state-of-the-art educational communication center. The building also received considerable private and organizational funding, including $2.4 million from the Thomas and Judith Pyle family, Epsilon Sigma Phi (the Cooperative Extension fraternity), and others. The building was named the Pyle Center and reopened in early 1999.

In 2000, everyone was busy learning a new language that contained terms like "digital media," "streaming media," "compressed video," "digital versatile disks (DVDs)," "Web-based content," "digital non-linear video," "random accessible" and others—not to mention bits, bytes, menus (no food involved) and processed words.

Along with other units in University of Wisconsin-Extension, Cooperative Extension was fully committed to an array of distance learning opportunities, allowing learners to travel short distances or not at all in order to obtain educational programs, up-to-date research information, and a host of other services via technology.

Distance education specialists such as Joe Eisele, Joan Cybela, and others worked with Cooperative Extension staff to help them understand and use the new technology in ways that enhanced teaching rather than merely providing a modern-day gimmick. Cybela prepared an on-line guide for the use of distance educators. She began the five-page pamphlet as follows: "You're a distance educator! At some time in your Cooperative Extension career you have been or will be responsible for facilitating learning at a distance. Whether the medium is satellite videoconferencing, interactive television such as compressed video, or two tin cans and a string, your role is critical to help ensure that 'education,' not just 'information,' does indeed happen!"[17]

But the old ways were not lost. There was still something to be said for the education that occurred when a County Extension agent made a house call and sat across the kitchen table to discuss a problem or concern. Demonstrations that showed a person how to do something and showed the results of an experiment continued to be important, even if reporting what had happened took new forms. Meetings also continued. People like to meet and learn. Some still like just being together.

As Cooperative Extension moved into the 2000s, the staff's bag of educational tricks had never been fuller or richer. But with so many options for carrying out educational programs, life for the Extension agent hadn't become easier. Not only did Extension staff members need to understand the multitude of available teaching approaches, they also needed to know which approach worked best with whom, and when and where to apply specific approaches. But then again, these are the questions Extension educators have faced from the very beginning.

CHAPTER 15

PROFESSIONAL DEVELOPMENT

E arly County Extension agents had to keep up to date in agriculture, translate complicated research findings into easily understood material, and teach this information in a way that kept farm people interested and involved. All three areas became grist for professional development.

Improving teaching approaches was a new idea for a college of agriculture. The college had excellent teachers in those who taught on and off campus, but the situation of the on-campus teacher was dramatically different than the situation of the county-based Extension agent. The on-campus teacher had a captive audience of students in classrooms who were working on degrees and earning grades. The exceptions were campus teachers who went on the road, traveled with the Extension trains, and spoke at farmers' institutes. In these off-campus sessions, the Madison professor had to show his mettle or he would have a considerably smaller audience the next time he appeared on the program.

With the exception of times when the county agent taught in the local agricultural school, the agent's province was not a formal classroom. The county agent's classroom was the cow barn and the cornfield, the pigpen and the hay field, the farm kitchen and the grass beneath the big elm tree in a farmer's yard.

Whatever form Extension professional development opportunities took, they usually included some combination of factual material (an updating of recent research), information about what peers were doing and with what success, and an attempt to provide something in the way of inspiration.

Early Extension leaders often spoke about the "Extension family," meaning that everyone worked together, shared what they were doing, and looked out for each other. Some disliked the use of the "family" metaphor, but few disagreed that the organization acted in many ways like an old-fashioned family with a strong-willed father at the top and mother and the children all pitching in to make sure the chores were done.

Annual Extension Conferences

In 1921, Wisconsin's county agents met in Rhinelander, marking the first time that all the agents got together in one place to share thoughts and ideas. State newspapers gave this meeting front-page coverage as if it were a major news story—and perhaps it was. The August 10, 1921, Superior *Telegram* published these headlines: "County Agents' Day Celebration" and "First County Agent in the World and the Two Men Who Succeeded Him." Photos of E. L. Luther, W. D. Juday, and C. P. West followed. These were the three men who had so far served as county agents in Oneida County. Incidentally, the paper was wrong. Luther was not the first county agent in the world. That honor went to W. C. Stallings, who had been appointed on November 12, 1906, to work in Smith County, Texas.

Agents from 52 Wisconsin counties attended the two-day confab, held on August 10 and 11. Also attending were K. L. Hatch, assistant director agriculture Extension; J.F. Wojta, state leader of county agricultural agents; and E. L. Luther, L. F. Graber, T. H. Campion, and G. M. Briggs, assistant state leaders of county agricultural agents.

Here are the counties that were represented at this first annual county agent gathering, with the names of the agents included:

Adams-E. V. Ryall	Marathon-W. W. Rogan
Ashland-M. H. Wright	Marinette-M. E. Sibole
Barron-W. A. Duffy	Oconto-Robert Amundson
Bayfield-V.E. Brubaker	Oneida-C. P. West
Brown-J. N. Kavanaugh	Ozaukee- G. S. Hales
Buffalo-Sidney P. Murat	Pierce- H. G. Seyforth
Burnett-E. H. Thompson	Polk-J. S. Klinka
Chippewa- P. D. Southworth	Portage- Warren Clark
Clark-H. M. Knipfel	Price-H. J. Rahmlow
Crawford-Merton Wright	Rock-R. T. Glassco
Dodge-A. A. Brown	Rusk-Leo Schoepf
Door-E. G. Bailey	St. Croix-A. W. Knott
Douglas-J. M. Walz	Sawyer-John H. Hill
Eau Claire-E. S. Leverich	Shawano-A. C. Murphy
Florence-A. J. Lonsdorf	Sheboygan-J. L. Wenstadt
Forest-A. W. Schmutzer	Taylor-R. A. Kolb
Grant-Paul F. Graf	Vernon-E. W. Schelling
Green Lake-James Lacey	Vilas-O. E. Gibson
Iowa-H. R. Noble	Walworth-L. J. Merriam
Jackson-G. W. Vergeront	Washburn-R. H. Rasmussen
Jefferson-J. M. Coyner	Washington-Milton H. Button
Juneau-Stanley Sand	Waukesha-J. F. Thomas
Kenosha-B. F. Wood	Waupaca-James Dance
La Crosse-W. E. Spreiter	Winnebago-G. A. Sell
Lincoln-A. H. Cole	Wood-R. A. Peterson
Manitowoc-R. R. Smith	

The front-page headlines of the Rhinelander *Daily News* for August 11, 1921, read: "Banquet To-Night Will Be the Grand Wind-up." The accompanying article began as follows: "The county agents got away to a flying start at about 8:30 this morning with a 20-car train of closely packed automobiles for their trip around the county." The paper reported visits to several Oneida County farms and a picnic dinner on the shore of "beautiful Pelican Lake, the dinner to be furnished in all its completeness by the Town of Schoekpe and its enterprising citizens."

Congressman Lever spoke to the group, falling over himself with praise and adulation. The county agent, Lever said, "is like unto John the Baptist, a man crying in the wilderness. Like John the Baptist, the county agent has too often met with rebuffs and opposition, but better counsel prevails and the county agent's position, his aims and strong desire for the betterment of agricultural conditions, is coming to be appreciated, and the day is at hand when the work of these men will be more generally understood."

Soon it was common for Extension agents to meet annually in order to be brought up to date on new agriculture and home economics research and learn new teaching approaches. But these annual meetings accomplished much more. Each meeting had a social dimension that provided agents, many of whom lived in rather isolated locations, an opportunity to share thoughts and ideas, and to reinforce each other concerning the importance of what they were doing. Many agents—myself included—worried at times that what we were doing was for naught, that nobody cared, and that our hard work and long hours made no difference. But after getting together and discovering our common feelings, we went home feeling better.

During the years that Henry Ahlgren led Cooperative Extension (starting in 1952), a highlight of each annual conference was Ahlgren's inspirational speech, delivered on the last day. He read poems, told stories, and wove together a message that had every Extension worker listening and engaged.

In 1972, the title of Ahlgren's speech was "The Impossible Dream." Early in his talk, he quoted Abraham Lincoln: "The dogmas of the quiet past are inadequate to the stormy present—as our case is new, we must think anew."

Toward the end of his speech he quoted George Bernard Shaw: "Life is no brief candle to me. It is a sort of splendid torch which I have got hold of for a moment and I want it to burn as brightly as possible before handing in it on for future generations." He even quoted an unnamed Chinese poet: "You ask me what is the supreme happiness here below?/It is listening to the song of a little girl as she goes down the road/After having asked me the way."

Along with a few other Extension people, Ahlgren had a gift for stitching together words that not only provided factual information—ideas for the head—but also emotional challenges for the heart.

Some people scoffed at Ahlgren's talks, saying he should stick to the facts and leave out the syrupy stuff. But even his critics had to agree that Ahlgren, an internationally respected agronomist, knew that Extension was more than plant varieties and fertilizer amounts, more than high-producing cows and well-managed households. Ahlgren said it well in the same speech, delivered just two years before his retirement: "There is one overriding consideration which has been held constant since the very beginning, and that is our focus. It has always been on people, not on things."

Professional development was a tough task. It is one thing to keep staff members up to date; it is quite another to keep them inspired and focused on a goal larger than merely passing on information.

District Meetings

By the time that most counties were staffed with male and female agents, the district meeting became another professional development opportunity. These meetings were usually held about once a month. Agents within a district met in a central location to discuss a wide variety of topics. The meetings started at 9 or 9:30 a.m. and continued to 3 p.m. They were organized and led by district supervisors (directors). A typical meeting included administrative announcements spelling out who hadn't turned in a required report, how the upcoming budget situation looked, and who had recently joined the staff. Afternoons were devoted to more meaty matters such as new issues in agriculture, new dietary research, and new 4-H youth program directions.

New Agent Orientation

Upon being hired, many agents were immediately given *A Handbook for Cooperative Extension Workers,* a publication that was revised over the years. The 1961 handbook included everything from standard information about retirement and health insurance plans to a listing of required reports. At the time, Extension agents were required to submit a monthly statistical and narrative report and an annual statistical and narrative report, plus in many cases monthly oral reports to the county board. The handbook also included information about the history of Extension, functions and responsibilities, the role of the county office, copies of interagency agreements with various organizations, and much more.

Sometime during their first year of employment, new agents were required to attend a "new agent conference" where they were introduced to the intricacies of the state organization and the College of Agriculture. There they met administrators and specialists and had a chance to socialize with other new agents. It was an initiation ceremony with a dose of "Here's what you do and how you do it."

District supervisors kept an eye on new agents during their first few years, not so much to check on them as to offer assistance as the agents worked their way into their positions. District directors often gave new hires the following words of advice: "Spend more time out of the office than in, especially the first couple years. Get to know the people." Program leaders worked with all agents, especially new ones, in helping them adjust to the organization and their duties.

Formal Courses in Extension Methods

The Department of Agricultural Education was established within the College of Agriculture in 1918, for the primary purpose of preparing young men to teach agriculture in the state's high schools. Later, as many young women as men were enrolled in the program.

In the 1940s Emil Jorgenson, a former agricultural agent and a district supervisor for Extension, began teaching a formal course on Extension methods in the Department of Agricultural Education. Many future vocational agricultural teachers took the course. Numerous agriculture teachers later became Extension agents.

When Henry Ahlgren took over as associate director of Cooperative Extension in 1952, he observed something that bothered him greatly. A considerable pay disparity had developed between County Extension people and those who taught on the Madison campus. Both groups were faculty members in the College of Agriculture, yet the pay difference was increasing. There also existed a certain amount of feeling that "those county agents do different things than we do, so maybe the pay difference is appropriate."

Ahlgren couldn't accept the argument. When he talked with campus administrators, he quickly learned that if he expected county agents to earn as much as campus faculty, then the agents would need comparable levels of formal education. At that time, the vast majority of county people had bachelor's degrees, while campus staff had master's and doctoral degrees.

Working with J. A. James, the chairman of the Department of Agricultural Education, Ahlgren proposed a plan to upgrade the educational credentials of county agents, so they would be seen as comparable to their campus-based colleagues. The department would broaden its purpose, change its name to Agricultural and Extension Education, and provide opportunities for county faculty to earn master's degrees. James polled the counties, and there was general agreement that the idea was a reasonable one.

Ahlgren surveyed Agricultural Extension directors nationally; they told him it was a terrible idea. However, a number of other states established departments of agricultural and Extension education several years later.

On July 1, 1954, the Department of Agricultural and Extension Education was organized, with Walter Bjoraker as chairman. James Duncan, who had recently completed a Ph.D., was brought in to teach Extension methods. Gale VandeBerg, county agent in Outagamie County, was hired to work in the department with an agreement stipulating that he simultaneously work on obtaining a Ph.D.

Ahlgren was a close personal friend of Conrad Elvehjem, dean of the graduate school, who helped work out the reorganization of the department and the approval of the new graduate program with an emphasis on Extension education.

Ahlgren was committed to making the plan work. He provided assistantship money, so county staff could be paid while they worked on degrees. He helped with

1953 Extension Summer School, Ur

budget for staff in the department as well as providing funds for expenses. The newly organized department scrambled to develop a new curriculum, obtain approval for the degrees, find space, and hire sufficient staff. The department also had to work out admission agreements with the graduate school, a task complicated by the fact that some county staff did not have undergraduate GPAs high enough for ready admission. Additional staff hired in the department included Frank Campbell, Patrick Boyle, Sara Steele, Mohammed Douglah, and Jerry Apps.

With the assistance of many, Ahlgren's plan was working. County staff began systematically returning to the campus to complete master's degrees. But not everyone was pleased. County board members often had difficulty understanding why it was necessary to take a perfectly good agent out of the county for a semester or more so he or she could complete another degree. Many county boards and county agriculture and Extension education committees didn't understand how another degree would make their agent a better one. Many weren't too keen on having to pay them more when they returned. To make matters worse some agents, armed with their newly earned master's degrees, found greener pastures and didn't return to their former positions. Some counties were infuriated with Ahlgren and his plan for upgrading county staffs.

But on balance, Ahlgren's vision resulted in higher salaries for county staff and recognition that they were full-fledged faculty of the College of Agriculture. Ahlgren's idea provided a foundation that made Wisconsin's Cooperative Extension Service one of the premier Cooperative Extension services in the country.

The Extension summer school in Madison was popular throughout the country for many years. Photo shows school in 1953.

of Wisconsin

National Extension Center for Advanced Study

Henry Ahlgren was becoming nationally known for his visionary attempts at upgrading County Extension staffs, and for encouraging state staffs to complete Ph.D. degrees. Ahlgren had friends in the W. K. Kellogg Foundation in Battle Creek, Michigan, and he and other Extension leaders wrote a proposal to create a national professional development center at Wisconsin. After several months, the Kellogg Foundation accepted the proposal and the center had begun.

The center was designed so Extension people from across the country could work toward advanced degrees. Administratively, it operated as a freestanding unit on the Madison campus, with Robert Clark as director. The first courses were offered in September 1955. The director reported to the dean of the College of Agriculture. Participants in the program earned their degrees through the Department of Agricultural and Extension Education.

The purpose of the center was "to provide academic courses, seminars, conferences, opportunities for research, pilot studies and demonstrations, and to assemble and disseminate information on administration and supervision in the Cooperative Extension Service."[1]

The staff for the center included three to six full-time faculty members, varying from year to year, and from five to seven part-time people plus secretarial support. The center soon developed a national and international reputation for far-reaching ideas about Cooperative Extension. It sponsored national, regional, and state seminars, many of them of 10 or 11 days long and covering such varied topics as personnel management, manpower development, budgeting, needed research in Extension, development of Extension leadership and administrative theory. Resource people were brought in from such far-flung disciplines (by traditional Cooperative Extension standards) as business management, psychology, sociology, political science, and higher education.

By 1961, 35 center participants had earned Ph.D. degrees and 49 had earned master's degrees. During that year, 23 additional persons worked on Ph.D. degrees and five studied for the master's degree. Several who earned degrees were Wisconsin people who went on to hold administrative positions in Cooperative Extension, including J. M. Mackey, Ava Marie Reuter (Peterson), Gale VandeBerg, George Dehnert, Marlys Richert, and Russell Robinson.

The center established a publishing unit that issued pamphlets and books with such titles as "Supervision in Extension" (translated into Spanish and Portuguese) and "Administration in Extension" which offered an emphasis on educational administration theory applied to Cooperative Extension. The center mailed a quarterly newsletter to former fellows, deans of colleges of agriculture and home economics, Extension directors, and others. The center also published a quarterly professional journal entitled *Journal of Cooperative Extension*, later simplified to *Journal of Extension*. G. L. Carter served as its first editor, followed by Jerry Apps in 1969. The journal's purpose was to provide research findings on Extension to administrators and staff throughout the country.

The center continued for 13 years and did much to elevate the professionalism of Cooperative Extension throughout the country. No longer could academic critics characterize Cooperative Extension as the "farmer outfit" that hired staff who didn't have what it took to teach on campuses.

The center helped Cooperative Extension look at itself in a thoughtful and systematic way. Additionally, the center encouraged Cooperative Extension to look outside of itself for new ideas and constructive criticism. Many graduates from the center went on to become top-level university administrators, Cooperative Extension directors, state 4-H leaders, and state home economics leaders. The National Extension Center for Advanced Study put the University of Wisconsin and its Cooperative Extension Service in a national leadership position.

The Role of Epsilon Sigma Phi

Epsilon Sigma Phi, a national organization for Cooperative Extension with state units, has long had an interest in the professional development of Extension staff. In the1970s the Wisconsin chapter, under the leadership of Gale VandeBerg, Robert Clark, and J. Mitchell Mackey, helped establish an Epsilon Sigma Phi Foundation to support agents who were doing graduate study. By the mid-1980s, Epsilon Sigma Phi had established a national foundation to enhance the professionalism of Extension workers. By 2000, the Wisconsin Epsilon Sigma Phi Foundation had a trust fund of $92,000, with a goal of increasing that amount to $400,000.[2]

Extension Summer School

The push for continued professional improvement of Extension workers took place on several levels. Starting in the 1950s and into the 1960s, district supervisors worked with county boards to effect agreements under which county staff could attend out-of-county meetings, workshops, and three-week summer schools that were being organized around the country. Two of the most popular regional summer schools were held at Colorado State University in Fort Collins and at the University of Wisconsin in Madison. An Extension winter school was later organized in Arizona.

Extension people from around the country came to Madison and studied the evaluation of Extension programs, program planning, leadership development, Extension communications, family finance, rural sociology, land-use planning, and Extension supervision. The instructors were drawn primarily from the University of Wisconsin and other land-grant universities. In addition to academic work, various evening and weekend social activities were highlights of these schools. Extension historian E. R. McIntyre reported that between 1950 and 1960, the Madison Extension summer school enrolled 435 county agents, 245 associate and assistant agents, 127 4-H agents, 299 home demonstration agents, 15 assistant home agents, 36 supervisors in agriculture, 32 supervisors in home economics, 12 directors of Extension, 33 farm and home agents, and 100 who were not classified.[3]

Ahlgren and others had worked out an agreement with the graduate school at the University of Wisconsin that enrollees in the Extension summer school could earn graduate credit for the courses they took. But even more important for out-of-state Extension workers was the opportunity to enroll in the Wisconsin graduate courses without paying hefty out-of-state tuition. Everyone who attended the summer school paid the same tuition.

Beginning in 1955, Extension summer school participants and Extension Fellows who were working toward degrees with the National Extension Center for Advanced Study were on campus at the same time. It was a rich time for the exchange of ideas among Extension persons from across the country who had gathered in Madison. Professional development had become accepted as necessary to ensure Cooperative Extension's continued success, particularly because this was a time when massive structural changes were occurring in agriculture and rural America.

Division of Staff Development

Several staff members in the Department of Agricultural and Extension Education taught campus courses and assisted with Extension professional development activities in the 1950s and 1960s. This was a time when evaluation, program planning, and leadership development courses were created for graduate credit and also were translated into workshop topics for county staff. The same people who taught the credit courses taught the off-campus workshops.

In 1965, when the Extension merger created University of Wisconsin-Extension, a Division of Staff Development was organized. Patrick Boyle became director, and several faculty members from the Department of Agricultural and Extension Education (and others) joined him. These faculty members included Sara Steele, James Duncan, and Jerry Apps. Later, Laverne Forest and Terry Gibson were added to the division. The faculty members who had been in the Department of Agricultural and Extension Education retained their campus teaching responsibilities but the budget for their Extension work was moved to University of Wisconsin-Extension.

Staff in the Division of Staff Development (later the Division of Program and Staff Development) organized workshops on a variety of topics, helped faculty learn new reporting requirements, assisted with evaluation studies, organized annual conferences, and helped develop new program approaches. Under continued pressure to show results, Extension nationally developed elaborate measurement, accountability, and reporting techniques. Program and Staff Development faculty had responsibility for implementing these new, often resisted approaches with county and state staff. Reporting systems such as the Extension Management Information System (EMIS) and a Wisconsin version (State Management Information System, or SEMIS) were introduced and implemented by the Division of Program and Staff Development. Although not uniformly accepted by Extension staff, these reports helped assure decision makers that Extension budgets were making a difference in the lives of people.

The Division of Program and Staff Development operated until the early 1980s, when reorganization eliminated the division and put staff development functions in the re-created Division of Cooperative Extension.

National Extension Leadership Development (NELD)

By the early 1980s, many national Extension leaders recognized that a leadership vacuum would occur at the top levels of state organizations within a few years. Many administrators who had started work in the 1950s were retiring. Under the leadership of Patrick Borich, Extension director in Minnesota, Ed Boone, Extension professor from North Carolina, and Patrick Boyle, University of Wisconsin-Extension chancellor, the national Extension Committee on Organization and Policy (ECOP) began discussing a new leadership development initiative.

Borich, Boyle, and Boone drafted a proposal to the W. K. Kellogg Foundation for money to create a center, somewhat after the fashion of the National Extension Center for Advanced Study, which had operated in the 1950s and early 1960s. However, NELD was not to be a graduate training program. It would be designed for those who already had graduate degrees and were interested in higher-level administrative positions.

For several months Boyle, Borich, and Boone wrote and rewrote sections of the proposal. Finally, the Kellogg Foundation agreed to fund the program. It was designed to operate for four years with Kellogg and Extension support. After that, all support would come from Extension. States were invited to apply to host the program.

University of Wisconsin-Extension was selected for the first four years (1989-1993), under the leadership of Jerry Apps as national coordinator, Judith Adrian as outreach specialist, Boyd Rossing as program evaluation coordinator, and Tim Neuman as graduate student assistant for evaluation. All staff worked part-time, including the national coordinator.

The NELD staff, along with its advisory committee and various national Extension leaders, worked out a curriculum for leadership development that focused on leadership for changing times.[4] NELD's program included: an internship program for those who had recently assumed an Extension leadership position; an administrative leadership workshop series for top-level state and national leaders; and a national forum for presidents of land-grant universities. The national forum, which was held in La Jolla, California, from February 28 through March 2, 1993, brought together land-grant presidents from around the country to discuss new directions for university outreach efforts. Three hundred participants attended, representing 52 institutions.

Three intern classes were organized while NELD was at Wisconsin, with workshops conducted at Tuskegee University (involving an opportunity to live with African-American families); Brussels, Belgium (involving a study of European economics); an Indian Reservation in North Dakota (an opportunity to live with Native-American Families); Mexico City (an examination of the North American Free Trade Agreement); and New Orleans.

Wisconsin Extension staff members participated as interns, attended administrative workshops held in Stowe, Vermont, and Olive Branch, Mississippi, and were heavily involved in the national forum. Some of the early participants in NELD activities who remained working in Wisconsin Cooperative Extension in 2000 included Sue Buck, Mary Brintnall-Peterson, and Carl O'Connor.

In 1994, NELD moved to Ohio State University and later to Colorado State University. It continued in 2001, with a new class of Extension interns selected each year.

Recreational Leadership Laboratory
The recreational leaders' laboratory was organized as a way to help Extension staff, volunteers, and others develop recreational skills. In 1938, a five-day recreational leaders' laboratory was held at Phantom Lake. Wisconsin churches, farm organizations, the rural YMCA, Works Progress Administration (WPA), and Cooperative Extension cooperatively sponsored the laboratory. The program featured crafts, games, folk dancing, and drama, and also included a section on the philosophy of recreation and the increasing importance of the use of leisure time.[5]

For many years, the recreational leaders' laboratory was held at the fairgrounds in Wausau, where participants stayed in dormitories. Later, the laboratory moved to Camp Upham Wood in Wisconsin Dells.

The 1963 workshop was held from April 15 through April 20 in Wausau. Forty-two people attended, including three 4-H agents, seven home economics agents, 10 county 4-H leaders, 15 county 4-H junior leaders, three College of Agriculture students, one representative from Campfire Girls, and a recreation leader from a children's home. Staff members included Jerry Apps, state 4-H staff and director; Robert Ellarson, specialist in wildlife management; Tom Echtner, art education; Marvin Hanson, state 4-H staff; Elda Schrader, elementary teacher; Carl Yoder, campus school music teacher at Wisconsin State College, Stevens Point; and Billie Howes, graduate student at the University of Wisconsin.

Each day started with a nature hike at 6:15 a.m. and ended with an evening program that concluded by 10:30 p.m. Topics included understanding nature; leading singing groups; how to do silk screening, block printing, and hand stenciling; leading games at meetings and parties; leading circle, folk, and square dances; and how to direct plays and other dramatic events.

Those attending the recreation workshops were expected to lead recreation efforts in their communities and teach others how to do it. It was a time when having fun was seen as an important part of living, and Cooperative Extension assumed some responsibility for helping with the endeavor.

Professional development has long been an important aspect of Wisconsin Cooperative Extension. During the 1950s and 1960s, Wisconsin was seen as a national leader in providing training opportunities and advanced degrees for Extension leaders across the country, in helping to establish new directions for the organization, and in establishing an unprecedented level of professionalism.

CHAPTER 16

HISTORICAL THEMES

Both positive and negative themes thread through the history of Wisconsin Cooperative Extension. Some themes emerged in the early 1900s, while others are as recent as the 1980s and 1990s.

Administrative Leadership

When Cooperative Extension was a part of the College of Agriculture, the head of Cooperative Extension was an associate dean responsible to the dean of the college. Leadership was certainly important, but not at the level of importance it has held since the 1965 merger that created University of Wisconsin-Extension. In 1965 Cooperative Extension, as a part of University of Wisconsin-Extension, developed a new relationship to the Madison campus. Although UW-Extension was still connected to the College of Agriculture and Life Sciences on the Madison campus, it was for all intents and purposes a separate division. Divisions had to fight for budgets, and Cooperative Extension had to fight for its very survival.

Since 1965, the leadership at the top has made all the difference whether the organization moved forward or slipped into an abyss—whether the Extension ship sailed or the boat wallowed and began taking water. At the time of UW-Extension's creation, University President Fred Harvey Harrington believed in the Wisconsin Idea and saw the creation of University of Wisconsin-Extension as a way of strengthening it.

Looking at Extension's history, it's clear that when a strong leader was at the helm, Extension prospered; when leadership was lacking, Extension was in trouble.

Reflecting on his own experiences, retired Chancellor Patrick Boyle said an Extension chancellor needed the following qualities:

• The ability to articulate and communicate a vision—a clear direction for the institution.

• An understanding of leadership with an engaging management style.

• Honesty and trust. A commitment to trust decisions that involved colleagues.

• Political astuteness. The ability to recognize the various political forces that affect the institution and be able to communicate a positive message to them.

Boyle believed that political astuteness was the most important quality.[1]

Structural Wars

When Cooperative Extension merged with General Extension and radio/television to form University of Wisconsin-Extension, the structural wars started. At times the wars went underground for a few years, but then they bubbled to the surface and the fight continued.

Many people inside and outside of Extension could not accept that Cooperative Extension was taken lock, stock and budget out of the College Agriculture in Madison. Starting in 1965, untold thousands of hours of faculty and administrator time went into deciding how Cooperative Extension should be organized, who should report to whom, where the budget would be controlled, what the titles should be, and who should fill the roles. Most Extension agents and specialists paid little attention to the organizing and reorganizing activities until the results affected them. Perhaps they reported to a different dean, or became part of a different unit or department. A needy public generally didn't care about structural changes, as long as Extension agents and specialists were doing their jobs.

Former administrators such as Vice Chancellor Gerald Campbell saw the University of Wisconsin-Madison's fight to retain its control over Cooperative Extension and its independence from campuses such as Stevens Point, Platteville, and River Falls resulting in "much less achievement than [there] could have been. There were so many hours spent trying to unbreak eggs that were broken."[2]

The Wisconsin Idea

Since the early 1900s, the Wisconsin Idea has been Extension's fundamental theme. The phrase associated with it, "The boundaries of the campus are the boundaries of the state," became Extension's slogan. Into the 2000s, literature about Extension and its activities was still liberally sprinkled with the words "the Wisconsin Idea."

The roots of the Wisconsin Idea are usually traced to three men: Governor Robert M. LaFollette, who was elected in 1900; Charles R. Van Hise, who became president of the University of Wisconsin in 1903; and Charles McCarthy of the Wisconsin Free Library Commission, who developed the Legislative Reference Library in 1901. McCarthy believed that university professors should help him as he provided information to state legislators for proposed legislation. McCarthy is said to have encouraged Van Hise to start a university Extension, which would be funded by the Wisconsin legislature. In 1907, Wisconsin became the first state in the nation to appropriate funds for an Extension division. In 1908, the legislature voted $30,000 to be provided annually for an agricultural Extension Service. By this time, College of Agriculture professors had already been actively involved in Extension activities throughout the state.

The phrase "the Wisconsin Idea" didn't appear until 1912, when McCarthy wrote a book with that title. The notion that "the boundaries of the campus are the boundaries of the state" was introduced later, by someone on the university's public relations staff.[3]

In 2000 some regarded the Wisconsin Idea as a bit limiting, since problems and programs often transcend state lines. But it still worked when a lawmaker needed a little convincing about what the university was doing away from its campuses.

Partnerships

From the 1980s, and especially during the 1990s, Cooperative Extension stressed partnerships with many agencies, institutions and organizations. However, partnership is an old idea for Extension. The "Cooperative" in Cooperative Extension relates to an official cooperating partnership among three units of government—federal, state, and county. County Extension agents and state specialists have long known that if their programs are to succeed, they must learn to work with each other, with other educational agencies, with farm organizations, and especially with local units of government. Extension has been quite successful working with others, but there have been problems, too. When developing a partnership with another tax-supported agency, the question of who got the credit usually came up. The quick answer—that there's plenty of credit to go around—usually didn't suffice.

Tradition sometimes got in the way of new partnerships, especially partnerships between Cooperative Extension and campuses other than Madison. Al Beaver, interim chancellor, believed that Cooperative Extension missed major opportunities for county people and state specialists to build more ties with campuses beyond Madison. Too many staff members had ties to the Madison campus, and loyalty got in the way—or these staff members were not comfortable with exploring other relationships. Sometimes, Madison-based faculty had too little respect for others who were well qualified.

A challenge in forming partnerships was making sure that a partner's agenda didn't supersede Extension's educational role. Carl O'Connor, dean for Cooperative Extension, expressed this fear well: " [Our] challenge is to find and to negotiate a meaningful educational role that is independent but complementary to the role of the partner. We have been able to do that with many of Wisconsin's agencies and municipalities. However difficult this may be, this will be one of our most important sources of funding in the future."[4]

Research-Based Information

Extension's strength has been its ability to rely on research generated by university scientists. In 2000, many commercial firms did research and offered the results to consumers, but the university's research was viewed as free of bias, because it came from an organization with no products to sell. Nevertheless, critics claimed that some university research did have a bias, and questions were raised. Ellen Fitzsimmons, associate dean for Cooperative Extension, said the public has changed its view of university research. She mentioned the BST-BGH controversy, involving use of technology to increase milk production, and other biotechnology as examples. "Our Extension specialists were used to delivering university information to people. In the area of biotechnology, having a specialist say it was so did not mean people believed it to be so. Specialists had to learn new skills in media and conflict resolution. This was a shock to some specialists, and to some field staff."[5]

Who did the research became an important question. Some university people believed that unless the research was done at the university, it lacked value. By 2000, the research model that appeared to work was a combination of research done by university researchers and that done by local people. Sometimes people tried to apply university research to their own situation, and sometimes they came up with entirely new ideas. "Indigenous research" was the label given to this research performed by local people. Some university researchers sneered at indigenous research, saying it came from non-scientific research procedures. However, if it worked, people used it. As Fitzsimmons said: "Community members have knowledge, and the university needs to value it, and [besides] people don't really believe research that isn't local."

The old model for Extension called for the university to generate knowledge and for Extension specialists to translate it and distribute it to county-based staff. Today, as Gerald Campbell, former vice chancellor for UW-Extension said, "The leadership role of campus-based specialists has been turned on its head. Extension specialists are caught in an ever-widening gap between faculty colleagues whose orientation is increasingly to the national and international research issues which bring dollars and distinction and the county-based faculty who need help with the specific problems of local communities."[6]

Jim Massey, general manager and editor of *Country Today*, offered reflections on Extension agents he has known: "If the Extension agents I worked with could have done anything differently, I think it would have been that they could have relied more heavily on farmers talking to other farmers . . . I spent too many meetings listening to Extension agents and state specialists talk about research results that weren't practical until there was a farmer there to say it worked for him or her. That was often the missing ingredient."

Massey, however, also recognized Extension as an independent research source. "Farmers and community people are so inundated with information from companies trying to sell them something that they need a neutral voice to help them sort through it all. That's where Extension has been valuable."[7] By the 1990s, Cooperative Extension agents and specialists were spending time with company representatives, to help them provide up-to-date information to their customers.

A further problem with university-based research is the time it takes for results. When problems emerge, people want answers, and they sometimes turn to non-institutional researchers because they can provide answers sooner. Pam Jahnke, a farm radio broadcaster, observed: "[The university's] independent research is still welcomed by all of agriculture, but it can take longer than the industry will tolerate."[8]

Program Focus
In the early days, the question of Extension focus was an easy one to answer.

Cooperative Extension worked on farm and farm-related problems. With the passage of Smith-Lever in 1914, focus broadened to include programs for women, boys, and girls. Two world wars and a depression changed Cooperative Extension's focus, and the massive changes in rural America that followed World War II greatly affected what Extension did. Several state and national planning efforts, including the "Scope Report," were mounted to figure out the best direction for Extension. As the years passed, additional legislation broadened the role of Cooperative Extension. And in 1965, with the formation of University of Wisconsin-Extension, the scope broadened still more. Expanded programming continued into the 2000s, especially in environmental programming, nutrition programs for low-income families, and community development efforts.

Extension's critics—especially some in the farm press—believed that Extension broadened its focus too much, thus losing sight of its historical mandate, which was working with rural people to help them solve their problems.

Kurt Gutknecht, editor of the *Wisconsin Agriculturist*, wrote an in-depth article in 1997 that was critical of Extension's expanded focus. "You can't fault the UW's Cooperative Extension Service for a lack of goals," he wrote, "and that may be part of the problem. For decades, the Cooperative Extension Service has fended off criticism that it's an organization in search of a mission. Moreover, there's the belief that 'mission creep' has diluted its ability to service production agriculture. Criticism of agricultural programs runs the gamut from producing outdated information to accelerating the industrialization of agriculture. The doubts about Co-op Extension's value to agriculture are widespread." In the same article, Gutknecht quoted Ben Brancel, a farmer and then Speaker of the Assembly, as saying, "[Extension] seemed to have lost focus of its mission." Gutknecht also quoted Ron Statz, the National Farm Organization's state director of membership said, "We feel their focus has been diverted from production agriculture into sociological aspects."[9]

The article prompted a flurry of responses, both in agreement and opposition. Al Beaver, chancellor of UW-Extension, wrote: "The lead article in your May issue suggests that agricultural programming has suffered as Extension programs have grown and changed over time. In reality, agricultural programs have been one of the primary beneficiaries of our efforts to adapt to the changes taking place in farming, agribusiness, and society as a whole."[10]

The *Wisconsin Agriculturist* has not been alone in criticizing Extension's expanded focus. Farm broadcaster Pam Jahnke said, "I'm afraid Extension is trying to be a 'jack of all trades and master of none.'"[11]

Joan Sanstadt, news editor of *Agri-View*, made the following observation: "My heart has always been with Extension. Today's role for Extension is changing, and not always in the right direction, in my opinion. Extension is caught up in obtaining outside funding, which may be necessary. But [they] may be forgetting their first mission is agriculture. [Extension] is going into areas like water quality to find money—maybe they shouldn't bend in these directions."[12]

John Oncken, who heads up Oncken Communications, worked as 4-H agent and later as agricultural agent in Clark County from 1957 to 1965. "I'm an Extension backer," he said, "but sometimes I think today's Extension is too busy doing to tell us what they are doing." Oncken is critical of Extension, especially of the state office, for not keeping people like him up to date on emerging Extension programs. "They [Extension administrators] seem very guarded," Oncken said. "They are reluctant to let people like me know what's going on. You'd think the state office people would call some of us in the press together once in a while and let us know what's happening—give us a chance to meet some of the new leadership in Madison. I do work with many County Extension people. And I'm generally impressed."[13]

The question of Extension's focus is one that is unlikely to go away. In 2001, the challenge for Cooperative Extension involved keeping old audiences happy and supportive while bringing in new ones.

Action Orientation

Extension people know how to get things done. They don't sit around theorizing and reflecting. Instead, they meet people, call meetings, and get on with helping people and communities solve problems. They leave reflection and theorizing to someone else.

Gerald Campbell wanted busy Extension people to stop doing once in a while and think about what they just did—and perhaps to write it down and tell others about it, so they wouldn't have to keep "reinventing the wheel." Campbell said he wanted Extension people to ask, when they completed a program: "What did we learn from doing this? This is not the usual kind of evaluation. [Staff] need to take the time to think carefully about what went on, what worked, what didn't, what could we teach someone else about this? [But Extension people] were disposed to keep running."

Campbell believed that Extension could have learned much from its many action-oriented efforts, if it had been willing to take some time for reflection—time to write down what happened and why. In his opinion, not nearly enough reflective scholarship took place. He also believed this was somewhat understandable. "Extension attracted action-oriented people. It rewarded action-oriented people. It didn't particularly reward academically oriented people who wanted to write and teach [about what they did]."[14]

Often, valuable lessons were not passed on to other Extension workers who might one day benefit from them. In many cases, even when Extension programs were carefully evaluated, measured for accomplishments, and reported, the behind-the-scenes information concerning what was done, with whom, and why and how, remained a mystery to those who might learn from these actions. This, too, has become something of a historical theme for Extension.

Supporters

Loyal support has been a constant for Cooperative Extension, especially during times of difficulty. Mention a budget cut or suggest eliminating a county position and Extension supporters rose up and did what had to be done. They usually prevailed. Even some of Extension's critics became supporters.

Many Extension supporters had their first contact with the organization as 4-H members. Joan Sandstadt, news editor with *Agri-View*, can be very critical of Extension's focus, but she says she got her start as a writer when she was in 4-H. "I was a 4-H member in the Happy Hustlers 4-H Club in northern Minnesota, where I wrote news articles for the Red Lake Falls *Gazette*."

Broadcaster Pam Jahnke also remembers fondly her 4-H days in Oconto County. "Four-H brought kids together from throughout the county. No competition. Just a bunch of kids/teens getting together for some project or another. I still keep in touch with a lot of those people."

Wally Hitt, Extension agent in Marinette County, described Jeff Brault, who started attending 4-H meetings when he was in second grade. He was so shy he wouldn't even raise his hand to second a motion. Over the years, Jeff participated in 4-H music and drama events with the Little River 4-H club. He entered the 4-H speaking contest as he slowly gained self-confidence, then became a club officer. As a teen, he helped promote 4-H by doing radio promos. Now Dr. Jeff Brault is a specialist at the Mayo Clinic, and he thanks 4-H for helping him overcome his extreme shyness and develop his self-confidence.

In Barron County, Wallace Jerome joined a 4-H Club in 1925, enrolling in the poultry project. In 1929, as a member of the Maple Grove 4-H Club, Wallace became the poultry champion of Wisconsin and won a trip to the National 4-H Club Congress in Chicago.

Wallace Jerome went on to become one of Wisconsin's largest turkey producers, contributing to Barron's status as "the Turkey Capital of Wisconsin."

Orion Samuelson, noted WGN radio and TV personality and longtime reporter of national agricultural events, credits much of his success to his start as a Wisconsin 4-H member.

But no matter what program area, those who have participated in Extension programs have become supporters. They are a force to be reckoned with when changes in Cooperative Extension are suggested.

Organization-Building

Cooperative Extension people are organizers. They know how to bring people together and show them how to accomplish more together than they could by themselves. Extension people have organized everything from 4-H clubs and homemaker clubs to feeder pig cooperatives, lake districts, writing clubs, arts groups, tourism committees, and much, much more.

Organizational skills have been a great strength for Extension and an exceedingly important theme. Unfortunately, Extension staff members have at times been burdened by organizations they helped form. They have served as executive secretaries, treasurers, and advisors, positions that required untold hours of their time. And sometimes an organization was formed when it wasn't needed. But most organizations served well, and they continue as one of Extension's many legacies.

Changing Staff Role

The success of Cooperative Extension has been due to its state and county staff. The organization's history is replete with stories of Extension men and women and what they accomplished—often under the most trying circumstances. Earlier chapters chronicled many examples of their work.

A great strength of Cooperative Extension, as opposed to other adult education agencies and organizations, was having staff located in each county, ensuring easy access. In the late 1990s, the role of community-based staff began changing, according to Ellen Fitzsimmons, associate dean for Cooperative Extension. Family living agents worked less with traditional audiences such as homemakers and 4-H, and more with public policy and community change. "They work with community coalitions and community influentials much more than in the past. Youth development is struggling . . . as they work to do broad youth development education beyond the traditional 4-H club. Agriculture agents don't set up chairs and make coffee for state specialists to come out and teach anymore. They are doing more . . . teaching at the local level and [sharing with agents in neighboring counties]." She explained that community natural resource and economic development agents in Wisconsin were among the first agents to work in new ways with community power structures and coalitions, and have become the best in the nation.[15]

Carl O' Connor, Extension dean in 2000, offered the following summation: "As community needs change and new educational programs emerge, Extension often finds itself needing to hire new educators. In 2000, as many as 150 recently hired academic staff worked with low-income families focused on nutrition education. Extension sought individuals who were well known and respected in their neighborhoods. In many cases, the new hires had little or no formal education past high school. As successful and important as the nutrition program is, it adds a complexity to the county office that was not there prior to the program. We have had some growing pains, but I am proud of the increased diversity of our programming and our staff. We are definitely a stronger and better organization as a result of this program, and the benefits to the community are huge."[16]

Final Comments

In spite of internal administrative turmoil and forces resisting change, change has always been central to Cooperative Extension—and to the Wisconsin Idea. As the issues and problems facing Wisconsin citizens have changed, Extension has modified existing programs, created new ones, and allocated resources to better serve people and maintain their support.

Wisconsin's Cooperative Extension continues to make history as it moves into the twenty-first century. The problems and challenges the organization has faced will continue. It will have its critics and its supporters. But when all the histories of Cooperative Extension are writ large and small, there will be no disagreement that the people always came first.

Appendix I

Extension Agent Organizations

During the early 1920s, at every February Farm and Home Week meeting, County Extension agents talked about organizing an agent association. Extension Director Hatch wasn't too keen on the idea and raised many questions about the need for such an organization. But in 1924, a group of county agents met and formed an agent association with eight committees. One activity the organization undertook was to review agent salaries. In 1928, the average salary among 52 county agents was $2,867, which included $1,167 from the county and $1,700 from state and federal contributions.

The County Agent Association remained active into the 1930s. At its October 18, 1934, meeting, Edith Bangham reported on the activities of homemakers clubs. By this time, several counties had home demonstration agents. Soon the group began discussing whether home demonstration agents should be allowed to join. The group agreed that they should, passing a motion to change the organization's name to Wisconsin Extension Workers Association.

However, at the February 6, 1935, meeting the group still called itself the Wisconsin County Agents Association. Another motion to change the name to Wisconsin Extension Workers Association passed, and this time the name was finally changed. Now home demonstration agents and agents with major responsibilities in 4-H work could belong. At the October 17, 1935, meeting the group elected L. G. Merriam as president, Emil Jorgensen as vice president, and Helene French as secretary-treasurer.

The group was active for many years, providing both social and professional development opportunities for Wisconsin Cooperative Extension staff members. When a huge old oak tree on Bascom Hill on the Madison campus died, Professor Walter Rolands obtained some of the wood. He made a supply of oak gavels, and each year presented one to the newly installed president of the Wisconsin Extension Workers Association. The last one was presented to Robert Stodola, Washington County 4-H and youth agent, in 1969. When the association was closed down in 1970, Stodola presented the gavel to the Wisconsin Association of Extension 4-H and Youth Agents. Each year, the gavel is passed on to the newly installed president of that organization.[1]

About 1967, the Wisconsin Extension Workers Association changed its name to University Extension Association of Wisconsin. The decision to rename the group reflected the 1965 formation of UW-Extension. It was hoped that members of the newly merged Extension organization would join their Cooperative Extension colleagues in this newly named University Extension Association, but it didn't happen. On November 16, 1970, the University Extension Association met to discuss its future. Joe Walker, county agricultural agent in Waupaca County, was president. Norman Everson was secretary.

At that November meeting President Walker offered the following remarks: "Now it seems that the University Extension Association has been in a somewhat confused state for a few years. As a matter of fact, about three years ago it was suggested we take one of three routes: 1) disband; 2) make minor revision of the bylaws so other Extension members could be eligible to join, but basically continue with the same programs; or 3) make major revisions which would change the dues structure, change honoree programs, and incorporate new functions and ideas.

"Our records show that only seven non-Cooperative Extension faculty joined UEAW during the three years [since the 1967 name change]. The reoccurring question at our board meetings has been: What are we going to do with UEAW?"

A motion was offered to dissolve the organization. The motion passed with little debate, and the remaining funds were given to a student loan fund, to the Wisconsin 4-H Foundation (Epsilon Sigma Phi), and to the three Wisconsin agents' associations that had continued to function. Many longtime Cooperative Extension workers were upset by the demise of the Wisconsin Extension Workers Association.[2]

Extension Organizations in 2000
In 2000, five organizations existed for Cooperative Extension members plus a sixth organization, Wisconsin Association of Extension Professionals, which provided a coordinating link among the various professional associations.

Wisconsin Association of County Agricultural Agents
Although records do not indicate a precise date, a second organization for county agricultural agents emerged in the very early 1960s. The first election of officers occurred in 1961. Elected were H.W. Kinney, president; M. P. Pinkerton, vice president; and Fred Field, secretary.

The association filed Articles of Incorporation in the early 1970s, probably 1973. The incorporated name was "Wisconsin County Agents Association." However, the name was changed to Wisconsin Association of County Agricultural Agents (WACAA) in 1993. Over the years, membership in the organization has ranged from 76 to 83 members.[3]

The membership of this organization includes county and area agricultural agents, specialists, and others maintaining membership in the National Association of County Agricultural Agents. The purposes of the organization are to improve agent effectiveness, provide professional improvement opportunities, recognize outstanding work, and provide for program exchanges. The association is affiliated with the National Association of County Agricultural Agents, which holds national meetings and sponsors distinguished service awards.

Wisconsin Extension Association of Family and Consumer Sciences
This organization began with a meeting held at the Memorial Union Building on the University of Wisconsin-Madison Campus on March 30, 1936. An earlier planning meeting had been held in Wausau in 1934. The organization was first known as the

Wisconsin Home Agents' Association. At the 1936 meeting, Helen Pearson was elected president, and dues of $1 per year were established. A total of $13 was collected at the first meeting.

The purpose of the organization in 2001 is to strengthen professional standards, exchange programs and accomplishments, and recognize leadership and professional abilities. The organization is also concerned about public policy and educating its members in public policy matters. WEAFCS promotes Extension family and consumer sciences and helps develop an awareness of family and community needs. State members are automatically members of the National Extension Association of Family and Consumer Sciences, which conducts an Extension awards program plus providing an opportunity to share outstanding research programs. Wisconsin had 85 members in 2001.

Wisconsin Association of Extension 4-H Youth Development Professionals

Wisconsin employed Extension agents who worked with youth programs as early as 1927. Agents with major 4-H responsibilities could belong to the Wisconsin Extension Workers Association starting in 1935. But 4-H agents, many of whom were known as assistant county agents, had special concerns: the future of the 4-H club agent as a career position; their status compared to other agents; long hours, low salaries, and rapid turnover. Several decided they needed their own organization, which began in 1948. Howard Knox was informally appointed chairman in 1948, and Marvin Hanson was elected president for 1948-49. This was the beginning of the Wisconsin Association of Extension 4-H and Youth Agents (WAE4-HYDP).

In 2000, membership was open to any person with full or partial responsibility for Extension youth programs. Members included faculty, academic staff (both state and county), state staff, program assistants, and university students interested in a career as a 4-H youth development professional. The organization was considering ways to extend membership to 4-H youth development professionals in state tribal colleges. The association provides professional development opportunities, promotes and shares research papers, and recognizes achievements. Membership in the national organization provides additional opportunities for professional improvement through annual meetings and a quarterly publication titled *News and Views*. As of 2001, the organization had 94 active members and 29 life members.[5]

Wisconsin Extension Community Development Association

In 2000, membership in WECDA was open to faculty, academic staff, and retirees of UW-Extension who currently or formerly had responsibility for community development. The association designs and sponsors an agent- and specialist-mentoring program. It also works to build collegial support and provides members an opportunity to share programs at the annual meeting, where awards are given for excellence and service.

The association began in September 1973 with 50 members. By 2000, the membership total had reached 76. Each year the Wisconsin Extension Community

Development Association awards four $250 scholarships to support the professional development of its members.[6]

Epsilon Sigma Phi—Alpha Sigma Chapter

Epsilon Sigma Phi (ESP) is a national honorary Extension fraternity that began in Wisconsin in about 1930. Nationally, Epsilon Sigma Phi began in 1938. The membership brochure states that "ESP provides opportunities for leadership, networking, fellowship, and collaborative effort among present and former Cooperative Extension employees. The chapter provides honorary recognition, grants, and loans to its members and monitors state and federal benefits programs that impact members."[7]

Major ESP activities have included raising money for the Pyle Center and raising funds to augment the chapter's endowment fund. The endowment fund supports Cooperative Extension employee professional development. Those providing early leadership for the fund included Gale L. VandeBerg, J. Mitchell Mackey, and Robert C. Clark. In 2001, ESP membership stood at 365.

Wisconsin Association of Extension Professionals

This organization began on May 11, 1978, when officers of the various Extension associations met to discuss creating a statewide "umbrella-type" organization. All of the associations expressed an interest.

On March 15, 1979, a steering committee of Wisconsin Extension agent organizations met and agreed to move the idea forward. The first minutes of the group were dated June 21, 1979. At that meeting, Louis Rosendick was elected chairman and Keith Nelson was elected secretary. The group agreed on who was eligible to belong, whether administrators could be members, and the purpose of the new organization. Members also discussed what other states with similar groups were doing and set the next meeting for September 6, 1979.[8]

In 2000, membership of this umbrella organization consisted of three elected or appointed representatives from each of the member organizations: Wisconsin Association of Extension 4-H Youth Development Professionals; Wisconsin Extension Association of Family and Consumer Sciences; Wisconsin Association of County Agricultural Agents; Wisconsin Extension Community Development Agents; and Epsilon Sigma Phi. The organization's board consists of a chairperson, chairperson-elect, secretary, and treasurer.

The purpose of the organization is to strengthen communications among all Extension faculty and administrators, and to encourage cooperation among the various Extension associations.

Extension organizations have served important functions over the years and continue to do so into the 2000s. Professional development of staff remains a major role played by these organizations, together with building esprit de corps.

APPENDIX II

ORGANIZATION OF UNIVERSITY OF WISCONSIN-EXTENSION (2001)

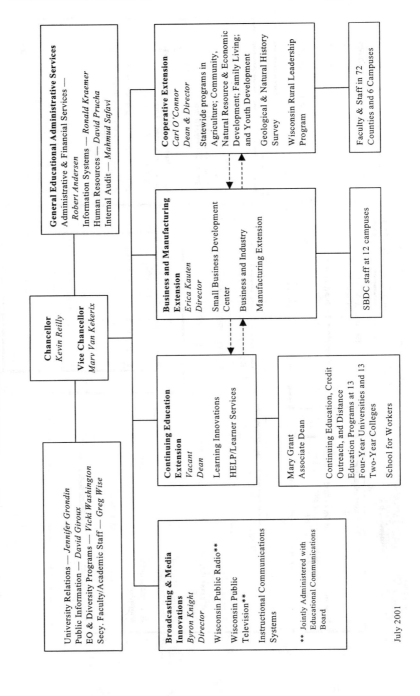

Serving Wisconsin People with Educational Programs Where They Live and Work

UNIVERSITY OF WISCONSIN-EXTENSION

Chancellor
Kevin Reilly

Vice Chancellor
Marv Van Kekerix

University Relations — *Jennifer Grondin*
Public Information — *David Giroux*
EO & Diversity Programs — *Vicki Washington*
Secy. Faculty/Academic Staff — *Greg Wise*

General Educational Administrative Services
Administrative & Financial Services —
Robert Andersen
Information Systems — *Ronald Kraemer*
Human Resources — *David Prucha*
Internal Audit — *Mahmud Safavi*

Cooperative Extension
Carl O'Connor
Dean & Director

Statewide programs in
Agriculture; Community,
Natural Resource & Economic
Development; Family Living;
and Youth Development

Geological & Natural History
Survey

Wisconsin Rural Leadership
Program

Faculty & Staff in 72
Counties and 6 Campuses

Business and Manufacturing Extension
Erica Kauten
Director

Small Business Development
Center

Business and Industry

Manufacturing Extension

SBDC staff at 12 campuses

Continuing Education Extension
Vacant
Dean

Learning Innovations

HELP/Learner Services

Mary Grant
Associate Dean

Continuing Education, Credit
Outreach, and Distance
Education Programs at 13
Four-Year Universities and 13
Two-Year Colleges

School for Workers

Broadcasting & Media Innovations
Byron Knight
Director

Wisconsin Public Radio**

Wisconsin Public
Television**

Instructional Communications
Systems

** Jointly Administered with
Educational Communications
Board

July 2001

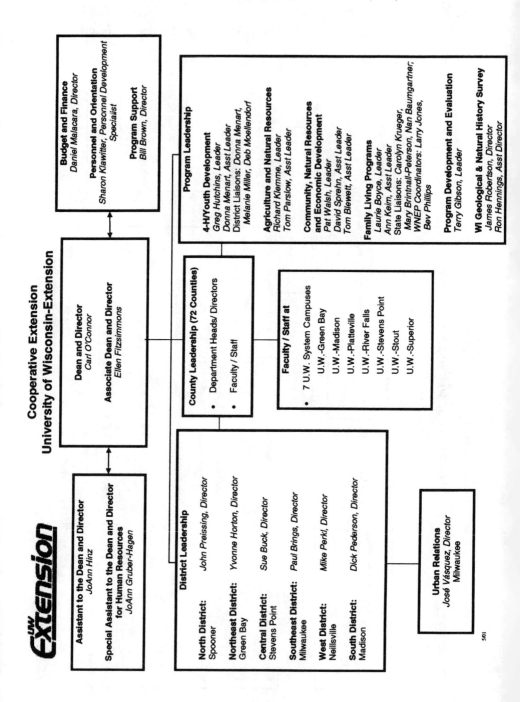

Cooperative Extension
University of Wisconsin-Extension

Dean and Director
Carl O'Connor

Associate Dean and Director
Ellen Fitzsimmons

Assistant to the Dean and Director
JoAnn Hinz

Special Assistant to the Dean and Director for Human Resources
JoAnn Gruber-Hagen

Budget and Finance
Daniel Malacara, Director

Personnel and Orientation
Sharon Klawitter, Personnel Development Specialist

Program Support
Bill Brown, Director

District Leadership

North District: *John Preissing, Director*
Spooner

Northeast District: *Yvonne Horton, Director*
Green Bay

Central District: *Sue Buck, Director*
Stevens Point

Southeast District: *Paul Brings, Director*
Milwaukee

West District: *Mike Perkl, Director*
Neillsville

South District: *Dick Pederson, Director*
Madison

County Leadership (72 Counties)
- Department Heads/ Directors
- Faculty / Staff

Faculty / Staff at
- 7 U.W. System Campuses
  U.W.-Green Bay
  U.W.-Madison
  U.W.-Platteville
  U.W.-River Falls
  U.W.-Stevens Point
  U.W.-Stout
  U.W.-Superior

Urban Relations
José Vásquez, Director
Milwaukee

Program Leadership

4-H/Youth Development
Greg Hutchins, Leader
Donna Menart, Asst Leader
District Liaisons: *Donna Menart,*
Melanie Miller, Deb Moellendorf

Agriculture and Natural Resources
Richard Klemme, Leader
Tom Parslow, Asst Leader

Community, Natural Resources and Economic Development
Pat Walsh, Leader
David Sprehn, Asst Leader
Tom Blewett, Asst Leader

Family Living Programs
Laurie Boyce, Leader
Ann Keim, Asst Leader
State Liaisons: *Carolyn Krueger,*
Mary Brintnall-Peterson, Nan Baumgartner;
WNEP Coordinators: *Larry Jones,*
Bev Phillips

Program Development and Evaluation
Terry Gibson, Leader

WI Geological & Natural History Survey
James Robertson, Director
Ron Hennings, Asst Director

5/01

Appendix III

Important Dates in Wisconsin Cooperative Extension History

1787-Congress passes Northwest Ordinance, creating the region that will include Wisconsin. Includes statement about importance of education for citizens in a democratic society.

1848-Wisconsin becomes a state.

1849-The University of Wisconsin begins operations.

1851-University Chancellor John Lathrop urges the university to offer agricultural education.

1851-Wisconsin Agricultural Society formed, organized by and for farmers.

1851-First state fair held in Janesville.

1851-Wisconsin Horticultural Society organized.

1862-Wisconsin becomes number two wheat-growing state in nation for first time.

1862-United States Department of Agriculture organized.

1862-Morrill Act creates land grant colleges to provide study in agriculture and mechanical arts.

1866-University of Wisconsin receives land grant designation after four years of debate.

1866-University receives 200 acres of land for agricultural research.

1868-William W. Daniells, a chemist, hired as first professor of agriculture.

1870s-Wisconsin switching to dairy farming and cheese making. Farmers seek help in understanding how to properly care for dairy cows.

1872-Wisconsin Dairymen's Association organized.

1878-Hiram Smith becomes the first farmer appointed to University Board of Regents.

1880-William A. Henry hired as professor of agriculture with duties to teach on and off campus.

1880-First farmers' institutes held in six locations around the state.

1883-Legislature acts to establish the Wisconsin Agricultural Experiment Station in Madison with an appropriation of $6,000.

1885-The university's Farm Short Course begins.

1885-Legislature appropriates $5,000 for farmers' institutes and assigns the money to the University Board of Regents.

1887-Congress passes the Hatch Act, making federal funds available to research stations.

1889-College of Agriculture organized at University of Wisconsin.

1892-First cooking schools become popular part of farmers' institutes.

1903-Ransom Asa Moore, an agronomist, begins forming corn clubs for young people. These clubs are forerunners of 4-H Club work in Wisconsin.

1904-Charles Van Hise becomes president of the University of Wisconsin. He begins advocating that campus resources should be available to all people in the state. This approach later becomes known as the Wisconsin Idea.

1904-05-First lecture trains bring experiment station results directly to farmers.

1904-One-week farmers' course begins in Madison. Later, the course becomes known as Farm and Home Week.

1905-Housekeepers' conference added to farmers' course.

1905-Agricultural experiment station receives tens of thousands of letters from farmers with questions about agriculture, farming, and rural life.

1906-First County Extension agent in the United States was hired in Texas.

1907-University Extension Division for General Extension work (not related to agriculture) is organized at the University of Wisconsin.

1908-Agricultural experiment station heavily involved in off-campus education. Staff members give 100 lectures around the state, write 45,000 letters answering questions, prepare 23,000 manuscripts, and distribute 102,000 sheets of mimeographed material.

1908-Legislature authorizes $30,000 annual appropriation to organize an agricultural Extension service in Wisconsin.

1908-Department of Home Economics becomes part of College of Agriculture.

1909-K.L. Hatch appointed head of new Agricultural Extension with title of Extension secretary.

1909-First branch Agricultural Experiment Station established in Spooner.

1909-Agricultural press service established within College of Agriculture.

1910-Thomas Bewick hired as first boys and girls club leader. Corn clubs become popular. Youth exhibit at 45 county fairs. Boys and girls enroll in animal care, food preparation, and sewing projects.

1912-First Extension agent in Wisconsin hired in Oneida County. Eau Claire and Barron Counties soon follow Oneida's example.

1914-Smith-Lever Act passed by Congress. The act creates the Cooperative Extension Service. It establishes cooperative relationship among counties, states, and the United States Department of Agriculture. It makes federal funds available to the states for Extension activities.

1914-Elizabeth Kelley hired as Wisconsin's first state leader for Extension home economics.

1917-In response to World War I, 27 war emergency agents are hired.

1917-More than 26,000 youth enrolled in Extension boys' and girls' clubs during World War I.

1918-Mary Brady, former war emergency agent, appointed on a full-time basis in Marathon County. She becomes the first home agent in Wisconsin with local tax support.

1924-4-H recognized as official name for Extension boys' and girls' clubs.

1928—Capper-Ketcham Act passed by Congress. Authorizes additional funds for Cooperative Extension, especially for salaries of agriculture, home economics, and 4-H agents.

1929-1940-Cooperative Extension adjusts its programs to assist people facing a depressed economy.

1930s-College of Agriculture and Cooperative Extension begin offering programs in the arts. College of Agriculture employs an artist-in-residence in 1936.

1938-Wisconsin's Cooperative Extension celebrates 25 years of service. Sixty-nine of Wisconsin's 71 county boards help fund 99 county agents, 4-H club agents, and home agents. Twenty-four agents are women.

1938-State enrollment in 4-H reaches 30,877 members—the largest number to this point. The most popular projects are dairy and field crops. Nearly 10,000 girls enroll in the clothing project.

1941-1945-World War II challenges Extension to increase farm production and at the same time promote victory gardens, homemade clothing, and food preservation.

1947-Wisconsin 4-H club enrollment reaches 36,486 members, including 18,200 boys and 18,286 girls.

1952-Henry L. Ahlgren becomes associate director of Cooperative Extension.

1954-First Farm Progress Days held in Waupaca County.

1955-Supported by the W.K. Kellogg Foundation, the National Extension Center for Advanced Study offers its first courses in September. The center operates for 13 years.

1958-The national Extension Committee on Organization and Policy (ECOP) publishes national plan for Cooperative Extension. This plan becomes known as the "Scope Report."

1960s-4-H programs introduced in several urban centers, including Milwaukee.

1960s-Extension becomes heavily involved in the tourism industry.

1964-College Week for Women is launched. Women from around the state come to Madison for several days of education.

1965-Cooperative Extension merges with General Extension and radio-television to form University of Wisconsin-Extension. Administratively, Cooperative Extension is no longer in the College of Agriculture. Donald McNeil is appointed first Extension chancellor.

1965-Educational Telephone Network becomes operational. Used for teaching as well as connecting staff for administrative meetings.

1966-Wisconsin Associated County Extension Committees (WACEC) is incorporated.

1966-Home economics subcommittee of the Extension committee on organization and policy produces "Focus," a plan for the future of home economics Extension. Extension home economics changes orientation from subject matter such as foods and clothing to a focus on family and community problems.

1967—Extension develops a series of half-hour television shows (*4-H TV Action*) on how to prepare for emergencies such as fire, cold, tornadoes, atomic radiation, and others.

1968-The Expanded Food and Nutrition Education Program (EFNEP) begins

1969-Henry Ahlgren becomes second chancellor of UW-Extension.

1960s-Cooperative Extension begins work on community and economic development in selected areas of the state. Programs become highly sophisticated by the 1970s and continue into the 1990s.

1970s—Many Extension agents become involved with public policy issues such as land use planning. This work continues into the 1990s.

1974-Jean Evans becomes UW-Extension chancellor.

1974-Legislature passes a law implementing a 1971 law that merges Wisconsin's two public college and university systems under one board of regents. This legislation forms the University of Wisconsin system.

1976-Master gardening program begins in Waukesha and Milwaukee Counties.

1980s-4-H/youth programs broaden to include an emphasis on the family. Also begin focusing on community youth development beyond 4-H clubs.

1981-The National Association of State Universities and Land-Grant Colleges and the USDA publish *Extension in the 80s*.

1983-Patrick Boyle becomes chancellor for Extension after serving as acting chancellor in 1982.

1984-First seminar for rural leadership program meets. The program continues into the 2000s.

1990s-Partnership becomes a key phrase as Cooperative Extension collaborates with public and private groups. Some partnerships result in new funding sources. Extension works with tribal colleges on a variety of programs.

1990s—For the first time, most 4-H literature is produced as a cooperative effort among 30 states.

1990s-Family living and Community, Natural Resource and Economic Development (CNRED) make substantial changes in program direction, including broadened audiences and an increased number of staff members.

1990s-E-Mail becomes popular and Internet access expands educational opportunities.

1991-Wisconsin satellite system becomes operational.

1993-Donald Hanna becomes chancellor of Extension.

1994-1995-Extension conducts welfare reform seminars for state lawmakers, staff, and agency professionals.

1996-Cooperative Extension develops special urban initiative involving Kenosha, Milwaukee, Racine, and Waukesha Counties.

1997-Albert Beaver becomes interim chancellor after Donald Hanna's resignation.

2000-Kevin Riley appointed chancellor when Beaver retires.

FURTHER READING

To learn more about Wisconsin's Cooperative Extension history, the following books are useful:

McIntyre, E. R. *Fifty Years of Cooperative Extension in Wisconsin, 1912-1962,* (Madison, WI: Cooperative Extension Service, College of Agriculture, 1962).

Shannon, Theodore J. and Schoenfeld, Clarence A. *University Extension* (New York: The Center for Applied Research in Education, 1965).

Somersan, Ayse, *Distinguished Service: University of Wisconsin Faculty and Staff Helping to Build Organizations in the State* (Friendship, WI: New Past Press, 1997).

White, Grace Witter, *Cooperative Extension in Wisconsin: 1962-1982* (Dubuque, Iowa: Kendall Hunt, 1985).

ENDNOTES

Chapter 1. EARLY HISTORY
1. Alice E. Smith, *The History of Wisconsin* (Madison, WI: The State Historical Society of Wisconsin, 1973).
2. James I. Clark, *Farming the Cutover: The Settlement of Northern Wisconsin* (Madison, WI: The State Historical Society of Wisconsin, 1956), p. 5.
3. Richard N. Current, *The History of Wisconsin, Volume II: The Civil War Era, 1848-1873* (Madison, WI: The State Historical Society of Wisconsin, 1976), p. 241.
4. "Transactions of the Wisconsin State Agricultural Society," (Madison, WI: Beriah Brown, State Printer, 1852), pp. 13-16.
5. Ibid., p. 16
6. World Wide Web. www.netins.net/web/creative/lincoln/speeches/fair.
7. J.W. Hoyt, "Transactions of the Wisconsin State Agricultural Society, Volume VII" (Madison, WI: Wisconsin State Agricultural Society, 1868), pp. 66-67.
8. Ibid.
9. Ibid., pp. 30-31.
10. Ibid., pp. 23-24.
11. Ibid. p. 42.
12. Jerry Apps, *Cheese: The Making of a Wisconsin Tradition* (Amherst, WI: Amherst Press, 1998).
13. I.O. Schaub, "Agricultural Extension Work: A Brief History," North Carolina Agricultural Extension Service, Extension Circular No. 377, November 1953.
14. Edmund deS. Brunner and E. Hesin Pao Yang, *Rural America and the Extension Service.* (New York: Teachers College, Columbia University, 1949), pp. 4-5.
15. John W. Jenkins, *A Centennial History: A History of the College of Agricultural and Life Sciences of the University of Wisconsin-Madison.* (Madison, WI: College of Agricultural and Life Sciences, 1991), p. 4.

Chapter 2. THE UNIVERSITY OF WISCONSIN AND AGRICULTURAL EDUCATION: 1851 to 1908
1. Vernon Carstensen, "The Birth of an Agricultural Experiment Station," in *The Growth of Agricultural Research in Wisconsin: A Lecture Series Commemorating the 75th Anniversary of the Wisconsin Agricultural Experiment Station, 1883-1958* (Madison, WI: College of Agriculture, University of Wisconsin, 1958), p. 7.
2. Glenn S. Pound, "An X-ray of a Century of Progress," in *Wisconsin Agricultural Experiment Station: Centennial Celebration, March 24, 1983* (Madison, WI: College of Agriculture, 1983), pp. 8-9.
3. W. H. Morrison & John Gould, eds., *Wisconsin Farmers' Institutes: Sessions of 1886-1887* (Milwaukee: Cramer, Aikens & Cramer, 1887), p. 1.

4. Ibid., p. 7.
5. Edith L. Clift, editor, *Wisconsin Farmers' Institutes: Cook Book No. 1* (Madison, WI: Office of Farmers' Institutes, 1908), p. 1.
6. Glenn S. Pound, "An X-ray of a Century of Progress," in *Wisconsin Agricultural Experiment Station: Centennial Celebration, March 24, 1983* (Madison, WI: College of Agriculture, 1983), p. 7.
7. Chris L. Christensen, "The Era of Deans Henry and Russell," in The Growth of Agricultural Research in Wisconsin: A Lecture Series Commemorating the 75th Anniversary of the Wisconsin Agricultural Experiment Station, 1883-1958 (Madison, WI: College of Agriculture, University of Wisconsin, 1958), pp. 16-17.
8. John W. Jenkins, *A Centennial History: A History of the College of Agricultural and Life Sciences at the University of Wisconsin-Madison* (Madison, WI: College of Agricultural and Life Sciences, 1991), p. 1.
9. Glenn S. Pound, "An X-ray of a Century of Progress," pp. 12-13.
10. W. A. Henry, director, *Twenty-Second Annual Report of the Agricultural Experiment Station of the University of Wisconsin, for the Year Ending June 30, 1905* (Madison, WI: Democrat Printing Co., 1905), p. 9.
11. Ibid.
12. H.L. Russell, *Report of the Director: Agricultural Experiment Station for 1911-1912* (Madison, WI: College of Agriculture, 1913), p. 67.
13. Ibid.
14. I. O. Schaub, *Agricultural Extension Work: A Brief History* (Raleigh, NC: North Carolina Agricultural Extension Service, 1953), p. 13.
15. "Farmers' Course in Agriculture," Bulletin of the University of Wisconsin, No. 105. December 1904, p. 3
16. Ibid., pp.3-4.
17. Ibid.
18. H. L. Russell, *Report of the Director, 1910: The University of Wisconsin Experiment Station* (Madison, WI: College of Agriculture, 1911), p. 46.
19. Franklin M. Reck. *The 4-H Story: A History of 4-H Club Work* (Ames, Iowa: The Iowa State College Press, 1951), pp. 4-5.
20. Ibid. p. 7.
21. Quoted in E.R. McIntyre, *Fifty Years of Cooperative Extension, 1912-1962.* (Madison, WI: Wisconsin Cooperative Extension, 1962), p. 189.
22. H. L. Russell, *Twenty-Fourth Annual Report of the Agricultural Experiment Station of the University of Wisconsin,* (Madison, WI: College of Agriculture, June 30, 1907), p. 14.
23. H. L. Russell, *Twenty-Fifth and Twenty-Sixth Annual Reports of the Agricultural Experiment Station* (Madison, WI: College of Agriculture, 1910), pp. 44-45.

Chapter 3. AGRICULTURAL EXTENSION
BEGINS: 1908 to 1914

1. H. L. Russell, *Twenty-Fifth and Twenty-Sixth Annual Reports of the Agricultural Experiment Station* (Madison, WI: College of Agriculture, 1910), pp.26-45.

2. John W. Jenkins. *A Centennial History: A History of the College of Agricultural and Life Sciences at the University of Wisconsin-Madison* (Madison, WI: College of Agricultural and Life Sciences, 1991), pp. 67-71.

3. "The Agricultural Extension Service: Agricultural Experiment Station," Circular Information No. 7, (Madison, WI: College of Agriculture, November 1909).

4. Ibid., p. 5.

5. Gladys Meloche. "History of Home Economics Extension Service: Wisconsin, 1885-1954," Unpublished paper, 1954.

6. James I. Clark. *Farming the Cutover: The Settlement of Northern Wisconsin* (Madison, WI: The State Historical Society of Wisconsin, 1956), p. 6.

7. Joseph Cannon Bailey. *Seaman A. Knapp: Schoolmaster of American Agriculture* (New York: Columbia University Press, 1945), p. 156.

8. Ibid., p. 177.

9. Clarence Beaman Smith and Meridith Chester Wilson, *The Agricultural Extension System of the United States* (New York: John Wiley & Sons, 1930), p. 36.

10. H. L. Russell, *Report of the Director, 1911-1912, Agricultural Experiment Station* (Madison, WI, 1913), pp. 63-64.

11. Ibid., p. 64.

12. Ibid., pp. 66-67.

13. H. L. Russell, *Report of the Director, 1912-1913, Agricultural Experiment Station* (Madison, WI, 1914), pp. 77-80.

14. Ibid.

15. Ibid. p. 79.

16. E. R. McIntyre, *Fifty Years of Cooperative Extension in Wisconsin, 1912-1962* (Madison, WI: Cooperative Extension, 1962), p. 52.

17. Ibid., p. 74.

18. H. L. Russell, *Report of the Director, 1912-1913, Agricultural Experiment Station*, pp. 82-83.

19. E. R. McIntyre. *Fifty Years of Cooperative Extension in Wisconsin, 1912-1962*, p. 46.

20. H. L. Russell, *Report of the Director, 1912-1913, Agricultural Experiment Station*, p. 83.

21. Ibid., p. 86.

22. Quoted in Franklin M. Reck, *The 4-H Story: A History of 4-H Club Work* (Ames, Iowa: The Iowa State College Press, 1951), p. 26.

23. Ibid., p. 98,

24. H. L. Russell, *Twenty-Fifth and Twenty-Sixth Annual Reports of the Agricultural Experiment Station*, pp. 8-9.

Chapter 4. YEARS OF DEVELOPMENT: 1914 to 1930

1. Clarence Beaman Smith and Meridith Chester Wilson, *The Agricultural Extension System of the*

United States (New York: John Wiley & Sons, 1930), p. 40.

2. Ibid., pp. 365-368.

3. Edmund deS. Brunner and E. Hesin Pao Yang, *Rural America and The Extension Service* (New York: Teachers College, Columbia University, 1949), p. 15.

4. H. L. Russell, *Report of the Director, 1914, Agricultural Experiment Station* (Madison, WI: College of Agriculture, 1915), pp. 83-90.

5. H. L. Russell, *Report of the Director, 1915, Agricultural Experiment Station* (Madison, WI, 1916), p. 66.

6. Ibid., pp. 72-74.

7. *Cooperative Extension Work in Agriculture and Home Economics, 1917* (Washington, D.C.: Government Printing Office, 1919), pp. 364-372.

8. Paul W. Glad, *The History of Wisconsin, Volume V: War, a New Era, and Depression, 1914-1940* (Madison, WI: State Historical Society of Wisconsin, 1990), p. 178.

9. E. R. McIntyre, *Fifty Years of Cooperative Extension in Wisconsin, 1912-1962* (Madison, WI, 1962), pp. 86-87.

10. Ibid., pp. 88-90.

11. *Cooperative Extension Work in Agriculture and Home Economics, 1917*, pp. 366-367.

12. Thomas Wessel and Marilyn Wessel, *4-H: An American Idea, 1900-1980. A History of 4-H* (Chevy Chase, Maryland: National 4-H Council, 1982), p. 40.

13. Ibid., p. 46.

14. Gladys Meloche, "History of Home Economics Extension Service: Wisconsin, 1885-1954," Unpublished paper, 1954.

15. Ibid.

Chapter 5. CRISIS AND CHALLENGE: 1930 to 1945

1. *Yearbook of Agriculture:1937* (Washington, D.C.: U.S. Government Printing Office, 1937), p. 4.

2. Paul W. Glad, *The History of Wisconsin, Volume V: War, a New Era, and Depression, 1914-1940* (Madison, WI: State Historical Society of Wisconsin, 1990), p. 363.

3. Superintendent's Journal. Archives, University of Wisconsin Experiment Station, Hancock, Wisconsin

4. E. R. McIntyre. *Fifty Years of Cooperative Extension in Wisconsin, 1912-1962* (Madison, WI, 1962), p. 134.

5. *Wisconsin Agriculture in Mid-Century* (Madison, WI: Wisconsin Crop and Livestock Reporting Service, Wisconsin State Department of Agriculture, Bulletin No. 325, 1954).

6. K. L. Hatch, *Basic Issues in Wisconsin Agriculture: Annual Report of the Extension Director* (Madison, WI: College of Agriculture, University of Wisconsin, Circular 251, February, 1932), pp. 33-34.

7. Wilfred Pierick, "Cooperative Extension in Grant County: The First Forty Years," Master of

Science Thesis, University of Wisconsin, 1963, pp. 104-105.

8. Paul W. Glad, *The History of Wisconsin, Volume V: War, a New Era, and Depression, 1914-1940* (Madison, WI: State Historical Society of Wisconsin, 1990), p, 494.

9. Chris L. Christensen. "Wisconsin Farming Under Adjustment" (Madison, WI: Extension Service, College of Agriculture, University of Wisconsin, Circular 269, May, 1934).

10. K. L. Hatch, *Basic Issues in Wisconsin Agriculture: Annual Report of the Extension Director* (Madison, WI: College of Agriculture, University of Wisconsin, Circular 251, February, 1932), p. 35.

11. Chris L. Christensen, *Wisconsin Farm Progress: 1938 Report of the Extension Service of the College of Agriculture* (Circular 293, June, 1939), p. 3 & 8.

12. Clarence Beaman Smith and Meredith Chester Wilson, *The Agricultural Extension System of the United States* (New York: John Wiley & Sons, 1930), p. 368.

13. Edmund deS. Brunner and E. Hsin Pao Yang, *Rural America and the Extension Service* (New York: Teachers College, Columbia University, 1949), p. 44.

14. K. L. Hatch, *Basic Issues in Wisconsin Agriculture: Annual Report of the Extension Director* (Madison, WI: College of Agriculture, University of Wisconsin, Circular 251, February, 1932), p. 30.

15. Warren W. Clark, *Serves State and Nation: A Summary of Extension Activities During the War* (Madison, WI: College of Agriculture, University of Wisconsin, Circular 370, February, 1946).

16. Ibid., pp. 18-21

Chapter 6. GROWTH AND EXPANSION: 1945 to 1960

1.*Wisconsin Agriculture in Mid-Century*, Bulletin No. 325 (Madison, WI: Wisconsin Crop Reporting Service, 1953), p. 21.

2. *Agricultural Extension in Wisconsin: Report for 1957* (Madison, WI: College of Agriculture, University of Wisconsin, Circular 558, March, 1958), p. 2.

3. Correspondence from Henry Ahlgren to Alfred Francour, September 22, 1955.

4. Correspondence from E.V. Ryall, county agricultural agent, Kenosha County, to members of the Special Committee, March 2, 1956.

5. John Hannah, *Joint Committee Report on Extension Programs Policies and Goals* (Washington, D.C.: U.S. Department of Agriculture and Association of Land-Grant Colleges and Universities, 1948), p. 1.

6. Ibid., p. 6.

7. *Agricultural Extension in Wisconsin: Report for 1952* (Madison, WI: College of Agriculture, University of Wisconsin, Circular 460, June, 1953), p. 10.

8. Gladys Meloche. "History of Home Economics Extension Service: Wisconsin, 1885-1954," Unpublished paper, 1954.

9. Clarence Beaman Smith and Meridith Chester Wilson, *The Agricultural Extension System of the United States* (New York: John Wiley & Sons, 1930), p. 365.

Chapter 7. NEW DIRECTIONS: 1960 to 1975

1. Edgar Boone and Clarence Ferguson, editors, *An Image of Cooperative Extension* (Madison, WI: National Agricultural Extension Center for Advanced Study, 1962), p. 23.

2. Ibid., p. 31.

3. Ibid., p. 59.

4. From *Public Papers of the Presidents of the United States, Lyndon B. Johnson, 1965* (Washington, D.C.: Government Printing Office, 1966).

5. Rachel Carson, *Silent Spring* (Boston, MA: Houghton Mifflin, 1962), p.15.

6. Reported in E. David Cronon & John W. Jenkins, *The University of Wisconsin: A History, 1945-1971, Renewal to Revolution, Volume IV* (Madison, WI: University of Wisconsin Press, 1999), p. 315.

7. See E. David Cronon & John W. Jenkins, *The University of Wisconsin: A History, 1945-1971, Renewal to Revolution, Volume IV* (Madison, WI: University of Wisconsin Press, 1999) for a detailed account of how the merger took place.

8. Ibid., p. 331

9. Bryant Kearl, "Who Killed the Wisconsin Idea?" Talk given to Madison Literary Society, March 9, 1992. Unpublished.

10. Laura Small, Gale L. Vandeberg (Madison, WI: University of Wisconsin-Madison Archives Oral History Project, 1988), transcription pp. 144-145.

11. Ibid., p. 140.

12. Statement accompanying December 12, 1973 correspondence from Glenn S. Pound to Regent John M. Lavine.

13. Lucille Braunschweig, "WACEC, a New Affiliate Profiled," *Wisconsin Counties*, June 1985, p. 20.

14. Grace Witter White, *Cooperative Extension in Wisconsin: 1962-1982* (Dubuque, Iowa: Kendall/Hunt, 1985), pp. 154-157.

15. Ibid., pp. 167-168.

16. A. E. Peterson, M.W. Burley and C.D. Caproon, "Frost Depth Survey: A New Approach in Wisconsin," *Weatherwise* (Volume 16, No. 2, April 1963), pp. 62-65.

17. Correspondence from Ray J. Antoniewicz, February 2001

18. Correspondence from Linda Kustka, 4-H Youth Development Department, 2001.

19. Mary E. Coleman, "Extension Home Economics: Focus" (Washington, D.C.: Extension Committee on Organization and Policy, 1966).

20. Marlys Richert, "Focus II: Extension Home Economics" (Washington, D.C.: Extension Committee on Organization and Policy, 1974) p.1.

21. Wisconsin Extension Homemakers Council, Inc. *The Impact of Her Spirit*, (River Falls, WI: River Falls Journal, 1989), p. 193.

22. Correspondence from Bonnie Hutchins, September 2000.

23. "Partners for Progress," (Madison, WI: University of Wisconsin-Extension), 1976.

24. Marvin Beatty,interview with Herman Smith, April 2000.

25. Ibid.

26. Ibid.

27. Ayse Somersan, *Distinguished Service: University of Wisconsin Faculty and Staff Helping to Build Organizations in the State* (Friendship, Wisconsin: New Past Press, Inc., 1997), pp. 81-91.

28. Correspondence from Eugene Savage, September 2000.

29. Rollin B. Cooper. "Recreation Resources Center, University of Wisconsin-Extension: History, Activities, Problems." Unpublished report, circa 1985.

30. E. David Cronon & John W. Jenkins, p. 521-596.

31. Correspondence from Glenn S. Pound to Regent John M. Lavine, December 12, 1973.

32. Draft Mission Statements, Memo from Donald K. Smith to Education Committee, Board of Regents, October 29, 1973.

Chapter 8. PROFOUND CHANGE: 1975 to 1990

1. Robert J. Battaglia, state statistician, *1998 Wisconsin Agricultural Statistics* (Madison, WI: Wisconsin Agricultural Statistics Service, 1998), pp. 76-77).

2. James W. Gooch, *Transplanting Extension: A New Look at the "Wisconsin Idea."* (Madison, WI: University of Wisconsin-Madison, Office of Outreach Development, 1995), p. 95.

3. Interview with Gerald Campbell, September 21, 2000.

4. Quoted in James W. Gooch, *Transplanting Extension: A New Look at the "Wisconsin Idea."*, pp.57-58.

5. Correspondence from Ray Vander Weele, chair of Faculty Select Committee to Dwayne Rohweder, chair, University Committee for UW-Extension, March 27, 1981.

6. Ibid.

7. Memo from Robert M. O'Neill to members of the President's Advisory Group on Extension, May 29, 1981.

8. Memo from Joint Faculty/Administrative Committee to Members of the UWEX Faculty and Academic Staff, June 12, 1981.

9. Memo from Robert M. O'Neill to members of the President's Advisory Group on Extension, May 29, 1981.

10. "Report and Recommendations of the President's Advisory Group on Extension," December 23, 1981, pp. 75-86.

11. James W. Gooch, *Transplanting Extension: A New Look at the "Wisconsin Idea."* p. 71.

12. Interview with Patrick Boyle, January 4, 2001.

13. James W. Gooch, *Transplanting Extension: A New Look at the "Wisconsin Idea."* p. 95.

14. Interview with Patrick Boyle, January 4, 2001.

15. *The Statewide Plan for Extension Programs in the University of Wisconsin System* (Madison, WI: Chancellor's Office, University of Wisconsin-Extension, 1988).

16. *Extension in the '80s: A Perspective for the Future of Cooperative Extension Service* (Madison, WI: Program Development and Evaluation of the Cooperative Extension Service, 1983).

17. *A Catalyst for Change-The Extension Service* (Washington, D.C.: United States Department of Agriculture, Extension Service, 1980).

18. Dale Lick quoted in *Extension in Transition: Bridging The Gap Between Vision and Reality* Blacksburg, VA: Virginia Cooperative Extension Service, 1987), p. 1.

19. Ibid., p. 6.

20. Interview with Russell Kiecker, February 16, 2001.

21. *The Wisconsin Idea: Extension Programs in the UW System, Fiscal Year 1986* (Madison, WI: University of Wisconsin-Extension, 1986).

22. Arthur E. Peterson, "Value of Cloud Seeding in Wisconsin," Unpublished paper, January 14, 1977.

23. Grace Witter White, *Cooperative Extension in Wisconsin: 1962-1982* (Dubuque, Iowa: Kendall/Hunt, 1985), pp. 157-158.

24. Laverne Forest & Barry Roberts, "Dane County Master Gardener Program Evaluation," (Madison, WI: Program Development and Evaluation, April 1986).

25. *The Wisconsin Idea: Extension Programs in the UW System* (Madison, WI: University of Wisconsin-Extension, 1989), p.26.

26. Interview with Russell Kiecker, February 16, 2001.

27. *The Wisconsin Idea: Extension Programs in the UW System,* p.20.

28. Correspondence from Beverly Henderson, July 2000.

29. *The Wisconsin Idea: FY 1988. Extension Programs in the UW System* (Madison, WI: Chancellor's Office, University of Wisconsin-Extension, 1988) pp. 20-21.

Chapter 9. THE CENTURY ENDS: 1990 to 2000

1. Wisconsin Number of Farms and Land in Farms, Milk Cow Numbers-Wisconsin, and 1999 Milk Production, Wisconsin (Madison, WI: Wisconsin Agricultural Statistics Service, 2001).

2. *The Wisconsin Idea: University Extension Programs in the UW System 1991* (Madison, WI: Chancellor's Office, University of Wisconsin-Extension, 1991).

3. Dave Riley, "Creating a Local Response to Children's Needs: An Empowering Approach." (Networking Bulletin, March, 1991,Vol. 2, No. 1), pp. 22-23.

4. David A. Riley, "Using Local Research to Change 100 Communities for Children and Families" (*American Psychologist,* Vol 52, No. 4, April 1997), pp. 423-433.

5. Dennis Frame, "Beginning Farmer Program Seeks Fourth Apprentice," press release, January 29, 2001.

6. *Impact 2000: 1999 University of Wisconsin-Extension Annual Report* (Madison, WI: Chancellor's Office, University of Wisconsin-Extension, 2000), p. 21.

7. Correspondence from Patrick Boyle, June 14, 2001.

8. Interview with Carl O'Connor, March 7, 2000.

9. *University of Wisconsin-Extension FY 1996 Annual Report* (Madison, WI: University of Wisconsin-Extension, 1996), pp. 6-7 and *Education for Life: FY 1995 Annual Report* (Madison, WI: University of Wisconsin-Extension, 1995), pp. 14-15.

10. Jennifer A. Galloway, "Fallout predicted over UW hiring: Gassman salary angers lawmakers," (Madison, WI: Wisconsin *State Journal,* January 23, 1997).

11. Stan Milan, "'Gassmangate' put UW System in hot water with lawmakers," (Janesville, WI: The Janesville *Gazette,* February 1, 1997).

12. "Former chancellor clarifies resignation," (Madison, WI: editorial page, *The Capital Times, Weekend,* July 5-6, 1997).

13. Phil McDade and Jennifer Galloway, "SAVE critical of Extension; cuts suggested," (Madison, WI: Wisconsin *State Journal,* January 22, 1995).

14. Ibid.

15. Phil McDade and Jennifer Galloway, "An organization overextended?" (Madison, WI: Wisconsin *State Journal,* January 22, 1995).

16. Correspondence from Mark Lederer, March 2001.

17. Ibid.

18. Correspondence Interim Chancellor Albert J. Beaver to members of Joint Finance Committee, May 27, 1997.

19. Interview with Mark Lederer, February 21, 2001.

20. Interview with Albert Beaver, May 22, 2000.

21. Interview with Patrick Boyle, January 4, 2001.

22. Correspondence from Laurie Boyce, March 5, 2001

23. Correspondence from Laurie Boyce, June 2, 2001.

Chapter 10. THE COUNTY EXTENSION OFFICE

1. Karl Knaus, *System in the County Extension Office* (Washington, D.C. USDA, March, 1951), p. 1.

2. Personal Correspondence from Gerry Campbell, October 4, 2000.

Chapter 11. THE EXTENSION AGENT

1. Don Jensen, "The Economy: Agriculture and Farming," in *Kenosha County in the 20th Century,* John A. Neuenshwander, Ed. (Kenosha, WI: Carthage College, 1976) pp. 151-152.

2. Clarence Beaman Smith and Meredith Chester Wilson. *The Agricultural Extension System of the United States.* (New York: John Wiley & Sons, 1930) pp. 47-48.

3. *The Home Demonstration Agent.* (Washington, D.C.:United States. Department of Agriculture, Miscellaneous Publication No. 602, April 1965), p. 5.

4. R.L. Reeder, *The People and the Profession.* (Epsilon Sigma Phi, Honorary Extension Fraternity, 1979), pp.85-86.

5. From unpublished personal memoir by Joseph Tuss, 1999.

Chapter 12. SPECIALISTS AND DISTRICT DIRECTORS

1. Clarence Beaman Smith & Meredith Chester Wilson. *The Agricultural Extension System of The United States.*(New York: John Wiley & Sons, 1930), p. 88.

2. Gladys Meloche. "History of Home Economics Extension Service: Wisconsin, 1885-1954," Unpublished paper, 1954.

3. Correspondence from Robert Hall to James D. McKean, Extension swine veterinarian, Iowa State University, November 19, 1999.

4. Walter L. Gojmerac, *History of Wisconsin's Bee Keeping and Honey Producing Industry* (Madison, WI: Department of Entomology, University of Wisconsin-Madison, 1995.)

5. From "Responsibilities of District Directors" (Madison, WI: Cooperative Extension, University of Wisconsin-Extension, 2000).

6. Correspondence from Donald Peterson to chairperson, Agri-Biotechnology Division, Moraine Park Institute, April 12, 1979.

7. Correspondence from Moraine Park Technical Institute to Donald Peterson, April 18, 1979.

Chapter 13. NOTABLE PROGRAMS

1. Correspondence, Al Francour, former La Crosse County agricultural agent, and district Extension director, March, 2000.

2. Correspondence from Eugene Savage, former Jackson County agricultural agent, September, 2000.

3. Correspondence from Ed Hass, Pierce County CNRED agent, August 2000.

4. David S. Liebl and Patrick Walsh, "Enhancing Industrial Waste Reduction Outreach: Wisconsin's University Extension Model," manuscript submitted to *Pollution Prevention Review,* Summer 1993.

5. Correspondence from Donald Last, August 2000.

6. Correspondence from Lowell Klessig, April 2000.

7. Mary Ellen Bell, "Cleaner Water and Higher Dairy Profits Result from UW-Extension Water Quality Programs" *Education for Life: FY 1995*

Annual Report (Madison, WI: Chancellor's Office, University of Wisconsin-Extension, 1995), p. 20.

8. Quoted by Nyla Musser in "Grace Frysinger Fellowship Report: Expanded Nutrition Program," 1970.

9. *Design for the Future: Human Health and Nutrition, 1987-1988* (Madison, WI: Cooperative Extension, 1989).

10. Memo to Extension home economists from Susan Nitzke, nutrition specialist, Jane Spriggs, EFNEP coordinator, Michael McIntosh, nutrition specialist, and Jane Voichick, nutrition specialist, October 1988.

11. Correspondence from Laurie Boyce, state program leader, October 2000.

12. "Mission Statement and Working Principles: Wisconsin Nutrition Education Program," University of Wisconsin-Extension, February 21, 2001.

13. Wisconsin Extension Homemakers Council, Inc. "The Impact of Her Spirit: An Oral History" (River Falls, WI: River Falls *Journal*, 1989), p. xiii.

14. Wisconsin Association for Home and Community Education: *Celebrating 60 Years of Caring About Families and Communities, 1940-2000* (Madison, WI: Wisconsin Association for Home and Community Education, 2000), iii, iv.

15. Correspondence from Winnie Joos, state HCE president, June 2000.

16. Correspondence from E.J. Lueder, who was responsible for volunteer and leadership development on the state 4-H staff from 1971 to 1990. December, 2000.

17. Material from JoAnn Stormer, executive director, Wisconsin Rural Leadership Program, January 2001.

18. Correspondence from Gerald Campbell, August 2001.

19. Correspondence from James Massey, September 2000.

20. Interview with Al Anderson, February 2001.

21. *Agricultural Extension in Wisconsin: Report for 1947* (Madison, WI: Cooperative Extension Service, College of Agriculture, University of Wisconsin, Circular 380, June 1948) p. 19.

22. "Upham Woods: Dedicated to Human Companionship and Fellowship With Nature" (fundraising circular circa 1951).

23. *Agricultural Extension in Wisconsin: Report for 1952* (Madison, WI: Cooperative Extension Service, College of Agriculture, University of Wisconsin, Circular 460, June, 1953), p. 13.

24. Information from Dick Vilstrup, September 2001.

25. Stephen M. Babcock, "A New Method for the Estimation of Fat in Milk, Especially Adapted to Creameries and Cheese Factories," *Seventh Annual Report of the Agricultural Experiment Station* (Madison, WI, 1890), pp. 98-113.

26. *Twenty-fifth and Twenty-sixth Annual Reports of the Agricultural Experiment Station* (Madison, WI: Agricultural Experiment Station, College of Agriculture, University of Wisconsin, 1910) pp. 24-25.

27. *Basic Issues in Wisconsin Agriculture: Annual Report of the Extension Director* (Madison, WI: Cooperative Extension Service, College of Agriculture, University of Wisconsin, 1932) p. 9.

28. Ibid., pp. 9-10

29. "Wisconsin Farming Under Adjustment" (Madison, WI: Cooperative Extension Service, College of Agriculture, University of Wisconsin, Circular 269,1934) p. 33.

30. George M. O'Connor, *Annual Report to Crawford County Board of Supervisors* (Prairie du Chein, WI: County Extension Office, 1938).

31. Clarence C. Olson, "What to Expect When You Join DHIA" (Madison, WI: Cooperative Extension Programs, University of Wisconsin-Extension, 1975).

32. Clarence C. Olson, "DHI Campaigns in Wisconsin," Proceedings for the sales marketing seminar for DHIA. Denver, Colorado, February 11, 1979.

33. "New Trend? Dairy Schools For Women" (*Dairymen's Digest*, Vol. 17, No. 4, April 1976), pp. 12-13.

34. Ronald Callaway Gee, "The Development of the Cultural Arts Programs in the Extension Services at the University of Wisconsin," Unpublished PH. D. dissertation, University of Wisconsin, 1958, p. 419.

35. *Basic Issues in Wisconsin Agriculture: Annual Report of The Extension Director,* 1932, p. 36.

36. Ayse Somersan, *Distinguished Service: University of Wisconsin Faculty and Staff Helping to Build Organizations in the State* (Friendship, WI: New Past Press, 1997), pp. 19-20.

37. *Basic Issues in Wisconsin Agriculture: Annual Report of the Extension Director,* 1932, pp. 34-35.

38. "Wisconsin Farm Progress: 1938 Report" (Madison, WI: Cooperative Extension Service of the College of Agriculture, the University of Wisconsin, Circular 293, June 1939), p. 36.

39. See Grace Witter White, *Cooperative Extension in Wisconsin: 1962-1982* (Dubuque, IA: Kendall Hunt, 1985), pp. 373-381.

40. Unpublished material from archives at Hancock Agricultural Research Station and interview with Charles Kostichka, station superintendent, January 18, 2001.

41. Minutes, "Vegetable Crops, Problems, and Possibilities in Wisconsin's Central Sand Area: Joint Conference, Extension and Research Personnel," Hancock Branch Experiment Station, January 13, 1954. From Hancock Agricultural Research Station archives.

Chapter 14. TEACHING APPROACHES
1. Joseph Cannon Bailey. *Seaman A. Knapp: Schoolmaster of American Agriculture* (New York: Columbia University Press, 1945), p. 155.

2. H.L. Russell, *Report of the Director: Agricultural Experiment Station for 1908-1909* (Madison, WI: College of Agriculture, 1910), p. 31.

3.Ibid., p. 43.

4. John Swenehart, "A Nitro Starch Mixture for Land Clearing," Bulletin Number 38 (Madison, WI: Cooperative Extension Work, College of Agriculture of the University of Wisconsin, 1920).

5. Hazel Hauck, "How to Gain Weight: Radio Circular" (Madison, WI: Extension Service of College of Agriculture, University of Wisconsin, Madison, November 1930).

6. Jerry Apps, *Symbols* (Amherst, WI: Amherst Press, 2000), pp. 99-101.

7. K. L. Hatch, *Basic Issues in Wisconsin Agriculture: Annual Report of the Extension Director* (Madison, WI: College of Agriculture, University of Wisconsin, Circular 25, February, 1932), p. 36.

8. Interview with Maury White, January 29, 2001.

9. Interview with Larry Meiller, March 9, 2001.

10. Dick Powers, "A Departmental History, Department of Life Sciences Communication (Formerly Agricultural and Life Sciences)" (Madison, WI: Department of Life Sciences Communication, 1983), unpublished paper.

11. Ibid., p.3.

12. K. L. Hatch, *Basic Issues in Wisconsin Agriculture: Annual Report of the Extension Director,* p. 36.

13. Interview with Maury White, January 29, 2001.

14. Linda A. Boelter & Joan E. LeFebvre, "Parenting the First Year: Evaluation Results" Unpublished report, June 1984.

15. James Gooch, *They Blazed the Trail For Distance Education* (Madison, WI: University of Wisconsin-Extension, Distance Education Clearinghouse, 1996).

16. William Lawrence, memo to county office department heads and other Extension personnel, January 31, 2001.

17. Joan E, Cybela, *Enhancing the Educational Impact of Distance Learning Experiences at the Local Level* (Madison, WI: Distance Education Clearinghouse, University of Wisconsin-Extension, rev. 1997), p. 1.

Chapter 15. PROFESSIONAL DEVELOPMENT

1. Dean Amory Worcester, *The National Agricultural Extension Center For Advanced Study: An Evaluation* (Madison, Wisconsin: National Agricultural Extension Center for Advanced Study, 1961).

2. Correspondence from Marvin Beatty, September 2000.

3. E. R. McIntyre, *Fifty Years of Cooperative Extension in Wisconsin, 1912-1962* (Madison, WI, 1962), p. 161.

4. See Jerold W. Apps, *Leadership for the Emerging Age* (San Francisco: Jossey-Bass, 1994).

5. "Wisconsin Farm Progress: 1938 Report" (Madison, WI: Extension Service, College of Agriculture, University of Wisconsin, Circular 293, June, 1939), p. 36.

Chapter 16. HISTORICAL THEMES

1. Interview with Patrick Boyle, January 4, 2001.

2. Correspondence from Gerald Campbell, October 4, 2000.

3. Joe Corry and James Gooch, "The Wisconsin Idea: Extending the Boundaries of a University," *Higher Education Quarterly*, Vol 46, No. 4, Autumn 1992, pp. 305-320.

4. Interview with Carl O' Connor, March 7, 2000.

5. Correspondence from Ellen Fitzsimmons, September 2000.

6. Correspondence from Gerald Campbell, October 2000.

7. Correspondence from James Massey, September 2000.

8. Correspondence from Pam Jahnke, September 2000.

9. Kurt Gutknecht, "Leading Wisconsin Agriculture? Critics say administrative structure, focus hamper Co-op Extension," *Wisconsin Agriculturist*, May 1997, pp. 12-22.

10. Albert J. Beaver, "Dear Editor," *Wisconsin Agriculturist*, June 1997, p. 4.

11. Correspondence from Pam Jahnke, September 2000.

12. Interview with Joan Sanstadt, November 26, 2000.

13. Interview with John Oncken, March 5, 2001.

14. Interview with Gerald Campbell, September 19, 2000.

15. Correspondence with Ellen Fitzsimmons, August 2000.

16. Interview with Carl O'Connor, March 7, 2000.

Appendix I. EXTENSION AGENT ORGANIZATIONS

1. Information from Kimberly Reaman, April 2001.

2. Correspondence from Norman Everson, January 2001.

3. Information from Craig Saxe, agricultural agent, Juneau County, past president Wisconsin Association of County Agricultural Agents.

4. "History of Wisconsin Association of Extension Home Economists," 1984.

5. Information from Kimberly Reaman, April , 2001.

6. Information from Charles Law, April 14, 2001.

7. From "Epsilon Sigma Phi Alpha Sigma Chapter" April 2000.

8. Minutes, Wisconsin Extension Association Council, June 21, 1979.

INDEX

Tlachac, Larry, 155
Tours and field days, as teaching approaches, 233
Tribal Colleges, 141
Tuss, Joe, 170, 172, 177

United States Department of Agriculture, 13, 41
University dairy barn, 20-21
University Extension Association of Wisconsin, 278
University Extension Division, 27-28
University of Wisconsin, establishment, 7-8
early curriculum, 8
Upham Woods, Camp, 216-217
Urban initiative, 142-143

Van Hise, Charles, 27, 270
VandeBerg, Gale, 90, 91, 108, 119, 125, 133, 143, 173-174, 196, 213, 261, 264
Vasquez, Jose F., 142
Vatthauer, Richard, 125
Viet Nam, 86-87
Vilstrup, Richard, 125, 190, 218, 219
Vocational Agriculture, 52

Wade, Suzanne, 139
W.K. Kellogg Foundation, 212, 263
Wagner, Peter, 246
Walker, Joe, 179, 190, 278
Walsh, Leo, 213
War on Poverty, 87
Washington, Booker T., 38
Watershed program, 138
Wedemeyer, Charles W., 91
Weiss, Sherman, 105, 193
West, C. P., 258
WGN Radio, 275
WHA Radio, 240
Wheat growing, 8

White, Grace Witter, 287
White, Maury, 106, 241-242, 246, 248
Wisconsin Agriculturist, 15, 273
Wisconsin Associated County Extension Committees (WACEC), 94, 118-119, 151
Wisconsin Association of
County Agricultural Agents, 279
Extension 4-H Youth Development Professionals, 280
Extension Professionals, 281
Wisconsin County Agents Association, 278
Wisconsin Dairyman's Association, 12-13
Wisconsin Extension,
Association of Family and Consumer Sciences, 279
Community Development Association, 280
Workers Association, 278
Wisconsin Idea Commission, 133
Wisconsin Idea Theater, 225
Wisconsin Idea, 27, 105, 148, 270-271
Wisconsin Nutrition Education Program (WNEP), 152, 206
Wisconsin State Fair, 9-10
Wisconsin Territory, 5
Wisconsin Works (W-2), 132
WLBL Radio, 241
Woelfel, Oscar, 197-198
Woeste, John, 195
Wojta, J. F., 62, 194-195, 258
Women s Programs, early, 18, 52
World War I, 47-48
World War II, 68-70

Yanggen, Doug, 202
Young, Edward, 112
Young, Elsie (Stein), 167
Young, Robert, 143

Zierl, Lori, 144